# THE GOLDEN DAYS OF TENNIS
# ON THE FRENCH RIVIERA
# 1874–1939

# THE
# GOLDEN DAYS
## OF
# TENNIS
## ON THE
# FRENCH RIVIERA
# 1874–1939

## Alan Little

WIMBLEDON
LAWN TENNIS
MUSEUM & TOUR

First published 2014

Published by
Wimbledon Lawn Tennis Museum,
All England Lawn Tennis Club,
Church Road, Wimbledon,
London, SW19 5AE

ISBN 978 0 906741 54 2

Designed by Roger Walker
Typeset in Gill Sans and Bembo

Printed and bound in Great Britain by
Butler Tanner and Dennis Ltd

# Contents

| | | |
|---|---|---|
| | Acknowledgements | 8 |
| | Introduction | 9 |
| | Early Days at Cannes | 11 |
| 1874 | Tennis Arrives on the French Riviera | 14 |
| 1879 | The Beau Site Hotel Tennis Courts | 19 |
| 1883 | The Renshaw Twins Discover the Beau Site Hotel | 22 |
| 1895 | Nice Stages First International | 34 |
| 1896 | George Hillyard Stars at First Monte Carlo Meeting | 36 |
| 1897 | The Doherty Brothers Raise the Game to International Level | 38 |
| 1898 | Golf is a Threat | 41 |
| 1899 | Reggie Doherty in Full Flight | 43 |
| 1900 | Only Two Tournaments Played | 46 |
| 1901 | Beau Site Hotel Holds First Open Tournament | 49 |
| 1902 | Menton Joins the Throng | 54 |
| 1903 | Top Class Entries from England | 57 |
| 1904 | The Metropole Hotel Joins to Make Five Tournaments | 61 |
| 1905 | London to Cannes in 25 Hours, First Class Return £10–10s | 64 |
| 1906 | English Ladies Win Titles | 69 |
| 1907 | Major Ritchie Leads the Way | 73 |
| 1908 | A Season of Outstanding Weather | 76 |
| 1909 | Frederick Alexander Dominates the Season | 80 |
| 1910 | Max Decugis and Major Ritchie to the Fore | 84 |
| 1911 | Max Decugis Versus Tony Wilding • German Players Challenge | 88 |
| 1912 | Twelve Year Old Suzanne Lenglen Makes Debut | 91 |
| 1913 | A New Year Start to the Season | 95 |

1914 Tournaments Double • Tony Wilding Too Good
for Everybody    99

1915 Tony Wilding Killed on Western Front    105

1916 Cannes is a Haven for the Army    108

1917 More Charity Matches    111

1918 André Gobert Meets Suzanne Lenglen    112

1919 Back to Normal • Big US Forces Tournament    114

1920 Riviera Offers Good Living and Excitement    118

1921 Gordon Lowe and Suzanne Lenglen Dominate    126

1922 More Tournaments, More Entries • Elizabeth Ryan Wins
Eleven Singles    133

1923 Many New Faces Arrive on the Scene    142

1924 Rain Affected Season • Henry Mayes and Elizabeth Ryan
Outstanding    152

1925 Henry Mayes and Elizabeth Ryan Continue to Shine    161

1926 Epic Match Between Suzanne Lenglen and Helen Wills    170

1927 Henri Cochet's Title Run • Many English Ladies Compete    184

1928 Henri Cochet Returns • Henry Mayes Wins Last Title at 47    195

1929 Esna Boyd and Emmanuel du Plaix Dominate •
Disastrous Weather    205

1930 Bill Tilden's Memorable Visit • Elizabeth Ryan Wins Nine
Singles Titles    215

1931 George Lyttleton Rogers and Phyllis Satterthwaite Share
Season's Honours    224

1932 Dearth of English Competitors    234

1933 Five Singles to Lolette Payot, Four to Sheila Hewitt    244

1934 Georgio de Stefani Wins Six Titles • The Ladies Share    253

1935 Simone Mathieu's Phenomenal Season    261

1936 Simone Mathieu Again Supreme • Fred Perry's Two Week Visit    269

1937 Simone Mathieu's Run Ends: • Kho Sin Kie Wins Five Singles    278

1938 Eastern Europeans Excel • Five Singles to Jadwiga Jedrzejowska
and Alice Weiwers    286

1939 Six Singles to Simone Mathieu, Five to Alice Weiwers, Four to
Constantine Tanacescu    294

The Summer Seasons    305

Epilogue    307

The Blue Train    309

History of Clubs Staging International Tournaments    313

| | |
|---|---|
| Antibes: | Provençal LTC |
| Beaulieu: | Beaulieu LTC |
| Cannes: | Beau Site Hotel, Cannes LTC, Carlton LTC (Carlton Hotel), Gallia LTC (Gallia Hotel), Metropole LTC (Metropole Hotel), New Courts Club |
| Hyères: | Hyères LTC (Golf Hotel), New Courts Club |
| Juan-les-Pins: | Juan-les-Pins LTC, Miramar LTC |
| Menton: | Menton LTC (Bristol Hotel) |
| Monte Carlo: | Hotel de Paris, Condamine, La Festa, La Festa Country Club, Monte Carlo Country Club |
| Nice: | Nice LTC (Platz Mozart), Nice LTC (Parc Imperial) |
| St Raphael: | St Raphael LTC |
| Val d'Esquières: | Val d'Esquières LTC (de la Residence Hotel) |

The Principal Characters    341

Renshaw Twins, Doherty Brothers, Major Ritchie,
Henry Mayes, Gordon Lowe, Charles Aeschliman,
Henri Cochet, Jacques Brugnon, George Rogers, Bill Tilden,
Wallis Myers, George Simond, Suzanne Lenglen,
Elizabeth Ryan, Phyllis Satterthwaite, Helen Wills,
Lili de Alvarez, Simone Mathieu

Winter/Spring Tournament Schedule, Year by Year, 1895–1939    359

Winter/Spring Tournament Event Winners 1895–1939    372

Summer Tournament Schedule, Year by Year 1928–1939    437

Summer Tournament Event Winners, 1928–1939    440

French Professional Championships, 1920–1932    452

Country Abbreviations    454

Picture Credits    455

Index of Players 1883–1939    456

Author Biography    464

# Acknowledgments

A book of this depth and magnitude would never have been possible to produce without the assistance of many people, some contributing in a small way, others by spending much of their time. To all the following I give my sincere thanks:

Roger and Diane Aeschliman, Upland, California, USA; Franco Alciati, Milan, Italy; Rita Boswell, Westminster School, London, England; Marie Brunel, Archives, Cannes, France; Francis Carline, SNCF, Paris, France: François Chopinet, Carlton Intercontinental Hotel, Cannes, France; Alain Cassaigne, Paris, France; Gianni Clerici, Como, Italy; Jean-Loup and Noele Coignard, Paris, France; Pierre Darmon, Paris, France; Peter Donnelly, King's Own Royal Regiment, Lancaster, England; Jacques Dorfmann, Juan-les-Pins, France; Geoff Felder, New York, USA; Margaret Firth, Ilkley, Yorkshire, England; Heiner Gillmeister, Bonn, Germany; Richard A. Hillway, Colorado Springs, Colorado, USA; Gem Hoahing, London, England; Paul Leppard, Cannes, France; Prof. Kenneth McConkey, University of Northumbria, Newcastle-upon-Tyne, England; Jorel Maurice, Nice, France; Henry Popp, Milton, Ontario, Canada; Alain Salpin, Nice, France; Michel Sutter, Paris, France; Frances Truchi, Monaco; John Woodcock, Ealing, London, England.

I also very much appreciate the assistance given to me by the staff of the Wimbledon Lawn Tennis Museum: Honor Godfrey (Curator) for her continuous encouragement, Matthew Glaze, Nazeea Elahi, Ashley Jones and Sarah Frandsen (Picture Researcher). I should also like to thank Kay Crooks (Library Assistant) for her many labours with the research, and Audrey Snell (Assistant Librarian), who over a very long period gave tremendous support, taking the many aspects of the production in her stride – much to my relief!

I am very grateful to Roger Walker of Middleton, Manchester, for his outstanding skill in designing this book.

*Alan Little, MBE*
*Honorary Librarian, Wimbledon Lawn Tennis Museum*

*January 2014*

# Introduction

Tennis first appeared on the French Riviera 140 years ago. This book relates the 'golden' days of the period, from the beginning in 1874 up to 1939 and the Second World War. It summarizes play at some 450 international tournaments spread along the shores of the Mediterranean, where over the years more and more players competed from all parts of Europe and a few from beyond. The main purpose was to spend a few weeks playing the game, generally in good winter weather, under blue skies and away from the dull and damp cities of the north. Of course the off-court activities were also an added attraction. The players were amateurs and as such paid their own travel and expenses.

At the rear of the book full tournament schedules and the names of the winners of all level events can be found. Also presented are histories of the participating clubs and brief biographies of the principal characters over the years.

The original intention was to bring the story up-to-date, but after spending untold hours I came to realise that the task would be too much and best left to others. I hope this book, which is primarily intended for reference purposes, will be the starting point on the subject for researchers in the future.

A.L.

*In collaboration with this publication, the Wimbledon Lawn Tennis Museum arranged a special exhibition entitled* **'On the Riviera: Tennis in the South of France, 1874–1939'**. *This exhibition, held in the Museum Gallery during 2013/2014, was organised by the Museum Curator, Honor Godfrey.*

# Early Days at Cannes

The French Riviera is the Mediterranean coastline of the south-east corner of France, generally accepted as extending from the west at Hyères past other resorts, St Raphael, Cannes, Juan-les-Pins, Antibes, Nice, Beaulieu, Monte Carlo, to Menton in the east, on the Italian border. This area is known by the French as the Côte d'Azur. From the 1860s Cannes continually expanded with the construction of many large hotels, such as the Bellevue (1861), Pension Gray (1863), Grand Hotel (1864), Beau Site (1868) and de Pins (1875), also fabulous private villas to accommodate the ever-increasing number of visitors enjoying the mild climate all year round and in particular during the winter. In 1874 lawn tennis was played for the first time on the Riviera at Cannes.

Forty years earlier, in 1834, Cannes was a completely different place, a poor fishing village with just a few streets scattered around the centre. That autumn, Lord Brougham and Vaux, a Scotsman born in Edinburgh who had just completed four years in the high office of Lord Chancellor of the United Kingdom, left London in his six-horse carriage and travelled to the South of France on his way to Genoa. When he arrived at St Laurent du Port, the crossing of the river Var into Nice and the border with the Kingdom of Sardinia at that time, he was refused admittance on account of a cholera epidemic. (Nice did not become French territory until 1860). The option he was given was to undergo 10 days' quarantine or write to Paris for permission to continue his travel. He decided on the latter and enquired where he could stay whilst awaiting the reply. He was directed to Antibes but here he found the boarding not to his liking and moved on to Grasse. However, on his way he 'discovered' Cannes and the small Hotel de la Poste, run by Pere Pinchinal.

Having days to spare, Lord Brougham spent time touring the district, to which he took an instant liking. Convinced of the mild winters, where frost was unknown and snow likely to fall perhaps only every ten years, he decided to purchase a piece of land and arrange for the building of a villa for the future. After searching just east of Cannes, he settled on the west side, purchasing a strip of land 50 metres wide, stretching down to the sea. The building of his Italian-style villa, Chateau Eleanor Louise, started in 1835 and was completed by 1839.

Lord Brougham

Lord Brougham and Vaux, a former Lord Chancellor of the UK, brought prosperity to the poor fishing village of Cannes.

In honour of Lord Brougham the people of Cannes erected a large statue on the waterside in his memory.

Lord Brougham continued to visit Cannes most winters and was responsible for requesting from the King of France a grant of money to be spent on providing a harbour and jetty for the town. A report was made to the Government with the result that a sum of two million francs was designated for the project. He was always in the forefront of bringing change to the town.

Because of Lord Brougham's influence on his friends and acquaintances at home he was able to convince them of the delights of the Riviera and, having seen for themselves, many decided to build a villa either for vacations or, indeed, permanent residence in the area. As a consequence, the town prospered. Lord Brougham died in Cannes on the 7th May, 1868, aged 89 and was buried in the Cimetière du Grand Jas. The people of Cannes erected a large statue in his honour on the waterfront.

Lord Brougham was never involved in lawn tennis but, among the many people he introduced to Cannes was Thomas Robinson Woolfield, who became a very influential member of the town and brought lawn tennis to the Riviera.

Of course, the most significant occurrence which brought about the prosperity of Cannes was the extension of the railway line along the coast from Marseilles to Cannes and Nice and then later on to Menton on the Italian border. The railway station at Cannes was opened on 10th April, 1863 and immediately visitors from all over flocked to the town. The journey time from Paris to Cannes was 20 hours, 20 minutes. A figure of an extra 100,000 visitors was recorded for the first year. This in turn called for more and larger hotels and supporting amenities. The railway also attracted royalty and nobility from many parts of Europe to travel in style and comfort.

British royalty led the way. Queen Victoria, with her entourage of between 60 and 80, first visited the area in 1882, followed by most years in the 1890s. Her son, the Prince of Wales, regularly spent three weeks there each spring, generally in Cannes from 1872, often patronising sporting events.

# 1874

# Tennis Arrives on the French Riviera

There is no doubt that the first lawn tennis court laid down on the Riviera was at Cannes, in the grounds of the Villa Victoria, the home of Thomas Woolfield, in September 1874.

After wandering around Europe for seven years, he finally settled in Cannes during 1845. The following year he purchased land and between 1852 and 1853 built the very large Villa Victoria, a replica of a rustic English cottage. In 1855 he built an English church adjacent to the house. At the bottom of his garden, which overlooked the Boulevard du Midi and the Mediterranean, he constructed a croquet lawn but unfortunately the coming of the Marseille to Nice railway in 1864 split the property, forcing a tunnel to be built under the lines to give access to the lawn.

Woolfield's passion for croquet gradually waned and in September 1874 he erected the first tennis court on the Riviera on part of the lawn. So keen were Woolfield's friends to play the game that the court was opened each day at 8 am and kept occupied all day. On some occasions the public were admitted to watch the matches.

The extensive Villa Victoria – home of Thomas Woolfield in Cannes.

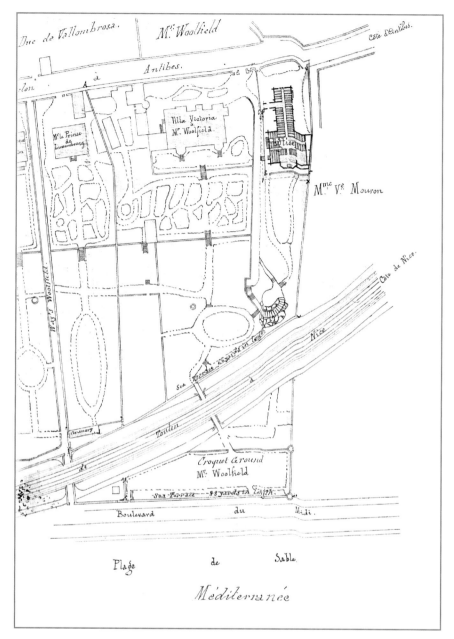

A plan of Thomas Woolfield's garden in the 1870s, showing the tunnel access under the railway to his croquet lawn. The first lawn tennis court was laid on the lawn in September 1874.

Woolfield continually entertained visiting royalty and dignitaries from many countries at the Villa Victoria, where he spent much time tending his beautiful garden. He contributed to Cannes and neighbouring areas, acacia, eucalyptus, palm and mimosa trees, the latter having originated from Hyères.

For over 40 years, Woolfield served the public of Cannes well and as a land and property developer encouraged the English to reside in the town. He died at Cannes on 28th April 1888, aged 88.

Also in late 1874 another court existed at Cannes at the French Club at Chateau St. Michael. The following year, by May, two other residences in Cannes were also playing the game, at Lord Cardross' Villa Flora and at St. John Blacker's Villa St. Cecile. Doubtless there were many others in the area who were enjoying the new-found sport.

Along the coast at Nice, some 30 kilometres east of Cannes, lawn tennis was probably first played around late 1874 at the residence of the very wealthy merchant and industrialist, Edward Cazalet (1827–1883), at Villa Liserb. The players must have taken to the game with great enthusiasm, for a short time after receiving the initial equipment, four dozen more balls were ordered. (It is possible that other residences were playing the game at the time, but there is no evidence of such.)

As early as the middle of April 1879, a small lawn tennis tournament was held at Nice. The organisers, who were visitors to the town, could not find a grass court available, so they adopted the St Phillipe Rink as being neutral ground. The final of the tournament was played on 21st April, but further details are not available. (Probably the rink was normally used for roller skating.)

Further east, at Monte Carlo, there is no record of lawn tennis being played at private houses during the mid-1870s. The first appearance seems to be in January 1880, when a lime court was first laid down in the grounds of the Hotel de Paris.

At this very early introduction of the game the playing equipment was supplied by Major Walter Clopton Wingfield through his agent, French & Co. of 46 Churton Street, a thousand or so miles away in London. Wingfield, a retired cavalry officer, who was appointed to the Honourable Corps of Gentlemen at Arms, the Queen's bodyguard on ceremonial occasions, was always looking for something new to pursue. For some time he had experimented with his new game, primarily played outside on grass, which brought healthy and energetic competition, so eagerly sought by Victorians of that period. People quickly realised that this recreation could replace the more leisurely game of croquet, utilising the ready made surface of grass.

By February 1874, Wingfield, encouraged by his friends, was ready to introduce to the public his new game of 'Sphairistike or Lawn Tennis'. In March, a letter appeared in the columns of 'The Field, The Country Gentlemen's Newspaper' signed by Gerald D. Fitzgerald, Secretary of the Marylebone Cricket Club, who explained that he had recently seen a new game played, which would be a great innovation as an outdoor amusement. He added that the rules were simple and clear and that he had enclosed copies of them with a short account of the game by the inventor. Although there were other notices in one or two periodicals, this particular letter

A Wingfield painted box containing poles, netting, four bats, balls and a book of rules for playing the game of Sphairistiké or Lawn Tennis, all for the price of 5 guineas. There is little doubt that Woolfield's tennis set originated in London from Wingfield's agents, French & Co.

was a great boost to Wingfield's enterprise, which quickly started to gain momentum.

All the items required for the game were contained in a painted box, 36×12×6 inches and included poles, pegs, netting, 4 tennis bats, a bag of balls, a mallet, a brush and, most importantly, an eight page book of the game, all for the price of five guineas, which was later increased to six guineas. There was also a larger size box containing extra bats, balls and a racket press for the price of ten guineas.

The book gave instruction on how to lay out the hour-glass shaped court (narrower at the net) and how to play the game, within the six listed rules. Apart from the shape of the court, one of the main features was that the server was required to always deliver the ball from the same end of the court but, in November of that year, Wingfield issued the second edition of his book and this laid down that the service should be delivered from alternate ends. Other changes included the number of rules being increased to 12.

By that time, the demand for Wingfield's sets increased dramatically – "selling like hot cakes" was one observation. Between early July 1874 and late June 1875, the French & Co. Day Sales book recorded well over 1,000 sets being sold at home and throughout Europe, with hardly a Royal Family or noble household being without the pastime. Soon the sets had filtered through to the United States and to the outposts of the British Empire.

In all, Wingfield produced five books and in the later editions he listed over 300 distinguished personages who had purchased a set and testified to the excellence of the game, headed by the Prince of Wales, the Crown Princess of Russia, the Grand Duke Czarevitch, the Duke of Edinburgh and so on, including those who were early purchasers on the Riviera.

By early 1875, many people were taking a great interest in lawn tennis and putting forward suggestions to improve the game. The MCC in London called a meeting of all interested parties and encouraged proposals, with the upshot that in the May the Club issued the first set of official rules, which were generally accepted. The hour-glass court was retained, a feature which pleased Wingfield, who continued merrily to sell his sets, incorporating the MCC rules into his own book. Quite a number of people claimed to have "invented" the game of lawn tennis and there is no doubt that many contributed in a manner of ways. However, certainly, Wingfield with his commercial instincts, popularised lawn tennis to such an extent that within a few years of evolution, the sport had grown to international status.

All was well for a couple of years until the All England Lawn Tennis Club decided to stage the inaugural Lawn Tennis Championship at Wimbledon. Going their own way, they appointed a sub-committee of three to produce a new set of rules, whereby the fundamental difference from the MCC code was the replacement of the hour-glass court in favour of a rectangular shape, 78 feet by 27 feet. A year later, in 1878, the AELTC and the MCC issued a combined set of rules.

With all these changes taking place, the game of tennis was also moving along on the Riviera. Because of the ideal winter weather, hotel residents now required the facilities to play tennis and one of the earliest hotels to supply this need was the Beau Site at Cannes, which for some twenty years or so became the centre for the game on the Riviera.

# 1879
# The Beau Site Hotel Tennis Courts

The Beau Site Hotel was opened in 1868, adjoining Lord Brougham's residence, situated at the west end of Cannes. The front faced the blue sea of the Mediterranean and the rear overlooked the Esterel Mountains.

The hotel was built on the site of a castle erected in 1840 for François Aymard Rollet. In early 1867 the castle was sold to Georges Gougoltz, who added to the property by purchasing further land. The main structure of the hotel was of rock, stone, masonry and plaster.

In 1873 a west pavilion was added and in 1879 a further floor gave the hotel a total of 300 rooms. A new Louis XIV dining room, designed by Charles Baron, with ceiling sculpted by Ernest Pellegrini, was inaugurated in January 1880. In 1885 the nearby Esterel Hotel was annexed and connected to the hotel by a gallery. A new lobby and restaurant were installed in 1902 and much later, in 1930, the hall was completely modernised. Eventually, the hotel was purchased by Eugene Schmid and transformed into a condominium in 1945.

Why the hotel was one of the first on the French Riviera to install lawn tennis courts within their grounds in 1880 is not certain. One possibility is that English guests visiting the area for the winter discovered, as others had, that the excellent climate was conducive to the game of lawn tennis and pressed the management to provide the facility. Also, the number of people owning lawn tennis sets in the Cannes area, having available space to play, must have increased considerably as the game grew in popularity and came to the notice of hoteliers. Another possible explanation is that the proprietor, Georges Gougoltz, a Swiss hotelier, was keen on lawn tennis and indeed occasionally his son took part in small tournaments held at the hotel.

A personal record of those very early days of lawn tennis at the Beau Site Hotel is recorded by John Simpson who, writing in 1900, stated that he was an annual visitor to the hotel each winter from 1879/1880.

Well-respected, he was to be found on the courts all day long, arranging and supervising the lawn tennis tournaments and practice sessions, plus providing handicap details for the players. His favourite seat overlooked the first court, but there was no evidence that he actually played the game. He was responsible for promoting the idea of a points system of scoring, instead of the normal games and sets formula, which became very popular with the

John Moyer Heathcote, an amateur real tennis champion, played on the Beau Site Hotel courts in January 1880.

players, particularly while contesting handicap events.

He recalled that in twenty years the courts had changed little, the only difference, of course, being that the nets were higher and the posts old-fashioned. There were few players then but in January 1880, John Moyer Heathcote appeared on the scene and, although not a regular lawn tennis player, he was much superior to anybody else and delighted in taking on any two players on the doubles court. He was resting from a severe strain he had contracted when playing real tennis and he used to play with his right hand in the morning and his left in the afternoon. Heathcote was many times amateur real tennis champion, a member of the MCC five-man sub-committee who framed the first official rules of lawn tennis in May 1875 and he was also the first to suggest India-rubber balls should be covered with white flannel.

The reference to the net is very significant in Simpson's article. In 1878 the Marylebone Cricket Club issued their first combined official rules of the game and these gave the height of the net at the centre as 3 feet and 4 feet 9 inches at the posts. In 1880 the height at the posts was reduced to 4 feet and in 1882 further reduced to 3 feet 6 inches – the same as today. Simpson in his description states that the nets were higher in early 1880 than at the time of his writing, which showed that the courts were constructed at that time.

The other factor is the mention of the posts being old-fashioned. This certainly implies that they were fixed by screws, not ropes as previously – another proof of the courts' installation date. Initially three courts were installed.

By late 1880 lawn tennis was in full swing at the Beau Site Hotel, with players competing in small tournaments organised by the hotel. A doubles event was played in hot sunny weather on their 'capital' courts, with the final being concluded on the 31st December. In a long hard-fought match, Messrs. Heberdon and Keene eventually defeated Messrs. Warn and White, 8–10 6–2 6–3. There was anticipation that further good play and hard-fought battles would take place when a singles event began on the 1st January.

The courts at the Beau Site Hotel were unique. They were made of a fine, almost silky sand, indigenous to that part of the Mediterranean, extracted from the Esterel Mountains. The sand had the property of binding well when watered and rolled and formed a magnificent playing surface, particularly when slightly damp. The courts had a good background of orange and eucalyptus trees and the light in the afternoon, when the sun was across the court, left nothing to be desired. Spectators were well accommodated with seats along the side of the court nearest the hotel.

Besides John Simpson's article, there is firm evidence that the tennis courts at the Beau Site Hotel were laid down in 1880, possibly in the early summer. The year before, in 1879, two neighbouring hotels in Cannes, the Central and the Prince of Wales, both advertised in the press throughout the year, offering the facilities they provided, including lawn tennis. The Beau Site Hotel also advertised during the same period and as late as November stated that the premises had been newly enlarged and improved, without any mention of tennis being provided. In April 1880 there was still no mention of lawn tennis in their advertising. However, by then, the hotel, normally commended for presenting innovations, must have realised that they were lagging behind and set about installing three courts.

John Simpson, a regular visitor to the Beau Site Hotel each winter, where for over 20 years he organised the tennis and arranged small friendly tournaments.

Further evidence of the date of 1880 is given by the presence for many years of two stone plaques attached to the hotel garden wall, adjacent to the courts. One is inscribed in English and states: "Lest we forget here on the Beau-Site terraces were invented and built in 1880 by the famous Renshaw brothers, the first and original hard tennis courts in the world." The other plaque, in French, reads: "Un peu d'histoire sportive. Dans les jardins de l'hotel Beau-Site à Cannes furent inventes et construits en 1880 par les fameux champions Renshaw frères les premiers tennis du monde en terre battue."

Significant is the date 1880. However, the reference to the Renshaw brothers' presence and intervention in the construction of the courts as early as given appears to be nonsense and based on legend and hearsay. This story has been perpetuated over the years to the present day. At that time the two brothers were less than 20 years old and surely would be lacking the experience required to be able to construct the courts, particularly in a strange environment with the unique materials being produced locally for the construction of the courts.

Also during this period the brothers spent considerable time serving with the Royal Lancashire Militia. Both were commissioned as 2nd Lieutenant in August 1878 and promted to Lieutenant in August 1880. However, with their tennis careers developing, they retired from the force, William in August 1881 and Ernest in May 1882.

# 1883
# The Renshaw Twins Discover the Beau Site Hotel

At the age of 20, William Renshaw won the Gentlemen's Singles at Wimbledon in 1881, a feat he repeated six times, 1882–1886 and 1889. The career of his twin brother, Ernest, followed a similar pattern and he won the Championship in 1888. During the 1880s the brothers completely dominated the game to become legendary figures.

More than likely the brothers, just starting out on their tennis careers, had learnt from friends and perhaps tennis officials or players that the Riviera could be reached in a day or so from London, where lawn tennis could be played every day in the winter in the most favourable weather, so different from England. Also, by becoming Wimbledon champion, William in particular must have attracted the friendship of many prominent and well-travelled people who were able to pass on information regarding the delights of the Beau Site Hotel. However, extensive research of English and French newspapers of the time and other records show no occasion when the brothers visited the area until late October 1883, when William journeyed to Cannes.

The brothers must have found Cannes much to their liking as, being very wealthy, they were able to visit regularly each winter for at least 14 or 15 years. Over that period there was only one occasion when each did not visit the hotel, then because of illness or injury. The length of their visits varied and quite often they stayed at different times. With the occasional game of golf and the round of dances and social events at the hotel each evening, the whole experience must have been delightful.

The continuing presence of the twins at Cannes encouraged enormous development of the game in the area. For much of the time they were the best two players in the world, with William holding the top place as Wimbledon champion, seven times, six of them consecutively. Spectators came to watch from the neighbouring towns and what they saw was the best, with the brothers and other good players constantly practising and indulging in the odd handicap event, to a very high standard, without the pressure and tension of tournament match play.

Over the years there were many top class players from England who wintered at the hotel with the Renshaws, thereby providing the necessary variety of play. Early on, players from America seeking a standard of

William and Ernest Renshaw, popularised the game of tennis on the Riviera by visiting Cannes each season.

competition seldom attained at home, began to spend a few weeks at Cannes, eager to participate in a much higher level of play and subsequently compete at English tournaments, including The Championships at Wimbledon. This was brought about following the visit to England in early July 1883 by Clarence and Joseph Clark, representing the Young America Club of Philadelphia, USA.

Although not carrying with them the status of a United States official team, they nevertheless had proved their prowess two weeks earlier by defeating the current American doubles champions, James Dwight and Richard Sears in two specially arranged matches in Boston and New York.

James Dwight, the first American to visit the Riviera in December 1883. He also visited in 1885–1887, bringing his wife on the last occasion.

*Below:* Richard Sears, eventual winner of the United States Championship seven times, arrived at Cannes during March 1884, after crossing the Atlantic aboard a 115 foot schooner. He returned to the Riviera in 1886.

The Clark brothers were warmly received by the All England Lawn Tennis Club and, although arriving too late to compete in The Championships, a match was arranged the day after on the Centre Court against the Renshaw brothers. Without striking their best form, the home side gained a comfortable win, 6–4 8–6 3–6 6–0. The visitors performed admirably at times but lacked the experience of their opponents at the crucial moments. They were keen to have a return match and this was arranged for a few days later at the same venue. On this occasion the Renshaw brothers were in excellent fettle and won easily 6–3 6–2 6–3 in 67 minutes. Surprisingly over 500 spectators watched the encounter.

Upon returning home, the Clark brothers no doubt enlightened their fellow players on the fine quality and conditions of the English game, sufficiently to persuade the top two players in the USA to cross the Atlantic to see and judge for themselves. Dr James Dwight, a non-practising medical doctor, who was President of the United States National Lawn Tennis Association

William Renshaw (left) and James Dwight practising on the Beau Site Hotel courts in very early 1885.

and generally regarded as the "Father of American Tennis", took up the challenge. He contacted William Renshaw, who made arrangements for them both to spend a sojourn practising at Cannes. Dwight arrived in London in mid-October and invited Renshaw to play a match against him and this was duly arranged on the asphalt covered court at Maida Vale. Renshaw, very familiar with this type of surface, won easily, 6–1 6–3 6–2, with reserve in hand. A week later, both were at the Beau Site Hotel where they were joined by top class English players, Claude Farrer, A.J. Mulholland and Arthur Stanley. Blessed with beautiful weather the visitors were able to relax and enjoy the surroundings and participate in practice most days. Renshaw, who often played Dwight, generally gave him 'fifteen' and, despite this, had little difficulty in winning. The American was a very good loser and always came up smiling.

Early in March 1884, Richard Sears, doubles partner of Dwight and eventual winner of the United States singles championship seven times in succession, 1881–1887, arrived at Cannes. His journey was quite novel. He had departed from Boston on 5th December on board the luxurious 115 foot schooner, 'Gitana', owned by millionaire William F. Weld Jr in company with two Harvard colleagues, Captain Sherlock and a crew of 12. Via Bermuda and Madeira, they reached Gibraltar on 6th February, set

for a tour of the Mediterranean, calling along the coast of Spain, Malta, South of France, Naples, Sicily, Algiers, Tangier and the Canary Islands before returning to America.

Sears' presence at the hotel, with his style of play, was a boost for the party, who during the many practice sessions could pit their ability against the two leading American players. Apparently some of the doubles routines were of a very high standard.

All the players were back in England by mid-April. The two Americans entered the Irish Championships in Dublin and tournaments at Bath, Cheltenham, the Northern at Liverpool and subsequently The Championships. A third American, Arthur Rives, also competed at Wimbledon to make his nation the first from overseas.

Towards the end of July, Dwight and Sears left Liverpool for the United States aboard the *City of Chicago* and arrived in New York, 4th August. Their return had an important effect on the game in America. Because of their association with many of England's leading players and administrators, they were able to report on the superiority of the English game and persuade the American tennis authorities to bring their rules of the game to coincide closely with the English rules.

The following winter, **1884/1885** Dwight returned to Europe in late January and together with William Renshaw took up residence at Cannes for a couple of months. Also at hand were Claude Farrer, Harry Grove, M.G. MacNamara and G.H. Taylor, allowing endless combinations for practice purposes.

In March a tournament for lawn tennis enthusiasts visiting the site was organised, but the 'crack' players were debarred from competing. The singles event attracted 11 players, from whom Stephen Winkworth beat Stubbs in the final, 4–6 7–5 7–5 6–2. William Renshaw presented the first prize, value £5. Renshaw and Dwight returned to London at the beginning of May. The American carried out a very tiring programme of 11 tournaments over the summer period, capturing five singles titles before returning home late summer.

Because of an injury William Renshaw delayed his departure to the Beau Site Hotel for the **1885/1886** winter trip. However, during the first week of January, his brother Ernest, in company with James Dwight and Richard Sears, who had just arrived in London, took the train to Cannes.

Two Englishmen, who were frequent visitors to the Riviera, Harry Barlow (top) and Harry Grove.

Grove was already there and Arthur Stanley, Mulholland and W.C. Taylor followed shortly. Reports suggested that many lively encounters took place, particularly a hard tussle resulting in Grove beating Dwight, 1–6 8–6 10–8 6–2.

A Scratch Pairs handicap event was arranged in which the majority of the top players entered. Local lady players were recruited and a merry time had by all – certainly in contrast to the daily round of practice. Dwight and a Miss Davidson won the event from 11 entries. Ernest Renshaw presented £10 as first prize for the lady of the winning pair, while her partner received £5 presented by Dwight (to himself!). Sears gave £5 for two second prizes.

In early March, William Renshaw with Charles Lacy Sweet joined the party at Cannes, enabling the scope of the practice format to increase further. Later that month, Sears, who had not been well, left Cannes for London and sailed home immediately, while the remainder of the players returned a few weeks later for the English summer season. Dwight played in five tournaments before withdrawing from The Championships, owing to injury.

The excellent facilities of the Beau Site Hotel, coupled with outstanding tennis courts and more often than not a cloudless sky made the resort, according to one, "the Elysium of Tennis". This attraction to the winter life in Cannes had spread across the Atlantic, as shown by this favourable comment made in the New York Times:

"Cannes presents the greatest possibilities for amusement. Nature certainly has done her best. One hotel, the Beau Site, presents the gayest appearances from morning till night. It is the centre of attraction in winter to the devotees all over the world of that attractive sport – lawn tennis. In the perfect courts are gathered the best players of England and America, who have built up for themselves a separate and distinct home. Crowds gather around the courts every morning to watch or engage in the play. Everybody at the hotel is clad in flannels from morning till dinner. The Renshaw brothers, the world's champions, can be seen at all times, hard at work, perhaps against Sears and Dwight, our American players. There are present many other noted tennis men from both sides of the Atlantic. Lately Frenchmen have joined in the sport, with amazing though often misapplied enthusiasm to the absolute vacuum of enjoyments at the other hotels. For the old gentlemen inside, the national American game of poker is provided every evening. Two open grass games are going on, one with a five-franc limit, the other with a two-franc limit."

That year, in another part of Cannes, a new tennis club known as the Reunion was founded by Capt. Clifton Percival. This small club possessed three gravel courts, which were occasionally visited during the winter by players such as the Renshaws, Harry Grove, Julien Robinson and others. No international tournaments were staged but handicap events featured. Unfortunately Capt. Percival died in 1892 and the club closed.

Ernest Renshaw, as keen as ever, was an early visitor in the **1886/1887** winter, being in residence at the Beau Site Hotel by the middle of January. Over the next few months the courts were fully occupied by many of the usual visitors, Grove, Stanley and MacNamara, in addition to the well-known names, B. Winthrop, J. Liddell, T. Attwood and Julien Robinson.

James Dwight, not tiring of the long journey to France, was present for the fourth year but this time bringing his wife along to see the splendour of the coast. Livingston Beeckman, another American, was present for the first time. During the middle of February a handicap tournament was arranged for all those present, which resulted in Ernest Renshaw defeating Livingston Beeckman in the final after five very close sets.

The players were delighted to welcome new company to the hotel, when Miss Constance Bryan arrived for a few weeks holiday. One of England's leading players, she found no other lady player at hand to give her some competition but she soon took full advantage of frequently practising with the men. Later two other top class players from England joined the party at the hotel, Miss E. Gurney and the 1884 and 1885 Wimbledon singles champion, Miss Maud Watson.

There was plenty to talk about at the hotel on the 23rd February, when the normal rhythm of life in the South of France was shattered early in the morning by several sharp earthquakes. These shocks extended along the Mediterranean coast from Marseilles into Italy, as far south as Rome.

At Cannes, three shocks moving east to west were felt. The strongest was observed at 5 am and lasted for 12 seconds, the second was more feeble and lasted for 5 seconds, while the third, which occurred at 8.15 am, lasted two seconds. There were also two short tremors the following day at 2 am and 4 am. There were no fatalities or significant damage to property, but there was much panic among the public, many of whom took to the streets. Eight special trains were provided to transport people away from the area, but the Prince of Wales, staying in the town, showed no intention of taking his departure. Despite all this upheaval, the courts at the hotel were still in continual use throughout the day.

The most violent tremors took place at neighbouring Nice, where some prominent buildings were destroyed and several people were killed. Over 9,000, mainly visitors, left Nice by train. Monte Carlo felt several shocks, but avoided damage to buildings, while at Menton several deaths were registered.

Maud Watson, champion at Wimbledon for the first two years, 1884 and 1885, made a surprise visit to the Beau Site Hotel in 1887, mainly for a short holiday and to practise her tennis.

During the second week of March a Scratch Pairs Handicap event was organised, which enlisted 10 pairs, including some seven local ladies. Ernest Renshaw and Constance Bryan won through to beat Grove and Miss Gurney in the final, 6–4 13–11. The winning pair had beaten Pennington and Maud Watson in the semi-final, 4–6 6–4 7–5. Ernest Renshaw presented a prize for the lady of the winning pair, while B. Winthrop gave one for the lady of the second pair. Over 300 spectators witnessed the final.

William Renshaw did not arrive in Cannes until late March. For over three months his mind had been mainly on matters other than tennis, including spending over three weeks in Scarborough, performing in various amateur theatrical productions. However, once on court, he was soon in good shape, with his daily practice sessions with Grove. Most of the players were back in England by May. Dwight decided to return to the United States, without competing in any of the English tournaments, including The Championships.

William Renshaw and Grove were the first visitors to the Beau Site Hotel for the **1887/1888** season, practising daily from the beginning of January. The courts had been thoroughly renovated since the previous season and were in excellent condition, playing as truly as an asphalt surface. The number of local spectators increased each week, and enjoying excellent weather did not require overcoats, in contrast to Londoners, who were suffering from a bad winter, shivering with cold and enveloped in black fog most days. A handicap event was organised and won by William Renshaw who was playing regularly and proving that he had recovered from the injury to his arm, which had put him on the sidelines during the last season. During January, Georges Gougoltz, the proprietor of the hotel, went bankrupt and was forced to run the establishment under the supervision of a commission presided over by the Mayor of Cannes. In February Ernest Renshaw, Harry Barlow, Farrer, McNamara and W.H. Harrison arrived to swell the party.

In March two tournaments were held, the first a handicap involving some local players and the second, a round-robin event in the 'American' format, which consisted of Ernest and William Renshaw, Barlow and Grove. However, after a few matches had been played, William injured his hand and was unable to participate. Fortunately, he soon recovered and in early April competed in a handicap event. When he arrived home later that month he was elected the first President of the Lawn Tennis Association, a position he held until 1896.

William Renshaw travelled to Cannes for the **1888/1889** winter but, on this occasion, he started out in the middle of December and did not return to London until mid-April. There were not so many top-class players visiting so early but he still found good form playing with E.W. Brook, Chippingdale , G.R. Corlett and Harry Bacon. Constance Bryan made a return visit to the site.

On the 16th February HRH The Prince of Wales commenced a private visit to Cannes, staying at the Reunion Club. A little later, William Renshaw had put his rackets away for the day, when the Prince honoured him with an invitation to lunch at his club in Monte Carlo. In March, MacNamara, A.E. Kennedy, Grove and Stanley joined William Renshaw at the Beau Site Hotel and further handicap events took place. Ernest Renshaw did not visit Cannes that winter.

During the season the players decided that in future they would generally cease to use the normal scoring method of games and sets during handicap competitions. Instead they adopted a system whereby the first player to reach 72 points (men) and 50 points (ladies) would be the winner of the match. The points were adjusted accordingly for handicapping. This proved to be a very popular move.

William Renshaw did not visit Cannes during the **1889/1890** winter, whereas Ernest Renshaw renewed his acquaintance. Arriving in early February he was soon joined by, among others, Stanley, Kennedy and left-handed Stephen Winkworth (he always played wearing a monocle), which ensured a high quality of play. Handicap events were arranged and a wealthy American, Rhinelander Stewart, became one of the winners.

The residents of the Beau Site Hotel received bad news on the 16th February when the death was announced at Cannes of Claude Farrer, at the young age of 25. He was a very accomplished and well-liked player, who made frequent visits to the hotel some years earlier. He had been quite unwell for some months. Ernest Renshaw travelled home at the beginning of March.

Very cold weather in London caused the players to migrate in early January to the Beau Site Hotel for the **1890/1891** winter, but on arrival they found the weather there just as uninviting, with the seafront at Cannes deserted for long periods of time. However, after a week or so the weather improved and Grove, Harry Bacon and James Crispe were testing each other, as usual. A little later they were joined by Winkworth, MacNamara, Manliffe Goodbody, Henry Guy Nadin and two very welcome players from the United States, Deane Miller and Marion Wright. As a break from playing at the Beau Site Hotel, Bacon, Grove and Winkworth supported a tournament held in conjunction with the opening of the neighbouring Metropole Hotel. Grove won the singles title.

Ernest Renshaw was due to arrive at Cannes, but an injury to his foot forced him to cancel his visit. William Renshaw arrived early in March when the weather was delightful and he was soon in action, contesting handicap events. However, in one event he was easily beaten by Miller. Wright also gave good account of himself. Spectators were in abundance.

The weather at Cannes throughout the **1891/1892** winter was glorious, with many top players flocking early to the Beau Site Hotel. Ernest Renshaw was quick off the mark and in situ by the middle of the first week in January. He was quickly followed by Bacon, MacNamara, Winkworth, Crispe and newcomers to the scene, George Hillyard and Oliver Campbell, the United States singles champion for the past two years. In the evenings many of the players indulged in billiards, with Renshaw, Hillyard and Crispe being outstanding performers.

In 1892 Oliver Campbell, United States Singles Champion for the past two years, visited the Riviera and played a few tournaments before sightseeing on the Continent. When he returned home he captured his national title for the third consecutive year.

At the close of February, William Renshaw and Harry Barlow joined the party and several high quality handicap events were staged. William Renshaw always mastered Oliver Campbell. Around this time Ernest Renshaw and George Hillyard returned to London, while Campbell decided to undertake a month's yachting cruise on the Mediterranean.

Other players joined the fray, including Deane Miller and Adam Wright (brother of Marion), plus Harry Grove and Julien Robinson. With all that talent available and with Campbell returning from his cruise, an outstanding entry of class players was obtained for a handicap event held in mid-March, where Adam Wright narrowly defeated William Renshaw in the final. The fine array of matches in this contest was described as probably the best ever seen on the Continent.

By the first week in April all the players had returned to London, except Campbell, who went sight-seeing on the Continent for a few weeks. He returned to England by mid-May and participated in tournaments, including The Championships where he lost in the second round to Arthur Gore.

During the winter a new golf course was opened a mile or so outside Cannes, offering an alternative to the continuous tennis being played at the Beau Site Hotel. Ernest Renshaw was uninterested and never played the game, whereas William was a keen golfer.

The majority of the top players heading for Cannes during the **1892/1893** winter arrived a little later than usual. By the end of January, Ernest Renshaw and Hillyard had settled in and were playing well. One match between the two players was described as superb and ended with Hillyard just winning, but with Renshaw owing 15 points.

William Renshaw decided to spend a short time in Monte Carlo before settling at the Beau Site Hotel, where MacNamara, Bacon and the Americans, Deane Miller and Adam Wright returning for a third season, joined the party. Several handicap events were organised using the 72 point system of scoring. The news of this innovation had so impressed some French players that the system was adopted for a tournament in Paris.

Ernest Renshaw and Hillyard returned to England by the end of February, but within a couple of weeks Renshaw came back and with his brother now in top form, many entertaining matches were fought, always before a capacity audience. At the beginning of April, William Renshaw returned home and the courts rapidly became deserted, allowing Ernest Renshaw and Bacon to enjoy the facilities by themselves. One day this pair went over to Monte Carlo for a change of scenery and formally opened new lawn tennis courts at the Casino. Ernest Renshaw was the last to leave on the 10th May and spent a few days in Paris before returning to London.

Not so many of the regular players were present during the **1893/1894** winter at Cannes. However, both Renshaw brothers, who were in great form, arrived very early in January, closely followed by Hillyard and Bacon. William Renshaw was back in London by mid-February, but Ernest and Bacon remained until the last week in April. Excellent weather prevailed throughout the months.

The brothers probably visited the Beau Site Hotel during the next two winters, but there is no evidence available to support this. By 1897 the Cannes annual tournament was being held alongside the new meetings at Nice and Monte Carlo.

William was listed to play at two events at Cannes in 1897, but withdrew, never to enter again. Although Ernest missed Cannes, he competed at Nice in 1897 and Monte Carlo in 1897–1899, generally restricting his participation to handicap events where, more often than not, he fell in the opening match. His last appearance was at Monte Carlo at the beginning of April 1899, where in a first round match he partnered Laurie Doherty against Reggie Doherty and Count Victor Voss. Although Ernest's side lost 6–3 6–4, the encounter was of the highest calibre and described as excellent.

The Renshaws' love affair with the Riviera was over. For more than a dozen years the brothers had developed and popularised the game of tennis with their annual visits. Nice in 1895 and Monte Carlo in 1896 were the first tournaments to feature international level events, which opened up a new era of play for the area. Fortunately, in the footsteps of the Renshaws came two other brothers, Laurie and Reggie Doherty, who visited for a decade and raised the game to the top international standard.

A very early advertisement in an English periodical, 1894, showing that the Beau Site Hotel had the best tennis courts on the Continent.

# CANNES.

## Hotel Beausite and Hotel de l'Esterel.

These magnificent establishments are situated in the West End of Cannes, **and are nearest the Golf Links**. They contain 350 bed and sitting-rooms, and **possess the best Lawn Tennis Courts** on the Continent.

Prices moderate. Arrangements made for a minimum stay of seven days.

G. GOUGOLTZ, Proprietor.

# 1895
# Nice Stages First International

The first occasion on which open tennis was played on the Riviera was at the inaugural international tournament staged by the Nice LTC from 11th to 14th March 1895. The Club was founded in 1890 when four courts were laid down in the Platz Mozart. Four events were held, just one level event, the men's singles, plus three handicap events, men's singles, men's doubles and mixed doubles.

The Committee hoped that a number of leading players staying in the neighbouring Cannes would compete but this did not materialise. However, several well-known players took part, including Count Victor Voss, the German champion, S. Blacker-Douglas and L.L. Whiteway (Nice LTC), as well as a few top players from Marseilles. The level men's open singles was won by H. Thomas from Marseilles, who defeated Voss in the final. Third prize went to Hitchcock (Marseilles) and fourth prize to Whiteway. The winner was presented with the Nice Cup, which became his absolute property. No details or scores of the matches are available.

The winners of the handicap events were: men's singles – J. Fall (Weymouth), men's doubles – Thomas and L. Hitchcock, mixed doubles – Blacker-Douglas and Miss K. Booth.

*Note: The first open event at the Monte Carlo tournament was 1896 and had level events. At the Beau Site Hotel at Cannes the first open tournament to have level events was in 1897 and then in 1901 etc, but international handicap tournaments were held there in 1899, 1900 and 1903.*

Count Victor Voss, the German champion, made his debut on the Riviera this season, when he was runner-up to H. Thomas at the first tournament staged at Nice.

*Right:* A very early poster advertising lawn tennis at the Grand Hotel Les Pins in Cannes.

# 1896
# George Hillyard Stars at First Monte Carlo Meeting

The 2nd international tournament held at Nice was staged in March. Despite extensive research, no details are available.

The first Monte Carlo open international tournament was held on the two courts of the Hotel de Paris from Monday to Sunday, 23rd to 29th March, during which four level and four handicap events were played. Details of matches leading up to the finals and, in some cases of the finals, are not available. The star of the meeting was George Hillyard, who beat Voss, in the final, 6–3 6–2 6–3. Hillyard also featured in partnership with Harry Bacon when defeating F.L. Fassitt and L.L. Whiteway in the final of the doubles, 6–3 6–0 6–6 6–7 7–6 8–7 9–7 (this score does not make sense but is given as recorded). In the other two level events Miss Booth and Miss Guillen reached the final of the singles, but the outcome is not recorded. Hillyard and his wife, Blanche, easily won the mixed doubles title.

As a further bonus Hillyard won the men's singles handicap event, eventually overcoming P. Whiteway in the final. Using a points system of scoring, Hillyard's handicap was -50, while Whiteway stood at +33, which meant that Hillyard was 82 points behind and this gap seemed impossible to bridge. However, he did and amidst a scene of great excitement from the spectators won by 72 points to 69. Other details known are the men's doubles handicap finalists, M. Collinet, Andre Fomberlaux, L.L. Whiteway and P. Whiteway, and that Blanche Hillyard took part in the ladies' doubles handicap final, but no further information is available.

The prizes amounting to 3,000FF were donated by the Société des Bains de Mer and the committee consisted of Messrs Smith, the English Vice-Consul, Dr Konte, Dr Tagge Milner-Gibson, Warren and F. Mattei, the Secretary.

George Hillyard was outstanding at the first international tournament held at Monte Carlo, winning the singles, doubles and mixed titles.

*Note: All records referring to Monte Carlo list the inaugural international tournament as taking place in 1897, the year the Doherty brothers first competed. In 1997 the annual tournament held at Monte Carlo celebrated the centenary. These landmarks are incorrect, as the first meeting was held in 1896.*

*References to the event hardly exist, but the German periodical 'Spiel und Sport', in an issue dated 4th April 1896, clearly states that at the gathering held from 23rd to 29th March an Englishman, George Hillyard, defeated the German, Count Victor Voss, in the men's level singles final. In all there were four level and three handicap events. This is confirmed by 'Lawn Tennis and Croquet', the official organ of the Lawn Tennis Association, in the issue of 19th May 1897, which gives a list of 'Prize Winners in Continental Tournaments for 1896'. Also, when the 1897 tournament was played, a report stated that the absence of Hillyard and his wife, Blanche, who last year took most of the prizes, was much regretted.*

# 1897
# The Doherty Brothers Raise the Game to International Level

This season entered a new phase of tennis on the Riviera. The decision of the newly established tournaments, Monte Carlo and Nice, to stage open events generally attracted a higher level of international play, but the foremost reason for the change of status was the presence of the two Doherty brothers, Laurie and Reggie, for the next ten years on the Riviera. There was always one present and quite often both. Between them they won the Championship Singles at Wimbledon nine times, Reggie, 1897–1900 and Laurie, 1902–1906, while as a pair they captured the Doubles Championship eight times, 1897–1901 and 1903–1905. They were the world's best players and consequently, they completely dominated the meetings and captured handfuls of titles. They set the standard for all to follow.

Cannes continued to be the centre of attraction for sport on the Riviera. With the support of the patronage given by the Grand Duke Michael of Russia and his wife, Countess Torby and Grand Duchess Anastasie Mecklenburg-Schwerin, tennis flourished and there were reports of the smaller hotels in the district providing a court or two for their guests. All this, despite the counter attractions of golf, bicycling, pigeon shooting or even roulette! The Duke, whose marriage was not in favour with the Czar, was particularly interested in golf and in recent years had given great support to the new Club at La Napole, just outside Cannes, where an outstanding course existed.

The first tournament of the year was staged during mid-January at the Beau Site Hotel where the three sand courts, admirably kept, were as level as a billiard table and perfectly drained. Rain tended to interfere with the play and there was some disappointment at the scratching of many of the entrants, including the trio of Irish players, Manliffe Goodbody, Harold Nisbet and Thomas Chaytor but, to counter this, Reggie Doherty was present, also Marion Wright from America and Count Voss.

Doherty was not pressed in the level men's singles and won through to defeat G. Gongoltz in the final, 6–2 6–4 6–3. The remainder of the programme consisted of handicap events at which Doherty gave support. In this category Doherty and Gongoltz won the doubles from Voss and Wright, while Miss Rooke took the top ladies' prize.

Reggie (left) and Laurie Doherty competed on the Riviera for over a decade. Apart from completely dominating the game, their personality and charm was the admiration of all who came in contact with them.

Just over five weeks later the scene shifted along the coast to Nice, where the second meeting of the season took place at the Nice LTC, situated in the Platz Mozart. Good class players entered, including Doherty, George Hillyard, Ernest Renshaw, Clement Cazalet, C.W. Blackwood-Price, Voss, Mrs Ruth Dyas, Miss Mildred Brooksmith and Countess Clara Schulenburg. Unfortunately, Hillyard had to return to London before play started and Renshaw contested only the mixed event.

Countess Clara Schulenburg of Germany made her debut on the Riviera and played at Nice and Monte Carlo. A very keen competitor.

There was little doubt that Doherty would win the level men's singles, but he was forced to concede a set against Voss before winning the Nice Challenge Cup, 6–2 6–4 3–6 6–1. Voss surprised all by eliminating Cazalet in the quarter-final, 6–2 6–3. The other five events were handicap affairs. In the ladies' division, Ruth Dyas beat Mildred Brooksmith in the last round, having knocked out Clara Schulenburg early on.

The Monte Carlo tournament followed closely after Nice. As regards entries, play and attendance, they eclipsed anything previously seen there. A total of 226 entries were received for the various events, with 95 players actually competing. However, there were reports that the events were badly managed, particularly the handicaps. Most of the competitors taking part had played at Nice, but there was a newcomer of note, William Cranston from the United States. As everyone expected, Doherty continued his domination in the men's open singles, accounting for Blackwood Price in the final, 6–2 6–1 6–1. He then partnered Voss to victory in the men's doubles – a foregone conclusion. Ruth Dyas, the only lady of first class status, was heavily handicapped and was eliminated at the semi-final stage by Clara Schulenburg, who in turn lost to a Miss Miles.

# 1898
# Golf is a Threat

The Beau Site Hotel tournament was not held during the season as there appeared to be a lack of support and suggestions that golf was a serious rival. Nevertheless, the courts at the hotel were much patronised each day.

The Nice meeting started badly by losing the opening day due to rain, but to compensate the final matches took place in delightful weather. Compared to the previous year the quality of the players entered was very poor, with only the two Doherty brothers rated as first class.

Drawn against his brother in the first round of the level men's singles, Reggie scratched and allowed Laurie to win through the four rounds to take the first prize with the greatest of ease, defeating J.R. Hay-Gordon in the final, 6–1 6–2 6–1. Laurie hardly appeared to move about his half of the court, whereas his opponents kept racing up and down their baseline as if performing a hundred yards sprint!

The five handicap events were well supported. An unknown, Miss M. Chalier, won the ladies' singles, beating Clara Schulenburg in the final, but the Dohertys, in partnership, were so heavily handicapped they never stood a chance.

The Monte Carlo tournament immediately followed Nice and was blessed with the sun shining most of the time. In the men's open singles 34 players started and, as expected, Reggie withdrew after finding himself due to play his brother in the third round. The latter moved through to defeat Victor Voss in the final after a fine contest in which the German surprisingly took the opening set, 6–4, before gradually fading, 6–3 6–3 4–0 ret'd. Voss' play proved to be the feature of the week as, in the lower half of the draw, he beat very experienced players, George Hillyard, 6–3 9–7, and George Ball-Green, 6–0 2–6 6–3, in successive rounds. Apparently, Voss had practised little in recent weeks as he had devoted his time to pigeon shooting, a sport where he was rated as one of the best marksmen in Europe. He had also earlier recovered from a severe attack of typhoid fever.

The men's doubles saw the Dohertys in tandem coasting through, their quality of play reflected in the 6–3 6–3 6–0 defeat of Blackwood-Price and André Fomberlaux in the final. In the handicap events Ernest Renshaw played in the doubles, while Miss Chalier proved to be the best in the ladies' singles. One afternoon society turned out in full to watch the play, among them being the Prince of Wales, who took great interest in the handicap events, particularly the doubles match between Reggie and Voss and Blackwood Price and Willie Lemaire de Warzee from Belgium.

As mentioned earlier, golf was very popular in Cannes during the spring and notable players like Hillyard, Reggie Doherty and Manliffe Goodbody were frequent visitors to the Cannes Golf Club at La Napole. The first mentioned proved himself to be the best golfer on the links, winning the gold medal for the lowest net score. He had the honour of receiving this from the Prince of Wales.

Early in the season, before the commencement of the international tournaments, a 17 year-old American, Frederick Alexander was holidaying with his family on the Riviera when he happened to be walking by the Nice Tennis Club in the Platz Mozart. He met the Secretary, another American, A.G. Morganstern, who suggested that he should enter the Nice Club Championship. This he did and in a not too strong field reached the final of the singles before losing to André Chalier. In the opening round he defeated Lemaire, who became a Belgian Davis Cup player in 1904. Another day he watched the Doherty brothers play at Monte Carlo and then moved on with his family to Rome. Some years later Alexander returned to the Riviera with outstanding effect.

# 1899
# Reggie Doherty in Full Flight

At the beginning of the year the only tournament that was certain to take place was at Nice. Whether meetings would be arranged at the Beau Site Hotel and at Monte Carlo was uncertain. However, after an announcement that the latter tournament would be held "under French management" and that the municipal authorities had granted the usual four-figure sum for the prizes, all was well. As regards Cannes it was feared that the ever-increasing interest in golf would drown the usual interest in tennis but, nevertheless, a small tournament was arranged during the last week of February. Thanks to Mr Simpson, who was able to arrange the attendance of Reggie Doherty and Count Victor Voss.

As usual, all the events at Cannes were handicap. Reggie and Voss were well above the class of the other competitors and, although both were handicapped heavily, they managed to pass all their opponents with ease to reach the final. Here a good match ensued but the Englishman, playing in his usual graceful and easy style, won comfortably, 6–3 6–3. When Doherty got to the net he had the Count at his mercy. The finalists paired to win the doubles handicap, but not without a fight in the final against Ernest Wills and Druce. The ladies' singles handicap was won by Miss Edith Riseley. A ladies' doubles handicap event was held and from the ten pairs entered, four were sisters, Misses Hudd, Faber, Debenham and Helen and Katie Pillans.

At Nice the men's and ladies' singles were both level events with the titles 'South of France Championships' added for the first time. Laurie Doherty did not take part in the tournament events as he had not been too well in recent months and had been advised by his doctor not to play singles matches. However, there were times he was seen practising on the courts.

Reggie Doherty was in full flight and with Voss had no bother in reaching the final of the singles. Here the Englishman was in phenomenal form to administer a 6–0 6–0 6–0 beating. Voss was by no means playing below his reputation but obviously Doherty had never played better. Mildred Brooksmith became the first holder of the new title, reaching the final via two walkovers then dismissing Miss M. Chalier, 6–3 6–0.

Doherty and Voss paired for the men's doubles handicap but fell early. In the same competition Harry Barlow and Ernest Renshaw entered but

Despite being a consistent visitor to the coast, Ernest Wills never won an open title although he was prominent in handicap events.

withdrew, sadly disappointing the spectators. The Allen twins, Charles and Roy, on their way back from Rome, called in at the tournament and on the last day played an exhibition match against Doherty and Voss. The latter won in three sets, dropping the opening set, 6–0. The brothers were great enthusiasts of the game and would normally travel anywhere to compete. They were what were called "pot hunters". People found difficulty in distinguishing between the two. They were a very good doubles pair, but in singles Roy was by far the better player and occasionally would put out a 'top crack'. They continued to play tournament tennis up to 1914.

Because of the earlier doubts whether the Monte Carlo tournament would be staged, the start was delayed until 4th April. For the third time in a couple of months, Reggie defeated Voss in the final of the men's open singles, on this occasion by 6–2 ret'd. They were both superior to the remainder of the field and, interestingly, Reggie put out Harry Barlow with ease in the opening round, 6–1 6–1. The two finalists combined to win the men's open doubles. In a different class they overwhelmed de Gordon and Willie Lemaire, 6–0 6–0 ret'd in the final.

Laurie Doherty consented to play in the doubles and, partnered by Ernest Renshaw, played Reggie and Voss in the opening round. This was a match of exceedingly high quality, which delighted all the spectators and resulted in victory to Reggie and Voss, 6–3 6–4. This was Ernest's last match ever on the Riviera. Laurie also played in the mixed doubles handicap with Clara Schulenburg. Miss E. Bosworth won the ladies' singles handicap. New players to the Riviera were the Italians, Count Minerti and C. Lamperti, who both showed promise.

NOTE. *Detailed match scores from the men's singles show that Reggie won the event. Laurie was frequently playing on the courts but did not take part in the tournament. Subsequently, annuals and record books show Laurie as being the champion that year, so it must be assumed that Reggie, having won, withdrew in favour of his brother who was champion the year before in 1898.*

*In 1900, Reggie won the event but the detailed results show that Reggie again retired in favour of his brother, but this time in what was listed as a Challenge Round. Laurie played in the tournament but not in the men's singles. Having 'won' three times, he made the Challenge Cup his own property. At that time, 'Lawn Tennis and Croquet', the official journal of the LTA, queried this procedure but did not pursue the matter.*

# 1900
# Only Two Tournaments Played

There was no Monte Carlo tournament this season. Problems with the management existed and there were reports that the courts were not in good shape.

Although generally very successful, the Nice meeting had much to contend with regarding the weather. Never had so much snow fallen at that time of the year, forcing the play which started on 19th March to be extended to two weeks and terminate on 31st March. The scheduling of the matches caused the Committee many problems.

In the men's open singles a Challenge Round had been established, which meant that the holder, Laurie Doherty, stood out to await his challenger. In the draw was Reggie, who with little effort won through to beat C.B. Weir in the final. In the Challenge Round, Reggie withdrew which left Laurie retaining his title. In the doubles the Dohertys paired and were never in any serious trouble to claim the event. They also played in handicap events. There were only five competitors in the ladies' open singles, which Countess Schulenburg took in her stride.

Towards the end of the week a magnificent exhibition match was staged between the Dohertys and Thomas Burke and Clarence Hobart. The play

A view of the entrance to the Nice Lawn Tennis Club, situated in the Platz Mozart.

was brilliant and resulted in the brothers happily edging out, 7–5 8–6 6–4.

Similar to the year before, it was doubtful whether the Beau Site Hotel tournament would take place. However, a committee led by L. de Goldstand, the Secretary, was indefatigable in obtaining entries and persuading local gentlemen to assist in providing prizes, with the consequence that a very small meeting transpired. As usual, all the events were handicap with Count Voss winning the men's singles, defeating Wills in the final, 3–6 6–2 6–4. Reggie Doherty played in this event but retired to Voss at the semi-final stage.

Both Dohertys contested the men's doubles handicap, Laurie with Edward Ditson and Reggie with Voss. In the end, Laurie and Ditson won the title over Lemaire and A. Taylor, 1–6 6–2 8–6. The ladies' singles handicap attracted a good entry, with Countess Schulenburg winning the top prize. Both Dohertys played in the mixed doubles handicap, which was won by Hobart and his wife.

Hobart, born in Waltham, Massachusetts, USA, but resident in New York, made a very favourable impression with his style of play when he visited Europe in 1898 and 1899. However, just before his first visit to the Riviera in 1900 he had not been too well and was advised by his doctor to avoid the stress of singles play and confine his activities to doubles, which he did. He had an outstanding record, being listed in the United States top ten singles rankings on ten occasions between 1890 and 1907 and becoming runner-up in the US Championships to Oliver Campbell in 1891. He also won the doubles championship twice and the mixed doubles with his wife, Augusta (née Schultz) in 1905. She established herself as a competent performer at the 1893 US Championships by reaching the All Comers' singles final and doubles final. Hobart was born on 27th June 1870 and died on 2nd August 1930, following a swimming pool accident

James Edward Ditson was the grandson of Oliver Ditson, the renowned music publisher from Boston, USA and a cousin of Henry Ditson, partner in the sports goods company, Wright & Ditson, who produced the lawn tennis annual from 1890 to 1940. Ditson died in Montreux, Switzerland in 1952, aged 73.

Clarence Hobart made his only visit to the Riviera this year and impressed all by his style of play. He was runner-up in the United States Championship in 1891 and twice a doubles winner. Unfortunately, he was recovering from illness and confined himself to doubles and exhibition matches.

Thomas Burke from Ireland playing on the Beau Site Hotel courts. He became an outstanding professional.

Voss did not compete on the Riviera again. He was the first top class German player, who had a good forehand and volleyed well, but on the other wing his strokes were comparatively weak. His service was hard, but not too difficult to return. He was born on 31st March 1868 in New York and married Marchesa Francesca Ricci in New York in 1911. He divorced in 1927 and married Clara Schulenburg a year later. He died in Warren, Mecklenburg, Germany on 9th August 1936.

# 1901
# Beau Site Hotel Holds First Open Tournament

For the first time the three tournaments were arranged to follow one another. Also, a great step forward was the decision of the Beau Site Hotel to hold open events which, to some degree, showed the rising standard of the play. The courts had been fully tested earlier in the season by the nobility of the area, which included the Grand Duchess Anastasie of Mecklenberg-Schwerin, the young Grand Duke, Countess Torby, Countess Schulenburg and Grand Duke Cyril of Russia, with the professional, Thomas Burke, being among the players.

There were two level events allocated, the men's and ladies' singles. In the former, Laurence Doherty won the first prize by holding the reins throughout against George Hillyard, who could not consolidate the chances he had in the second set and went down, 6–3 6–3 ret'd. The day before Hillyard had played very solidly to cause the exit of Wilberforce Eaves, 6–2 6–2. Born in Australia, but resident in England, Eaves was a highly qualified doctor who had earlier returned after service in the South African War. Earlier, Hillyard had accounted for a newcomer from the United States, Basil de Garmendia, 6–4 6–0. Reggie entered but withdrew from the event in favour of his brother in the second round. Blanche Hillyard was far too strong for all the other competitors in her division, beating Miss Gladys Duddell in the final, 6–2 6–2. In addition there were five handicap events in the programme. The Doherty brothers entered the doubles, but withdrew.

The Monte Carlo meeting was back in full swing this year at the Hotel de Paris, where the two courts had been completely overhauled. In particular the background behind the players was fitted with green curtains fixed on wiring, which kept off the wind and dust. The soil, which was different to Cannes and Nice made the courts harder and more gravelly and consequently affected the bounce of the ball. New challenge cups designed by Taburet of Paris were introduced. Keen to attract players from England to compete in the tournament, the organisers, a couple of months beforehand, placed an advertisement in 'Lawn

An open international event was played at the Beau Site Hotel for the first time. The courts were tested very early in the year by the local nobility, including the Grand Duchess of Mecklenburg-Schwerin (below), a great patron of the game who regularly practised with Clara Schulenburg.

A view of the two courts at the Hotel de Paris, Monte Carlo. On the left are Reggie and Laurie Doherty who are playing Roy and Charles Allen in the men's doubles handicap event.

Tennis & Croquet', the official journal of the Lawn Tennis Association, detailing the events and prizes. From then on annually the majority of the tournaments on the Riviera followed suit.

The meeting lasted 10 days and consisted of four level events and six handicap events, well-supported by the Doherty brothers, Allen brothers, George and Blanche Hillyard and Eaves, to mention just a few leading players.

In the men's level singles, Reggie withdrew in the opening round to Hillyard who advanced to meet Laurie. This match featured high-class

Wilberforce Eaves, born in Australia but resident in England, visited the coast for the first time. Although he did not win any singles titles he gave great promise for the future by stretching the Dohertys.

play, but Hillyard, not at his best at the start, missed chances on his service in the second set to lose, 6–3 6–4. Laurie met Eaves in the final and won the opening set comfortably, 6–2, but then, leading by five games to three, his opponent pulled up marvellously by reeling off the next four games. His volleying was superb. Laurie then mastered the situation to win the third set, 6–1.

The Doherty brothers won the doubles final from Eaves and Hillyard, 2–6 7–5 6–4 6–1. The latter pair had beaten the Allens in the round before, 2–6 6–4 6–2.

Blanche Hillyard was in a class of her own during the season and had little bother winning the singles at the Beau Site Hotel, Monte Carlo and Nice.

Blanche Hillyard was expected to win the ladies' singles and this she did with ease, defeating Mildred Brooksmith in the ultimate match, 6–2 6–1. In the ladies' singles handicap, Blanche Hillyard was a match point down before beating Gladys Duddell in the final, 6–2 2–6 8–6. As expected, George and Blanche Hillyard won the mixed doubles. On the last day of the meeting, Leopold, King of the Belgians and his daughter, Princess Clementine, watched the play, having driven over from Cimiez.

The Nice tournament ended the season with a similar list of competitors to Monte Carlo. The men's singles was a repeat of a week earlier, with Reggie withdrawing and Laurie going through to beat Eaves in the final this time, 6–3 6–3 6–2. The men's doubles saw the Dohertys eliminating Eaves and Hillyard, 3–6 6–4 6–3, before conquering the Allens in the final, 7–5 6–2 6–0.

A good entry in the ladies' singles resulted, as expected, with Blanche Hillyard on top again. Clara Schulenburg fought well throughout the final and the score of 6–4 6–3 reflected the balance of play.

A very welcome guest to the Riviera during the season was Dwight Davis, the American player who a couple of years earlier donated the Davis Cup for international competition. He played several exhibition matches at Cannes, Nice, San Remo and Monte Carlo, but did not take part in the tournaments.

# 1902
# Menton Joins the Throng

The Beau Site Hotel tournament at Cannes was not held this year and no satisfactory explanation was forthcoming. Possibly the entry was poor, with many favouring golf. However, the courts at the hotel were reported to be in great demand daily by visitors. A new international meeting was staged at the Menton Lawn Tennis Club which, from a tentative start, developed into a regular fixture for many, many years.

Monte Carlo became the opening meeting of the season on the 1st March at the Hotel de Paris. The courts were in excellent condition and the weather throughout had never been better for the time of year, with the temperature ideal for outdoor play. Even the mistral, which usually blows along the coast in the afternoons, kept off. The entries were more numerous than in recent years, with all striving to win a trophy, the Challenge Cups being to the value of 5,000 FF and the prizes exceeding 5,500 FF.

Some of the players stayed at the Hotel de l'Europe, which was five minutes distance from the courts and three from the railway station. This gave full board and lodging with wine from 10 FF a day, according to the situation of the room. Others were attracted to the Hotel Metropole, which was first class, and could arrange 'all-found' from 16–20 FF a day.

Neither Laurie Doherty nor Blanche Hillyard were able to defend their titles, although Laurie visited in the concluding stages of the meeting. Reggie arrived late from Switzerland, where at St Moritz he had played some tennis with Miss Lottie Dod (five times Wimbledon singles champion) and her brothers, who were on holiday.

Although his health was not particularly good, Reggie still held his own throughout the men's singles, which concluded with him defeating George Hillyard, 6–4 6–4 6–3. The latter had been spending much time playing golf and was out of practice. The remainder of the competitors were not really in the class of the two finalists.

In a small field, Clara Schulenburg comfortably beat Mildred Brooksmith in the final, 6–3 6–3. When Reggie paired with Hillyard in the men's doubles the outcome seemed certain. So it was, but Xenophon Casdagli and Willie Lemaire gave them a run for their money and even captured a set before falling, 6–0 8–6 4–6 6–3. Reggie and Clara Schulenburg won the mixed doubles.

Nice followed and experienced ideal weather. Both Doherty brothers were present and competed in the men's singles. Casdagli's game had noticeably improved and, with a very severe forehand, he put aside Charles Allen, 6–1 6–4, before facing Reggie in the semi-final and going down 6–3 6–4. Earlier, Laurie really had to exert himself to win against unknown Captain Alderson, the score telling the tale, 9–7 7–5. As expected, Reggie withdrew from the final to let Laurie retain his title.

With Blanche Hillyard not entered, Clara Schulenburg had little trouble in winning the ladies' singles title in a field of four, beating Mildred Brooksmith at the last stage in two sets of nine games. The Dohertys had little opposition in axing the doubles, while Reggie and Clara Schulenburg, solid from the baseline, won the mixed doubles handicap, despite owing 40.

During the last two days a small professional tournament took place in which Thomas Burke (Cannes) beat Charles Haggett (Stockholm), 6–2 6–3 6–4, beat Tom Fleming (Beau Site), 3–6 6–4 6–3 6–2. Haggett beat Fleming, 6–1 6–0 6–1. Burke won the £100 prize donated by a wealthy American.

The new international tournament staged at Menton, the most easterly town on the Riviera, next to the Italian frontier, was successful with well-known players competing, such as the Allen brothers, Charles and

A view of the Beau Site Hotel courts.

Louise Martin, an eventual eight times Irish champion, visited the area for a few weeks. She did not compete in tournaments but participated in a number of friendly and exhibition matches – and played a lot of golf.

Roy, Lemaire and Basil de Garmendia. In the final of the men's open singles Lemaire outlasted Charles Allen, 3–6 6–2 6–4 7–5, while Miss V. Henshaw won the ladies' singles. The Club had made great progress since the opening just a year earlier and their place on the Riviera schedule was made secure for many years under the title of the Riviera Championships.

There was a very well-known player who visited the area that season. Miss Louise Martin, eight times Irish champion, stayed at Monte Carlo for ten days, where she played in some arranged friendly matches before moving on to Cannes and devoting much of her time to golf. However, a special exhibition match was arranged with her partnering Hillyard against Reggie Doherty and Clara Schulenburg, but unfortunately the rain came and the duel was cancelled. Clara Schulenburg also 'knocked-up' several times in singles with Louise Martin and in one semi-serious match won a single set match, 6–3.

# 1903
# Top Class Entries from England

The Monte Carlo tournament was the starting point of the season and, with an excellent entry, which included many of the top class English players of the day, was ensured of success from the start. The presence of Frank Riseley, Major Ritchie, Sidney Smith, George Hillyard, plus the two Allens and Dohertys, enabled great matches to take place. In the men's singles one of the outstanding contests was the final, when defending champion, Reggie, won through against Riseley, 6–1 14–16 ret'd. The first set was won comfortably by Reggie but in the second he led 5–3 only to be pulled back. After a struggle for supremacy between the two, in which the play was of the highest level, the score reached 14–all and Reggie proceeded to lose his service to 15, and with not too much effort his opponent served out for the set at 16–14. At that point Riseley retired, leaving Reggie the winner. No reason was given. In the semi-final Riseley put out Ritchie in four sets, 6–3 6–3 6–8 6–4. When the latter won the third set, he seemed to be in control but Riseley quickly brought matters to a conclusion. In the other semi-final Laurie gave a walkover to Reggie. The round before, Laurie playing from the back of the court, beat Smith at his own game, 6–2 6–2. Hillyard withdrew from the singles without playing.

The presence of Englishmen Frank Riseley and Sidney Smith (far left) for the first time ensured major opposition would be given to the two Doherty brothers. Riseley against Reggie and Smith versus Laurie produced classic encounters. In doubles the brothers were beaten on one occasion at the Monte Carlo meeting.

A new visitor to the Riviera, Miss Toupie Lowther, carried too much armoury for the remainder of her opponents in the ladies' singles and with great confidence beat Mildred Brooksmith in the final, 6–3 6–1. In the round before, Mildred Brooksmith put out Clara Schulenburg in a fierce struggle, 10–8 6–3, while Toupie Lowther passed Mlle de Robiglio, 6–3 6–3. In the men's doubles Smith and Riseley defeated Laurie and Ritchie at the last stage, 13–11 6–4 6–4.

By general acclaim the outstanding encounter of the meeting was in the second round of the men's doubles handicap, where the Doherty brothers faced Smith and Riseley. Both pairs handicapped at 0–40, started

Toupie Lowther was too strong for the remainder of the ladies as she won the Monte Carlo and Nice singles titles.

even and, because of the great interest in the match, it was agreed to play the best of five sets. At The Championships at Wimbledon the previous year the Dohertys had been surprisingly beaten by this pair and the question was could they repeat the performance? The court was very crowded and the play worthy of the occasion. After a wonderful display the brothers were beaten, 11–9 6–3 6–4. The mixed doubles title was won by Smith and Mrs Ruth Winch, who edged out against Laurie and Toupie Lowther, 6–3 7–5. Without question, this was a meeting to be cherished.

A few months before the Nice tournament was due to commence, a situation arose in which the status of amateurs and professionals in the game came under scrutiny. The Nice Club Committee had issued a prospectus proposing that a combined competition be held between amateurs and professionals, whereby the former would receive prizes of stated value and the latter, money. In other words, both classes would play in the same competition.

The British LTA, to whom the Club was affiliated, stated that they could not sanction this tournament as proposed. Also, they added that if the Nice Club wished to find out whether the best professional was better than the best amateur, a competition could be held between professionals for money prizes and another competition for amateurs for ordinary prizes, after which there would be no objection to the winning amateur playing the winning professional, provided that no prize of any kind was offered.

The Nice Club Committee, without any hesitation, replied agreeing to remodel their programme on the lines suggested by the LTA and so the competition was duly staged. The winning amateur received a prize to the value of 1,000FF and the winning professional received 2,000FF in money. Other prizes were given for second and third places.

During the season the Allen brothers, Roy and Charles, won the men's doubles title at Menton, a feat they repeated in 1904 and 1905. They visited the Riviera frequently and were very popular. Being identical twins the umpires were often puzzled as to which was which. They were sometimes referred to as Tweedledum and Tweedledee.

The whole tournament lasted a fortnight from 9th to 22nd March and every day experienced beautiful weather. Play started each day at 8.30 am. The outstanding match of the meeting was undoubtedly the men's singles final between Laurie Doherty and Smith, which developed into a test of strength. Laurie withstood the bombardment of Smith's marvellous drives, being able to return anything. The first two sets went up and down and could have been captured by either, but Smith prevailed to take the lead. At this point he appeared to tire and Laurie, pressing most of the time, reached two sets all. Both suffered from fatigue in the deciding set, with Smith being in greater distress. The gallery, in a state of great excitement, saw Laurie eventually lead 4–3 before Smith conceded the last two games, winning just one point. The final score in Laurie's favour was 5–7 3–6 6–3 6–4 6–3. This gave him his sixth consecutive South of France Championships and the possession of a second Challenge Cup. In other matches of the event, Laurie beat Ritchie, 6–3 6–3, before being given a walkover by Reggie. Smith at the same stage accounted for the Austrian, Rolf Kinzl, 6–2 6–2. Toupie Lowther, certainly in a class above all the other contestants in the ladies' singles, duly won the title but not before dropping the first set to

Clara Schulenburg, 1–6 6–1 6–2. Toupie Lowther's volleying was superb. The men's doubles was won by the Dohertys and the mixed by Reggie and the Countess.

The competition for amateurs/professionals resulted as follows: Amateurs – two groups of four players playing each other resulted with Reggie 3 wins, Ritchie 2, Rolf Kinzl 1, Clement Cazalet ret'd. Laurie 3 wins, Hillyard 2, Lionel Escombe 1, Willie Lemaire O. Professionals – one group of three players playing each other, Thomas Burke 2 wins, George Kerr 1, Charles Hierons 0. In the play-offs, Laurie beat Kerr, 6–3 6–2 7–5, and Reggie defeated Burke, 1–6 6–1 6–0 6–0. The better side was plainly seen.

For the second year running the Beau Site Hotel did not organise an open tournament. Most of the top players had left for home or were engaged in golf contests at the nearby La Napoule. However, following the Nice meeting handicap events took place, with the Doherty brothers, Hillyard, Clara Schulenburg and Ruth Winch participating. Hillyard won the handicap singles and received a ruby and diamond pin from the Grand Duchess Anastasie. Ruth Winch was prominent among the ladies. Earlier in the year, on 30th January, the proprietor of the hotel, Georges Gougoltz, troubled with financial problems, shot himself.

The Menton tournament was staged for the second year and an enjoyable time was had by all. Many players had left for other locations and it was left to Roy Allen and Mildred Brooksmith to take the major singles honours, while the Allen brothers were too good in the doubles.

# 1904

# The Metropole Hotel Joins to Make
# Five Tournaments

With the Beau Site Hotel tournament back in the fold and the addition of the Metropole Hotel at Cannes, plus the usual Menton, Monte Carlo and Nice, the total meetings for the season reached five, the largest to date.

Instead of being the last gathering, Menton opened up the play on 18th February and lasted a week. There were three open events and three handicap events. In the men's open singles, Major Ritchie won the Challenge Cup by beating Roy Allen in the final, 6–4 6–2 6–1. He was also given a bronze goblet as first prize. Miss Henshaw won the ladies' title and the Allen brothers won the men's doubles.

In the ladies' singles final Miss Henshaw regained the title she held in 1902 by overcoming Miss Rooke after conceding the opening set, 5–7 6–2 6–1. Besides receiving the Challenge Bowl she was presented with a silver mounted umbrella. The Allen brothers, Charles and Roy, held too many guns for Ritchie and Evan Gwynne Evans in the final of the men's doubles, winning in straight sets, 6–2 6–2 6–2.

Monte Carlo was plagued with much rain on several days, which meant that some of the handicap finals did not take place. The meeting could not boast of the same excellent entries as the year before but, nevertheless, with the Dohertys, Allens, Wilberforce Eaves, Clement Cazalet and Ritchie engaged, there was some fine play. Both the Dohertys seemed at times to be in remarkable form, although Reggie appeared to be rather stale at the end of the week when he met Ritchie in the singles final, which very nearly proved to be a five set match. But for a point given against Ritchie, which was disputed, at the close of the fourth set, there was no knowing what the result may have been. Reggie looked exhausted at the end, but won, 6–1 7–5 3–6 7–5. The Dohertys were drawn to meet each other in the second round, but Laurie withdrew and Reggie went on to beat Roy Allen, 6–2 9–7, before receiving another walkover into the final.

Paired, the Dohertys comfortably beat the Allens in the doubles final, 8–6 6–2 6–4. This match attracted the largest crowd of spectators the courts had seen, fully a thousand people being present, including Princess Stephanie of Austria. In the ladies' singles final, Mlle de Robiglio confirmed how much she had improved by defeating Clara Schulenburg, 6–2 6–2. Laurie and Miss K. Kentish won the mixed doubles title when Reggie and the Countess withdrew. In all, 5,000FF worth of prizes were given, while Reggie carried away the 3,000FF silver cup for his third victory in a row.

The Nice tournament followed, commencing on 7th March and lasting 10 days. On the whole, the weather was quite favourable but on the final day the gate suffered on account of a very high wind.

Disappointingly, Cazalet and Evans scratched. This left the two finalists in the men's singles as predictable, with Laurie Doherty against Ritchie. The match was quite one-sided with Ritchie unable to pass his opponent at the net. Laurie's marvellous powers of anticipation enabled him to win comfortably, 6–2 6–3 6–3. This was the seventh time in succession that Laurie had been champion. Both Allen brothers reached the semi-final, with Charles giving Laurie a walkover and Roy falling, 6–3 6–4, mainly because of his mistake in trying to play Ritchie from the baseline.

As quite often happened, the Doherty brothers found themselves in the same half of the draw. This time Reggie retired early on to Laurie. Lurking in the second round of the event was Henry Slocum, the United States champion of 1888 and 1889. He was defeated by Charles Allen, 6–3 6–3.

For the second season running Major Ritchie gave good account of himself, pushing both Dohertys hard in finals. As consolation he gained the singles titles at Menton and the newly established Metropole Hotel meeting.

The final of the ladies' singles between Clara Schulenburg and Mlle de Robiglio was one of the finest encounters ever played at Nice, with the hitting from both being quite severe, but in the end the Countess got her revenge for her loss at Monte Carlo, to the tune of 8–6 7–5. A splendid match enjoyed by all.

The Dohertys easily confirmed their superiority over the Allens in the final of the men's doubles. The Allens won the opening set, 6–1, but then their opponents settled down to win, 6–3 6–3. Reggie and the Countess captured the mixed doubles title.

The reappearance of the Beau Site Hotel tournament, with the three perfect courts available, was rewarded with a very high level of support from the players, with names such as the Doherty brothers, Eaves, Ritchie, Frederic Payn, Gwynne Evans, Arthur Stanley, Slocum, Clara Schulenburg, Ruth Winch, Miss Kentish, Miss Amy Ransome and Miss Miles, etc. The hotel was reported to be full of youth, beauty, fashion and endless gaiety and, what with tennis, golf, dancing and bridge, time went only too quickly. The play was good and the rallies exciting and the gaily dressed throng that witnessed the matches gave proof with their unbiased enthusiastic applause.

To assist with the whole operation the weather during the week was excellent. George Simond undertook the duties of Referee and handicapper for the first time and all were very satisfied with his performance. Laurie Doherty won the men's singles as expected and it appeared that Ritchie, who faced him in the final, was a beaten man from the start, all confirmed by the score, 6–1 6–1 6–1. Laurie was given a walkover by Reggie in the second round before dispatching Eaves in the semi-final, 7–5 6–1 1–6 6–3. Ritchie at the same stage put aside the left-handed Payn, also in four sets, 6–3 5–7 6–1 6–1.

Ruth Winch won the ladies' title from Clara Schulenburg in the final, 6–3 7–5, and if it had not been for her annoyance at one or two of the umpire's decisions the game would have ended earlier!

The Dohertys won the men's doubles event by demonstrating the superiority of their service and overhead shots against Ritchie and Simond in three sets of ten games each. Besides the three open events there were five handicap competitions, all extremely well supported.

The last meeting of the season was the new tournament held at the Metropole Hotel in Cannes. There were six events but only the men's singles was open. Unfortunately, only six competitors entered and in the end there were just three matches. Reggie Doherty and Eaves had a bye in the first round, but then both withdrew in the semi-finals against Gwynne Evans and Ritchie respectively, who went on to contest the final, won as expected by Ritchie, 6–2 6–3 8–6. The weather was not good, but the new venue was voted a success.

# 1905
# London to Cannes in 25 Hours,
# First Class Return £10–10s

The travel facilities for players from London to the Riviera were advertised that year as follows: the cheapest, shortest and best route was by the London Brighton Railway and l'Ouest (Newhaven-Dieppe) and PLM Railways of France. Travelling first class, passengers would leave Victoria or London Bridge by the 10am service or by the 8.10pm service and be in Cannes in 27½ hours by the former and 25¼ by the latter. Travelling second class the journey was lengthened by about 10 hours in each case, though Paris was reached in the same time. The fares were – first class return £10–10s-6d, second class return £7–11s-8d and free allowance for 66lb registered luggage. Customs examination took place at Dieppe.

During the season there were four tournaments played, one less than 1904, as the Metropole Hotel gathering did not take place. The Menton tournament opened the proceedings on 21st February – event winners were Major Ritchie, Amy Ransome, Charles and Roy Allen and Roy Allen and Mildred Brooksmith.

Frederick Alexander had arrived from America a couple of weeks earlier with his wife, Florence Lousnbury, whom he married on 16th January at St Thomas' Church, New York. He entered the Nice Club Championships, starting on 6th February, and disposed of R. Chalier, 6–3 6–4, Roy Allen, 9–7 4–6 6–3, Charles Allen, 6–4 9–7, and Ritchie in the final, 10–8 6–4 6–4. He then decided not to enter at Menton but practised at Monte Carlo, during which he played two or three exhibition matches, one of them in partnership with Ritchie against Reggie Doherty and Clement Cazalet, a match repeated in the afternoon.

Monte Carlo had splendid weather throughout the tournament, which commenced on 3rd March. Luckily rain fell the week before and returned just after. There were a number of players who intended to compete but subsequently withdrew, having become engaged to be married, including

Two-time Wimbledon champion, Dorothea Chambers, made her first visit to the Riviera. She practised for a few days on the Beau Site Hotel courts (far left) before winning the singles at Monte Carlo (left). A week later at Nice she sprained her wrist and was forced to withdraw from the meeting and the Cannes Club tournament which followed.

Reggie Doherty playing with Countess Clara Schulenburg in the mixed doubles at the Beau Site Hotel.

Sidney Smith, who made all the arrangements to attend with Frank Riseley, his doubles partner, Max Decugis and E.D. Robinson, who met his 'fate' at the hotel where he was staying at Nice. There was also the German, Otto von Muller, who had come south especially to play all the Riviera meetings, but met a charming countrywoman of his at Bordighera and suddenly lost all interest in the game. Apparently, instead of posting his entry he sent the Referee an announcement of his engagement!

As well as these 'deserters' the biggest blow to the organisers was that Alexander was recalled without explanation to New York just before play began, much to the disappointment of the organisers who were looking forward to the possibility of him facing the Doherty brothers.

Consequently, he made his way with his wife to Le Havre to catch the *SS 'La Touraine'* on 4th March, en route to New York. Writing later, Alexander stated that he always remembered the entrance to the Monte Carlo dressing rooms, composed of blocks of stone, upon each of which were chiselled the names of the winners of the tournament and all he could see was the name DOHERTY.

There was a fine men's entry at Monte Carlo. Besides both Doherty brothers there were the Allen twins, Ritchie, Gwynne Evans, Simond and

Wills. Cazalet was also in the draws but fell ill and left for London two days later.

Reggie Doherty, having retired the men's singles trophy the previous year, stood aside for his brother Laurie, who beat Roy Allen with the loss of one game to meet Ritchie in the final. The latter, in great shape, had defeated Gwynne Evans, Wills and Simond with the loss of only five games in six sets and therefore an exciting final was in prospect. The match did not disappoint and unravelled in an exciting manner containing many long rallies, but Laurie, always in control, won through, 6–4 8–6 6–4.

The ladies' singles event was bolstered by the first time appearance on the Riviera of the 1903 and 1904 Wimbledon singles champion, Miss Dorothea Douglass and her compatriot, Miss Constance Wilson. These ladies were in a far higher class than the remainder of the draw and both reached the final with little difficulty, where Dorothea Douglass, as expected, took the title, 6–4 6–1. In the semi-finals, Constance Wilson put out Clara Schulenburg after a 'hiccup' in the second set, 6–4 6–8 6–1, while the Wimbledon champion dismissed Amy Ransome, 6–3 6–1. The Countess had a notable win against Miss Gladys Eastlake Smith earlier on, 6–1 6–1.

Clara Schulenburg posing for the cameras at Monte Carlo.

The Doherty brothers beat the Allen brothers in the doubles final after quite a rousing match, 7–5 6–3 9–7. Roy Allen and Dorothea Douglass took the mixed doubles title.

This was the last occasion that the Monte Carlo tournaments were held on the two courts of the Hotel de Paris. Soon after, the decision was taken to utilise the area to build an annex to the hotel and the venue for the next tournament was moved to the Condamine. The meeting was also the last time Charles Voight carried out the duties of Referee, a position held since 1897.

The 11th Nice open tournament was highly successful, both from a point of view of entries, which numbered 208 and the high class play. The only title in the open events which seemed in doubt was the mixed doubles, which resulted in a tremendous struggle between Reggie Doherty and Clara Schulenburg and Charles Allen and Dorothea Douglass, with the former pair, the holders, eventually winning by 6–4 2–6 12–10. The three sets lasted the better part of two hours and the match having started at 11.30am, many in Nice were late for lunch. The grandstand was full to the end.

Unfortunately, Dorothea Douglass had the misfortune to sprain her wrist in the mixed final, an accident which cost her the chance of winning the ladies' singles from which she was obliged to scratch to Clara Schulenburg in the semi-final on the following day. In the other semi-final Constance Wilson beat Amy Ransome, 6–3 6–1, and went on to defeat the German lady, 6–1 2–6 6–4, in the final, which was an exceedingly tight encounter.

In the men's singles Laurie sailed through to defeat Roy Allen in the title round, 6–3 7–5 7–6, the loser having eliminated Ritchie, 6–3 7–5. Charles Allen withdrew in the semi-final.

Two days of rain had stretched the meeting to 13 days. Unfortunately, this ran into the Beau Site Hotel tournament, where the latter stage of the mixed doubles handicap was eventually decided. There was a request from Nice to Cannes to give a little more time between their meetings in the future.

The gathering at the Beau Site Hotel was, as usual, very enjoyable despite one or two 'old faces' missing. Dorothea Douglass was unable to take part and scratched from all events on account of her sprained wrist. However, she remained to the end, watching the play each day.

Ritchie won the men's singles title with a walkover in the final against Laurie, who had played six sets that day and did not want to overtire himself for the Golf Spring Meeting the following day! Reggie was listed in the draw but retired in the opening round. In the semi-finals Laurie beat Wills, 6–1 6–2, while Ritchie defeated K. Sanderson, 6–2 6–3.

There were no outstanding matches in the men's doubles until the final, when the Dohertys beat Ritchie and Simond, 6–4 6–1 4–6 7–5. As expected, Constance Wilson and Clara Schulenburg duelled to win the title in the final of the ladies' singles, which was comfortably won by the Englishwoman, 6–3 6–3. Reggie and Clara Schulenburg won the mixed doubles, also as expected. Strangely, three matches in a day ended with net cord strokes, two were ladies' doubles and one a men's singles.

During the Monte Carlo tournament an exhibition match between the professionals, Thomas Burke and Tom Fleming was staged, which attracted a good audience. Burke, owing 15 each game, beat his opponent, 6–4 5–7 6–2 5–7 6–4. They played a return match later at the Beau Site Hotel and with the same odds, Burke narrowly lost 6–3 5–7 6–4. The first match was for 575FF and the second 700FF, which they shared.

# 1906
# English Ladies Win Titles

Instead of Menton hosting the opening tournament of the season, it was replaced by Monte Carlo, which staged their Championships for the first time on the three new courts at the Condamine. This meeting was as enjoyable as ever, with over 1,200 spectators present on the day the finals were concluded. The newly appointed Referee was George Simond, whose task to programme the matches was made easier with the extra court available. Despite a very large entry the meeting was finished on time, though on the second day no play took place due to rain.

Naturally, followers of the game were disappointed on hearing the news that Reggie Doherty would not be visiting the coast this year, but his brother, Laurie, was present to carry all before him in the open events, winning all three and for the majority of the time being on top form.

On the way to winning the men's singles title, Laurie defeated Major Ritchie, 6–1 6–2 8–6, W. de Gladky, 8–6 6–1 6–4 and Anthony (Tony) Wilding from New Zealand, making his debut on the Riviera, 8–6 6–3 0–6 6–0, before dismissing Wilberforce Eaves in the final, 6–3 11–9. Eaves, who volleyed well throughout, had comfortably defeated Roy Allen in the other semi-final, 6–2 6–1 6–3.

Laurie and Eaves in partnership won the men's doubles title in an entertaining final against Ritchie and Wilding, 6–2 7–5 6–4. Gladys Eastlake Smith had noticeably improved since last year and won the ladies' title without dropping a set. In the last two rounds she accounted for Miss Rosamund Salusbury, 6–0 6–2, and Amy Ransome, 6–4 6–2. She won a second title with Laurie in the mixed doubles.

The 5th Menton tournament ran very smoothly thanks to a very energetic committee and the tireless efforts of the Referee, A.E. Madge. The men's open singles was won by Wilding, who defeated Ritchie in the last match.

In an entry of 12 for the ladies' singles, Miss Vera Warden from the United States achieved a well-earned victory over Amy Ransome in the final, 8–6 6–3. Vera Warden showed great pluck in this match as her opponent actually stood at 5–2 40–30 in the first set! The winners of the men's doubles were Ritchie and Simond and in the mixed doubles, Wilding and Vera Walden.

This season the venue for the Monte Carlo Championships was changed from the Hotel de Paris to the Condamine courts (right), situated near to the harbour. Laurie Doherty won the men's singles title and Tony Wilding from New Zealand made his debut on the Riviera.

The annual tournament at Nice was brought to a successful conclusion on 19th March. The victory of Laurie over Wilding in three sets in the final gave him the South of France Championships for the ninth successive year and a Challenge Cup for the third time. This final was undoubtedly the match of the week, with Wilding's strokes adapting themselves very much to the fast and high bound of the ball on the gravel courts. His great asset was his fitness. However, Laurie produced all that was required to win, 6–3 8–6 6–2. What surprised the crowds during the week was the splendid form shown by Wilding in dispensing with Ritchie, 6–3 6–0,

Wills, 6–2 8–6, and Arthur Gore, the 1901 Wimbledon champion, 6–2 6–0. Roy Allen was unable to take part in the meeting owing to an injured foot.

The ladies' singles final was very absorbing and this eventually resulted in Toupie Lowther getting the better of Gladys Eastlake Smith, 6–4 5–7 6–3. Toupie Lowther generally seemed to have a little in hand. In the men's doubles division, Eaves and Laurie beat Charles Allen and Wilding, 8–6 8–6 6–8 6–4, in the final, a match in which most people thought the reverse would occur. Allen was the outstanding man on court. Laurie and

Clara Schulenburg comfortably won the mixed doubles for the fourth year running.

The Beau Site Hotel tournament at Cannes, the last of the season, was very much spoilt by the rain, which halted play completely on four days. However, all ended well under the guidance of Simond, the Referee.

For some reason, Laurie decided not to compete in the men's singles, which left the title wide open for Wilding. He had greatly improved his game in recent months, particularly his forehand drive, and defeated Eaves decisively in the final, 6–3 6–1 6–3.

The round before he passed Ritchie, 9–7 6–2, while Eaves had too much in hand for Wills, 6–3 6–0. Toupie Lowther won her second singles title in a row by being in her best form to beat Clara Schulenburg in the final, 6–4 6–4. Toupie Lowther's victims en route were Amy Ransome, 6–3 6–0, and Gladys Eastlake Smith, 2–6 6–4 6–0. A good week's work indeed!

The men's doubles resulted in a comfortable exercise for Ritchie and Wilding, who held too many guns for Gore and Hillyard in the final, 6–4 6–2 6–3. Laurie and Eaves were eliminated by Ritchie and Wilding, 6–3 6–3. Another shock occurred in the mixed doubles final, when the team of Laurie and the Countess were dismissed by Eaves and Ruth Winch, 1–6 6–4 6–4 – the real upset of the meeting.

During the season a Frau Hedwig Nerescheimer from Munich played the ladies' singles as well as handicap events, where she won several prizes. She was to play regularly on the Riviera in the next few years.

At the end of the season Simond stated that he had decided not to compete at any tournament where he was acting professionally as Referee. (There were occasions he still took up the racket!) He had recently acted in that capacity at the Monte Carlo tournament and was already officiating at the Beau Site Hotel and within a short period was in charge of all the Riviera meetings, apart from Menton. He eventually took over that tournament. Simond continued as Referee on the Riviera until the mid 1930s.

This was the last season Hillyard competed on the Riviera, having first played in 1892. He was a first class player, winning numerous titles at home and abroad. At The Championships at Wimbledon he reached the Challenge Round of the Doubles and at the same venue later, won an Olympic gold medal in the doubles. An all-round sportsman he played cricket for Leicestershire and Middlesex and excelled at golf, swimming, pigeon-shooting and billiards. He served in the First World War and rose to the rank of Commander in the Royal Navy. He was a well respected administrator, who was Secretary of the All England Lawn Tennis Club from 1907 to 1925. He married Blanche Bingley, six times Wimbledon singles champion, in 1887. Hillyard died in 1943, aged 79.

# 1907
# Major Ritchie Leads the Way

There were five tournaments held in the 1907 season, four of them won by Ritchie. The first, starting on 21st February, was at Menton, where Ritchie captured outright the singles challenge cup, valued at £10, comfortably defeating George Simond, taking a rest from his refereeing duties, in the last match, 6–2 6–2 6–4. George de Bray, the Russian champion, was in the draw and fell to Simond in two close sets.

Rosamund Salusbury beat Miss Hampshire to take the ladies' singles event, which included two Hungarians visiting the Riviera for the first time, Miss Katalin Czery and Miss Margit Madarasz. Both seemed out of form, but the latter showed good style and promise for the future.

The following Monte Carlo meeting at the Condamine had four courts available, one more than the previous year. Apart from one day, the weather was excellent and, as expected, Laurie Doherty and Ritchie had no difficulty in overcoming the opposition on the way to the final. In this contest, played in dazzling sunshine, Ritchie achieved a famous victory in straight sets of fine quality, which was labelled as the sensation of the season. His service, lobbing and clever passing shots against an opponent obviously giving his best, but decidedly on this occasion not on form, resulted in the score of 8–6 7–5 8–6. This was Doherty's first and last appearance in singles that year.

In the semi-finals, Ritchie beat Gordon Lowe, making his first visit to the Riviera, 6–2 6–3 6–0, and Doherty put aside Robert Powell, 6–1 6–3. Powell, a left-hander from Victoria, Canada, played well, with his volleying being particularly praiseworthy. Daniel Rhodes, a visitor from Boston, USA, never really settled down and lost in the second round to Ritchie, 6–0 6–1 6–1.

Max Decugis was due to play but his entry arrived too late. Gladys Eastlake Smith, the holder, retained her title by outlasting Rosamund Salusbury in a match of three sets, each containing 10 games.

A thoroughly representative entry was received at Nice. Ritchie had the unique distinction of taking two love sets from each of the Wright brothers, Beals and Irving, visitors from the United States. The score against Beals Wright was quite a shock as he was the third ranked American player and was national champion in 1905. He had also won the Olympic singles

medal in 1904 at St Louis. A report suggested that the pair treated the exercise as a holiday.

As expected, Tony Wilding won through to annex the singles title for the first time. After accounting for Powell, 6–0 6–2, he eventually edged out against Decugis in the semi-final after a tremendous struggle in the second set, 6–4 11–9. This was the Frenchman's only appearance on the Riviera that season. Wilding's opponent in the final was Ritchie, who himself had to suffer the rarity of losing the opening two sets, 6–0 6–0, before returning to normality and losing the third set, 6–3. Doherty, playing with Ritchie, beat Wilding and Decugis in the final of the men's doubles, 3–6 7–5 6–1 6–1, but lost in partnership with Countess Clara Schulenburg at the conclusion of the mixed doubles.

Gladys Eastlake-Smith was outstanding in the ladies' singles, winning the title for the first time, accounting for Rosamund Salusbury, Clara Schulenburg and then the surprise finalist, Margit Madarasz, 10–8 6–1.

American visitors to the coast were the Wright brothers Beals and Irving. Beals (above) was the outstanding player, having won the United States Singles Championship in 1905 and an Olympic gold medal in 1904. Both brothers entered Monte Carlo and Nice, but reports suggested that they treated the exercise lightly and more like a holiday.

Ruth Winch had an outstanding tournament at the Beau Site Hotel, winning the ladies' singles title, defeating the holder, Toupie Lowther in the final, 6–0 6–1. Ruth also won the title in 1904.

Ritchie turned the tables on Wilding a week later at the Beau Site Hotel gathering, which attracted 22 competitors to the men's singles event. This occurred in the quarter-final, when the Englishman, employing assiduous lobbing, gained success after dropping the opening set, 2–6 6–4 6–2. From then on nobody could stop Ritchie and he beat Rhodes in the final, 6–4 6–3 ret'd. The Wright brothers entered the singles and then withdrew, but paired, reached the final of the men's doubles, losing to Ritchie and Wilding in four sets.

Ruth Winch was unstoppable when she successfully passed Rosamund Salusbury, 7–5 6–3, Gladys Eastlake Smith, 8–6 6–3 and in the final, the title holder, Toupie Lowther, 6–0 6–1.

The last of the meetings was also at Cannes, where the Metropole Hotel was back on the scene after an absence of three years. There were two open singles events and five handicap events. Ritchie and Clara Schulenburg each had an easy passage to win the major titles.

# 1908
# A Season of Outstanding Weather

The weather for January on the Riviera was quite exceptional with every day, without exception, being bright and mild. Nice in particular took advantage of this with the inhabitants spending much time out of doors and bathing in the afternoons. Those with automobiles made the best of the weather, with trips in all directions. Added to the pleasure for the people, the authorities had recently tarred all the most used thoroughfares, making them free from dust. No one expected the good weather to continue, but generally during the season the weather was quite acceptable apart from a few showers affecting Menton, allowing all venues to be completed on time.

The same five tournaments as in the previous year took place but, instead of Menton opening the proceedings, Monte Carlo led the way. Here an excellent entry was achieved and included newcomers to the Riviera. Laurie Doherty did not enter the singles, which brought Tony Wilding and Wilberforce Eaves to the final, the former having disposed of the Cup holder, Major Ritchie, with conspicuous ease in the semi-final, 6–1 6–3 6–3. Eaves was unexpectedly stubborn, showing great strategic skill and Wilding able to win only by his superior physical condition, 6–3 2–6 6–3 4–6 6–0.

The Doherty brothers scratched from the men's doubles, won by Ritchie and Wilding. Reggie Doherty figured in the handicap singles but was not able to survive the opening round. Laurie Doherty played in the mixed doubles.

Gladys Eastlake Smith won the ladies' singles for the third consecutive time to claim the Cup as her own property by beating Miss Evelyn Dillon in the final, 6–3 6–4. Two months later she became Mrs Lamplough.

The Menton meeting was somewhat marred by intermittent rain for three days, although the programme was completed on time and exciting matches took place, Ritchie's defeat of Wilding, who had routed him the week before, came as a big surprise. The winner showed great pertinacity and sound judgment to triumph in the final, 1–6 6–2 7–5 2–6 8–6. He then joined George Simond to win the men's doubles Cup outright.

The two Dillon sisters, Maude and Evelyn, reached the ladies' singles final, where the latter retired without striking a ball. The sisters were twins

The popular Gladys Eastlake Smith won the Monte Carlo Singles Championship for the third year running to possess the Cup outright. Gladys and Laurie Doherty also won the mixed title for the third consecutive year. A couple of months later she won an Olympic gold medal and married Dr. Lamplough. She is shown earlier on the Beau Site Hotel courts.

and daughters of a retired army Lt. Colonel. Rosamund Salusbury did not defend.

There were two outstanding features of the Nice tournament, the weather remaining favourable for the ten days and the pleasure of seeing the Doherty brothers playing in tandem for the first time in public since 1906. They reached the final but were forced to submit to Ritchie and Wilding in four sets, 6–1 6–4 7–9 6–2. The interest in this memorable match was so overwhelming that the largest crowd ever assembled on the Riviera to watch a tennis match.

The men's singles brought Ritchie and Wilding together once again. Here the latter's fierce driving to the corners of the net became the dominating factor as he won easily, 6–0 6–1 6–3.

Returning to the Riviera after an absence of three years, Dorothea Chambers (Douglass) was accompanied by her husband Robert, who participated in the handicap events. As expected, she won the ladies' singles but was given quite a surprise in the semi-final when Miss Jessie Tripp came within two points of winning in the second set. In the final,

A view of the Beau Site Hotel courts at Cannes, now showing the small marquee provided for important guests.

Rosamund Salusbury played pluckily but managed just three games. Hedwig Neresheimer lost in the second round to the eventual winner.

For the third time in a row Ritchie and Wilding faced each other over the net at the Beau Site Hotel meeting in the final of the men's singles, where Wilding came out on top to register a straight sets victory, 6–3 6–4 6–0. Neither finalist was troubled earlier. Eaves entered the draw but withdrew without playing.

By common consent the best match of the week was the final of the men's doubles, when Ritchie and Wilding came within two points of defeat by Ball-Greene and Eaves, 6–2 3–6 3–6 6–2 8–6.

In a small field Dorothea Chambers beat Hedwig Neresheimer, 6–1 6–0, in the semi-final before defeating Maude Dillon, 6–1 6–4. In a surprise result in the opening round, Jessie Tripp beat Ruth Winch over three sets, but lost to Maude Dillon in the other semi-final.

The Cannes Metropole Hotel tournament brought the season to a close with the usual two open singles events. Support could have been better but rumours of a fever in Cannes drove many of the visitors back to England early. However, there were about 30 competitors to share the three courts which were in excellent condition.

Wilding, who set himself a handicap of owe-30, coasted through the men's singles, beating Hubert de Bertoult in the last match, 6–1 6–3 6–1, while Ruth Winch won her division commandingly over Mrs Eveline Nutcombe Quicke, 6–2 6–1.

By coincidence the Duke of Devonshire, a patron of the game in England, died at the hotel on the eve of the tournament.

There were other features that season. At the Metropole tournament umpires were scarce at certain periods and on one chilly afternoon there was the strange sight of the Referee officiating on one court, the Club Professional, Tom Fleming, on another, while the third was presided over by a young lady, carefully coached by the senior ball boy.

On 21st February the new Cannes Croquet and Lawn Tennis Club was opened by Grand Duchess Anastasie of Mecklenburg-Schwerin. Afterwards the Duchess partnered Reggie Doherty against Simond and Clara Schulenburg in a couple of sets, ending all square. Many other celebrities were present.

Apparently, Manliffe Goodbody the Irish veteran who surprisingly entered the Monte Carlo tournament had remarkable luck in the Casino – a lifetime coup. Reduced to his last five franc piece he backed No.6, which won. The next turn of the wheel brought him another *en plein*, also No.6. Moving to 45 with a *louis* he got another double and was the richer by over £100.

During the Nice tournament, M. Primat, proprietor of the Hotel du Louvre, where the majority of the competitors stayed, instructed his staff to discreetly hide copies of the daily papers containing critical accounts of his guests' previous day's performance, until dinner was served.

# 1909
# Frederick Alexander Dominates the Season

The reputation of the Riviera to have a warm and genial climate during the early months of the year was severely tested. The first three tournaments at Monte Carlo, Menton and Nice suffered unkindly, with very cold weather, mixed with aggressive winds, spasmodic rain and hardly a glimmer of sun. Somehow the management and the players pulled through and all events were completed. However, by the time the Beau Site Hotel's turn came, the real Riviera weather had arrived at last. Handicap events were at the peak of popularity with six being held at each tournament. There was disappointment all round when Wilding decided not to play the Riviera for the season following his visit to Australia and New Zealand.

The outstanding personality of the season was Frederick Alexander, who was making his third visit to the Riviera. He arrived in early February from Australia, via the Suez Canal, having participated in the Davis Cup Challenge round, Australia v USA, in Melbourne during the closing days of November and in the Australian Championships held a week later at Sydney, where he captured the singles and doubles titles.

The opening tournament at Monte Carlo, which started on 22nd February, was particularly affected by the cold, with players shivering in blanket coats while waiting to go on the Condamine courts, spectators huddled together and the ladies wrapping themselves in extra furs. Another problem was that the balls dispatched from London went astray and for a couple of days supplies had to be obtained from local clubs. All was well in the end.

Without a shadow of a doubt the overwhelming feature of the meeting was the defeat of Laurie Doherty, endeavouring to win the Monte Carlo Cup outright, in the final of the men's singles by Alexander. The Englishman started the event confidently by defeating Friedrich Rahe. He then dropped a set to Wallis Myers and then a further one to Major Ritchie in the semi-final, a match played mainly from the back of the court between two men not in the best of form. In the meantime, Alexander moved confidently forward, passing Gordon Lowe in four sets.

In the final the American played throughout with great determination and energy. Doherty led 4–2 but from then on was unable to control the play, and his opponent in attacking mood, particularly on the volley, went from strength to strength to claim a meritorious victory, 7–5 6–4 6–1. This was the only occasion Laurie Doherty lost to an American.

Miss Alice Greene won the ladies' singles for the first time, after being given a close fight by Clara Schulenburg in the final, 4–6 6–2, 6–4, the loser having recorded a good win over Rosamund Salusbury in the round before. The men's doubles title was won by Doherty partnering Ritchie. There was a surprise in the mixed doubles when Myers and Jessie Tripp beat Doherty and Clara Schulenburg and then Ritchie and Alice Greene in the concluding round.

A week later Alexander simply romped through the men's singles at Menton, even to the point of inflicting two 6–0 6–0 victories to enter the final. In this he showed little mercy to Ritchie who, after leading 4–2, felt the full weight of his opponent's sweeping service, incisive cross-volleys and well struck forehands before retiring unwell in the third set at 6–4 6–2 3–0. In the first round Ritchie was taken to the brink of defeat by Rahe in a match where foot-faulting provoked much argument.

For good measure Alexander won a second title when, partnered by Myers he defeated Simond and Ritchie after an uphill struggle in the men's doubles final, 2–6 3–6 6–3 6–4 6–3. Rosamund Salusbury recaptured the singles title which she won in 1907, when Alice Greene retired from the final due to indisposition. In the round before, Alice Greene had dismissed Jessie Tripp, 4–6 6–1 6–2. Myers and Jessie Tripp repeated their success of the previous week at Monte Carlo by winning the mixed doubles.

The weather at Nice was particularly unkind early in the week, which caused the meeting to be drawn out and the normal support from the spectators below par. Alexander continued his domination for the third week as he went through five rounds without any bother, pushing aside Gordon Lowe, 6–1 6–4, and Artemas Holmes 6–3 6–1, before defeating Ritchie decisively in the final, 6–2 6–1 6–2. Together the two then proceeded to win the men's doubles by two advantage sets against Simond and Gwynne Evans in the final.

Alexander's hard hitting and speed about the court no doubt surprised his opponents. His service delivery certainly bothered them, with few being able to master his 'screw service', as the stroke was called. (In the United States this was known as the 'reverse twist').

Clara Schulenburg deservedly won the ladies' singles Cup outright, defeating Jessie Tripp in the final, 6–1 6–8 6–0, but progress was not easy and she had to put the loss of a set behind her. Laurie Doherty and Clara Schulenburg retained their high reputation in winning the mixed doubles.

Fred Alexander's third visit to the Riviera was an overwhelming success as he notched three singles titles in devastating style. He won the Monte Carlo singles by defeating Laurie Doherty in the final, to become the only American to beat the Englishman. At Menton and Nice he showed no mercy to Major Ritchie in both finals.

The delays at Nice caused the Beau Site Hotel meeting to fall behind schedule. Although Alexander had entered the lists he decided to scratch, so as to be able to keep an appointment in Paris with his wife and young son to sail from Cherbourg to New York on the *'Oceanic'* on 31st March. Later in the year Alexander captured the United States doubles championship, for the third time in a row, in partnership with Harold Hackett. This pair also won the title in 1910. Alexander won his fifth title with Harold Throckmorton in 1917.

Alexander's absence from the Beau Site Hotel was very much regretted by the management but, to compensate, the number of players taking part was the best for many years, and the weather throughout was also delightful. There were few surprises, but one was the defeat of Robert Powell by Ferdinand Boelling who really had a 'peak' day. Rahe also played well to dismiss Lowe and went on to meet Ritchie in the final. Here the Englishman was back to his true form and he won, 6–1 4–6 6–2 6–2. This was indeed an exhilarating and absorbing match.

Alice Green and Ruth Winch fought a fierce battle, which was played either side of lunch. Ruth Winch eventually wore down her adversary, 6–8 7–5 6–1 but, being indisposed, was unable to meet Clara Schulenburg in the ultimate match, so the Cup went to Germany. Laurie Doherty and Clara Schulenburg retained their mixed doubles title. This was the last time the name of Doherty appeared on a draw sheet on the Riviera.

The last meeting of the season at the Metropole Hotel attracted a very large entry, although the standard did not rise to that of the earlier meetings. All aspects of the meeting were a great success. Rahe came out on top in the men's singles, but was given a stiff fight by C. Andrewes from England in the final, 9–7 6–1 5–7 6–3. Alice Greene coasted through the ladies' singles, which had only seven competitors, having no problem in beating Eveline Nutcombe Quicke in the final, 6–0 6–2. Rahe and Holmes won the men's doubles, which was being staged as an open event for the first time.

Fortunately the change of weather at Cannes, which allowed the Beau Site Hotel tournament to be played out under beautiful blue skies, was much welcomed by all. By general consent, to be at the hotel during the wonderful spring weather was a delight not only for the players, but also the spectators and guests, who were 'getting away from it all.'

Alice Greene from England adapted well to the conditions on her first trip to the coast, winning two singles titles. She beat Clara Schulenburg at Monte Carlo and Eveline Nutcombe Quicke at the Metropole Hotel.

Reports at the time nicely summed up the attraction of the hotel. "The Beau Site Hotel has now become the leading hotel for the sporting community of Cannes. Before it was turned into an English company, it was owned by Georges Gongoltz, who shot himself one morning. Afterwards it was managed by Henri Pruge, who now runs the Savoy in London, and next year by Weber, now owner of the Hotel de France in Nice. How delightful to be awakened in the morning by the strains of some itinerant band of Italian musicians playing *'Funiculi, Funicula'* or *'O Sole Mio'* and how glorious to fling open one's shutters and look down upon the stately palm, orange and mimosa trees in the garden below, with the tall eucalyptus of the Villa La Rochefoucauld in the background and the blue Mediterranean on the horizon beyond as far as the eye can see and then, after breakfast, the *dolce far niente* of squatting down on the terrace facing the courts in sunshine next to a pretty girl, with an umpire calling 'love all' from his perch on high. Yes indeed, a morning at the Beau Site is a thing to remember. There's nothing like it on this whole Côte d'Azur." Someone else wrote "There are outstanding memories of dancing in the evenings, plus the other little harmless diversion which a tennis community knows so well how to enjoy."

# 1910
# Max Decugis and Major Ritchie to the Fore

The weather was very mixed on the Riviera, where the number of tournaments was increased from five to seven, with the addition of the Cannes Croquet and Lawn Tennis Club and Hyères – an excellent sign of a growing game and the attraction of the Riviera. There was hope that Wilding would visit the area for the season, following his absence in 1909, when he visited Australia and New Zealand, but instead he decided to go to South Africa to compete in their Championships on 24th March.

Following recent practice, Monte Carlo began the programme and for the first time in its history the men's singles was captured by a Frenchman, Max Decugis, who was not only successful, but won with comparative ease against Major Ritchie. Playing to perfection he controlled the first set 6–3 and then in a great charge, took the next two sets, 6–0 6–0. In grand form, Decugis, leading up to the final match, outplayed both Kleinschroth brothers from Europe making their debut on the Riviera, Robert, 6–4 6–1 and Heinrich, 6–2 6–4. Ritchie had beaten Stanley Doust, 6–0 6–4, in the semi-final.

Rosamund Salusbury was on top in the ladies' singles, but dropped a set to Amy Ransome in a fierce struggle, 2–6 7–5 7–5, and another to Mildred Brooksmith in the final, 4–6 6–2 6–2. Doust and Wallis Myers took the men's doubles, while Decugis and his wife, Marie, were successful in the mixed doubles.

A week later, lovely spring weather blessed the Menton meeting. Decugis and Ritchie were too good for most of the competitors and ended facing each other in the final. The Frenchman was leading 4–2 in the first set, when he slipped and strained his foot but, in a very generous action, Ritchie decided to withdraw, leaving Decugis the winner. Rosamund Salusbury retained her title beating Eveline Nutcombe Quicke in the final, 6–3 6–2 and then joined Ritchie to win the mixed doubles Cup outright.

Dreadful weather ensued at Nice, when for four days no play was possible. Once again the protagonists in the final of the men's singles were Decugis and Ritchie. In a very interesting match watched by a large crowd, including the King of Sweden, Ritchie looked like winning despite losing the opening two sets, but Decugis held on and just edged through, 6–3 6–4 3–6 13–11. Ritchie appeared a little tired at times, having played a long

contest with Doust in the semi-final, 6–2 0–6 6–4, while at the same time Decugis got ahead of Heinrich Kleinschroth, 6–1 6–3. Rosamund Salusbury gained her third victory in a row by outlasting Clara Schulenburg, 6–4 3–6 6–3. Decugis and Ritchie never looked like losing the men's doubles.

The Beau Site Hotel tournament had a record entry and splendid weather. Once again Decugis and Ritchie fought out the final of the men's singles but on this occasion Decugis, after winning the opening two sets, 6–4 6–4, retired after losing the third set, 8–6, for no apparent reason. Neither player was pressed in their earlier matches. Rosamund Salusbury was supreme again, beating Clara Schulenburg, 6–3 6–3, and Ruth Winch, comfortably, in the last round, 6–1 6–4. Decugis and Ritchie won the men's doubles title.

The first open meeting of the Cannes Club, held on five courts, was eventually brought to a successful conclusion after adverse conditions and for other reasons. The starting date of 16th March was postponed to 21st when it was known that the Beau Site Hotel had unfortunately fixed the same date and, had their fine weather continued, all would have been well. But Nice dragged on due to the rain and then the Beau Site and the Metropole tournaments clashed, so in the end some players actually found themselves competing in three tournaments!

There were many well-known players competing for the new Côte d'Azur Championships, but few were really in the top class. Artemas Holmes was the successful winner of the men's singles, beating Robert

The Nice Lawn Tennis Club in the Platz Mozart where there was a total of four courts.

A view of the spacious lounge of the Nice Lawn Tennis Club.

Kleinschroth by a walkover and defeating G.H. Nettleton in the final, 4–6 6–2 7–5 6–4. Clara Schulenburg held control throughout against Eveline Nutcombe Quicke in the final, 6–4 6–3. The Referee was Capt. Dawson.

At the Cannes Metropole Hotel meeting which followed, no-one was capable of extending Ritchie although Ferdinand Boelling withstood him pluckily for a time before going down in the final, 6–0 6–0 7–5. In the ladies' singles, the retirement of Clara Schulenburg in the semi-final assisted Rosamund Salusbury to win her fifth successive victory of the season in singles, over Miss E.S. Rose in the final, 6–1 5–2 ret'd. In the past year she had advanced her game consistently and added just that little bit of extra finish in tactics and execution to bring it to first class status.

The two Kleinschroth brothers won the men's doubles, while the scheduled all-German mixed doubles final between Heinrich Kleinschroth and Hedwig Nerescheimer and Boelling and Clara Schulenburg was never contested as the latter pair retired before a ball was struck.

The other new tournament that season was held at the Golf Hotel at Hyères, the town of palms. There was a good entry but not of a very high standard, where the singles titles were annexed by John Flavelle and Mme Regine Vlasto. Five sets had to be played in the men's doubles final before L. Hitchcock and René Gheerbrandt won through. Mr Zick, the proprietor of the hotel, provided two challenge cups and prizes to the value of 1,400FF, while the town of Hyères gave a challenge cup for the men's singles and the golf club a similar one for the ladies.

Apart from a fleeting appearance in 1914, this was the last season that Clara Schulenburg regularly played on the Riviera, having made her first appearance in 1897. For some years she was the outstanding German player, winning several important tournaments including Nice, four times, Monte Carlo, Cannes Club and Cannes Metropole.

Clara possessed firm ground strokes, with her forehand being her best side. Her length was generally good and she served underarm with a twist of the racket. In the early days she quite often played under the pseudonym of 'Mrs Adams'. She was born Clara Kusenberg on 24th July 1874 in Dusseldorf and married Count Hartwig Schulenburg on 16th November 1895 in Berlin. In 1906 they divorced and much later, on 28th March 1928, she married Count Voss in Berlin. Clara died on 26th February 1951 in Berlin. Clara had an elder sister, Antoine Kusenberg (Mme Popp), who played in a number of tournaments on the Riviera at the early part of the century.

# 1911
# Max Decugis Versus Tony Wilding •
# German Players Challenge

A first class entry was received for the Monte Carlo tournament, possibly the best on record. There were some splendid matches in the run through which, as expected, resulted in Max Decugis and Wilding battling out the final of the men's singles, the latter returning to the Riviera after missing two seasons. The Frenchman pressed hard at the start and led by two sets to love, but Wilding's staying power saw him triumph, 5–7 1–6 6–3 6–0 6–1. The winner had eased past Robert Kleinschroth in the round before, 6–2 6–1, but Decugis had a tougher time at the same stage passing, Friedrich Rahe, 6–3 7–5. Rahe, a German from Rostock, had built up an admirable record in Europe over the past few years. In 1908 he represented his country at tennis and hockey at the Olympic Games. Decugis eliminated Major Ritchie rather easily, 6–0 6–1. New to the Riviera were two Americans, Craig Biddle from Philadelphia, who inherited a million dollar fortune from his grandfather, and Richard Williams, born in Geneva, Switzerland – a name to note for the future.

Rosamund Salusbury retained the Ladies' Vase, but she was hard-pressed by Eveline Nutcombe Quicke, 7–5 5–7 6–4, before dismissing Hedwig Neresheimer, 6–4 6–3, and Gladys Colston (Duddell) in the final, 6–2 6–4. Ritchie and Wilding took the men's doubles title but not before spending five sets overcoming Decugis and Rahe, 2–6 6–4 1–6 6–2 6–2. A surprise in the mixed doubles saw the downfall of Decugis and his wife, Marie, to Heinrich Kleinschroth and Hedwig Neresheimer in the final, 6–3 6–1.

Menton provided a week of excellent play in attractive weather. Not surprisingly Decugis and Wilding reached the men's singles final, but both dropped a set on the way, the former to Curt Bergman, 6–2 2–6 7–5 and the latter to Biddle, 6–1 4–6 6–2. A five set match ensued, with Wilding winning 6–2 6–2 3–6 5–7 6–3. Ritchie was fighting, as usual, but was no match for the winner in the semi-final, 6–2 6–4. Rahe retired at the same stage to Decugis. Ritchie and Wilding won the doubles.

Jessie Tripp won her first open singles on the Riviera. Certainly a day she would remember for, in the final, Rosamund Salusbury took her the full distance at 6–2 6–8 7–5. A title well earned. She had won some hard fought matches earlier, notably beating Hedwig Neresheimer, 6–4 6–4,

and Mildred Brooksmith, 7–5 6–2. Ritchie and Wilding and Kleinschroth with Hedwig Neresheimer were successful in the doubles events.

Rain interrupted play several times at Nice but the saga of Decugis and Wilding continued and, as expected, in the final Wilding proved invincible and triumphed without dropping a set, 9–7 6–0 6–3. The New Zealander, therefore, won the Nice Cup outright. Earlier, Williams pressed Decugis severely, 5–7 6–4 6–3. Wilding had beaten Rahe without effort, 6–4 6–1.

The two German ladies contested the singles final with hard-hitting Frl Dagmar von Krohn outwitting Hedwig Neresheimer, 6–2 2–6 6–3. Jessie Tripp lost to the winner, after a tremendous struggle in the quarter-final, 4–6 6–1 7–5. Ritchie and Wilding won the men's doubles again and Kleinschroth and Hedwig Neresheimer were surprisingly beaten by Decugis and his wife, Marie, in the final.

There was a high wind present during the last two days at the Beau Site Hotel meeting, but not sufficient to cause serious problems. This time Decugis and Wilding did not meet in the final of the singles, as the Frenchman lost after a fierce match in the semi-final to Rahe, 6–1 5–7 7–5. Wilding held control in the last match to crush Rahe, 6–1 6–4 6–1. Williams again gave further proof of his advance by extracting a set from Wilding.

Hedwig Neresheimer was in great form, beating Miss Margaret Tripp, the younger sister of Jessie, 6–1 6–4, and Rosamund Salusbury, 6–4 8–10 7–5, to secure the ladies' singles. In the mixed doubles final the German

Tony Wilding (above left) met Max Decugis (right) three times during the season, in the finals at Monte Carlo, Menton and Nice, with the New Zealander triumphant on each occasion. They are seen here playing on the Condamine courts at Monte Carlo.

Hedwig Neresheimer from Germany was prominent during the season, winning the ladies' singles title at the Beau Site Hotel and the Cannes Club. The photograph shows Hedwig playing at Monte Carlo.

partnership proved again to be the best. Ritchie and Wilding won the men's division.

The second annual meeting organised by the Cannes Club, where extensive improvements had been carried out in the previous years, drew an excellent entry, with two Australians, Alfred Dunlop and Rodney Heath, taking part. However, Wilding decided to withdraw from the singles and Rahe proved to be the best player, fending off Heath in the singles final, 6–4 6–4 7–9 6–4. Hedwig Neresheimer beat both Tripp sisters, Jessie, 6–3 6–4 and Margaret, in the final 6–0 6–2. A stale Wilding, paired with Wallis Myers, was beaten in the final of the men's doubles by Rahe and Theodore Mavrogordato, 6–4 6–4. The German pair won the mixed doubles for the fourth time in the season.

For some unexplained reason the Metropole Hotel did not stage a tournament. The Hyères meeting concluded the play for the year, with Frederic Warburg and his wife, Emmeline, dominating all the events.

At the conclusion of the season representatives of the eight clubs constituting the Riviera Tennis Committee (this included Bordighera and San Remo in Italy) met at Menton on 10th April to discuss the programme for 1912. Besides setting the dates they considered how best to avoid the dragging on and overlapping that had occurred in the last two seasons. One of the firm decisions taken was to start each tournament programme one week earlier.

# 1912
# Twelve Year Old Suzanne Lenglen
# Makes Debut

Monte Carlo, the first tournament of the season, was originally scheduled to commence on 19th February at the Condamine, but the Committee agreed to start earlier on 12th February to allow the European middleweight boxing championships to take place. This occurred on 29th February, when George Carpentier (France) defeated Jim Sullivan (Great Britain) in the second round.

For nearly a month before the tournament there was much rain and the players had scarcely been able to practise. Wilding and Decugis, easily the pick of the contenders in the men's singles, met in the semi-final when the New Zealander, despite a bad fall at the end of the first set, won a fine match, 9–11 7–5 6–1.

In the final, Wilding having eased through the first set, 6–3, showed no mercy to his opponent, C. Moore of Britain, and reeled off the next 12 games without reply.

In the ladies' singles, Jessie Tripp was never threatened, with her sister, Margaret, withdrawing from the final. Hedwig Neresheimer, now being listed as Frau Hedwig Satzger, was unable to appear owing to an accident while skating. Wilding did not enter the men's doubles, where the title went to the French pair, Decugis and Maurice Germot. However, Wilding and Frl Magdaline Rieck surprisingly defeated Wallis Myers and Jessie Tripp in the mixed final, 6–0 6–3. The Allen brothers reappeared and had a new veterans' handicap event at their mercy.

Menton, which followed, was devoid of the services of Wilding who, having injured his hand at Monte Carlo, was only able to compete in the mixed doubles. In his absence the men's singles was won by Roy Allen, after a five set final against Myers, 6–0 3–6 6–1 6–8 6–0. Myers had beaten Count Ludwig Salm in the round before.

In an upset in form, Jessie Tripp lost in the second round of the ladies' singles to Magdaline Rieck, 2–6 6–3 6–1. The German, playing steadily, went on to beat Margaret Tripp in the final, 1–6 7–5 6–3, but as the score indicated, it was a hard-won victory. Tony Wilding, partnered by Lady Domini Crosfield, never passed the opening round of the mixed doubles, but they put up a good fight against Salm and Magdaline Rieck, 4–6 6–3 6–4.

Wilding, not recovered, did not defend his singles title at Nice and the honours were carried by France when Decugis beat Germot in the last match, 10–8 4–6 6–2, the former's stamina being the deciding factor. Jessie Tripp gained her revenge over Magdaline Rieck, 6–4 6–4, in the quarter-final and sailed on to win the title when once again her sister, Margaret, defaulted from the final. Hedwig Satzer entered but, still unfit, retired to Miss E.M. White after one set, 7–5. Mrs Maud Barger-Wallach, who was United States National Singles Champion in 1908, lost to Margaret Tripp in the semi-final, 6–2 6–1. In the men's doubles Decugis and Germot were too good for the rest of the field.

Among the competitors for the ladies' singles handicap event was the name Suzanne Lenglen, who was making her debut in a Riviera tournament. After a bye and two walkovers, this 12 year-old girl,

The beginning of an outstanding career in tennis – 12 year old French girl Suzanne Lenglen played her first Riviera tournament in the handicap singles at Nice, losing in the quarter-final to Maud Barger-Wallach of the United States.

*Right:* Magdaline Rieck of Germany appeared for the first time on the scene and gave good account of herself, winning the ladies' singles title at Menton.

born in Paris, lost to Maud Barger-Wallach, 6–1 6–3, in the quarter-final, having played stubbornly in the second set. For eight years after the First World War, Suzanne Lenglen was the undisputed top lady player in the world.

At Cannes, the Beau Site Hotel meeting was ushered in by wet weather and very little play was possible for two days and then came a glorious spell of fine weather. However, with a very large entry it was impossible to finish by the end of the week and play went on until the Tuesday. Decugis and Germot disputed the final of the men's singles, but the latter did not show anything like the form of a week earlier and, to some degree, was overwhelmed, 6–1 6–2 6–4. Jessie Tripp won her fourth title of the season (including San Remo on the Italian Riviera), managing to keep Magdaline Rieck at bay, 6–3 6–1. Decugis and Germot were successful again with the men's doubles, fencing off the two Allen brothers, 6–4 6–2 6–3. By general acclaim the Beau Site meeting was tremendously successful and most enjoyable.

At the other Cannes tournament, the Cannes Club, the leading Frenchmen had left for home but, irrespective, a good entry resulted in the German, Ferdinand Boelling, taking the major honours in beating Myers in the final, a ding dong struggle from beginning to end, 6–2 3–6 6–3 3–6 6–4. Gladys Colston won the ladies' singles and Simond and Myers, the doubles.

At the last of the season's tournaments, played at Hyères, Salm, after vain efforts to win elsewhere, at last won his first open singles on the coast. To celebrate he also won the men's doubles title. Mrs Perrett was outstanding in the ladies' singles.

Lord George Rocksavage, accompanied by Clement Cazalet, arrived at the Beau Site Hotel in late December, well before the start of the season, for the express purpose of raising his game by receiving coaching from the hotel professional, Tom Fleming. A very keen player, he competed up to the First World War and after, regularly until the late 1920s. He was a left-handed player.

Richard Williams, a competitor on the Riviera in 1911, was a survivor from the White Star Line *'Titanic'*, which on her maiden voyage

Maurice Germot, a leading French player excelled without winning a singles crown, but his doubles partnership with Max Decugis was outstanding as they captured the titles at the Beau Site Hotel, Monte Carlo and Nice.

from Southampton to New York struck an iceberg, 400 miles south of Newfoundland, 15 minutes before midnight on 14th April. By 2.20am the next morning the ship had sunk. A total of 1517 passengers perished and 705 survived. Williams, accompanied by his father Duane, was travelling to the United States to enter one of the universities. After entering a lifeboat he spent several hours in freezing conditions before being picked up by the *'Carpathia'*. His father was lost in the disaster, but Karl Behr, a notable American Davis Cup player survived. Williams fully recovered and went on to achieve much at the top of the game.

# 1913
# A New Year Start to the Season

A total of nine tournaments were held during the season and for the first time the experiment of holding a New Year meeting was attempted, with the result proving an unqualified success, although the number of entries was small.

Staged at the Beau Site Hotel in Cannes from 30th December to 5th January, there were two open and four handicap events. Cambridge University, past and present, contested the men's singles final, where the greater energy of Hope Crisp accounted for the old Blue, Clement Cazalet, 6–4 6–2 3–6 6–2. The ladies' singles event could muster only four contestants and in the final Miss Adele Topham beat her younger sister, Doris, 6–1 3–6 6–1. Both stayed in the family villa, 'Haute Rive', while at Cannes. Adele became Mrs Bayon and Doris, Mrs Farlaine, before she emigrated to Canada. The pattern of Christmas/New Year tournaments was set.

The next tournament, beginning on the 3rd February, was at Beaulieu, the latest addition to the Riviera list. This was held at the Bristol Hotel, where three excellent courts, all with ample space, were provided in a beautiful garden adjoining the hotel. This was the start of a campaign by the three German players who practically dominated the season. The leading singles exponent was Friedrich Rahe, who was joined by Heinrich Kleinschroth to attain a very high standard of doubles play, which led them to win the title at Wimbledon a few months later. Heinrich's elder brother, Robert, completed the trio. The

American Elizabeth Ryan, making her initial visit to the Riviera, continued to impress during the season and ended with four singles tournament successes, Beaulieu, Cannes Club, Monte Carlo and Metropole Hotel, Cannes.

Friedrich Rahe returned to the scene and brilliantly captured the singles titles at the Beaulieu, Cannes Club and Beau Site Hotel meetings and just lost in the final at Nice. His partnership with fellow countryman Heinrich Kleinschroth during the season was unbroken as they excelled at six meetings, Beaulieu, Monte Carlo, Menton, Nice, Cannes Metropole and Beau Site Hotel. No wonder they went on to reach the Challenge Round at Wimbledon a few months later.

singles winners were Rahe, who beat Ludwig Salm for the men's singles title, 3–6 6 2 8–6 6–2, and Miss Elizabeth Ryan who accounted for Miss M. Towler in the final, 6–2 6–1.

This was the first season Elizabeth Ryan had played on the Riviera. Born in California, USA, she and her sister, Alice, had visited England a year earlier. For the next 20 years or so Elizabeth Ryan continually competed everywhere and except for the years 1919 and 1926, was present on the Riviera, where she captured scores of titles, predominantly in doubles. An outstanding legend of the game.

The next meeting was held at the Cannes Club, but was restricted to two days, owing to some difficulty with the French governing body. Only the men's singles and ladies' singles events were staged. Rahe easily defeated Robert Kleinschroth in the final, 6–3 6–4 6–2, while Elizabeth Ryan was too good for her opponents, apart from being given a tough fight in the opening set in the final against Frl Dagmar von Krohn of Germany before coasting through, 4–6 6–2 6–0.

At Monte Carlo, Rahe fell to Decugis in the second round, but now Wilding had joined the fray to really coast through the event and defeat Frenchman, Felix Poulin, with ease in the final, 6–0 6–2 6–1. Elizabeth Ryan defeated the holder, Jessie Tripp in the semi-final, but a great surprise awaited her in the final, when Mrs Madeline O'Neill, making her first appearance at a Riviera tournament, beat her, 6–3 8–6.

A week later, at Menton, Wilding was again most convincing, dismissing Decugis in four sets in the last round. Madeline O'Neill was still in great form, but fell to Dagmar von Krohn at the end, 1–6 6–2 6–4.

A large entry at Nice, requiring six rounds in the men's singles, resulted in Decugis, the holder, eventually winning a long and brilliant five set match against Rahe in the final, 7–9 6–2 6–3 1–6 6–3. Wilding did not enter the lists. Dagmar von Krohn regained the title she won in 1911.

Gordon Lowe competed in this tournament. Usually each year he visited the Riviera earlier, but this was his first meeting of the season, having just arrived a day or two earlier from Australia. On 12th September 1912 a British Isles team of four left London for Melbourne to challenge Australasia for the Davis Cup. This team of 'forlorn hope' consisted of

Charles Dixon (Captain), Arthur Beamish, James Parke and Lowe. In a tremendous upset the visiting team won by 3 matches to 2, with Parke beating Norman Brookes and Rodney Heath, and Dixon also overcoming Heath. Lowe was not selected to play but afterwards said that if he had played, his country would have lost the Cup.

The team had taken five weeks and five days for the outward journey via the Cape, but on the return had decided to travel via Colombo and the Suez Canal, taking less than a month. The 'Omrah' reached Suez on Saturday, 1st March and after a very rough crossing of the Mediterranean reached Naples on the Thursday. Early Saturday morning, 8th March, they docked at Toulon, where Dixon and Parke decided to travel overland to London, while Beamish travelled on to Gibraltar. Lowe had other ideas and took the train along the coast to Nice in time for the tournament, hoping to quickly lose his 'sea-legs' and again be competitive. However, there is little doubt that foremost in his mind was to renew his close acquaintance with Mrs Margaret Laverton, his mixed doubles partner.

In the men's singles, Lowe was far from his best, submitting to Rahe in the third round, 6–3 7–5, also making scant impression in the doubles with Alfred Hunter.

The Cannes Metropole Hotel tournament was successfully revived after two years. Most of the leading Continental players did not compete and the German team retired from the singles. Lowe beat Salm in the semi-final and after losing the first set, eased through against Crisp in the final. Elizabeth Ryan always looked like taking the ladies' singles.

The main Beau Site Hotel meeting for the Championship of Cannes saw Rahe in the ascendancy again and with hard-hitting tactics he won through to beat Robert Kleinschroth in the final, 6–3 6–2 1–6 3–6 6–0. The runner-up had seen off Decugis in the semi-final, while the surprise of the week was the easy defeat of Lowe by Heinrich Kleinschroth, who gave a dazzling exhibition of volleying, ensuring that the Englishman failed to win a game. He was then forced to retire from the other two events owing to indisposition, after being listed with Robert Kleinschroth and Margaret Laverton, the latter for the third consecutive tournament. This association had a future. Jessie Tripp won the ladies' singles.

There was one further tournament that season at Hyères, starting on 31st March. Many of the top players had returned home, leaving Crisp to beat the Frenchman, A. Resuge, in the men's singles final, 6–0 6–1. Miss White was successful in the ladies' singles event.

The Rahe-Heinrich Kleinschroth partnership had been unbroken throughout the season, having won six tournaments, at Beaulieu, Monte Carlo, Menton, Nice, Cannes Metropole Hotel and Beau Site Hotel.

In October Lowe was cited as co-respondent in a divorce case held in London, when Margaret Laverton was petitioned by her husband, Major Henry Laverton. This was after the Major had found letters that his wife had written to Lowe and both were seen booking into a London hotel. The Major was granted a decree nisi.

# 1914
# Tournaments Double • Tony Wilding
# Too Good for Everybody

Over the previous few seasons the Riviera had witnessed a steady rise in the number of visitors to the area. Some took residences for the winter, while others spent two or three weeks' sojourn, confident of escaping from the wet and gloomy weather of central and northern Europe.

Generally, the attraction of tennis to people as a pastime had grown accordingly and those with sufficient time and money could afford the travel and hotel expenses involved in being able to participate in tournaments away from home. This movement in the game was well reflected by 12 tournaments staged in 1914, compared to five years earlier when just five meetings were arranged. Also, the standard of play of the competitors had considerably improved as shown by the number of entries received and from a wider range of countries. The keenness for competition evident by the number of handicap events held at the majority of the tournaments. The demand for ladies events was much higher. For the first time on the Riviera a ladies' doubles event was added to an open international tournament programme. This occurred at Monte Carlo and was copied by Nice.

Tony Wilding's success during the season was phenomenal. He entered 10 tournaments and took part in the singles event in nine, which he duly won, beating Gordon Lowe in six of the finals. In addition he captured seven doubles titles.

There were two new tournaments added to the 1914 list, the Carlton Club and the Nice Country Club, where each venue had five courts available. The experiment of holding a New Year tournament was maintained at the Beau Site Hotel, where Gordon Lowe and Suzanne Lenglen dictated the play to capture the singles in cold and cheerless weather.

Dorothea Chambers visited the Riviera for the third occasion in late February and stayed for a little over four weeks. She won all the singles titles, defeating Elizabeth Ryan at Monte Carlo and Menton, Miss Stuart at Nice and Jessie Tripp at the Nice Country Club – all with the greatest of ease.

Wilding's success during the season was phenomenal, as week by week he continued to overwhelm the opposition. A summary of his achievement shows that he entered 10 consecutive tournaments (missing the Metropole Hotel) and in nine of these took part in the singles event, which he duly won. Throughout this period he lost only two sets in all, one in the final against Lowe at Nice and the other against the same player at the Beau Site Hotel second meeting.

He did not rest there for, in addition, he won seven doubles titles, five with Craig Biddle and one each with Norman Brookes and Count Salm. Wilding and Biddle were beaten by Robert Kleinschroth and Felix Poulin in the final, over four sets at Monte Carlo which, by common consent, was

# CHAMPIONSHIP OF THE SOUTH OF FRANCE.
## LADIES' OPEN SINGLES.
### THE NEW LADIES' CUP, offered by A. G. Morganstern, Esq.

*32 Entries.*

Best of 3 advantage sets throughout.

HOLDER FOR 1911-1913 Fraülein Von KROHN. 1912 Miss J. TRIPP.

First Prize value 150 frs. — Second Prize, value 75 frs. — Two 3rd Prizes, value 40 frs. each.

| No. | 1ˢᵗ ROUND | 2ⁿᵈ ROUND | 3ʳᵈ ROUND | PENULTIMATE | FINAL | WINNER |
|---|---|---|---|---|---|---|
| 1 | Mrs. J. O'Hara Murray | Miss E. Kelsey (w.-o.) | | | | |
| 2 | Miss E. Kelsey | | Miss E. Kelsey 6/4—4/6 retired | | | |
| 3 | Miss M. A. Wright | Mrs. Fletcher 6/3 - 7/5 | | | | |
| 4 | Mrs. Fletcher | | | 3rd Prize. | | |
| 5 | Miss Cadle | Miss Cadle 6/1 – 6/1 | | Mrs Perrett 6/1 – 6/3 | | |
| 6 | Miss F. Rogers | | Mrs Perrett 6/1–6/4 | | | |
| 7 | Mrs. Perrett | Mrs. Perrett (w.-o) | | | | |
| 8 | Miss M. Ward | | | | 2nd Prize. | |
| 9 | Miss Ryan | Miss Ryan 6/0–6/4 | | | Miss Stuart 6/4 - 6/2 | |
| 10 | Mrs. Sturtz | | Miss Ryan 6/2 retired | | | |
| 11 | Miss E. M. White | Miss E. M. White 6/0 - 6/2 | | | | |
| 12 | Hon Mrs Barker Mill | | | Miss Stuart 7/5—1/6 - 6/1 | | |
| 13 | Mme M Gondoin | Mme M. Gondoin 6/4 – 6/3 | | | | |
| 14 | Miss O. Ranson | | Miss Stuart 6/1—6/4 | | | |
| 15 | Mme R. Neveu | Miss Stuart 6/0 6/0 | | | | 1st Prize. Mrs. Lambert-Chambers 6/2 - 6/0 |
| 16 | Miss M. E Stuart | | | | | |
| 17 | Mrs. Lambert Chambers | Mrs. Lambert-Chambers (w. o) | | | | |
| 18 | Mrs. L. Boys | | Mrs Lambert-Chambers 6/1 – 6/1 | | | |
| 19 | Mlle de Gladky | Mlle de Gladky (w.-o) | | | | |
| 20 | Mrs. Hall Walker | | | Mrs Lambert-Chambers 6/2 - 6/0 | | |
| 21 | Mrs. A H. Crosfield | Mlle Isnard 6/1 – 8/6 | | | | |
| 22 | Mlle L. Isnard | | Mlle Isnard 6/2 – 6/3 | | | |
| 23 | Mlle A Visart de Bocarmé | Mlle Visart de Bocarmé 6/0 – 6/1 | | | | |
| 24 | Mrs. F. A. Jackson | | | | Mrs. Lambert-Chambers 6/3 – 6/3 | |
| 25 | Mlle N. Xantho | Miss Street 6/0 - 6/3 | | | | |
| 26 | Miss Street | | Mlle S. Lenglen 6/1—6/1 | | | |
| 27 | Miss M. Tripp | Mlle S. Lenglen 6/1 – 6/3 | | | | |
| 28 | Mlle S. Lenglen | | | 3rd Prize. | | |
| 29 | Mme Cezilly | Miss Kelsey 6/2 – 6/2 | | Mlle S. Lenglen 6/1—6/3 | | |
| 30 | Miss M. Kelsey | | Miss Towler 6/0 – 6/1 | | | |
| 31 | Mrs. A. A. Hall | Miss Towler 4/6 – 6/2 – 7/5 | | | | |
| 32 | Miss Towler | | | | | |

The draw for the ladies' singles at Nice, showing the first prize won by Dorothea Chambers.
She was given a good match by Suzanne Lenglen.

the outstanding feature of the gathering. The pair were given a shock in the first round of the Nice Country Club tournament, when they fell to Lowe and Max Decugis. Biddle was a very close friend of Wilding. He had a small house in Cannes in which Wilding stayed for a few months during the season. Biddle, an all-round sportsman, was born at Philadelphia, USA, into a wealthy family. At the age of 21 he inherited $1 million from his grandfather. He married three times and died in 1947.

Wilding's main antagonist in singles was Lowe, an outstanding player on the sand surface. He was able to overcome, in his stride, most of his rivals but against the New Zealander could never take control in the six finals contested at the Carlton Club, Beaulieu, Cannes Club, Monte Carlo, Menton and Nice. He was never able to force an advantage set. As some compensation Lowe won the singles event at Hyères, but then Wilding was not competing.

In two other finals, Wilding beat Brookes decisively. At the Beau Site Hotel (second meeting) he lost only seven games and at the Carlton Club he conceded just six, both matches scheduled over five sets. This proved that Wilding was superior on hard sand courts, as was the Australian on grass courts. At the Nice Country Club, Wilding, with accustomed ease, defeated Poulin in the last match after a very tight first set.

As well as his Riviera exploits, Wilding travelled just over the border to Italy during mid-January to win the singles and doubles at Bordighera (the oldest club in that country) and the doubles at San Remo, without entering the singles. He was just too good for everyone that season!

Still not 15 years of age, Suzanne Lenglen played her first full season on the Riviera. She won the singles title at the first two low-key tournaments at the Beau Site Hotel and the Carlton Club by defeating respectively Miss M. Ward and Ruth Winch in the finals. At Monte Carlo she met Elizabeth Ryan for the first time and, although she played admirably, the result was not in doubt and she lost, 6–3 6–4. However, at the last tournament of the season at the Carlton Club, Suzanne Lenglen beat the American for the first time by driving beautifully and constantly out-manoeuvring her, 6–3 3–6 6–2, in the final.

With six Wimbledon singles behind her, Dorothea Chambers visited the Riviera for the third time and played in four meetings, Monte Carlo, Menton, Nice and Nice Country Club. Clearly in a class of her own she won the singles titles without losing a set, defeating Elizabeth Ryan twice, Miss M. Stuart and Jessie Tripp in successive finals. At Nice Suzanne Lenglen excelled in extracting three games in each set against the champion. The next occasion these two players met was at Wimbledon five years later, when one of the most dramatic matches ever played by ladies took place. Jessie Tripp's standard considerably increased during the season when she

Tony Wilding (centre) is about to partner Arthur Balfour, former British Prime Minister (right), in the handicap doubles at Nice. Looking on is Craig Biddle from America, a great friend of the New Zealander.

reached four finals. She lost twice to Elizabeth Ryan but in a very long tussle edged out against her at Beaulieu, 6–4 9–11 6–4.

There were other features that season. Former British Prime Minister (1902–1905), Arthur Balfour partnered Wilding in the men's doubles handicap event at Nice. In one of the early rounds the pair were playing Biddle and Prince Bahram of Persia. All of a sudden, when the Prince began to serve, the tones of a soprano practising singing rang out from a neighbouring flat. Balfour, the receiver, raised his hand to the side of his face to listen, but the Prince continued to serve and the point was allowed to stand. Balfour and Wilding lost in the final, but the former was at a distinct disadvantage, as on the way to the courts by car, a youngster had thrown a stone and injured his eye. Balfour also paired with Dorothea Chambers in the mixed doubles handicap event, but they failed to pass the opening round. Apparently, just before they played, Balfour said to his partner "I shall be as nervous as you would be if you had to make a maiden speech in the House of Commons."

Watching the play daily at the Carlton Club tournament were the Duchess of Marlborough, Marquis of Blandford, Lord Ivor Spencer Churchill, Admiral Lord Beresford, Lord Cheylesmore and his two sons, also Prince Philippe de Bourbon and Prince Bahran of Persia. Former British Davis Cup player, Frank Riseley, who also played in the men's doubles at Monte Carlo, was making his first appearance on the Riviera since 1903.

C.H. Ridding, the popular coach at the Beau Site Hotel, was ordered to take a rest and proceeded on a long sea voyage to Australia.

The Duke of Westminster and the Marchioness of Headfort practised daily at the Carlton Club, under the watchful eye of Tom Fleming, the coach. Later in the season, the Duke organised a very successful private invitation tournament at the Club, in which he partnered Adele Topham.

As soon as the season was over, Lowe returned to London and married Margaret Laverton on 4th May at Kensington.

As spring turned to summer the threat of war loomed. Some years earlier the nations of Europe had aligned themselves into two hostile alliances with the Central Powers, Germany, Austria/Hungary and Turkey on one side and France, Great Britain, Russia and Italy on the other. The trouble came to a head when a Serbian nationalist assassinated Archduke Franz Ferdinand of Austria at Sarajevo on 28th June, which started off a chain of events, culminating in the First World War.

The fateful day was 4th August when, at dawn, the German troops crossed the French border in Lorraine. So began the 'Great War', as it was known, which was to last over four years and account for the slaughter of eight million men, when casualties from both sides were added together. There was constant misery, hardship, austerity and probably, more than anything else for those at home, the constant worry for the wellbeing of their loved ones 'over there'.

The first week or so on the Riviera passed as normal but, by mid-September the reality of the fighting up north, some 600 miles away, became vividly apparent as hotels in the area were requisitioned and the steady flow of officers requiring medical treatment or convalescence increased significantly.

Nice was the first town to open its doors but was soon followed by Cannes, Hyères and Menton. Although Monaco remained neutral, establishments were allowed to become hospitals and rest homes. By the end of September some 5,000 injured officers were being treated and by the end of the year, many more hotels were requisitioned to deal with the increasing flow.

# 1915
# Tony Wilding Killed on Western Front

Early in February, George Simond reported from Monte Carlo that, apart from the presence of the War casualties and the absence of the international tournament programme, life was somewhat normal. The courts at La Festa and the Condamine were in perfect condition and, although there were few good players around, the courts were occupied from early morning until dusk by 20 to 30 enthusiastic rabbits! Suzanne Lenglen, although hard at work at school, had visited recently and played a few matches with him. Also, American visitors were staying at the Hotel de Paris and the Hotel Windsor and taking exercise on the courts. Simond also reported that the Riviera was "wonderfully cheap" this year to stay en pension for 8 shillings and he suggested the experience for visitors travelling from home would not be unpleasant. Apparently, some of the professionals were still in post, with Thomas Burke and his son at Cannes and Henton at Menton, but Monaco, the late professional at Monte Carlo had been killed in action.

At the Beau Site Hotel at Cannes there was a series of exhibition matches held on 30th March between Suzanne Lenglen, Simond, L. Relecom, Charles Hatch, R. Dunkerley and the professionals, Ridding and Thomas Burke. There were two small prizes offered to the players who had the best average result. Simond took the first and Suzanne Lenglen the second. Apparently the courts played very well and the grounds of the Beau Site Hotel were looking their best. The matches were much enjoyed by the visitors to the hotel, numbering about 60. Among the spectators was Prince Phillipe de Bourbon.

In April two tournaments were staged to raise money for charity. The first was held at the Cannes Club from 22nd to 24th, with the proceeds divided between the Continental and Sir Charles Hospitals in Cannes. There were four handicap events, won by D. Martin, Suzanne Lenglen, Desprez and I. Relecom, and L. Relecom and Suzanne Lenglen. The referee was George Simond, who also took part in three men's doubles exhibition matches.

A few days later, from 27th-29th, a further meeting was held at the Beau Site Hotel, in aid of the South African Ambulance Hospital at Cannes. A similar schedule of handicap events was won by P.A. Smuts, Suzanne Lenglen, Desprez and L. Relecom and R. Dunkerley and Suzanne

Lenglen. 940 FF was raised for the hospital. One of the problems was the acute shortage of new balls but, from "somewhere", two dozen balls arrived from Monte Carlo, which were augmented by six dozen used ones donated by two wellwishers.

News of Wilding's death in the trenches on the Western Front must have come as a shock to many tennis lovers, particularly those on the Riviera, where his annual visits gave so much pleasure. As a newly promoted Captain in the Royal Marines he was serving at Neuve Chapelle in France when, around 4.45pm on 9th May, a German shell struck and he was killed instantly. Lying intact, blown out of his pocket was a gold cigarette case, a souvenir of the Riviera from 1914, presented to him by his great friend, Craig Biddle.

This very popular, athletic player from New Zealand had dominated the game for many years prior to the War, during which he captured the singles crown at Wimbledon four times from 1910–1913 and the doubles title also on four occasions, 1907, 1908, 1910 and 1914. Apart from these successes he is credited with winning over 110 singles titles, plus numerous doubles events from 1901 to 1914. He also represented Australasia several times in the Davis Cup.

He was a regular visitor to the Riviera from 1906 to 1914 with the exception of 1909 and 1910, during which period he amassed 23 singles titles, nine of them during the 1914 season. He won the Monte Carlo meeting five times, the last four consecutively. He also won 16 doubles and five mixed doubles titles.

Born at Christchurch, New Zealand on the 31st October 1883, he first visited England in 1903 when he attended Trinity College, Cambridge. He was called to the English Bar in 1906, also qualifying as a barrister in New Zealand. In 1913 he entered business as a continental representative of a tyre company. Apart from his tennis, his great interest was motor cycling, which he used continually for his travels to tournaments abroad. For some years he was very close to Maxine Elliott, an American stage actress, but they never married.

Late summer another morale boosting charity venture was held, again organised by George Simond. A match was arranged at Monte Carlo, between Nice and Monte Carlo, with 6 players per side participating. Monte Carlo won by 7 matches to 1, 15 sets to 3 and 111 games to 61, with a thunderstorm terminating play for the day. A sum of 234 FF was raised. Suzanne Lenglen played in this encounter for Nice and took part in exhibition matches with leading players of the area.

There was an abundance of spectators watching the play, including the Grand Duchess Anastasia, Prince and Princess Mirza Khan, Lord and Lady Waleran, Lord and Lady Wallscourt and many other notables. Besides this tournament, Simond had managed to run a small weekly handicap event for the past three months, when each competitor was charged two FF to pay for the balls and ball boys. During the year there were probably other charity events where the details have been lost through the passage of time.

The Clubs in the area did their utmost to provide facilities for recreation for the troops, but other than the occasional friendly contest, the possibility of holding a top class tournament was out of the question.

# 1916
# Cannes is a Haven for the Army

On 18th March a benefit meeting was held at the Cannes Club for the Club professional, Thomas Burke, who had suffered severely through the exigencies of the War. There were three handicap events, Singles (combined men and ladies) won by Suzanne Lenglen who beat Charles Hatch 6–2 6–1 in the final, ladies' singles won by Miss M. Nativelle and mixed doubles won by O. de Carfort and Miss Nativelle. There was also a series of doubles matches, in which Suzanne Lenglen and George Simond took part. Over £40 was taken at the gate.

Shortly after lunch on 24th March, the 'Sussex', a cross-channel ferry from Folkestone to Dieppe, was approaching the French coast when she was struck by a torpedo from a German submarine. Of the 258 passengers and approximately 50 crew, 52 people were killed and of these, two were tennis personalities who had played on the Riviera. Manliffe Francis Goodbody was a distinguished former Irish international who in 1894 was

Strolling along the Promenade des Anglais in Nice, (left to right) Lt. De St Cyr, Bobette and Max Decugis and Suzanne Lenglen.

*Facing page:*
*Top:* A group of mainly British soldiers on leave or convalescing from the fighting in the north, relaxing by playing tennis at the Nice Lawn Tennis Club in Platz Mozart. In the centre of the photograph is Suzanne Lenglen, who lived in one of the adjoining houses.

*Below:* Spectators take a break from watching the charity matches staged by Baron de la Barrière and M. Lenglen at the Cannes Club on 18th March.

runner-up at the United States National Championships at Newport. He won many other tournaments and competed on the Riviera in 1903 and made a fleeting appearance in 1908. Prince Bahram of Persia was an ardent devotee of the game who played regularly in mainly handicap events on the Riviera and was an hospitable host off court.

Georgio Gault, a leading French player who competed on the Riviera in 1913 and 1914, was killed by a shell on the Western Front in France in the autumn.

On 26th April and following days, a charity tournament was held at the Beau Site Hotel at Cannes, in aid of the South African Ambulance Hospital, which provided replacement limbs for wounded soldiers. As usual Simond was in charge of the proceedings. There were three even events and five handicap events. A rare spectacle was seeing Suzanne Lenglen playing four singles matches against men. The outcome was 2 all with victories over Bertram Marion-Crawford, 6–0 6–1, and Simond, 6–2 6–4, and losses to Ridding, 4–6 3–4 ret'd, and Thomas Burke, 5–7 0–3 ret'd. There was a large attendance of wounded French and British officers. This very successful meeting raised 1,800 FF.

# 1917
# More Charity Matches

As the intensity of the War increased, the feelings of the 'neutral' United States people gradually hardened against Germany. Following the sinking of the '*Lusitania*' by submarine in 1915 and other international incidents, the United States eventually declared war on 6th April 1917 and on 24th June troops first landed in France. Eventually, an army of one million men was in Europe and in the end this figure had risen to two million. During this period thousands of officers were sent to the Riviera for medical treatment or leave.

At the same time as the United States was entering the War there was tremendous support for the charity tournament held on the Beau Site Hotel courts at Cannes in April, which resulted in over 2300 FF being handed to the Russian Hospital in the town. About 400 spectators witnessed the play. As usual, Suzanne Lenglen offered her services and without too much difficulty won the level mixed singles from an entry of 28, defeating Bertram Marion-Crawford by default in the final. There

Robert Powell (left) and Kenneth Powell

were also four handicap events and one exhibition in which Suzanne Lenglen and Marion-Crawford beat Thomas Burke and Charles Hatch, 6–2 7–5. The prizes were presented by the Duchesse de Noailles and the Sultan of Morocco. George Simond, as usual, was the referee.

In May a very notable player, Lt. Robert Banks Powell, was killed on the Western Front at Vimy Ridge. He was born in Victoria, Canada, on 2nd April 1881 and represented his country in the Davis Cup in 1913, 1914. He won numerous tournaments in the United States, Canada, British Isles and Europe and also played in the Olympic Games. He will be remembered at Wimbledon for being runner-up in the 1910 All Comers' Doubles in partnership with his namesake, Englishman, Kenneth Powell, (no relation), who was also a left-hander and predeceased him in Flanders in February 1915. Robert Powell played on the Riviera in 1907 and 1909.

# 1918
# André Gobert Meets Suzanne Lenglen

As the year progressed, many more thousands of servicemen found their way to the Riviera, either for hospital treatment, convalescence or leave. Presumably some of them found time to play a game of tennis – that is if there were balls available! Maybe a few charity tournaments were staged and other 'get-togethers', but records of these have been lost over the years.

André Gobert of France, on leave from the Western Front, visited Cannes and played some exhibition matches, including partnering Suzanne Lenglen (facing page).

However, there is a short story regarding André Gobert, the 1911 French champion, who made his first visit to the Riviera in late May. Early in March, while serving in the French Army as a photographic officer, he was returning from a mission over enemy lines when anti-aircraft fire severely damaged his aeroplane. The pilot lost control, but they crashed on home territory and both were injured.

After a short period in hospital, Gobert spent the next two weeks on leave at Cannes where he was able to play a little tennis. After a week his play improved and he entered a small three-day tournament at the Beau Site Hotel, where he reached the singles final before being beaten by Marion-Crawford after a "very amusing match". Gobert played in exhibition matches and was very impressed by the appearance of Suzanne Lenglen who partnered him. In a practice match, Suzanne beat Gobert, 6–1 6–1, with the "greatest of ease". Gobert never returned to compete on the Riviera.

# 1919
# Back to Normal • Big US Forces Tournament

With the signing of the Armistice on 11th November 1918, the War finally came to an end. At that time the American Expeditionary Force numbered around two million officers and men and the General Staff soon realised that a serious problem existed.

Previously, the men were 'keyed up' by the continuous preparation for taking part in the fighting but, with that behind them, what could be done to ensure that the troops kept fit and had alert minds, now that there was so much idle time?

Col. Wait Johnson, on the General Staff and Chief Intelligence Officer of the Army, had studied this situation for some time and suggested that all physically fit personnel should engage in some form of play, whatever the sport or activity. General John Pershing, the Commander in Chief, approved the scheme and Johnson went about the task of arranging a series of sporting programmes. As regards tennis, he appointed Harry Graff, a physical director with the YMCA, to arrange an American Officers' Tennis Championship, and selected Cannes as the ideal venue, bearing in mind the generally wonderful climate experienced during the winter.

After qualifying tournaments, or in some cases straight selection, held in January across all areas, a total of 181 players hailing from 41 American states, descended upon Cannes. The entry (singles and doubles) was of the highest quality and included such names as Lt. Col. William Larnard (seven times US champion), Lt. Col. Dwight Davis (donor in 1900 of the famous international cup), Major George Wrenn (an early Davis Cup international), Capt. Richard Williams (the 1916 US Champion), Capt. Watson Washburn (No.2 in the US rankings), Lt. Dean Matthey (No.10 in the same list), Capt. Douglas Watters, Lt. Henry Breck and many others.

All competitors were ordered to be in Cannes by 16th February. Arrangements were made to accommodate all taking part at the Carlton Hotel, while the Carlton Club and the Cannes Club put their combined number of 13 courts at the disposal of the organisers. The local Red Cross and YMCA also contributed with another five courts.

For the convenience of players, arrangements were made with Spalding to open a fully equipped tennis shop in Cannes.

Practice started as soon as the players arrived in Cannes. Col. Johnson, who also competed, took charge of the play at the Carlton courts, while Graff ran the Cannes Club operation. Play commenced on 19th February at 9am and finished that day at 5pm, when 94 matches had been contested. Unfortunately, the next two days were completely rained off but, apparently, the men were not too disturbed as they were enjoying themselves, particularly at the evening dances organised by the YMCA, where they were able to practise their 'footwork' on the polished hard-wood floor.

On 22nd February, play was resumed and another 47 matches were played until the finals were reached on 3rd March. Each day the stands were full of spectators, many of them allied servicemen on leave or recuperating. A very interested Suzanne Lenglen watched the matches on several occasions.

There were some very interesting matches played (over the best of three sets, except the last two rounds of five sets). Towards the end, in the singles, Washburn beat Capt. Frank Payne in a dull encounter, 6–2 6–2 5–7 6–2, while Williams defeated Breck in a very lively affair, 8–6 9–7 6–1, to reach the final. Here the result was never in doubt as Williams outplayed Washburn, 6–2 7–5 6–2. The doubles final never sparkled as Washburn and Williams combined to crush Davis and Chaplain Burnham Dell, 6–1 6–1 6–2.

Cups were presented to the winners and runners-up by the YMCA, with Williams being given a beautiful trophy by the City of Cannes. The following day everyone set forth to return to their units, having enjoyed a super time and participated in probably the largest tournament the game had known.

All these famous American players served in the First World War and were at Cannes to take part in the American Officers' Tennis Championships during February. (Left to right) Lt.Col. Dwight Davis, Maj. George Wrenn, Maj. William Larnard, Capt. Watson Washburn, Capt. Richard Williams, Capt. Douglas Watters, Lt. Dean Mathey and Col. Wait Johnson. The singles title was won by Williams and the doubles by Washburn and Williams. A week later Watters won the men's singles at the Carlton Club tournament, the first regular meeting after the War.

That winter, owing to lack of time to plan and co-ordinate the scheduled dates, the Tennis Regional Commission for the Côte d'Azur was only able to arrange seven meetings between March and early May. Players were attracted in good numbers and gave enthusiastic support to all the venues, where at each the programme was extended to include at least four handicap events. Some competitors were eager to re-establish their annual visit to the coast.

Nicholas Mishu, a Romanian diplomat, made his first venture to the Riviera with great success. He won three tournaments by beating Max Decugis in the finals at Monte Carlo, Menton and the Beau Site Hotel, but lost to his opponent at Nice. Mishu had eight different variations of service.

The honour of staging the first open tournament on the Riviera since the War belonged to the Carlton Club. The meeting was arranged to follow the American Army tournament, but bad weather delayed the former and with some of the players engaged in both, the management was set a hard task. However, the fine weather arrived and with the redoubtable Simond taking up his pre-War duties as Referee, the schedule was completed on time.

An excellent entry was obtained with as many as 52 challenging in the men's singles. Max Decugis was the clear favourite to win, but after defeating a young newcomer to the scene, Nicholas Mishu, he was indisposed and withdrew from the final against Watters.

At the next four meetings, Decugis and Mishu disputed the men's singles final, with the Romanian winning three. At Monte Carlo, instead of the meeting being held on the Condamine courts near the harbour, play took place on the high level La Festa courts, a smaller but much more select environment. Here, Mishu beat Decugis. 6–2 6–0. At Menton, Mishu won again, this time in a tremendous struggle of five sets, 6–3 6–2 10–12 2–6 7–5. A week later at Nice, Decugis was in charge from start to finish,6–3 6–2 6–1, thereby winning outright the 100 guineas Challenge Cup, which he had previously put his name on in 1912 and 1913. In their final meeting at the Beau Site Hotel, five sets were required before Mishu won, 6–8 6–4 4–6 6–3 6–0.

Mishu was a diplomat by profession, whose lively play included eight totally different variations of service, employing cuts, chops, slices and twists of all kinds. The strength of Mishu's game lay in the power of his drives, backhand and forehand, particularly down the lines, which enabled him to overcome Decugis. The Romanian rarely went to the net.

Suzanne Lenglen, keen to demonstrate her ability after four years' waiting, was in a class of her own, decisively winning the five singles finals, three of them without conceding a game. Also, a number of doubles titles came her way. The Monte Carlo Easter gathering was restricted to men's and mixed doubles events but, at the second Beau Site meeting, a very unusual invitation doubles event took place, whereby Suzanne Lenglen, partnered by Charles Hatch, won two matches before defeating W.H. Grace and B.I. Williams in the final.

Charles Phillips Hatch, an American from Newport, who was educated at Harvard, married wealthy Baroness Marie Van Haeften in 1909 and purchased the Villa Florence in Cannes. He played in tournaments before the War and during the conflict competed in charity matches and occupied himself with work at Cannes hospitals. He was also a good golfer.

This was the last season Decugis played on the Riviera, having made his debut in 1907. He dominated French tennis from the turn of the century, winning the national singles eight times, 1903, 1904, 1907–1909, 1912–1914, plus the doubles on 13 occasions and the mixed seven times. Throughout the years he won scores of titles throughout Europe and played Davis Cup between 1904 and 1919. He was Wimbledon doubles champion in 1911. During the First World War he served as a lieutenant in the French forces.

# 1920
# Riviera Offers Good Living and Excitement

This year was the dawn of a new era for tennis on the Riviera, a period which was to last about 20 years. People had generally shrugged off the drudgery and austerity of the War and had adjusted to the loss of their loved ones. They were looking for good living and excitement, which had deserted their lives earlier. The wealthy, who had free time and a flair for tennis, were attracted to the tournament scene for a few weeks each winter, as the ideal means of escaping the hubbub of the city, indulging themselves in comfort and enjoying the delightful weather.

Players did not have to be in the top class category to enter the tournaments, as there were plenty of handicap events available, in addition to the normal five open events, which allowed all classes of ability to compete and mix socially. The ladies could find themselves partnering a Prince or a Lord, while the men could probably arrange to play with a 'beauty' who had caught their eye. Naturally, many romantic affairs began in this manner.

The hotels were there to provide first class service and entertainment, with regular evening dances, bridge parties, billiards etc. For those who sought a little more adventure, a casino was generally not far away for a 'flutter'. There were also quite a number of golf courses within easy reach. Normality had returned.

Once again the Tennis Regional Commission for the Côte d'Azur was able to construct a full schedule of open tournaments for the season, commencing the first week in January and finishing the first week in May, with a total of 15 tournaments, with two of the venues in Cannes, Beau Site Hotel and Carlton Club, holding three each.

The first tournament of the season at the Beau Site Hotel was due to commence on 3rd January, but a storm of unusual violence delayed the start for three days, resulting in the ground being strewn with fallen oranges and the courts out of commission. Although thereafter brilliant sunshine favoured the week, a continuous high wind generally spoilt the play. Unfortunately the weather for most of the season, especially late on, was unkind and tournaments suffered delays and in some cases encroached on those that followed. After an absence of nine years, Major Ritchie returned to the Riviera to compete in the early tournaments. Even at the age of 49 he was clearly the favourite to win and this he did with ease. His fine passing shots and great steadiness gave him victory over Major Ambrose Dudley in the final, 6–1 6–2.

Suzanne Lenglen was eager to demonstrate that she was the world's top player, following her formidable performances at Wimbledon the previous July, when she won the singles crown against the seven times holder, Dorothea Chambers, after being two match points down. She certainly produced her best in front of the very appreciative audience, losing only three games in all, with just one in the final against Madeline O'Neill. The men's doubles title was won by the Frenchmen, Pierre Albarran and Alain Gerbault.

The Carlton Club meeting, which immediately followed, was favoured with fine weather, except for the last three days being affected by a troublesome wind. As before, Ritchie and Suzanne Lenglen took the singles without losing a set, but the former was forced into an advantage set in the final against Alfred Hunter. Suzanne Lenglen's opponent in the final was Elizabeth Ryan, back on the Riviera after six years. She was expected to display sturdy resistance, but the American was in poor form, winning just one game in the final, which was completed in 20 minutes. Albarran and Gerbault repeated their doubles victory but in the mixed doubles, the crowd was unhappy with the outcome. Albarran, paired with Suzanne Lenglen, reached the final, where their opponents were Ritchie and Elizabeth Ryan. The French pair lost the opening set 6–1 and trailed 3–4 in the second, when Suzanne Lenglen surprisingly announced her retirement. Subsequently it transpired that she had expressed a desire to

A magazine advertisement listing the tournament schedule for the season and the name and address of each Secretary.

# Lawn - Tennis - Côte d'Azur
## 1920 ∴ TOURNOIS INTERNATIONAUX ∴ 1920

| DATE | CLUB | SECRÉTAIRE | DATE | CLUB | SECRÉTAIRE |
|------|------|------------|------|------|------------|
| Janv. 5 | Cannes, Beausite | Propriétaire Hôtel Beausite. | Mars 15 | Nice | Ch. LENGLEN, Nice L. T. Club |
| » 12 | Cannes, Carlton | DE ROULET, Carlton Ten. Club | » 22 | Cannes | G. JENNER, Cannes L. T. Club |
| Fév. 9 | Hyères | Cap. RESUGE, Hyères L. T. Club | » 29 | Cannes, Beaus'te | Propriétaire Hôtel Beausite. |
| » 16 | Cannes, Carlton | DE ROULET, Carlton Ten. Club | Avril 5 | Cannes, Métropole | E. ROBINSON, Hôtel Métropole. |
| » 23 | Beaulieu | C. M. RIDDING, Hôtel Bristol | » 11 | Nice | Ch. LENGLEN, Nice L. T. Club. |
| Mars 1 | Monte-Carlo | G. M. SIMOND, La Festa T. Cl. | » 26 | Cannes, Beausite | Propriétaire Hôtel Beausite. |
| » 8 | Menton | A. E. MADGE, Menton L. T. | Mai 3 | Monte-Carlo | G. M. SIMOND, La Festa T. Cl. |
| | | & Croquet Club. | | | |

Les Championnats et les Critériums Régionaux seront joués à Nice, le 12 Avril (dimanche) et jours suivants.
Les Championnats et Critériums Régionaux des Concours Officiels Inter-Clubs par Équipes seront disputés à des dates à fixer ultérieurement.
COMMISSION RÉGIONALE, *Le Secrétaire.*

# LAWN-TENNIS DE MONTE CARLO
## Affiliated to the U. S. F. S. A.

## *Ordre des Parties pour Mercredi 10 Mars*

**A 9 heures :**

M. J. Relecom et Mlle Fau  c.  M. ....ugen et Miss Judd  **H.**
M. L. Balbi  c.  Capt. Cartwright  **H.**
M. Olsen et Mme Fick  c.  M. Hatfield et Mlle Donnet  **H.**

**A 10 heures :**

*Finale Championnat Simple Messieurs :*
M. J. G. RITCHIE  c.  Capt. F. GORDON LOWE.  **H.**

Miss Bishell  c.  Miss Layton Blunt  **H.**
M. Cox et M. Graham  c.  M. Glen Walker et Mlle Maubert

**A 10 h. 45 :**

M. Wills et Miss Brocksmiths  c.  M. Dunkerley et Miss Howkins  **H.**
M. English et Miss Mercer  c.  Lord Ch. Hope et M. Lowe  **H.**

**A 11 h. 30 :**

*Finale Championnat Simple Dames :*
Mlle S. LENGLEN  c.  Miss E. RYAN.

Capt. Gavin et Mlle Vermeulen  c.  Si A. Crosfield et Lady Crosfield  **H.**
M. Watson et Miss Eddis  c.  Capt. Greig et M. Fowler  **H.**

**A 2 heures :**

*Demi-Finale Championnat Mixte :*
Miss E. RYAN et M. J. G. RITCHIE  c.  Mme BEAMISH et Major DUDLEY.

Miss Harrison  c.  M. Gordon Lowe  **H.**
Miss Mercer  c.  Miss Howkins

**A 2 h. 45 :**

*Finale Championnat Double Dames :*
Mlle S. LENGLEN et Miss E. RYAN  c.  Mme BEAMISH et Mme FICK.

*Finale Championnat Double Messieurs :*
M. ALBARRAN et M. GERBAULT  c.  M. DUDLEY et M. LOWE.

Com. Leach et M. Hunt  c.  Admiral Palmer et M. Hobson  **H.**

**A 4 heures :**

*Finale Championnat Mixte :*
Mlle S. LENGLEN et M. ALBARRAN  c.  Miss RYAN
et M. RITCHIE ou Mme BEAMISH et Major DUDLEY.

MM. Relecom et Relecom  c.  MM. Cox et Sherman  **H.**
M. Covell  c.  M. English  **H.**

**A 4 h. 45 :**  **H.**

M. Lippmann  c.  M. Playfair  **H.**
M. Wills  c.  M. Y. Resuge  **H.**
M. Greig  c.  Lord Charles Hope

*The SLAZENGER HARD COURT BALL is being used*

The final programme at the delayed Monte Carlo tournament showing the names of the contestants in the five main events.

withdraw from the match some time before being put on court, as she was not feeling well. Reluctantly she had agreed to play at the request of the Referee, who pointed out that the large crowd present would be so disappointed.

After an interval of three weeks, during which a week on the schedule was allocated to Club Championships, the Hyères tournament was staged at the Golf Hotel. The feature of interest was the appearance of Gordon Lowe, playing in his first open tournament since the end of the First World War. He had just arrived home via the Suez Canal from Mesopotamia, where he had served from 1917 to 1919. He had originally joined the Indian Army Reserve of Officers in 1916.

Although short of practice, Lowe easily retained the men's singles title he won six years earlier, by beating Gerbault in the final, 6–4 6–0 6–1. Mrs Winifred Beamish, making her first venture to the Riviera, found no opponents in her class and took the singles without the loss of a game.

The second meeting at the Carlton Club attracted a large gathering, with the total number of entries from both sexes adding up to around 150. Unfortunately the weather left much to be desired. Lowe took the men's singles title by showing vigour and keenness to defeat Ritchie in the final, 6–4 6–2. Gerbault conceded to Ritchie in the round before, after disposing of Dudley. He then paired with Albarran to display smart volleying and comfortably defeat Lowe and Ritchie in the doubles final, 6–4 6–1. Suzanne Lenglen was indisposed and this allowed Elizabeth Ryan to win the singles title, downing Mrs Winifred Beamish at the last stage, 6–1 6–0.

At Beaulieu, Ritchie turned the tables on Lowe, who had experienced quite an exhausting passage through the singles draw. Lowe beat Nicolas Mishu, 3–6 6–2 7–5, and Gerbault, 8–10 6–2 6–4, before falling to Ritchie, 7–5 3–6 6–3. Again, Albarran and Gerbault were imposing, coasting through the doubles final, ousting Dudley and Lowe, 6–1 6–2. Suzanne Lenglen, fit again, smartly dismissed Elizabeth Ryan in the singles final, 6–2 6–0, passing Madeline O'Neill without the loss of a game, while Elizabeth Ryan was too good for Winifred Beamish, 6–3 6–3.

The Monte Carlo tournament which followed was played on the Condamine courts instead of La Festa and was affected by a rail strike which kept away among others, Max Decugis and Mrs Phyllis Satterthwaite. Lowe, well in the driving seat, beat Gerbault, 6–3 7–5 6–3, before gaining the ascendancy over Ritchie in the singles final, 7–5 6–2. Possibly the surprise of the meeting was the defeat of Albarran and Gerbault in the final of the doubles by Dudley and Lowe, 7–5 6–4. Suzanne Lenglen allowed Elizabeth Ryan just two games in the final of the singles but in the round before, Winifred Beamish, in great form, managed to notch up seven games against the winner. Suzanne Lenglen paired with Elizabeth Ryan to win their first ladies' doubles title on the Riviera. (They had joined once before in 1913, but this was a handicap event.)

At Menton, Ritchie did not enter and Lowe, with little effort reached the final to face the holder, Mishu. Unfortunately Lowe, leading 3–2, tripped and tore a tendon in his leg, forcing him to retire two games later at 4–3. The day before, Lowe had beaten the Italian, Count Mimo Balbi di Robecco, 6–4 4–6 6–2. With Lowe also retiring from the doubles and the two Frenchmen not competing, the title went to C.W. Murray and Balbi. Suzanne Lenglen and Elizabeth Ryan were absent, which left the field clear for Winifred Beamish.

A week later at Nice, Lowe had not recovered from his injury and took no part. There was much rain during the beginning of the week, but with the full cooperation of the players the meeting finished on time. Count Mikhail Soumarokoff, the last winner of the Russian title in 1913, won the men's singles final, 7–5 6–2 2–6 3–6 6–1, from Gerbault after having survived another long match earlier against Ritchie, 3–6 6–4 6–4. Soumarokoff, a left-hander, possessed an unorthodox stroke in that he turned his wrist over for his forehand shot, hitting the ball with the reverse side of the racket. Suzanne Lenglen withdrew from the singles final against Winifred Beamish on medical advice, following participation in the protracted mixed doubles final.

Lowe returned to the fray a week later at the Cannes Club, but he was still nursing his injury, which impeded his mobility against Ritchie in the semi-final. Ritchie surprisingly was pushed hard to beat Dudley in the final, 3–6 6–0 6–4 5–7 6–1. Elizabeth Ryan overcame the loss of the first set to beat Winifred Beamish in the final, 4–6 6–2 6–2.

The last important gathering of the season at the Beau Site Hotel was considerably delayed by rain but, as so often was the case, George Simond succeeded in getting the heavy programme through with his usual patience and tact. The men's singles was captured for the first time by an Australian, Lewis Barclay, who experienced a straightforward route to the final to beat Fisher over five sets, 6–2 7–5 3–6 7–9 6–1. Barclay was the fitter of the two and certainly the younger. Fisher had produced a fine win over Ritchie, 2–6 6–3 6–2 and then Lowe, 2–6 6–3 6–1. He then paired with Ritchie to win the men's doubles. For the second week in succession, Elizabeth Ryan was too good for Winifred Beamish, to the tune of 6–2 6–2. Francis Marion Bates Fisher, born at Wellington in 1877, was a former New Zealand Cabinet Minister. His tennis career dated back to 1896 when he won his first tournament in his native country. A great enthusiast for the game and a respected administrator, he won many events in England and Europe.

'Napoleon', the famous head ball boy at the Beau Site Hotel since the very early days, was feared lost during the First World War. However, after being demobilised from the French Army at the beginning of the year, he took a job at a perfume factory at nearby Grasse before asking to be allowed to resume his duties on the courts. The management and the players were delighted to welcome him back at the end of the March meeting.

The Metropole Hotel tournament felt the full force of the dreadful weather on the Riviera, with fierce winds and continuous heavy rain, so much so that one day hardly a match was decided, followed by two days when not a ball was struck. Eventually most events were concluded, with Lowe near his best, beating Fisher in the final of the singles, 7–9 6–2 1–6 6–3 6–2 – a very gruelling affair.

The closing stages of the ladies' singles fell apart when Winifred Beamish, having to leave for London, withdrew at the semi-final stage to Phyllis Satterthwaite, who in turn retired to Madeline O'Neill in the final, owing to a sprained foot.

The bad weather continued to plague the coast, with the third Carlton Club meeting greatly affected. Scheduled to conclude on 18th April, play actually finished on 23rd. In a small entry, Lowe was too consistent for Hunter in the final, particularly in the second set, 6–4 6–1. The top ladies

Although Major Ritchie excelled at tournaments before the First World War he was able to win four singles titles during the season, three at Cannes – Beau Site Hotel, Carlton Club and Cannes Club and at Beaulieu. His last visit to the Riviera was in 1923 at the age of 52.

Winifred Beamish visiting the Riviera for the first time competed for the majority of the season, always featuring in the closing stages of the events, leading to victories in singles at Hyères, Menton and Nice.

had left the area and in the final of the singles, Mrs Sigrid Fick of Sweden defeated Miss Dorothy Shepherd, 6–3 6–3. In between the confusion caused by the bad weather, the second tournament at Nice took place with a restricted draw. Lowe won the singles beating Leonce Aslangul, a French ranked player born in Armenia, in the final, 6–3 6–1 6–0. Mme Marcelle Gondoin, also from France, had no real opposition in the ladies' division.

The last tournament of the season, and the third at the Beau Site Hotel was, like others, delayed. Lowe had departed leaving Hunter to achieve a good win over Gerbault by three sets to love. Suzanne Lenglen made a late season appearance, but with no player around worthy of her skill, beat Sigrid

Fick in the singles final with the loss of just two games, to take her fifth title of the season. Albarran and Gerbault were in a class of their own and took their sixth doubles title. In an interesting exhibition match, the King of Sweden, partnered by Suzanne Lenglen, beat Albarran and Sigrid Fick, 6–4 6–2.

Lowe performed extremely well during the season, winning six singles titles and would have most probably added to the total had he not been injured halfway through. His wife, Margaret, also had some success, winning the handicap singles at the Cannes Club and Monte Carlo. The Monte Carlo tournament scheduled to follow was cancelled – the weather had won in the end.

Two weeks before the conclusion of the season, the Tennis Regional Commission of the Côte d'Azur met in Nice on 17th April to discuss plans for the future. In the Chair was the President, Comte de Bourbel, overseeing representatives from nine tournaments: Beau Site Hotel, Beaulieu, Carlton Club, Cannes Club, Hyères, Menton, Metropole Hotel, Monte Carlo and Nice. There was discussion whether tournaments should be accorded 10 days instead of seven, but this was not agreed. The meeting expressed the wish that the directors of the tournaments would, where limited courts were available, restrict the number of events or the number of entries, to ensure a finish before the next tournament began.

The tournament dates were agreed for the 1921 session, starting on 3rd January at the Beau Site Hotel and finishing on 18th April at Monte Carlo. The Beaulieu Club proposed that a tournament be held for the professionals attached to the clubs and offered a Challenge Cup to the value of 1,000 FF. The idea was warmly accepted and it was agreed that the first meeting should take place at Beaulieu from 27th to 30th December 1920 and that future tournaments should be held at the Club to which the winner was attached.

Subsequently, the initial tournament attracted an entry of 11 professionals, with the winner emerging as Romeo Acquaron of France (Carlton Club), who defeated Joseph Negro of Italy (Nice) in the final, 3–6 7–5 5–7 6–2 6–3. This match was watched by a distinguished company, including the Grand Duke Michael, the Grand Duke Boris and the Grand Duchess Anastasie. The Honorary Referee was George Simond. This tournament continued annually at the various venues until 1932 when the event was transferred to Paris.

# 1921
# Gordon Lowe and
# Suzanne Lenglen Dominate

Unlike much of the bad weather of the previous season, the Riviera generally experienced very propitious conditions during the three months of competition. Naturally, there was a little rain and some wind which interfered with the play, but all the tournaments finished on time, bar one at Hyères.

The number of tournaments was maintained at 15, the same level as the year before. Overall, entries had risen and a glance down the draws clearly indicated that the vast majority of the competitors were British. Towards the latter half of the season more Frenchmen and others took part.

Two players registered outstanding performances. Lowe competed in the first nine meetings and won eight singles titles. Not unexpectedly, Suzanne Lenglen also captured eight singles titles, conceding just 27 games in the process.

The opening gathering of the season, held at the Beau Site Hotel, started on 3rd January and attracted a good class entry with competitors clearly showing their freshness and eagerness to perform. All were rewarded with splendid weather, only the Saturday night storm breaking a spell of cloudless days.

Lowe never lost a set in claiming the men's singles title, although he was given a good run for his money in the final by Francis Fisher, before winning 6–3 7–5 6–3. The New Zealander had his chances, particularly in the second set when he three times had a point to clinch matters. A name lurking in the draw was the American, Jimmy van Alen who some forty years later developed the van Alen Simplified Scoring System (VASSS), which led to the present tie-break scoring system, adopted internationally.

The presence of Suzanne Lenglen left little hope for the other competitors in the ladies' singles. She was brilliant to the degree of playing four matches without conceding a game! In the final, Gladys Colston reached deuce twice and at one point actually led 40–15 in a game. Lowe won a second title pairing with Fisher, as did Suzanne Lenglen partnered by Wallis Myers.

The following week the Carlton Club had a similar entry, but there was quite an upset which surprised many spectators when Douglas Watson defeated Fisher in the quarter-final, 3–6 6 –3 7–5. There was a further

A view of the main courts at La Festa, where the Monte Carlo Championships were played.

upset when Charles Aeschliman of Switzerland then beat Watson, 6–3 5–7 6–0, his chief weapon being his backhand drive, using excessive top spin, forcing Watson to go to pieces in the deciding set. In the meantime, Lowe passed George Rocksavage, 6–2 6–4, and crushed Aeschliman in the title round, 6–1 6–2 6–1. In a match played almost entirely from the back of the court, Suzanne Lenglen allowed Elizabeth Ryan just one game in the final of the ladies' singles.

The Cannes Club's first meeting of the season drew a very large entry. Suzanne Lenglen's not entering had a corresponding effect upon the attendance but, with favourable weather and 12 courts available, the meeting was a complete success. Lowe continued his good fortune and pocketed three titles. Once again he did not drop a set in capturing the singles title, his last three opponents being Jack Hillyard, son of George Hillyard, 7–5 6–2, Aeschliman, 6–2 6–2, and in the final, Alain Gerbault, 6–1 6–1 6–4. In the latter match the Frenchman made no headway until the third set when his volleying markedly improved, but Lowe's superior resources were evident to close out.

Elizabeth Ryan won the ladies' singles event after dropping the first set to Phyllis Satterthwaite in the final, 1–6 6–1 6–2. In the semi-finals the winner beat Gladys Colston, 6–3 6–4, while Phyllis Satterthwaite accounted for Sigrid Fick, 6–2 6–1.

During the Beau Site Hotel tournament the spectators were entertained by two exhibition matches involving two Kings. (Left to right) Winifred Beamish, King Gustav of Sweden, Suzanne Lenglen and King Manuel of Spain. In turn, Suzanne partnered each King to victory.

After a week's break, when the club Championships were held, the Hyères Club became the centre of tennis. The weather was most unkind, with rain falling on the first and last two days and in the end only the men's singles final was contested. This allowed Lowe to win his fourth title of the season and take permanent possession of the Hyères Cup, having won in 1914 and 1920. In the one-sided final, played in the rain, Jack Hillyard was well beaten, 6–1 6–0 4–0 ret'd. Gladys Colston won the ladies' singles title when Phyllis Satterthwaite retired.

The first meeting at the Nice Club was chiefly notable for the entry of Lt. Col. Algernon Kingscote, making his final visit to the Riviera. The weather was cold but fine except for the last day. Nothing outstanding occurred in the men's singles to stem the progress of Lowe, Gerbault, Kingscote and Soumarokoff reaching the semi-finals, where Kingscote beat Gerbault, 3–6 6–1 6–1 6–3, but the other encounter was a different matter when Lowe after a great struggle beat the Russian, noticeably tiring, 3–6 10–8 3–6 7–5 3–0 ret'd, after two and a quarter hours. In the final, Lowe, more than his opponent's match at the back of the court, won in three sets, 6–3 6–4 6–1.

Suzanne Lenglen towered above her rivals. After a succession of 6–0 6–0 victories she defeated Elizabeth Ryan in the final of the ladies' singles, 6–0 6–2. An interesting newcomer to the Riviera was Miss Eleanor Goss, ranked second in the USA in 1919 who, unused to the conditions, fell to Elizabeth Ryan, 6–2 8–6. Lowe and Kingscote eased through the doubles final against Gerbault and Soumarokoff, 6–0 6–4 6–4.

The second and most important meeting of the Carlton Club drew an entry of unprecedented size. The men's singles ended in another encounter between Kingscote and Lowe. Before a record gallery the former was quick and decisive at first to lead by a set and 4–1, but Lowe's defensive play wore him down and eventually he won, 3–6 7–5 6–3 6–3.

As anticipated the ladies' singles title went to Suzanne Lenglen, who triumphed over Elizabeth Ryan, 6–0 6–2. Madeline O'Neill and Phyllis Satterthwaite were the other semi-finalists. Suzanne Lenglen and Elizabeth Ryan won the ladies' doubles, an event which featured Dorothea Chambers, who was on a six weeks tour of the area. Unfortunately for much of the time she met with little success. She suffered from 'tennis elbow', which restricted her to playing doubles only. On returning to England she announced her retirement from singles but would continue to compete in doubles events. She visited the Riviera each winter up to 1928.

Beaulieu was the scene for a marathon struggle in the final of the men's singles between Kingscote and Lowe on 27th February. These two were on court for four solid hours, 10.45 am to 2.45 pm, without a break, under a hot midday sun. For two sets Lowe played superbly, producing drives of unfailing precision, to which generally his opponent had no answer.

He continued in the same vein in the third set until leading 5–2 and Kingscote 15–40 down on his service, but with great fortitude the set was salvaged and from then on Kingscote's superior fitness gave him the edge and Lowe soon tired. The final score in Kingscote's favour was 3–6 9–11 9–7 6–3 6–1. This contest constituted the longest singles match ever played on the Riviera at that time.

Suzanne Lenglen restricted her appearances to winning both doubles events, which left the way open for Elizabeth Ryan to win the singles. A very disappointed crowd saw Phyllis Satterthwaite lose the opening set 6–0 and then scratch.

A week later there was another record entry at Monte Carlo, the matches being played on the high-elevated La Festa courts. Lowe gained his revenge over Kingscote, this time in four sets, 6–1 0–6 6–4 6–2, and

Leading English player, Algernon Kingscote, made a brief visit to the Riviera and at the Beaulieu meeting fought a marathon match in the singles final to defeat Gordon Lowe, taking four hours. At that time, this was the longest singles match played on the coast.

Henry Mayes, a Canadian by birth, settled in England after serving in the First World War. Devoted to physical fitness he was always a difficult opponent to beat. He played on the Riviera from 1921 to 1928, winning 21 singles titles.

proved he was a superior match player on the clay courts. Kingscote changed his all out attacking game which gave him an initial advantage to win the second set, but Lowe, consistent from the back of the court and occasionally venturing to the net, took command. There were some surprising results in this event, with Rocksavage beating Leonard Lyle and Ambrose Dudley in the same day. Also, Mishu was beaten by Gerbault who later was the equal of Kingscote, but only for two sets. Suzanne Lenglen, back in singles contention, showed no mercy to Elizabeth Ryan in the final, dropping two games in the first set. In the semifinals, Suzanne Lenglen beat Winifred Beamish, 6–1 6–0, while Elizabeth Ryan overcame Eleanor Goss after quite a struggle, 6–4 7–5. There was no stopping Suzanne Lenglen who, as expected, won the two doubles titles. The men's doubles title went to Kingscote and Myers.

At the close of the meeting, Kingscote left for home and never played on the Riviera again. He had a very distinguished military career, serving in the First World War, 1914–1918, during which he was awarded the Military Cross and rose to the rank of Lieutenant Colonel. He represented Britain several times in the Davis Cup. At Wimbledon he reached the final of the All Comers' Singles in 1919 and a year later the final of the doubles. He won numerous tournaments, at home and abroad, including the Australian Singles Championship in 1920. He was born in 1888 and died in 1964.

Lowe stayed on to compete at the Menton tournament, which since the previous year had added two courts and extended the accommodation. He found a worthy opponent in Major John Rendall in the semi-final of the men's singles and was forced to concede the middle set. In the other half of the draw, Mishu, the holder for the past two years, was not consistent enough to be dangerous against Gerbault and lost quite easily. In the final, Lowe was far too consistent for the Frenchman, as he made light work of his 6–1 6–3 6–4 victory. Suzanne Lenglen entered only the doubles events. She won easily with Elizabeth Ryan and withdrew in the final of the mixed event. The latter beat Phyllis Satterthwaite in the final of the singles, 6–3 6–4.

Around that time Lowe was given the distressing news that his wife, Margaret, had been arrested by the police and charged with stealing a pocket-book containing FF 5,000. After being held for two days she was brought before the Magistrate at Nice, who referred her case to the court at Grasse on 5th April, where she was found guilty. Apparently, for some time past, complaints had been received by the police at Nice and Cannes that considerable sums of money had been taken from coats, which had been lying about at tennis clubs. The thefts had occurred at times when the general public was not present, so suspicion had been attached to some players. However, two detectives disguised as gardeners were placed on watch at the Carlton Club during some practice sessions and saw Mrs Lowe pick up a coat and remove from a pocket-book, banknotes which had been marked.

She was arrested and when questioned stated that she had lost heavily on the gaming tables at Monte Carlo and had stolen the money as she did not wish to tell her husband. Enquiries had been made into eight thefts and Mrs Lowe admitted to six. She was sentenced to one year's imprisonment and a fine of FF 500. However, she was given the benefit of the First Offenders' Act with respect to the year's imprisonment, which was immediately suspended. Lowe took steps to replace the stolen money and he and his wife left for London.

Lowe had been entered for the South of France Championships at Nice, but withdrew in the first round of the singles against Glen Walker. This left Soumarokoff as the strongest player in the men's singles, as he confirmed by defeating Jack Hillyard in the semi-final, 6–3 6–2, and Balbi, without any strain, in the final, 6–1 6–1 6–0, to retain the title. Balbi had beaten Gerbault after a struggle, 6–3 3–6 7–5. Suzanne Lenglen beat Mlle Septier, 6–1 6–1, in the final of the ladies' singles in a contest described as an object lesson in graceful movement.

Good weather persisted at the Cannes Club where the Côte d'Azur Championships were contested. The English entry in the men's singles was not of a very high standard and the final brought together Balbi against Felix Poulin of France. The former won by his superior steadiness, 6–2 9–11 6–3 6–1. The winner had great difficulty in shaking off Aeschliman in the semi-final, 6–4 5–7 6–2, while Balbi beat Hunter, 6–3 6–4. Suzanne Lenglen only played in the ladies' doubles, giving Elizabeth Ryan the opportunity to beat Phyllis Satterthwaite in the singles final, 7–5 6–2.

The Beau Site Hotel meeting which followed had a large entry but did not contain the quality of past years. Balbi won his second title of the season when he defeated Resuge, a young Frenchman, in the final after five strenuous sets, 6–3 4–6 6–1 2–6 7–5. On her first visit to the Riviera, Miss Phyllis Howkins imposed a strong volleying attack to defeat Phyllis Satterthwaite, 2–6 6–1 6–3, in the final battle for the ladies' singles. Suzanne Lenglen decided not to compete in any of the events but played two notable exhibition matches, one with King Manuel of Spain against the King of Sweden and Mrs Winifred Beamish and the other, swapping partners. The last day crowd were delighted with the entertainment.

The Cannes Metropole gathering was affected on some days by rain. The Canadian, Henry Mayes, won the men's singles defeating first A. Kramet, 8–6 8–6, and then Cotah Ramaswami of Cambridge University in the final, 6–2 6–2. Winifred Beamish and Phyllis Satterthwaite shared the ladies' singles title.

Rain made the third meeting at the Carlton Club difficult but Aeschliman coped best to beat Rocksavage in the semi-final of the men's singles, 1–6 6–4 7–5, and then took the honours against Kramet, 6–1 6–3 6–1. Suzanne Lenglen was back and, as usual, crushed Phyllis Satterthwaite in the final of the singles, 6–1 6–0. There was an unusual outcome in the mixed doubles when Rocksavage and Suzanne Lenglen withdrew from the final, owing to Rocksavage having to leave for Paris in his motor, with a view to breaking the time record!

The last meeting of the season at Monte Carlo, starting on 18th April, encountered unsettled weather. Jack Hillyard won his first open singles title in France, defeating Aeschliman in a five-set final of uneven tennis, 6–3 6–2 3–6 4–6 6–2. Suzanne Lenglen again showed no mercy to Phyllis Satterthwaite in the final of the singles, 6–1 6–0.

# 1922
# More Tournaments, More Entries •
# Elizabeth Ryan Wins Eleven Singles

The attraction of players to the Côte d'Azur considerably increased this year, as shown by the record number of entries, with tournaments being staged continuously from the opening at Monte Carlo on 26th December (1921) to the third Monte Carlo meeting, concluding on 23rd April. This total of 17 meetings was the most to date.

The two players who dominated the previous year did not repeat their performance during the following months. Lowe decided not to pay a visit, while Suzanne Lenglen did not play competitively until late March as a result of being unwell for six months, following her ill-fated visit to the United States the previous September. When she did appear, her outings were restricted to doubles and handicap matches and her only singles venture was at the last meeting of the season. Her absence for the early weeks certainly had a profound effect on the weekly 'gate'. Elizabeth Ryan became the star performer of the season.

The day after Christmas heralded a new tournament at the La Festa courts at Monte Carlo, which was favoured with glorious weather. An uneventful start to the men's singles event climaxed with an outstanding victory for Rocksavage, when he registered his first ever title on level terms. He became the holder of a newly-instituted Challenge Cup, which carried with it the Championships of Monaco. His win over Hillyard in the final required five sets and called for courage and endurance to recover from two sets down before the duel was settled, 2–6 2–6 6–3 6–4 6–3. Rocksavage also featured in the final of both doubles, but lost both. Phyllis Satterthwaite and Madeline O'Neill had the field to themselves in the ladies' singles, the former getting the better, 7–5 6–3.

The Beau Site Hotel meeting attracted nearly a hundred entries but, with two new courts available and fine weather, the Referee had few problems. A dual success was obtained by Sam Hardy, who was the United States Davis Cup captain in 1920. He won the singles title beating Aeschliman in the final, 8–6 6–1 6–4 and then paired with Myers to take the doubles title from Aeschliman and Hillyard, 7–5 15–13 3–6 6–3. Elizabeth Ryan was on top form, giving little quarter to Phyllis Satterthwaite in the singles final, 6–1 6–1. The latter had considerable difficulty in disposing of the very promising 17 year-old French girl, Mlle Sylvia Jung, from Le Havre, 7–5 6–2, in the previous round. At the same time, Elizabeth Ryan beat Madeline O'Neill, 6–2 6–3.

Good weather prevailed at the Carlton Club meeting, except for a dust storm on the Thursday. Hardy and Hillyard decided not to compete, but the entry was strengthened by the arrival of two Australians, Harold Hunt and Rupert Wertheim but, not being acclimatised to the local conditions, both fell early in the men's singles. The surprise of the event was the exit of Fisher beaten by Rocksavage in the semi-final, 6–3 6–4. The winner's very crisp driving, often to his opponent's weaker backhand, scored many a point. However, he was defeated in the final by Aeschliman by two sets to one, but had his chances when leading 5–4 in the fourth set. The score was 6–2 6–3 3–6 8–6.

After a prolonged battle with Madeline O'Neill, Sylvia Jung won through, 7–5 4–6 6–4 and then put up a gallant fight against Elizabeth Ryan before losing, 6–3 6–4. The French girl's ground strokes tended to let her down but, overall, she continued to impress. Fisher captured the the men's and mixed doubles titles.

Two days of unceasing rain delayed the Cannes Club meeting, with the result being excessive pressure towards the end of the week and, generally, some rather ragged play. However, Aeschliman again was in good form to dispose of Rocksavage and Ernest Lamb to reach the final against Charles Roupell, whom he had beaten the previous week. Now the role was reversed as the Englishman gained a straight set victory, 6–1 6–2 6–4. Aeschliman launched a volleying attack towards the end but it was too late, with his opponent standing his ground.

Elizabeth Ryan won her third singles title in as many weeks, beating Sylvia Jung, 6–1 6–1, and in the final, Phyllis Satterthwaite, who in the first set won four games and then retired, evidently reckoning the winning of the next two sets was beyond her capability. The attendance on the last day was excellent.

At times the rain interfered with the progress of the first Menton meeting but, despite some delays towards the end, all events were completed. The entry was below expectation and the tennis not of a very high standard. Hardy was the outstanding performer, winning three titles without the loss of a set. Opinion favoured Wertheim, his opponent in the final of the men's singles, as the match was best of five sets, but Hardy appeared to be at particular pains to win and this he did in three tight sets, 6–3 6–4 6–4, a feat well accomplished at the age of 45. This success added to his earlier triumph at the Cannes Beau Site Hotel. Miss Margrethe Kahler, a former champion of Denmark, won the ladies' singles event. Following a noteworthy performance against Madeline O'Neill, 4–6 6–4

Elizabeth Ryan had a tremendous season throughout without being beaten in singles. In all she won 11 titles, the last eight consecutively.

6–1, she volleyed well to beat Miss Aylmer, somewhat overawed in the final, 6–1 6–0.

Rain delayed the start of the Hyères tournament, played on the courts of the Golf Hotel, and the matches had to be hurried through to finish on time. The Referee, Simond, was unwell and a Miss Logan acted in his place. Resuge, a resident in the area, won the men's singles. His opponent in the final was Hillyard, who started poorly and could not recover sufficiently to avoid being beaten in straight sets, 6–1 6–4 8–6. The two paired to win the men's doubles in a very long drawn out final. The best two ladies in the singles draw faced each other across the net in the final, with Phyllis Satterthwaite beating Madeline O'Neill in a not very interesting duel, 6–2 6–2.

The first Nice tournament of the season was played on the courts at Platz Mozart for the last time. There was sadness at the departure from the venue, which had been the Club premises since 1890. However, the area was too small, with only four courts available, this being reduced to three to provide spectator accommodation during international tournaments. Simond was still unwell and his place was taken by Cordery, who performed well.

The crowds were very disappointed that Suzanne Lenglen did not make her comeback at her own club, but she seemed content to indulge in a few practice games.

The standard of play was not very high. In the men's singles, the better of the French players, Gerbault and Gerard Manset, were short of practice.

Count Mikhail Soumarokoff, the Russian champion of 1913, won the men's singles title at the South of France Championships held at Nice for the third year in succession.

Resuge retired and other non-starters were Aeschliman, Hardy and Wertheim. Soumarokoff, the holder, retained his cup without much trouble, beating Hillyard and Rocksavage on the way to the final, where he overawed the Swiss player, G.M. Morier, who played with a very large racket, 6–1 6–1 6–0. The runner-up had played well when he accounted for Gerbault in the second round, 7–5 6–4. Elizabeth Ryan and Phyllis Satterthwaite advanced unscathed to the final of the ladies' singles, with the former winning with only limited pressure, 6–2 6–0. Margrethe Kahler reached the semi-final but fell victim to the American, 6–1 6–1.

Dorothea Chambers and Winifred Beamish made an appearance during the week, but only in the ladies' doubles. They could make little impression in the final on the winners, Elizabeth Ryan and Phyllis Satterthwaite, and went down 6–4 6–1.

The second Carlton tournament at Cannes was favoured with fine weather, apart from the last two days when a very high wind prevailed. The entry was large and required much effort to get through. Simond was still not in post and Alfred Hunter took over control of the scheduling. Aeschliman proved he was the best player in the men's singles, disposing of Lamb, Gerbault and Rocksavage before downing Myers in the final, 3–6 10–8 6–1 6–3. Myers had six points for the second set, but once this was concluded, his physical resources proved inadequate against an opponent twenty years his junior.

Winifred Beamish entered the ladies' singles and reached the final and, with a large gallery in attendance, took the opening set from Elizabeth Ryan with very accurate passing shots. However, the American changed her tactics and played mainly from the back of the court, to wear her adversary down, 3–6 6–2 6–2. For the second week running Winifred Beamish and Dorothea Chambers proved disappointing as they lost the doubles final to Elizabeth Ryan and Phyllis Satterthwaite, 6–3 6–2.

Other than the third day, when rain fell piteously, the weather at the Bristol Hotel courts at Beaulieu was perfect. Simond was not quite fit enough to resume as referee and his place was taken by C.H. Ridding. Making his first appearance of the season, Balbi captured the men's singles title. To reach the final he was given a severe test in the second set before passing Wertheim, 6–1 8–6. His opponent, David Morgan, home on leave from India, was also pushed hard by Lamb and Hillyard before reaching the last stage, where a very unusual incident occurred. Balbi led Morgan by two sets to one, then in the next set Morgan led by 3–1 but the umpire, by some mischance, called 3–2 in Morgan's favour and directed the players to change ends. Morgan questioned the umpire, who kept to his decision. Eventually the set went to Balbi at 6–4 and with it the match, when only nine games had actually been played in that set. By this time, the umpire had examined the score sheet at the suggestion of an onlooker and found out his mistake, but the players had left the court and the light had faded. Accordingly it was decided to consult Simond, who was convalescing at Monte Carlo, and the decision was taken to resume the match the following day, with the score at 5–4 in favour of Balbi. When the match was restarted, Balbi won the first game, and the match and title were his.

Elizabeth Ryan won the ladies' singles but was hard-pressed by Winifred Beamish who, driving brilliantly, led 5–1 in the opening set and was within a stroke of winning the second, but still the American won through, 7–5 8–6. For the third week running, Elizabeth Ryan and Phyllis Satterthwaite beat Winifred Beamish and Dorothea Chambers in the final of the doubles, this time 6–2 6–2.

With over 150 individual players from many countries entered for the second Monte Carlo meeting there was a need to use both the championship courts at La Festa and the old courts at the Condamine. Fortunately Simond, better in health, was able to resume his duties as referee and expertly managed the programme. The courts were busy all day.

For the first time the Monte Carlo Cup was won by an Italian, Balbi, who thoroughly deserved his success. His path to the final was via Hillyard, Morgan, Crawshay Williams and Lamb, all whom he passed without dropping a set. His opponent in the final was Gerbault, who distinguished himself by beating his compatriot, Jean Samazeuilh, the French champion, who had previously disposed of Aeschliman.

In the final, Balbi had only to play steadily in order to win, while mistakes by Gerbault did the remainder. The match score was 6–1 6–4 6–3.

Elizabeth Ryan always seemed to have something in hand as she won the singles title. Phyllis Satterthwaite came within a point of winning a set before falling in the semi-final, 6–2 8–6. In the final the American met Winifred Beamish for the third week running and had a comparatively easy victory, 6–2 6–1, despite a nasty fall early on, which damaged her knee. Margrethe Kahler was beaten by the runner-up, 6–1 6–0.

Gerbault and Samazeuilh fought courageously to come back against Balbi and Wertheim in the final of the doubles, 5–7 5–7 6–1 6–3 6–1. Once more Elizabeth Ryan and Phyllis Satterthwaite were far too good for Dorothea Chambers and Winifred Beamish in the doubles final, winning 6–3 6–1.

Like so many tournaments during the season, Menton, staging the Riviera Championships, suffered patches of rain. With an easy draw in the men's singles, Balbi was the clear favourite to secure his third successive title. All was as expected until he reached the semi-final against P. Marsden, a tenacious player, home on leave from India. The Italian took the opening set after 12 games and led 4–2. At this stage he broke a string in his racket and was evidently very disturbed. With the wind assisting him, Marsden, driving severely and shrewdly lobbing, won the set, 8–6, and reached 4–1 30–love, when Balbi gave up and retired. In the final, Marsden played well but Wertheim was too aggressive for him to win, 6–2 6–1 6–4. In the second round a fierce battle took place between Wertheim and Morgan, which fluctuated several times. In the second set, Wertheim was within two points of winning the match, but Morgan survived and actually led 7–6 in the deciding set before the Australian finally ran out, 6–3 7–9 9–7. Morgan had certainly been the surprise of the season.

Elizabeth Ryan strode on magnificently to win another singles title, on this occasion defeating Phyllis Satterthwaite in the final, 6–3 6–3. In the previous round the runner-up received a walkover from Winifred Beamish, who was suffering from a cold and the effects of her marathon encounter the day before with Madeline O'Neill, which she eventually secured, 6–3 15–13. Elizabeth Ryan's semi-final win was over Margrethe Kahler, 6–4 6–3, over two sessions. Hardy and Hillyard played a very long match to beat Balbi and Murray in the doubles final, 4–6 3–6 7–5 6–2

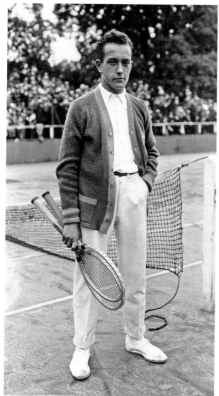

The season heralded the arrival of two young Frenchmen, Henri Cochet (left) and Jean Borotra, who both became legendary in the game. Cochet was a frequent visitor to the coast, whereas Borotra very seldom appeared.

11–9. Elizabeth Ryan lost her first match of the season in partnership with Wertheim in the semi-final of the mixed doubles.

The meeting at Nice for the South of France Championships was made distinctive by two features, the first being the change of club venue from Platz Mozart to the Parc Imperial, where 15 courts were available instead of four, along with far superior accommodation. The second was the reappearance of Suzanne Lenglen. She did not compete in the singles event, but won the ladies' and mixed doubles, with Elizabeth Ryan and Count Soumarokoff, respectively.

There was a large crowd assembled on the last day to watch the men's singles final between Soumarokoff and the 20 year-old Frenchman, Henri Cochet, fresh from his record victory in the World's Covered Court Championships, who had accounted for Rocksavage in the semi-final, 6–3 6–4. The Russian started in a hurry, winning the opening two sets with loss of two games. Then, after being within three points of losing the third set, he took command to win, 6–0 6–2 7–5, and so take the title for the third year running. In the third set Cochet played some beautiful all-round tennis, which included some outstanding forehand drives.

Elizabeth Ryan was quite often given a hard match by Winifred Beamish and on this occasion had to concede the opening set in the singles final. She had to fight hard to square the match but, having done so, the deciding set was hers all the way. The ladies' doubles was robbed of much of its interest by the withdrawal of Dorothea Chambers, owing to her being indisposed. The men's doubles final was a long drawn-out affair, with Cochet and Rocksavage eventually winning, 4–6 3–6 7–5 6–4 10–8.

There was a big programme, ably carried through by Simond at the Côte d'Azur Championships, staged at the Cannes Club. The weather for most part was cold and cheerless, with more than a day's play being lost to rain, but all involved counted their blessings to be escaping the blizzards and storms raging in the north of the country. Interest centred on Cochet, who won the men's singles with masterly ease. In the final, Morgan led 6–5 in the first set and got four games in the second, but his steady back court game was an inadequate defence against his opponent's unremitting volleying and the match ended in the Frenchman's favour, 8–6 6–4 6–2. In the third round Morgan had survived three very tough sets against Aeschliman to pass, 5–7 7–5 6–4. Suzanne Lenglen did not compete in the three main events. Once again Elizabeth Ryan was too good for Winifred Beamish in the ladies' final, recording a 6–4 6–3 victory.

A large crowd assembled on the Saturday to witness an exhibition match with Suzanne Lenglen and Elizabeth Ryan playing Winifred Beamish and Phyllis Satterthwaite. Most present were of the opinion that the match would have been more interesting if Suzanne Lenglen had partnered one of her opponents, instead of Elizabeth Ryan but, apparently, she would not agree. As expected, the outcome was most one-sided. Distinguished spectators at this match were the King of Sweden, ex-King Manuel of Spain and Lord Balfour.

Much rain fell on the Friday and Saturday at the main Beau Site Hotel tournament, held at the end of March, which involved an unbroken series of matches throughout the Sunday for some of the winners. Frenchman, Jean Borotra, destined to be another of the game's legends, made his debut on the Riviera. He arrived direct from a match on covered courts in Paris, where very different conditions of light and surface existed. Naturally he did not show anything approaching his true form but, nevertheless, managed with much exertion to win the men's singles title. Cochet was expected to be his adversary in the final but he had to contend in the round before with Morgan, who surpassed himself to win, 6–4 7–5. He continued in this vein in the last match and stood at 5 all in the fifth set against Borotra who just won the last two games and the title, 7–5 6–4 2–6 3–6 7–5.

Immediately after this marathon, Borotra had to leave for Paris to play on the following Monday in an Army football match, which meant he had to scratch from the men's doubles semi-final and the mixed doubles final, the latter where he was due to play with Suzanne Lenglen. In this event, Jimmy van Alen and Sylvia Jung played well and just failed to reach the semi-final.

The ladies' singles final brought together the usual two players, ending with the same result, with Elizabeth Ryan conceding eight games in two sets to Winifred Beamish, 6–4 6–4. This was her 11th singles title of the season, with the last eight being in succession. In the round before, Phyllis Satterthwaite retired to Elizabeth Ryan, while Winifred Beamish coolly passed Miss Honor Woolrych, 6–2 6–1.

Borotra, returning to the Riviera was the main attraction at the Metropole Hotel, Cannes, tournament. Over the weekend he had suffered a sprained ankle, but still beat Gerbault very easily, then lost a set to Mayes before a five-set victory over Rocksavage in the singles final, 6–1 6–3 1–6 3–6 6–2. Borotra eased up his volleying attack when he seemed to have the contest in hand, but renewed his control in the final set.

Sylvia Jung had a narrow win over Phyllis Satterthwaite in the singles semi-final, 6–1 4–6 8–6, and went on to win the title with an impressive win over Honor Woolrych, 6–0 6–1. Suzanne Lenglen played only mixed doubles. Her partnership with Borotra was far too good for any other combination.

Many of the leading players had left the Riviera before the Carlton Club's third meeting and consequently the entry was not too strong. An early upset was the defeat of Aeschliman by Williams, who was quickly dismissed by Gerbault. With a comfortable win over J. Nielsen, the Frenchman reached the final to produce his best performance of the season against Morgan, 6–4 6–2 7–5.

Sylvia Jung won the ladies' singles, beating Margaret Tripp and then Madeline O'Neill in the final, 6–3 7–5. The men's doubles was captured by Aeschliman and the Argentinian, Ronaldo Boyd, while van Alen and Sylvia Jung won the mixed title with a series of tight matches.

The third Monte Carlo tournament brought the very long season to an end. At last Suzanne Lenglen participated in the ladies' singles, which she won in masterly fashion without losing a game to four opponents, Miss M. Smailes, Miss Grace Bristed (USA), Margaret Tripp and in the final, Eleanor Goss, ranked fifth in the United States. In the last encounter, the American won just four points in the first set and eight in the second.

The other honour of the meeting fell to Aeschliman who, due to his fighting spirit, gradually wore down Gerbault in the final of the singles, 4–6 6–4 6–3 6–3. Aeschliman and Boyd won the doubles and, as expected, Gerbault and Suzanne Lenglen won the mixed doubles.

# 1923
# Many New Faces Arrive on the Scene

The number of tournaments for the season was reduced from the previous year's total by three to 14. After the opening three meetings play ceased for the last two weeks in January and for those who remained the interval was pleasantly filled with club matches, invitation mixed doubles events and practice games. When, a little later, the more important gatherings were held, the quality of the entries was of a very high standard, possibly overall the best ever to that date.

There were the 'regular' names participating, Aeschliman, Balbi, Dudley, Fisher, Gerbault, Hillyard, Mayes, Morgan, Rocksavage and Soumarokoff, besides Lowe and Ritchie, who were returning to their happy hunting grounds, plus a number of top level players competing for the first time on the Riviera. There were two Englishmen, Leighton Crawford, who learnt most of his tennis in India as a police officer, and Randolph Lycett, who although born in England spent his early life in Australia before returning home to win numerous tournaments. He was a top-class player, reaching the singles challenge round at Wimbledon in 1921 and winning the doubles championship, 1921–1923. From the Continent came two leading players, who both represented their country in the Davis Cup, Baron Uberto de Morpurgo from Italy and Erik Tegner from Denmark.

The ladies' standard was also impressive, with Suzanne Lenglen, Elizabeth Ryan, Winifred Beamish, Phyllis Satterthwaite and newcomers, Miss Kathleen McKane, Britain's leading player, Miss Molla Mallory, seven times United States singles champion, Miss Leslie Bancroft, the No.2 American player, and two young and rising players, Mlle Diddie Vlasto from France and Srta Lili de Alvarez from Spain. Also, there was Dorothea Chambers supporting many of the doubles events.

For the first time on the French Riviera, a regulation was introduced to ensure that draws for the events were seeded, which generally resulted in the better players reaching the concluding stages. In the past there had been a number of cases where all the top players were assembled in one half of the draw and this led to very one-sided and dull finals.

The first of the season's tournaments commenced on Christmas Day on the La Festa courts at Monte Carlo, with the Monaco Championships at stake. Although heavy rain had fallen just prior to the start, two of the

courts, newly dressed, were firm and fast, but the third court, with the open trellis background intercepting the falling sun, remained a severe handicap. The weather throughout was fine if a little chilly. The spectators were numerous and they were rewarded with some splendid matches.

Crawford won the men's singles and the doubles in partnership with Hillyard, showing an ability to quickly acclimatise to the local conditions with ease. In a 32 draw he beat Mayes in the semi-final, 6–2 6–3, and then proceeded to capture the title by overwhelming Fisher in a very disappointing duel, 6–0 6–4 6–4. Fisher had beaten Rocksavage, who capitulated after a strong opening, 8–6 6–2.

As expected, the ladies' singles finalists proved to be Phyllis Satterthwaite and Madeline O'Neill, the latter retiring without taking the court. Earlier, the winner was far too strong for Lady Domini Crosfield, while Madeline O'Neill survived a hard fought match with Miss M. Smailes, a baseline player from the local Nice Club.

The New Year Meeting at the Beau Site Hotel, which followed, was another success for Crawford, who in turn eliminated Gerbault, 6–1 6–4, and Aeschliman, 6–2 8–6, before facing Douglas Watson, a Northumberland county player, in the final. No one expected the score to

On 6th June Alain Gerbault set out single-handed in his 39 foot boat for New York, where he landed 101 days later. In 1924 he started to circumnavigate the world, arriving home nearly five years later. The Frenchman is seen playing on the La Festa Courts at Monte Carlo.

be 6–0 6–0 6–0. This constituted a record for the best of a five set match at the tournament and was remarkable in view of Watson's physical fitness and normal capacity to stay the course and hit hard most of the time. Crawford pursued an aggressive game from start to finish with power and accuracy to win game after game. Earlier, Watson inflicted an excellent 2–6 6–4 6–4 win over Mayes, who narrowly won the round before ousting Morgan, 4–6 6–2 13–11.

As usual Suzanne Lenglen was in a class of her own and won the singles title without any stress, although she was somewhat shaken in the final by Phyllis Satterthwaite who, after a good opening set, went down 6–4 6–2. In the semi-final, Madeline O'Neill made no impression on the champion and left the court without winning a game.

The first Carlton Club meeting was affected by rain towards the end and Simond was forced to overrun the programme into a second week. The courts were reported to be appreciably improved with new dressing, which yielded a more tractable bound of the ball than in the past.

Crawford won his third title in a row beating Gerbault on a very slow court in the final, 6–1 6–4 6–1. The winner employed 'safety first' tactics to good effect and was really only pressed in the second set when the Frenchman produced some fine shots. Crawford was given much to think about in the semi-final by Mayes, who was within a point of 5–3 in the third set, but he missed out and his opponent won the next eight points for victory at 3–6 6–3 6–4.

Hillyard had two very close matches, beating Aeschliman, 4–6 6–2 10–8 and then conceding to Gerbault, 6–8 6–4 6–2.

With Suzanne Lenglen not competing in the singles, the final was inevitably fought out by Elizabeth Ryan and Phyllis Satterthwaite, which the American won after a very dull match, 9–7 6–2. Domini Crosfield played well in the previous round to stretch Elizabeth Ryan to 6–3 6–4. Suzanne Lenglen played in both doubles events, winning the ladies' division with Elizabeth Ryan over Madeline O'Neill and Margaret Tripp in the final, 6–3 6–1, and the mixed with Fisher, a pairing which was in a different class that day in overwhelming Hillyard and Phyllis Satterthwaite in the final, 6–3 6–1.

After the two week break the serious business of the season began with the meeting at Hyères, where the weather for once was consistently fine. The programme was organised by Miss Logan.

The outstanding feature of the play was the triple victory of Jack Hillyard who, after a week's boar hunting with the Duke of Westminster in the forests at Landes, returned to the court with vigour to win the final of the singles from Brame Hillyard, who captured the opening set. But from then on the winner settled down to an accurate and aggressive game, which was far too strenuous for his opponent, to record the score, 4–6 6–3 6–3 6–3. The Hillyards were not related, with Brame a veteran, who had won the Plate event at Wimbledon, way back in 1902. The pair combined to win the doubles. Phyllis Satterthwaite, head and shoulders above the rest of the field, won the ladies' singles title without bother, also the mixed doubles with Jack Hillyard.

The first Nice tournament heralded the return of Ritchie, who was winning singles titles on the Riviera way back at the turn of the century. At the age of 52 he demonstrated his capability to still hold his own with some of the best players of the day. He reached the semi-final of the singles with victory over Dudley, 6–1 6–3, before eventually bowing to de Morpurgo in a very long tussle, 6–4 8–10 6–3, after missing two points to be 4 all in the deciding set. de Morpurgo had survived a tough struggle in the third round versus Rocksavage, 12–10 1–6 6–4. All were agreed that the Englishman's standard of play increased each time he went on court. The other finalist was Mayes, who was in fine fettle, passing Morgan and Gerbault, losing just five games to each, before taking the title with unexpected ease from de Morpurgo, 6–0 6–1 9–7. The Canadian showed wonderful control of the ball and throughout his lobbing was a telling factor.

Uberto de Morpurgo, Italy's top player for a number of years, entered the arena and successfully won many titles in the coming years.

Suzanne Lenglen competed in three events and won them all. The crowd was very disappointed in the outcome of the singles final as Elizabeth Ryan withdrew, suffering from a sore throat, preferring to concentrate on the doubles events. In the semi-final Suzanne Lenglen beat Miss Lesley Cadle, 6–0 6–0, while Elizabeth Ryan had a simple win over Madeline O'Neill, 6–1 6–1. Mayes and Suzanne Lenglen paired for the first time and as expected took the mixed event without being pressed.

The main meeting at the Carlton Club, plagued by adverse weather conditions for the first few days, had an outstanding entry. Simond was given a harassing time but, as usual, he was able to cope with the demanding situation. The men's singles title was captured by Mayes who, for the second week running, conquered de Morpurgo in the final. On this occasion he required four sets, 6–0 7–5 5–7 6–4. The Italian looked like turning the tide when he won the third set but thereafter Mayes was the fresher of the two. The Canadian was given little concern when ousting Dudley in the semi-finals, while de Morpurgo was pushed to two very close sets by Tegner. In earlier contests, Mayes crushed Ritchie, 6–0 6–2, de Morpurgo beat Rocksavage, 8–6 6–4, and Tegner outlasted Jack Hillyard, 4–6 6–2 8–6, the latter having eliminated Gerbault in the third round, 0–6 6–4 6–2.

With Suzanne Lenglen competing in three events, the outcome was predictable. She won the singles for the third time, defeating the holder, Elizabeth Ryan, 6–3 6–1. In the semi-finals the winner beat Mrs Doris Craddock, 6–1 6–1, and Elizabeth Ryan defeated Margaret Tripp, 6–1 6–2. Miss Kathleen McKane and Winifred Beamish arrived on the scene by train from Barcelona where the two had contested the singles final of the World's Covered Court Championships. The former won, 6–3 4–6 6–2, and as the prize took away a magnificent Cup donated by the King and Queen of Spain. Both players decided to restrict their energies to doubles at the Carlton Club, where Kathleen McKane in partnership with Dorothea Chambers reached the final of the ladies' event.

The standard of competition was raised further a week later at Beaulieu when Lowe joined the circuit and Crawford returned after an absence of several weeks. Also appearing for the first time during the season was Balbi, the holder of the men's title. He lost his Cup but had the satisfaction of knowing that his conquerer became his successor, for Lowe went on more or less comfortably to the final, where he beat Crawford, 6–3 6–2 2–6 6–3. Lowe's other victims included Gerbault, to whom Ritchie retired after losing the opening set, 6–4. Gerbault himself retired in the semi-final when Lowe was leading 6–3 4–1. He appears to have been upset by an aeroplane entertaining a crowd in connection with the local 'battle of flowers', dropping large squares of paper over the court. Morgan defeated Jack Hillyard to reach the semi-final, where Crawford was too steady for him.

Suzanne Lenglen appeared in only the ladies' doubles, which left Winifred Beamish and Elizabeth Ryan vying for the title. The latter, tired from earlier matches, conceded 6–4 6–3, losing to her opponent for the first time in her career. Kathleen McKane competed in the doubles events only.

The Monte Carlo meeting was highly successful in many respects. The men's singles entry totalled 60, of which British participation was unusually large, while the show of ladies was probably the highest quality ever seen on the Riviera. These, plus good weather attracted large crowds, which were almost unwieldy at times. Tennis in Paris kept a number of leading Frenchmen away but, irrespective, there was little doubt that Lowe would win through – and so he did. In a disappointing final he defeated Crawford in straight sets, 6–2 6–4 6–4, to win the Monte Carlo Cup outright, having succeeded in 1920 and 1921. Lowe never dropped a set throughout but was pushed to a tight second by Tegner in the semi-final, 6–2 7–5. Crawford eliminated the holder, Balbi, in the third round and went on to beat Morgan and de Morpurgo.

Kathleen McKane, displaying her fine talent in singles for the first time on the Riviera won the title, overcoming Elizabeth Ryan in the final, 7–5 4–6 6–2. Her play was something special, but the American might have altered the outcome had she had not served 19 double faults. Phyllis Satterthwaite played her best to beat Molla Mallory, struggling to acclimatise, in the fourth round, 6–2 6–1, but then fell away at the vital stage to Elizabeth Ryan in the semi-final, 4–6 7–5 6–2. Kathleen McKane reached the final with a brilliant display against Winifred Beamish, 6–1 6–4.

The match of the tournament was undoubtedly the duel for the ladies' doubles title, when Suzanne Lenglen and Elizabeth Ryan eventually defeated Dorothea Chambers and Kathleen McKane, 6–1 3–6 6–4, in which the winners found themselves in the unfamiliar position of being led by 4–3 in the final set. All four players were in grand form. (This was the only occasion that the winners ever lost a set as a combination.)

For the third week in succession the same two protagonists reached the final of the men's singles at Menton, with Lowe emerging the winner over Crawford, 6–2 6–3 7–5, to win the Menton Cup for the second time. The winner mixed his game well, using almost every stroke at his command

Four top personalities of the game meet in the final of the ladies' doubles at Monte Carlo when Elizabeth Ryan and Suzanne Lenglen narrowly defeated Kathleen McKane and Dorothea Chambers. The winners drop a set – the only occasion this occurred in their long partnership. This was the only season that Kathleen McKane visited the Riviera.

and fought back well when being led 5–2 in the third set. In the fourth round, Lowe was given a fine fight by Balbi, who had many chances before falling 9–7 6–4. The Englishman then beat de Morpurgo, a very narrow winner in his opening match against C.P. Lock, who had played much tennis in India. The score of 6–8 11–9 6–4 tells the story. Lycett, making his debut on the Riviera, gave good account of himself, beating Ritchie in a baseline battle, 6–2 6–3, before going down to Crawford in the semi-final, in two sets of ten games.

The showpiece of the meeting was the final of the ladies' singles in which Suzanne Lenglen defeated Kathleen McKane, 6–2 7–5. Postponed because of rain, the match was played at the same time as the men's final, but attracted a large crowd. This was their third meeting in twelve months and only the second set was uncertain, when the players stood at 4–all. Kathleen McKane was unlucky not to have won the next game, but at a critical point the Frenchwoman had an unreturnable net cord. However, the score reached 5–all, but Suzanne Lenglen's fine temperament in the crisis won through, as usual. In the semi-final the winner crushed Phyllis Satterthwaite, 6–0 6–0, despite her trying to drop shot her way out of trouble, while Elizabeth Ryan, the holder, won the middle set with great confidence against Kathleen McKane but then faded, 7–5 2–6 6–2. A shock win in the second round of this event occurred when Lesley Cadle defeated Molla Mallory, 6–0 7–5.

Suzanne Lenglen and Elizabeth Ryan coasted through the ladies' doubles, while in the men's division Jack Hillyard and Crawford came out on top – but only in the 14th game of the fifth set of the final.

The South of France Championships at Nice saw Lowe maintain his unbroken record when he beat Lycett in the singles final by displaying one of his best performances. Lycett was also on top form, but could not match his opponent's steadiness and stamina and fell, 9–7 3–6 6–3 6–2. Lycett beat de Morpurgo in the semi-final by playing a strong game, 6–1 6–4, while Lowe was give a walkover by Rocksavage, owing to the death of his father, the Marquis of Cholmondeley. Earlier, in a battle of two Italians, de Morpurgo beat Balbi in a marathon contest, 6–4 5–7 8–6.

Suzanne Lenglen defended her three championships and was successful in only two. With ease she put aside Diddie Vlasto, 6–1 6–1, Molla Mallory, 6–0 6–0 and in the final, Elizabeth Ryan, the holder, 6–1 6–0. The match between the winner and Molla Mallory was their fourth encounter and was concluded in 25 minutes and won by 50 points to 18. Kathleen McKane entered for the two doubles events only, reportedly feeling the cumulative strain a little.

In the final of the ladies' doubles, Suzanne Lenglen and Elizabeth Ryan had a simple victory against Dorothea Chambers and Kathleen McKane,

6–4 6–2, but the Frenchwoman and her partner, Soumarokoff, were given quite a shock in the semi-final of the mixed event when eliminated by Lycett and Elizabeth Ryan, 6–3 7–5. This upset stopped the losers winning the title three times in a row. This was a very rare defeat for Suzanne Lenglen.

The Cannes Club meeting, always very popular, drew an entry which involved nearly 600 matches – quite a total for Simond to handle. The Club had 14 courts but only eight were available as the stands surrounding the gallery court took up considerable space. Lowe and the Italians had left the scene and Crawford and Mayes were the obvious finalists. Mayes won the title by beating Aeschliman in the semi-final, 7–9 6–2 6–3 and then Hunter with ease, 6–3 6–2 6–0. Crawford retired earlier.

The feature of the ladies' singles was the defeat of Kathleen McKane by Molla Mallory in the fourth round. The Englishwoman was three times within victory in the second set at 5–3 and 5–4, but the American held on to eventually win, 4–6 7–5 6–4. Surprisingly Winifred Beamish eliminated Molla Mallory the following day in the semi-final, 6–2 9–7, but then fell to Phyllis Satterthwaite in the last match, 8–6 6–4. Elizabeth Ryan withdrew after a poor showing against Lili de Alvarez in the fourth round, where she dropped a set. A famous name appeared in the ladies' singles draw – that of Mrs Clementine Churchill, wife of Winston.

There was a slight decline in the quality of the competitors for the Beau Site Hotel meeting, but the lists were as large as ever. The weather was excellent, but the courts were described as unusually dusty. Borotra was not defending his title in the men's singles, but another newcomer to the Riviera, Frenchman Roger Danet, showed great promise before falling to Aeschliman in the fourth round, 6–2 6–3. However, the Swiss met his match against Jack Hillyard, who at one stage won 11 consecutive games to notch up a 6–2 6–0 victory. This gave Hillyard a place in the final, where Mayes playing a balanced game, won in four sets, 6–2 6–1 5–7 6–4, after missing a match point in the third set. Earlier, the Canadian had disposed of Gerbault, 6–3 3–6 6–3, after the last named had beaten Ritchie, 6–4 6–4. Rocksavage

Molla Mallory, seven-times singles champion of the United States, made her first of many visits to the Riviera, where initially she had difficulty acclimatising to the conditions.

returned to the Riviera as the Marquess of Cholmondeley and competed in the doubles.

Although Suzanne Lenglen and Elizabeth Ryan did not contest the ladies' singles, the event attracted considerable interest. Diddie Vlasto brought off a notable success by patiently outlasting Molla Mallory, 8–6 9–7, a task which occupied the court for over two hours. She then proceeded to the semi-final against Lili de Alvarez, 2–6 6–4 6–4, before falling to Winifred Beamish, 6–3 6–2. In the other half of the draw, Kathleen McKane was given a walkover by Phyllis Satterthwaite, prior to winning the title over Winifred Beamish, by displaying her volleying skills to the full to win, 6–2 6–2.

Suzanne Lenglen and Elizabeth Ryan retired from the ladies' doubles and the event was taken by Dorothea Chambers and Kathleen McKane, a fitting end to the latter's last tournament on the Riviera. Danet and the Swede, Sune Malmstrom, were the surprise winners of the men's division.

After playing assiduously all through the season, Brame Hillyard had his reward at the Cannes Metropole Hotel tournament, where he won the men's singles title. With ridiculous ease he beat Jack Hillyard, 6–1 6–1, and Ritchie, 6–0 6–1, to reach the final against Malmstrom. After winning the first two sets he was pulled back, but rallied in the fifth set to win the match, 6–3 6–2 1–6 1–6 6–3.

Elizabeth Ryan won another singles title, when Phyllis Satterthwaite scratched to her in the final. The winner had comfortably passed Eleanor Goss in the round before, 6–3 6–3, while at the same stage Lili de Alvarez withdrew, having earlier beaten Leslie Bancroft, 5–7 6–0 6–2. The two Americans had recently arrived in Europe for a summer tour.

Jack Hillyard won the men's doubles final with Julien Lezard, beating Aeschliman and Roland de Graffenried of Switzerland. He was also runner-up in the mixed doubles with Phyllis Satterthwaite to Frederick Scovel and Elizabeth Ryan.

The third meeting at Monte Carlo, and the last gathering of the season, ending on 15th April, was noteworthy for the surprise win in the ladies' singles by Lili de Alvarez who, driving vigorously throughout, defeated Phyllis Satterthwaite in the final, 6–3 7–5. Her progress during the past few weeks had been extraordinarily rapid and being still not 18 promised much for the future. The two Americans were dismissed at the semi-final stage, Leslie Bancroft by Phyllis Satterthwaite without the loss of a game, and Eleanor Goss, by Lili de Alvarez, 6–2 7–5.

Brame Hillyard followed up his triumph of the week before by capturing the men's singles title, with victory over Aeschliman in the last match, 8–6 6–8 6–0 8–6 – a very unusual score. His was a very polished performance. Jack Hillyard and Aeschliman won the men's doubles and Aeschliman took a second title paired with Lili de Alvarez.

After competing at the second Beau Site Hotel tournament, Alain Gerbault put his rackets away and turned his attention to fulfilling a lurking ambition for long distance sailing. Having earlier purchased a 39 foot boat named *'Firecrest'* he left for Gibraltar, where on 6th June he set out single-handed for New York and arrived there on 15th September after 101 days at sea. Back home in France he was awarded the Légion d'Honneur. He returned to New York and on 1st November 1924 started his long journey to circumnavigate the world via Panama, Tahiti, Indian Ocean, Durban, St Helena and the Azores to eventually return to Le Havre nearly five years later on 26th July 1929, after 700 days at sea and a distance of 40,000 miles. For the next three years he mixed sailing and bridge with tennis. He last played tennis on the Riviera in 1930. He realised that he missed the life of the South Pacific and left Marseille in a new boat on 28th September 1932 and never returned. He died at East Timor on 16th December 1941, aged 48. During the First World War, Gerbault served in the French Army Flying Corps and was decorated several times. He never took a day's leave.

# 1924
# Rain Affected Season • Henry Mayes and Elizabeth Ryan Outstanding

For the second season running the Riviera attracted many top class players, particularly in the men's division. Unfortunately, the weather refused to cooperate and the 16-week schedule suffered, many programmes being continually interrupted by rain, to the displeasure of the competitors and, most of all, Simond. Of course there were some bright periods but the last month or so saw little of these.

Beautiful windless weather favoured the opening meeting held over Christmas at Monte Carlo, where the six courts of the Condamine were used to supplement the three La Festa courts. The former played the better, but the latter had to be used for the show matches, being equipped with the necessary stands for spectators. Naturally, some of the competitors were short of practice, with those new to the scene finding difficulty with the surface and light. Arthur Lovibond, an American who had made his mark in England just after the War was, despite lack of competition, able to hit the ball crisply and with consistency to race through two rounds of the singles before embarking on a long match to overcome J.N. Lowry, the previous year's Cambridge University captain, 4–6 6–2 7–5. This put him in the final against Col. Charles Brierley, who won after an uphill fight, 6–2 1–6 7–5 6–3. In the earlier rounds Lowry beat Jack Hillyard, 9–7 6–3. Unfortunately, Aeschliman had to withdraw owing to a severe chill.

Phyllis Satterthwaite made a gallant effort to win the singles cup outright and seemed in sight of success when she led Elizabeth Ryan, 4–1 40–15, in the deciding set. However, she failed to win another game, mainly due to exhaustion, and the American secured the title, 3–6 6–4 6–4. In the semi-final the winner accounted for Margaret Tripp, 6–4 6–1, and the runner-up ousted Miss Audrey Wright, 6–0 6–2. Jack Hillyard and Lovibond won the men's doubles.

The New Year tournament, held at the Beau Site Hotel, saw the reappearance of Mayes, who won the men's singles, after a somewhat one-sided final against Brame Hillyard, who was beaten for consistency on the baseline, 6–0 6–4 6–2. In the semi-final Mayes easily defeated Jack Hillyard, while in the other match van Alen gave way to Brame Hillyard after being four times within a point of taking the duel in two sets. An unexpected result in the third round was when Brierley, the winner the

week before, fell to the Marquis of Cholmondeley, who moved on to push hard van Alen, 6–3 6–3.

Suzanne Lenglen entered but did not take part in the singles, which left Elizabeth Ryan and Phyllis Satterthwaite as the main protagonists. However, the latter decided to withdraw at the semi-final stage, preferring to reserve herself for the mixed doubles. The conclusion was that the American beat Lesley Cadle, 6–3 6–3, for the title. Suzanne Lenglen partnered Aeschliman to victory over Jack Hillyard and Phyllis Satterthwaite in the mixed final, 10–8 3–6 6–0. The result could have been different if the losers had won the first set, where they were within a point of doing so. Jack Hillyard and Mayes won the men's doubles after a terrific struggle over Aeschliman and Watson, 7–5 7–5 3–6 9–7.

The following week the scene of the action moved to the first Carlton Club meeting, which initially was affected by rain swamping the courts. However, by continuously staging matches the event was concluded on time. Mayes again dominated the play, beating in sequence both Hillyards to claim the singles title, Brame, 6–2 5–7 6–1, and Jack, 7–5 6–1 6–1. The latter accounted for Brierley in the semi-final, 6–4 6–2. The ladies' singles event was very disappointing as Phyllis Satherthwaite again retired to Elizabeth Ryan, on this occasion in the final. The semi-finalists were Mrs W.P. Keays and Lesley Cadle. Aeschliman and Watson proved the best pair

The first Gallia Lawn Tennis Club international tournament was held in January, with the singles titles won by Henry Mayes and Elizabeth Ryan. The Club was opened in late 1922 when five courts were constructed.

in the men's doubles, while Jack Hillyard and Phyllis Satterthwaite always looked like winning the mixed doubles.

After a week's break for the Club Championships the new Gallia Club at Cannes promoted their first open meeting. They were rewarded by fine weather, a good entry and an appreciative crowd daily, filling the well-provided accommodation. The courts' surface was not provided locally, with the material being transported from Paris. Although slow, the courts dried rapidly. Simond was unwell and G.A. Saulter acted as referee.

For the third consecutive tournament, Mayes won the singles, overcoming newcomer Leonce Aslangul in the final, 6–2 6–2 4–6 6–3. The Frenchman led 3–1 in the fourth set, but his opponent steadied to regain control. In the round before, Mayes beat Cholmondeley effortlessly, 6–2 6–0, while Aslangul struggled hard to defeat Crawford, 3–6 6–2 6–3. Earlier Mayes beat Brame Hillyard, 9–7 6–1 and Aslangul accounted for Brierley in a long match, 2–6 7–5 6–4.

Mrs Phyllis Covell (Howkins) returned to the Riviera with newcomer, Mrs Dorothy Shepherd-Barron. The two were great friends, who shared a double wedding in Bombay during September 1921. Both reached the semi-final of the singles, the former losing to Elizabeth Ryan, 8–6 6–4, and the latter to Lesley Cadle, in a marathon match, 2–6 6–0 14–12. Dorothy Shepherd-Barron led 8–7 40 love on her service in the deciding set and was twice within a point of victory. Lesley Cadle's response was truly gritty. In the final, Elizabeth Ryan beat Lesley Cadle, 6–3 6–2.

Suzanne Lenglen did not compete in the singles but, as expected, won both doubles titles. There was a very interesting incident in the final of the ladies' doubles when Suzanne Lenglen was footfaulted by a linesman, whereupon she stopped playing and declined to resume until the linesman was replaced – which he was. Her reason for adopting this stance was that she should have been given a previous warning. Apparently, at that time in France, this was the custom. The mixed doubles final took one hour and a half to settle, the third set going to 28 games, with Suzanne Lenglen and Mayes edging out against Aeschliman and Elizabeth Ryan, 6–4 1–6 15–13. That was the most games the Frenchwoman ever played in a set during her career.

The Hyères meeting, though relatively small in entry, provided a week of enjoyable tennis and was favoured with warm and windless weather. Jack Hillyard retained the singles title but only after five close sets with Ernest Lamb, who at 4–all in the final set missed a great opportunity when his opponent stood at 15–40 on service. Phyllis Satterthwaite's third win in a row in the singles at the tournament gave her the Cup outright. By concentrating on Lesley Cadle's backhand and varying the strength of her forehand, she won 6–4 6–2 in the semi-final and then proceeded to

Four of the leading lady contenders for honours during the season, (left to right) Lili de Alvarez, Phyllis Satterthwaite, Helen Contostavlos and Diddie Vlasto.

overcome Phyllis Covell in the last round, with surprising ease, 6–3 6–1. Jack Hillyard and Lamb won the men's doubles.

The winter Nice meeting had a small entry in the level events. Aslangul shone during the week, disposing of Brame Hillyard, 2–6 6–2 6–2, de Morpurgo, 6–2 7–5 and in the final beat Mayes, 6–2 6–1 7–5. The Frenchman's steadiness was his telling factor. Suzanne Lenglen entered the singles event and, as expected, coasted through beating Phyllis Satterthwaite, 6–3 6–1, and in the last encounter, Dorothy Shepherd-Barron, who was allowed just one game in the second set. The event lost some interest when Elizabeth Ryan withdrew owing to a bad cold, Aeschliman and Suzanne Lenglen won the mixed doubles.

Apart from some unsettled weather the main Carlton Club tournament was an unqualified success. Of the large field of 64 entered for the men's singles, Lowe and Aslangul were reckoned to be the finalists but, surprisingly, both were eliminated in the third round respectively by Jack Hillyard, 3–6 8–6 8–6, and Aeschliman, 6–3 6–4, respectively. This was Lowe's first outing on the Riviera and he appeared a little rusty, while the Frenchman failed to cope with the very damp court. Jack Hillyard continued to shine in the semi-final, eliminating Crawford, 1–6 6–3 6–3, but disappointingly played poorly in the final against Mayes, who on the day was superior all round to register a drubbing, 6–1 6–2 6–2.

Elizabeth Ryan was far from her best at the meeting but, nevertheless, took the honours in the ladies' singles, accounting for Phyllis Satterthwaite in the final, 6–2 7–5. The majority of the earlier contests were settled in straight sets, including the semi-finals, where Elizabeth Ryan was always in command against Diddie Vlasto, 6–2 6–1, and Phyllis Satterthwaite overcame a close first set to dispatch Miss Ermyntrude Harvey on her first visit from England, 7–5 6–2. Suzanne Lenglen won both doubles events.

A very full entry with only three courts available gave Simond an exacting task at Beaulieu. Lowe had still not recaptured his best form as he struggled to beat Crawford and Lamb, before falling to de Morpurgo in the last four, 6–1 2–6 6–4. Lowe led 4–1 in the final set.

After beating Aslangul in the semi-final, 7–5 6–4, Jack Hillyard played superbly for the title, outvolleying de Morpurgo in straight sets, 6–3 6–4 6–2. Suzanne Lenglen did not compete and in the singles the title was won by Elizabeth Ryan without any worry, beating Phyllis Satterthwaite, who once again retired, this time after losing the first set, 6–4. The American won both doubles titles.

The Monte Carlo gathering on the La Festa courts was badly interrupted by rain during the week, leaving the Sunday a complete washout and only half a day's play possible on the Monday, causing the men's singles final and the closing stage of the mixed doubles to be cancelled. However, at a later date both events were concluded on the Nice Club courts.

The entries were similar to the previous week, with Mishu and Friedrich Rohrer from Czechoslovakia being fresh new faces and Crawford returning after a week's rest. Because of the rain many of the matches were forced to be 'stop and start' and this upset some contestants. Crawford was certainly one of the favourites, but he was very near defeat in the second round by Rohrer, who won the opening set and was 2–1 up in the third on the previous day, when darkness fell. On resumption he led 5–1 and had a match point at 5–2 but, somehow, Crawford held his nerve and won through. The winner then proceeded to the final but not before being extremely hard pushed by de Morpurgo, 6–3 10–8, and Brame Hillyard, 6–3 3–6 9–7. In the other half of the draw Aslangul, full of confidence, disposed of Lowe, the holder, 6–3 3–6 6–4, and Jack Hillyard easily 6–0

Henry Mayes had an outstanding start to the season by winning the singles at his first four meetings. He had a decisive win over Jack Hillyard in the singles final at the Carlton Club meeting.

6–2. When the event was decided, Crawford was back to his best form to beat the Frenchman, 6–4 3–6 6–2.

Elizabeth Ryan and Phyllis Satterthwaite reached the final, but both had narrow escapes on the way before the American won the title, 6–2 6–2. However, the semi-final matches were in deep contrast with Elizabeth Ryan crushing Mrs M.F. Ellis, 6–0 6–0, while Phyllis Satterthwaite was taken to the limit by Ermyntrude Harvey before finally edging out, 6–1 13–15 6–4 – no wonder the loser was not at her best the following day. Earlier, Elizabeth Ryan beat Dorothy Shepherd-Barron, 1–6 6–3 6–2, and Ermyntrude Harvey accounted for Diddie Vlasto, 6–4 8–6. This was a good field with only Phyllis Covell missing. The delayed mixed doubles title was won by Lamb and Dorothea Chambers.

The Riviera Championships at Menton were favoured with a fine week. The task of the referee, Madge, was not easy when scheduling many of the matches, as several leading players elected to stay long distances from the courts. If the trains or other conveyances were late, the programme was soon thrown out of gear.

Lowe, the holder of the men's singles title, was back to his winning way, although not without some worries. He lost the opening set to the Belgian champion, Jean Washer, before playing a strong deciding set, 3–6 11–9 6–3. He then dismissed Aslangul, 6–3 6–1 3–6 2–6 6–2. The champion should have won in straight sets as he led in the third, 3–0, but was distracted by cheers on the neighbouring court which upset his concentration. By winning for a third year, Lowe retired the Cup.

Suzanne Lenglen returned to the ladies' singles and on the way to beating Elizabeth Ryan in the well-contested final, 7–5 6–1, had to pass both Dorothy Shepherd-Barron and Phyllis Covell. The first lady won four games, the second, three games. Ermyntrude Harvey lost to the defeated finalist, 7–5 6–4.

A mixed doubles international invitation event was inaugurated, which necessitated pairs being of the same nationality. In a very restricted draw, Cochet and Suzanne Lenglen triumphed. Strangely this was the Frenchman's only appearance at the tournament.

The main Nice meeting drew one of the finest entries ever, with Aeschliman, Cochet, Crawford, de Morpurgo, Lacoste, Lowe, Mishu, Washer and, newly arrived from Australia, Norman Brookes, the 1907

In great form during the season, Gordon Lowe won the Menton tournament for the third time.

and 1914 Wimbledon champion. Suzanne Lenglen was present plus the four English international players. Brookes still had his 'sea-legs' and after playing one singles match, retired, no doubt realising that the court surface was far from his liking.

There were some excellent matches, with the upshot being that the young Frenchman, René Lacoste took the title, defeating Washer in the final after just recovering in the fifth set, 6–1 6–0 3–6 7–9 6–3. Lacoste's victim in the semi-final was Aeschliman, who earlier was quite brilliant in passing Aslangul and Brame Hillyard in the same day, having arrived late and then, the following morning, put out Lowe, the holder, 5–7 6–1 6–3. All this took too much out of the Swiss as he fell to Lacoste in the semi-final, 6–1 6–1. Washer had overcome Cochet at the same stage, 1–6 6–3 7–5.

Suzanne Lenglen's victory in the ladies' singles was assured from the start and in the last three rounds she beat Mrs Ellis, 6–0 6–0, Dorothy Shepherd-Barron, 6–1 6–2, and in the final, Phyllis Covell, 6–2 6–1 – it was all so easy! To the singles she added the two doubles crowns.

The Cannes Club meeting for the Côte d'Azur Championships was bigger than ever, as may be judged by the mixed doubles handicap event which drew an entry of 98 pairs. Unfortunately, after three perfect days, the rain set in and this forced Simond to decide on two rounds of both singles on the same day. Obviously, this was an advantage for youth.

Aeschliman was in tip-top form throughout, capturing three events. In the singles his last three victories were over Lacoste, 6–2 6–4, Jack Hillyard, 3–6 6–3 6–1, and in the final, Brame Hillyard, 6–2 6–4 6–2. His cunning defensive play ruled the day. Brookes entered but retired after a couple of rounds and Lowe fell victim to Jack Hillyard, 10–8 6–1.

Lili de Alvarez made a deep impression in the singles, particularly against Phyllis Covell, where her tactical play and placements saw her through, 4–6 6–4 6–2. After beating Mlle Yvonne Bourgeois she lost to Elizabeth Ryan in the final, 6–3 10–8. Here she had many chances in the second set and possibly more experience would have told her how to deal better with the American's dropshots.

A disappointed crowd saw little of Suzanne Lenglen, who entered only the ladies' doubles with Elizabeth Ryan, especially as they were given walkovers in the last two rounds! Brookes and Suzanne Lenglen paired but withdrew in the third round as the Australian suffered an attack of influenza.

The last week of March at the Beau Site Hotel, where the Cannes Championships were contested, was again very wet and on the day the

In December at Boston, USA, Charles Aeschliman married Leslie Bancroft, the former American No.2 player, who had visited the Riviera for the past two seasons.

semi-finals were due, play was abandoned. By general agreement the best two players seen on the Riviera during the season were the two young Frenchmen, Cochet and Lacoste. After them came the remainder, half a dozen or so players who were all capable of beating each other on their day. Cochet beat his compatriot in the final transferred to the Gallia LTC courts, in three very close sets, 7–5 6–4 6–4. To reach this stage, Cochet had outclassed Crawford, 6–0 6–2, while Lacoste really had no problems with Aslangul, at 6–1 7–5. Earlier, Cochet beat Malmstrom, 7–5 6–3 and Lacoste defeated Jack Hillyard, 6–2 6–4.

There was an unusual ending to the Aslangul versus de Morpurgo match, when the latter retired at match point down, 3–6 8–6 5–3. A report stated "this unusual act was the culminating incident of a long and bitter struggle conducted without the customary dignity and decorum of Beau Site matches".

Elizabeth Ryan won her fourth singles title at this tournament, and ninth of the season, receiving a walk-over in the final from Lili de Alvarez, given for no reason. Diddie Vlasto pushed the winner to the full in the opening set of the semi-final before fading, 8–6 6–0. At the same stage the French lady's cousin, Mlle Hélène Contostavlos, proved quite a handful to Lili de Alvarez, to the tune of 6–2 8–6.

Suzanne Lenglen played in both doubles events, winning easily with Elizabeth Ryan and then defeating her and Cochet in the final of the mixed doubles in tandem with Brookes, 6–2 6–4.

The Metropole Hotel tournament was another badly affected by rain but, as usual, Simond coped exceedingly well. The feature of the meeting was an invitation mixed doubles event, made clear by the organizers "for this occasion only", whereby six pairs played each other. The two stars who won were Brookes partnered by Suzanne Lenglen. They captured all six matches and indeed never dropped a set! Their opponents were all top class, Aeschliman and Elizabeth Ryan, Jack Hillyard and Phyllis Satterthwaite, de Morpurgo and Diddie Vlasto, Aslangul and Lili de Alvarez and van Alen and Phyllis Covell.

With Cochet and Lacoste no longer present, de Morpurgo proved himself the best of the remainder, in narrowly defeating Crawford in the semi-final, 4–6 6–3 8–6, and then Aslangul comfortably in the deciding match, 6–4 6–0 6–2. Aslangul had expended all his energy against Jack Hillyard the day before, 6–3 4–6 7–5.

Other than Suzanne Lenglen, few people could claim to have beaten Elizabeth Ryan in singles, but in the semi-final this was achieved (for the second time) by Phyllis Covell in two tough sets 8–6 6–4. However, try as she might, she could not get the better of Lili de Alvarez in the final and after an arduous match went down 9–7 2–6 7–5.

The doubles winners were de Morpurgo and van Alen and Suzanne Lenglen and Elizabeth Ryan. The weakened mixed event was taken by the French pair, Antoine Gentien and Mme N. Descleres.

The third meeting at Monte Carlo was noteworthy for Phyllis Covell's defeat over Lili de Alvarez in the singles final, 5–7 6–3 6–1, to reverse the result of the previous week. The Spaniard made many errors as the match proceeded. In the semi-final, Phyllis Covell dismissed Eleanor Goss, a member of the United States Olympic team, 6–0 2–6 6–4.

In the men's singles final, Aeschliman beat Brame Hillyard after five sets, 6–2 7–5 4–6 3–6 6–3. Youth ultimately won through!

The first Juan-les-Pins tournament held at Easter was extra to the original schedule. David Morgan, just home from India, coasted through the men's singles to defeat Alfred Hunter in the final, 6–1 6–4 6–3, but the great surprise occurred in the ladies' singles final when Lili de Alvarez was ousted by Mme Sylvia Lafauric (Jung), 7–5 6–2. Suzanne Lenglen made a brief appearance and partnered Mrs Florence Gould to victory in the doubles.

# 1925
# Henry Mayes and Elizabeth Ryan
# Continue to Shine

The season contained the greatest number of tournaments ever played during the winter on the Riviera, with 18 weeks of play, stretching without a break from 8th December to 12th April.

The first venture, starting earlier than ever before, was held at the Nice Club, and attracted a small entry, with many of the contestants not generally known. A visitor from Australia, Lyle Terrey, won the men's singles with a straight sets win over the Italian, Roberto Bocciardo, 6–2 6–3 6–2, while Phyllis Satterthwaite just as easily beat Margaret Tripp in her last encounter, 6–2 6–2.

The first of three tournaments held at Monte Carlo followed and featured the Monaco Championships, staged on the La Festa Courts. There was an outstanding performance by Lili de Alvarez, who won three titles but it was her crushing defeat of Phyllis Satterthwaite in the final of the singles, with the loss of just one game in the second set, which sent waves of surprise through the crowd. The Spaniard joined her opponent to win the doubles and Marian-Crawford to capture the mixed. The men's singles winner, Placido Gaslini of Italy, had too many strokes at his command to dispatch D. Straten, with the loss of five games, 6–1 6–2 6–2. During the latter half of the week the Duke of Connaught was present.

The season started with a meeting held at Nice. From a small entry an unknown Australian, Lyle Terrey, won the singles title.

The Christmas meeting was scheduled to be held at Beaulieu, but the seven new courts recently constructed were not ready and the Metropole Hotel in Cannes stepped into the breach and held a very successful gathering. The weather was good, except for heavy rain on the last day.

Mayes, head and shoulders above the others in the men's singles, won through five rounds losing only two sets, with his steady ground strokes dictating the play against van Alen in the final, 6–0 6–2 0–6 6–3. A much improved van Alen had accounted for Brame Hillyard, 8–6 6–3, conqueror of Gaslini, 6–3 5–7 6–1. Elizabeth Ryan was unbeaten during the week, winning the three events. She was too severe for Phyllis Sattherthwaite in the final of the singles to the tune of 6–2 6–4.

While England was being swept by gales and floods, the Riviera was enjoying almost continuous sunshine and the only check to the progress of the New Year meeting at the Beau Site Hotel came on the opening day. This had been preceded by one of only two wet days in December and rain had left four of the six courts waterlogged, with just the newer two fit for play. However, from then on the schedule was maintained and Simond was able to close down on time.

The five main finals were generally one-sided. Mayes continued where he left off the week before and comfortably retained the men's singles title, by overcoming Cholmondeley in the final, 6–3 6–3 6–4. In the semi-finals, his Lordship inflicted a 6–4 6–2 over van Alen, who in the round before just got the measure of his Cambridge colleague, Keats Lester, 4–6 6–0 6–4. Mayes beat Brame Hillyard, 6–2 8–6. Jack Hillyard, suffering from arthritis, was resting.

Margaret Tripp played extremely well, defeating the 17-year old Miss Eileen Bennett, the Middlesex junior champion, in the singles, 6–2 8–6, then Phyllis Satterthwaite, 6–1 6–3, before taxing Elizabeth Ryan in the final, 6–2 6–4.

The event of the week was undoubtedly the reappearance of Suzanne Lenglen, having her first outing anywhere since retiring due to illness from The Championships at Wimbledon the previous July. She played only in the doubles with Elizabeth Ryan, where the pair lost just four games. Large crowds watched the Frenchwoman play every match.

Beautiful weather each day favoured the first Carlton Club meeting, although at night there was quite often a frost. Besides the usual five level events, there were three handicaps, but no player was allowed entry to more than four. This was to ensure that the players were not put under undue strain.

The entry for the men's singles was much the same as the week before, except that van Alen restricted himself to doubles. Strangely, Mayes was handed the easier half of the draw. Not that he needed this assistance, for once again he dominated the play to win for the third week running, again without losing a set. In the other half of the draw were Cholmondeley, Brame Hillyard, Lester, Watson and Aeschliman. The latter emerged, but in the final he could not overcome the accuracy of Mayes who, hitting harder than ever, lost only two games in each of the three sets. Aeschliman was making his first appearance of the season on the Riviera with his new bride, the former Leslie Bancroft. They had met in Paris during the 1924 Olympic Games and married in December of that year. They made their home at Cannes.

Elizabeth Ryan, although never in jeopardy in the singles, was given a good game by Mrs Annie Neville-Smith (Rimington) in the semi-final

and by Mrs Eveline Crundall-Punnett (Nutcombe-Quicke) in the final, the winner's score in each case being 6–2 6–3. The runner-up was 52 years of age. Eileen Bennett again showed great promise and took a set from Annie Neville-Smith. Suzanne Lenglen entered both doubles events and, as expected, was successful with much to spare.

The Hyères meeting enjoyed perfect weather during the week but the entry was not up to the usual standard in the three level and two handicap events. (Most players opted to compete in the Cannes Club members' tournament, in which Mayes and Elizabeth Ryan took top singles honours). Lieut. René Jaureguiberry won the men's singles final against M. Harvey after trailing by two sets to one, 6–3 5–7 2–6 6–3 6–3, while the ladies' division was captured by a young French player, Mlle Cosette Saint Omer Roy, without dropping a set.

The Gallia Club was the next on the list and the main topic of conversation into the week was on the introduction of an 'American' ball, which proved rather embarrassing to many of the British players, who found difficulty in coping with the different bound and flight and in consequence unexpected results occurred. Mayes and Aeschliman played

In December the professional tournament for the annual Bristol Cup was decided at the Carlton Club and resulted in Albert Burke (left) defeating Roman Rajuch in the final. Suzanne Lenglen presented the Cup.

their third consecutive final, with the former inflicting a severe defeat, 6–1 6–1 6–0. The Swiss fought gamely but somehow all accuracy had gone. Mayes never lost a set throughout and indeed never lost more than two games in a set. In the semi-final he passed W. Cumming, while Aeschliman accounted for Brame Hillyard. Van Alen and Lester were not in the field and Cholmondeley chose to compete only in doubles.

The ladies' entry was excellent with Elizabeth Ryan winning yet another singles title. She was tested to the full by Leslie Aeschliman in the semi-final, but having just edged through the opening 14–game set, was never again threatened and won six games on the trot. Winifred Beamish, who played sound tennis to beat Eileen Bennett, 6–4 6–2, moved on to the final where, despite a cold, she produced her best, but still went down, 8–6 6–3. Unfortunately for her Elizabeth Ryan was at her very best. Earlier, Leslie Aeschliman and Lesley Cadle had a spirited match with the American just winning through, 9–7 6–3.

After a month of excellent weather the second Metropole Hotel meeting felt the full force of the rain for the first three days in which only an odd match could be decided. Aeschliman did not compete in the singles but Mayes, despite a hurried journey to Paris and back, continued his domination to beat Brame Hillyard, 6–3 6–4, and following on, Cholmondeley in the final with a procession of points, 6–1 6–1 6–1, to win his sixth successive tournament (including the Cannes members' tournament).

Diddie Vlasto, wearing the mantle of French champion, made a welcome return to the circuit. After winning three singles matches in one day she then opposed Winifred Beamish in the semi-final. There was a great struggle with the Frenchwoman, twice at match point, at 6–5 in the third set, before her opponent edged back to win 4–6 6–2 8–6. Interestingly both players had acquired overhead services recently to strengthen their game and when under pressure reverted to underhand deliveries. Winifred Beamish, as usual, gave Elizabeth Ryan a hard game in the final, but the result for the American was 7–5 6–3. In the semi-final Elizabeth Ryan inflicted a 6–0 6–0 victory over Lesley Cadle, exactly the same score the latter had secured over a disappointing Eileen Bennett. Suzanne Lenglen bypassed the meeting.

With the return of the good weather the second Nice gathering ran smoothly. Suzanne Lenglen entered all three events, with the singles competition being the first she had undertaken for seven months. Unfortunately, any form of 'opposition' had disappeared as Elizabeth Ryan was having a week off, while Winifred Beamish, Phyllis Satterthwaite (arm problems) and Diddie Vlasto confined their energies to doubles events. Suzanne Lenglen won five rounds for the total loss of two games. Her last two matches against Eileen Bennett and then Margaret Tripp, never bothered the scoresheet.

At last Mayes met his match against de Morpurgo in the singles final. The Italian, playing for the first time during the season, produced a difficult service and volleyed well, both which he exploited with great success. Mayes pushed the ball back instead of hitting it normally and so his length and pace suffered. He led 5–4 in the third set but de Morpurgo held on to win, 6–1 6–2 7–5. The day before, de Morpurgo had survived a lengthy match against Brame Hillyard, 6–2 5–7 6–3. The latter had accounted for Cholmondeley, 8–6 6–1. Maurice Germot, the ex-French champion, competed in the doubles, the event eventually won by Mayes and Lamb.

An unsettled February continued at the Carlton Club meeting, when following intermittent showers for a couple of days, the Friday produced a swamping storm and on the Saturday the courts were swept by a hurricane. All this caused several retirements and made some of the finals an anti-climax. Mayes and Cholmondeley both withdrew from the singles. Aeschliman and Brame Hillyard received walkovers to the semi-final, where the Swiss won, 7–5 6–2. Waiting for him was Lowe, back in action on the Riviera following a spell in London. After taking a set to find his length, he went forward with some outstanding ground strokes, to win the title, 4–6 6–3 6–3 6–1.

Diddie Vlasto retired in the fourth round, which gave Elizabeth Ryan an easy passage into the final and here she met Winifred Beamish who had lost the middle set to Ermyntrude Harvey, 6–3 5–7 6–1. The Englishwoman again demonstrated that she was capable of extending her opponent, but in the end she mustered eight games, at 6–3 7–5. There was a strange finish to the mixed event, when Aeschliman and Elizabeth Ryan won the last two rounds without taking the court, while in the ladies' doubles the result was a foregone conclusion for Suzanne Lenglen and Elizabeth Ryan.

Three-times Wimbledon doubles champion, Randolph Lycett and his new bride, Joan Austin were married in London on 12th February and for their honeymoon travelled to the Riviera where they both entered the Beaulieu tournament.

Beaulieu attracted a good entry and spectator support, and although showery at times, generally had kind weather. Lycett with his new bride, the former Joan Austin, joined the throng and progressed through the singles to meet Lowe in the semi-final. Here, the latter serving well and scoring on his opponent's backhand, won in two tight sets, 8–6 7–5. At the same stage Terrey pushed de Morpurgo to the limit before going down 6–0 3–6 9–7, but he had his chance in the deciding set when he led 6–5 and 7–6 but on each occasion lost his service.

In the final Lowe won the first two sets and should have won in the fourth but, going in to a decider, led 4–3 when de Morpurgo gave up after losing a 25 stroke rally.

Elizabeth Ryan and Winifred Beamish met once again in the singles final, where the American, in tip-top form inflicted a crushing defeat to win the title four times in five years, 6–0 6–1. Joan Lycett fell victim to Margaret Tripp in the second round, 1–6 7–5 6–2. The winner eventually lost to Winifred Beamish in the last four, 6–2 6–4. De Morpurgo and Lycett paired to win the men's doubles. Suzanne Lenglen and Elizabeth Ryan coasted past Dorothea Chambers and Ermyntrude Harvey in the ladies' doubles final.

Over 400 matches were scheduled for the main Monte Carlo tournament played on the La Festa courts, but several blank days due to rain caused most events to be abandoned.

The men's singles was divided, with the last four being Lacoste and Mayes, Lowe and de Morpurgo, while the ladies' singles final had been reached, with again Elizabeth Ryan and Winifred Beamish due to meet. All other events were abandoned except the Butler Cup final, which was postponed for a week until 10th March. Gaslini returned from Genoa for the match, while Cholmondeley and Mayes came over from Cannes. In the end de Morpurgo and Gaslini beat Mayes and Cholmondeley, 6–4 6–1 6–4. February had been a terrible month for weather.

The following meeting at Menton, where the Riviera Championships were at stake, fared well with the weather and on the last day the stands were packed with spectators.

Lowe was never in danger winning the men's singles title for the third successive year. In the semi-finals he was too accurate for Lycett, who struggled throughout to produce his best ground strokes and could only manage two games in each of the two sets. Lowe took the first two sets easily from de Morpurgo in the final, revelling in the pace provided by his opponent. The Italian then countered with aggressive shots to take the next set and lead 4–2 in the fourth, but Lowe's greater tenacity came to his aid to win through, 6–2 6–0 4–6 7–5. The runner-up had eliminated Brame Hillyard in a very tight fight, 6–4 5–7 6–3.

Playing in her third tournament on the Riviera, Honor Woolrych reached the final of the ladies' singles and with a faultless display of driving took the first set from Elizabeth Ryan, 6–3. The effort tired her and the next six games went to her opponent. She held the American to 3–2 in the deciding set and then faded, 6–2. In the semi-final Honor Woolrych led Ermyntrude Harvey, 6–4 5–4 30 love, when the match was interrupted for 10 minutes, owing to the noise from the adjoining court, following the conclusion of the men's singles final. On resumption Ermyntrude Harvey

pulled back to win the set, 8–6, but Honor Woolrych, unperturbed, drove her way to 4–1, when her opponent after arduous chasing, retired. In the other match Elizabeth Ryan had a walkover from Joan Lycett. The inaugural invitation mixed doubles event had been won the previous year by Cochet and Suzanne Lenglen. However, with Cochet being ill, Lacoste took his place and, as expected, the pair won easily. In the championship event, Suzanne Lenglen participated only in the doubles with Elizabeth Ryan, with the result as expected.

Although the sun shone every day at the South of France Championships, held at the Nice Club, there was a constant chill about the air. Without any threat of defeat, Lacoste retained his singles title with a decisive victory over Lowe, 6–1 6–4 6–3. With the Frenchman playing at the top of his form, Lowe managed to counter on two or three occasions, but seemed to accept the situation as the match progressed. Both semi-finals were resolved in two sets, Lacoste over Cholmondeley, 6–4 6–2, and Lowe passing Terrey, 6–2 6–1.

In the ladies' singles Elizabeth Ryan's withdrawal before playing left the event a natural gift for Suzanne Lenglen, but the situation could have been more interesting if Ermyntrude Harvey and Honor Woolrych had been well. They were keen to show what they could do, but both had to retire, Honor Woolrych in the quarter-final after playing just one game,

People taking advantage of a fine sunny spring day as they stroll along the Promenade des Anglais at Nice.

and Ermyntrude Harvey forced to take to her bed just before the final. The latter's match in an earlier round before did not assist her task as she was pushed to the limit by Yvonne Bourgeois, 6–4 6–8 6–4. Earlier, Diddie Vlasto beat Winifred Beamish, 7–5 6–2, before falling to the champion, 6–2 6–0. As expected, Suzanne Lenglen won both doubles titles, easily with Elizabeth Ryan and comfortably the mixed with Aeschliman.

The Côte d'Azur Championships, staged at the Cannes Club, involved some 500 matches, which imposed quite a heavy strain on Simond. Fortunately good weather was on hand with the sun present all week if, at times, being quite chilly.

Similar to the week previously, Lacoste fully deserved to win the men's singles. As before, he faced Lowe in the final, but he found his opponent much more stubborn. The Englishman played a great first set but his fine form was not maintained and gradually Lacoste got the upper hand to win, 4–6 6–0 6–3 6–4. There was little to chose between the two men.

There were other entertaining matches. Early on, Brame Hillyard took a set from Lacoste and in the semi-finals, Lowe beat Mayes who persisted in playing the contest from the back of the court, 6–4 6–2, while Lacoste always had the measure of Aeschliman, 6–0 6–3.

Neither Suzanne Lenglen nor Elizabeth Ryan competed in the singles and to some degree the surprise winner was Lili de Alvarez, who returned to competition after spending some weeks at St Moritz. The expectation was that she would meet Winifred Beamish in the final, but the young English player, Miss Cristobel Hardie had other ideas. In the fourth round she led, 6–3 2–1, when her opponent retired, feeling the effects of a severe cold. In the semi-final, Cristobel Hardie faced a sterner task, but eventually managed to outplay Yvonne Bourgeois, 1–6 6–3 7–5. However in the final she made little impression on the Spaniard, who won with much to spare, 6–0 6–2. There was a rare upset in the mixed doubles final when de Morpurgo and Elizabeth Ryan beat Aeschliman and Suzanne Lenglen, 6–3 6–3 – the Frenchwoman's first loss in any competition since Wimbledon, 1923.

The Championships of Cannes, decided at the Beau Site Hotel, were ruined by rain and the committee was obliged to abandon the tournament for the first time. Some play was possible on two days of the week but not enough to make any impression on the programme and, when on the Friday morning heavy rain fell and the courts were waterlogged, only the first two rounds of the singles had been completed. Sadly an excellent entry had been received which included Heath of Australia and newcomer, Eduardo Flaquer of Spain and, returning to the scene for the first time since 1914, Count Salm. Lacoste, Myers plus Lili de Alvarez and Suzanne Lenglen and Elizabeth Ryan were also present.

The second birthday of the Juan-les-Pins tournament enjoyed a week of springtime at its best. The men's singles entry was most imposing on paper, but Cholmondeley, Lacoste, Salm and de Morpurgo stood down or retired, thus the men's doubles for which the three first-named stayed, became the most interesting event.

In the singles the best two players, Jean Augustin of France and Brame Hillyard fought out the final in very hot weather, with the Frenchman winning in five sets, after losing the first two, 3–6 3–6 8–6 6–3 6–2. The ladies' singles finalists were Lili de Alvarez and Cristobel Hardie. The latter made a much better showing against the Spaniard than two weeks earlier at Cannes. She led 4–1 but gradually Lili de Alvarez achieved the necessary control in time to save the set. Cristobel Hardie continued to run for everything but could only score two more games. Earlier the runner-up had dismissed Lesley Aeschliman, 6–0 6–2. The men's doubles final was one of the highlights of the meeting, with Cholmondeley and Lacoste beating Aeschliman and Salm, 6–2 7–5 6–3.

At the last tournament of the season at Monte Carlo, Mayes was at his best and, after accounting for Aeschliman in the semi-final, 6–2 6–2, proceeded to defeat Brame Hillyard, with the loss of the second set in four, 6–1 4–6 6–3 6–1. Hillyard had scored a 6–2 6–3 victory over René Gallepe of France, who earlier had surprised Cholmondeley, 6–4 8–6.

In the absence of Suzanne Lenglen in the singles, Phyllis Satterthwaite won the title against an improved Domini Crosfield, 6–1 6–4. Suzanne Lenglen won the two doubles, in partnership with Phyllis Satterthwaite and Aeschliman.

During the main Monte Carlo tournament held from 23rd to 29th February, a presentation was made to George Simond to mark the occasion of his twenty first year of office as referee and handicapper of the tournament. The testimonial took the form of a pair of pearl studs and a portable dressing case. The list of subscribers contained over a hundred names, headed by the Duke of Connaught. The presentation was made by Wallis Myers and Suzanne Lenglen.

# 1926
# Epic Match Between Suzanne Lenglen and Helen Wills

The season opened on 14th December at Monte Carlo with the Monaco Championships, played on the La Festa Courts, where a distinguished gathering of players assembled.

As expected, Jacques Brugnon was outstanding among the men and duly won the singles, beating newcomer to the Riviera, Donald Greig, over four well-fought sets, 6–4 1–6 6–3 6–3. The latter had a good win the day before in disposing of Gaslini 6–1 6–3, while at the same mark, Brugnon was taken to 9–7 6–3 by Cholmondeley. Earlier the rising Italian star, ambidextrous Giorgio de Stefani, came into the limelight by surprising Fisher, but then falling to his Lordshiip.

All the level events were concluded by the Saturday, with the exception of the ladies' singles final, which was scheduled for the Sunday, between Phyllis Satterthwaite and Mrs Elizabeth Macready but, owing to heavy rain for two days, the match never came off. The prizes were divided and, under the rules, Phyllis Satterthwaite retained the Cup, having won it twice before. In the semi-finals, Phyllis Satterthwaite found Mrs L. Pitman easy prey, 6–0 6–0, and Elizabeth Macready dropped a set to Miss Eden Petchell, 2–6 6–1 6–4. Other than Phyllis Satterthwaite, the ladies were making their debut on the Riviera. Brugnon and Suzanne Lenglen each won their respective doubles events.

There was no Christmas tournament arranged this year and the next assembly of players was at the New Year Beau Site Hotel tournament commencing 28th December. The week had beautiful weather for the first five days and a large entry. Mayes won the men's singles for the third year in a row, by convincingly beating Greig, trying to force the pace, in the final, 6–3 6–1 6–1. Two of the regular players, Aeschliman and Cholmondeley, reached the semi-final, with the former going down to Mayes, 6–4 6–3, and the latter falling to Greig after a tight struggle, 8–6 4–6 6–1.

Eileen Bennett won only two games in the first set against Phyllis Satterthwaite in the final, but she proved her match-winning ability earlier by surviving two close matches with Mlle Pat du Cross and Mrs Keays, the latter leading 5–0 in the deciding set. The semi-final resulted in Phyllis Satterthwaite beating Domini Crosfield, 6–2 6–0, and Eileen Bennett defeating Sylvia Lafaurie, 6–3 6–2. Aeschliman and Cholmondeley won the doubles and Suzanne Lenglen retired from the doubles and mixed doubles due to indisposition.

The Hyères tournament scheduled for 4th-10th January was abandoned, owing to the combined effects of frost, snow and rain, which stopped the courts being in playing condition. However, since the week was also devoted to Club Championships on the Riviera, there was little slackening by the tennis enthusiasts.

The first tournament promoted by the New Courts Club in Cannes, which followed, felt the full force of bad weather, where frost and rain put the courts out of commission for varying intervals. The Club, founded the previous season by wealthy American Frank Jay Gould, was described as a delectable spot, admirably equipped in every way, indoor and outdoor.

Jacques Brugnon, one of the great doubles players and a considerable force in singles, was attracted to the Riviera every year from 1926 to 1939, during which he amassed a total of 58 titles. He was very popular.

Cochet won the men's singles title but found himself in a difficult position more than once. In the semi-final he was pushed hard by Greig who, before losing 9–7 7–5, had a chance to win both sets. Mayes gave the Frenchman much to think about before he finally triumphed in an entertaining match, 3–6 6–3 6–3 3–6 6–4. In his half Mayes comfortably ousted the Pole, Stanislav Czetwertynski, an indefatigable retriever of the ball, 6–3 6–3. Another encounter worth noting was Greig's victory in the quarter-final over de Stefani, 3–6 6–3 6–3, a match where there was so little between the two players.

Phyllis Satterthwaite added yet another singles title to her tally by overcoming Eileen Bennett in the final, 6–2 6–1. The latter tried her hardest but could not make any headway. The semi-finalists were Lesley Cadle and Margaret Tripp.

Cochet with Brugnon, who did not enter the singles, captured the men's doubles, just defeating Brame Hillyard and de Stefani in a long five set duel. Suzanne Lenglen, passing up the singles, took both doubles titles in partnership with Phyllis Satterthwaite and Cochet. Elizabeth Ryan was not available to partner Suzanne Lenglen as she had decided, unusually, to remain in America for the spring.

There was a buzz of excitement along the Riviera when confirmation was received that the top American player, Miss Helen Wills, would be

competing there during the season. Ever since her visit to Europe in 1924, when she reached the singles final at Wimbledon and captured the gold medal at the Olympic Games, hopes had been high that a meeting with Suzanne Lenglen would take place. In the previous autumn she had captured the United States singles crown for the third successive year. Now at the age of 20 she had proved herself at home and was keen to tackle Europe and pitch her skill against the supreme Suzanne Lenglen. Helen Wills crossed the Atlantic and reached Le Havre on 15th January. The boat train was met in Paris by Pierre Gillou, President of the French Tennis Federation and Borotra, and later that day she caught the overnight Blue Train to Nice, in good time to compete in the Metropole Hotel meeting. The local community were quick to offer hospitality to her as she was soon a guest at a *matinée dansante* and on another day presented the prizes to the winners of a polo match at Mandelieu.

At the beginning of February, Suzanne Lenglen and Helen Wills met for the first time when they contested the mixed doubles final at the Nice meeting. Suzanne, paired with Uberto de Morpurgo (right) decisively defeated Charles Aeschliman and Helen, 6–1 6–2.

Helen Wills decided to enter the singles only, whereas Suzanne Lenglen followed her usual practice early in the season of playing just in doubles. Although the American won the singles event without the loss of a set, her form did not reveal a sign of dominance. In the semi-finals she lost four games in the two sets to Hélène Contostavlos, and in the final against Diddie Vlasto, eventually found her way out of a continuous string of backhand exchanges to win, 6–3 7–5. There was no shortage of spectators watching her matches.

Brugnon, after a slow start, used his pace and volleying skills to defeat Mayes in the final of the men's singles, 3–6 3–6 6–1 6–1 6–1. In the matches before, Mayes beat Czetwertynski, 6–3 8–6, and Brugnon defeated Aeschliman, 6–2 6–1. Suzanne Lenglen was in wonderful form in the doubles, losing just three games in the two finals.

Still in Cannes, the play moved to the Gallia Hotel. Suzanne Lenglen did not enter any event as her father was unwell, and Helen Wills, in a not too strong field, won the ladies' singles final defeating Helene Contostavlos, suffering slightly from a strained side, 6–3 6–2. The only time the American was give a tough ride was against Mrs Elsa Haylock in the quarter-final 9–7 6–2. There was a surprise loss for Helen Wills in the mixed doubles, when paired with Jack Hillyard, they fell in the semi-final to the American, Allister McCormick and Eden Petchell, 1–6 6–4 7–5. Mc Cormick, whose Chicago family manufactured farm implements, died in 1981, aged 100.

Cochet and Mayes met again in the final, where the Frenchman's volleys countered his opponent's well-placed drives, 6–4 6–3 2–6 7–5. Cochet was under some pressure to pass Brame Hillyard in the semi-final, 6–1 7–5.

So on to Nice at the Parc Imperial, the home club of Suzanne Lenglen. Helen Wills opted to participate only in the doubles, whereas Suzanne Lenglen entered all three events. The latter's participation in the singles was made at the last moment, obliging the committee to redraw the event. Her entry did much to quell the press, who for some weeks had suggested that she was trying to avoid the American.

Suzanne Lenglen produced a notable victory in the singles, as she won the title, playing five rounds without the loss of a game! To some degree the spectators were not completely disappointed that the clash with Helen Wills had not taken place, as the players faced each other across the net for the first time in the final of the mixed doubles. However, this match was over quickly with the Frenchwoman and de Morpurgo defeating the American and Aeschliman, 6–1 6–2. A second meeting of the two was avoided in the doubles, when Suzanne Lenglen's partner, Phyllis Satterthwaite, withdrew in the second round owing to an injury, sustained when her car collided with a tram.

With all the interest being taken in the ladies' play, the men were slightly overshadowed. Their entry was weak compared with earlier meetings and de Morpurgo ruled throughout the singles, beating an unknown Serbian, Gyorgy Dungyersky, in the final, 6–4 6–1 6–4. A young Canadian, David Morrice, caught the eye of many by eliminating Czetwertynski, 5–7 6–4 6–2 and Jack Hillyard, 4–6 6–3 6–4, before losing to Dungyersky in the semi-final, 6–8 6–1 6–1.

During the tournament, Simond announced that Suzanne Lenglen and Helen Wills would both play in the singles at the Carlton Club tournament beginning on the following Monday, 8th February. This began an upsurge of worldwide interest that had hitherto not been accorded to ladies' tennis. Scores of journalists descended upon Cannes during the following week, all working overtime to obtain their exclusive stories of the daily happenings of the two players. Certainly most newspapers in the United States carried the stories, likewise many countries in Europe.

The Club had six courts situated at the side of the Hotel, with the entrance in Rue Canada. The remote possibility that the two star players would not meet in the final was ignored by the authorities as they set about doubling the seating accommodation around the main court to 3,000, by erecting a temporary stand on the adjacent court.

Unfortunately, the weather disregarded the programme and when the rain poured for three days, Tuesday to Thursday, the meeting was forced into

There was an upsurge of worldwide interest in ladies' tennis when Suzanne Lenglen and Helen Wills met in the final of the Carlton Club tournament at Cannes in February. This was a case of the master versus the pupil and after much drama the Frenchwoman won, 6–3 8–6. Pictured here Suzanne and Helen shake left-hands before the match.

a second week. English players fared badly in the singles. Eileen Bennett and Ermyntrude Harvey were easily beaten by Helen Wills and Diddie Vlasto, respectively, while Honor Woolrych, playing in her first tournament of the season, fell victim to Mme Taunay of Holland. Suzanne Lenglen and Helen Wills reached the singles semi-final where the Frenchwoman dispatched Hélène Contostavlos with no bother, 6–0 6–2, but the American, having won the first set against Diddie Vlasto, 6–1, trailed 1–4, before recovering to win the next five games – much to the relief of all concerned.

The final was decided on the following Tuesday, 16th February. All seats were sold in advance, with the front row occupied by numerous titled supporters from the top echelon of 'Who's Who'. Every vantage point was

Suzanne Lenglen (left) verus Helen Wills. Every vantage point around the court was taken up during the tense playwith many of the spectators risking injury while perched on the adjacent building roof.

taken up by spectators, some sitting perilously on the roofs of adjoining buildings and others perched on the branches of trees. Simond ensured that all linesmen were neutral and appointed George Hillyard as Umpire.

Both players came on court around 11am and were besieged by dozens of photographers. Suzanne Lenglen served first, but fell behind at 1–2,

before leading 4–2 and taking the set, 6–3. The play was mainly from the back of the court, with the American trying to break down her opponent's defence. In the second set, Helen Wills took risks to forge ahead, 3–1, but Suzanne came back to 3 all. In the eighth game, the Frenchwoman hit a forehand drive, which Helen Wills considered had gone out, but

Another view of the historic match between Suzanne Lenglen and Helen Wills, with the towering Carlton Hotel in the background.

the ball was not called, which meant that her chance of leading 5–3 had gone. Suzanne advanced to 6–5 and reached 40–15 on her service and, following a very long rally, the American hit a drive which struck the line. The linesman remained silent but someone in the crowd called "out" and, thinking the match over, Suzanne Lenglen advanced to the net and shook hands. Immediately the court was invaded by photographers but Aeschliman, sitting at the sideline, came forward to the Umpire to indicate the ball was in and that the match was not over. Hillyard confirmed this was the case and announced to the crowd that the match would continue. Suzanne still had a match point at 40–30, but put the next ball over the baseline. Somehow, noticeably exhausted, she eventually captured the American's service for 7–6. In the following game she double faulted within a point of winning but her coolness and experience at this stage triumphed on her fourth match point, 8–6. The contest lasted 63 minutes.

The court was swamped with people and attendants brought on huge baskets of flowers. A weeping Suzanne Lenglen was too agitated to take much notice. The old regime had maintained superiority over the new. To some historians this was the 'match of the century'.

Later in the afternoon Suzanne Lenglen returned to the court for the doubles final where, partnered by Diddie Vlasto, she defeated Helen Wills and Helen Contostavlos, 6–4 8–6. Most of the time, Suzanne Lenglen appeared too tired to be very effective but, luckily, Diddie Vlasto was on top form. Suzanne Lenglen and Helen Wills were never again to compete against each other.

To some degree the foregoing matches overshadowed the men's singles event, which drew a good entry. The final between Aeschliman and de Morpurgo was a long drawn-out and fluctuating affair of two hours, resulting in the Italian winning, 6–4 3–6 5–7 9–7 6–2. There were two outstanding matches, where de Morpurgo triumphed against Charles Kingsley, making his first trip to the Riviera, after dropping the middle set, 6–4 1–6 6–2. The Englishman had evened the contest with his surprise volleying, but for some reason he abandoned his attack in the deciding set and this was his downfall. The other match which drew much attention was Aeschliman's inspired mood which enabled him to draw Lowe from his favourite baseline position, with the clear use of the drop shot. This was Lowe's first outing of the season and he was a little rusty. The score to the Swiss was 6–4 6–1.

Judged the most successful meeting to date on the Bristol Hotel courts at Beaulieu, the week enjoyed ideal weather. Newcomer Bela von Kehrling of Hungary and Kingsley came through the men's singles field, which included Lycett, Lowe and Crawford. Von Kehrling put out Lycett after a protracted opening set, 10–8 6–0, while Kinglsey's greater activity had the better of Lowe, 5–7 6–2 6–0, and Crawford, 2–6 6–1 6–3. In the final between the Hungarian and Kingsley, play was even for two sets until the Englishman lost his speed and stamina to fall, 7–5 3–6 6–1 6–4. The men's doubles final saw an unexpected victory for von Kehrling and Lowe over de Morpurgo and Lycett, 6–3 6–3 6–3.

Public interest in Helen Wills showed no diminution as she sailed through four rounds of the singles without losing more than one game

The match between Suzanne Lenglen (left) and Helen Wills appeared to be all over when the American offered her congratulations at the net. But this was not so. The last point had been incorrectly called. The match was restarted and a couple of games later Suzanne finally triumphed and they shook hands again.

in each set. Phyllis Satterthwaite was her opponent in the final and she suffered the fate of the others, 6–1 6–1. The American earlier beat the English opposition by crushing Audrey Wright, 6–0 6–0, Joan Lycett 6–0 6–1, and Ermyntrude Harvey, 6–1 6–0. Frau Nelly Nepach, the German champion, competed in both doubles events. Suzanne Lenglen made the briefest appearance, paired with Phyllis Satterthwaite but, after winning their opening match the Frenchwoman retired, indisposed.

The weather continued to be kind at the following main Monte Carlo meeting at which a first class entry was received. Von Kehrling was too good for Kingsley for the second week running in the final, his unusual break service doing much damage, 6–4 6–1 6–3. Kingsley avenged his defeat by de Morpurgo at Cannes in the semi-final, 6–4 6–4, while the Hungarian beat Brame Hillyard, 6–0 6–4, although he was four times within a point of being led 5–4 in the second set. Lowe, far from producing his best form, went down to de Morpurgo in the quarter-final, 6–4 6–0.

Helen Wills continued in her winning vein, but she was offered strong opposition by Eileen Bennett in the semi-final to the tune of 6–3 6–2, and then by Lili de Alvarez in the title round, 6–2 6–3. The quality throughout this match was high, by the speed of the rallying and, if the Spaniard had not consistently hit most of her shots to her opponent's backhand, she might have taken the match into three sets.

Suzanne Lenglen played only in doubles, the new international competition for the Beaumont Cup, corresponding to the Butler Cup for the men. With Diddie Vlasto she won the final against Phyllis Satterthwaite and Eileen Bennett, 6–4 8–6, but as the score indicates, the winners were given much to think about. At one stage there was a possibility that Suzanne Lenglen would meet Helen Wills across the net in this event, but the American and Mrs Leslie Aeschliman were eliminated by the runners-up at the semi-final stage. The Butler Cup was retained by de Morpurgo and Gaslini.

The Riviera Championships at Menton were decided in perfect weather apart from the Mistral, which blew during part of the Friday. The galleries were crowded throughout the week. The men's final brought together France and Hungary in conflict and was judged to be one of the best matches of the season. Five sets were needed before Cochet outlasted von Kehrling, 6–4 3–6 7–5 3–6 8–6, but the deciding set could have gone either way when the Hungarian led 5–4 and 0–30 on his opponent's service. However, he netted two vital drives and the Frenchman went on to serve out. In the semi-final Lowe won the opening set against von Kehrling who, using his top-spin drives, brought matters level and then, in an up and down situation, won through 5–7 6–1 6–4. Cochet at the same stage handled Kingsley well, 6–1 6–4.

Helen Wills faced Lili de Alvarez in the final of the singles for the second week running, but the match failed to reach the heights of the earlier encounter. The American, suffering from a cold, played defensively and only when threatened in each set raised her game by attacking with her usual vigour to win in two 10 game sets. Earlier she had a succession of easy matches, overwhelming Ermyntrude Harvey in the last four, 6–0 6–1. At the same stage, Lili de Alvarez defeated Diddie Vlasto in two very tight sets, 7–5 8–6.

The international mixed doubles event, known as the Coupe des Nations, was won by Cochet and Diddie Vlasto. Suzanne Lenglen did not appear. The stress of the past few weeks had taken its toll on her and she readily accepted an invitation from wealthy Count Alberto Bonacossa to relax for a few weeks in Italy.

The South of France Championships at Nice was the fourth tournament in succession to be favoured with a week of rainless weather with just a couple of days being windy and chilly. The chief interest as far as the singles was concerned, by way of a change, involved the men, who mustered a strong entry. The four semi-finalists in the singles were Cochet, Kingsley, de Morpurgo and André Aron and their arrival was well predicted. Both matches were one-sided and the winners were at the top of their game, Cochet in defeating Kingsley 6–0 6–2 and de Morpurgo beating Aron 6–1 6–3. The final was a real triumph for the Italian, who beat Cochet, 1–6 6–2 6–2 6–3. The encounter was notable for the speed and accuracy of the players and the domination of Cochet in the first set. The Frenchman must have been very surprised by the outcome. De Morpurgo had been given a tough fight by Brame Hillyard in the quarter-final, 6–4 6–4.

In the ladies' singles Helen Wills ploughed on relentlessly, trailing disaster for the English players. First Miss Shirley, 6–1 6–0, followed by Miss Sally Maynard, 6–1 6–0, and Miss Joan Ridley, 6–0 6–2. In the semi-final the pattern continued over Mrs Ilona Peteri of Hungary, 6–2 6–2, and finally an American in the final, Miss Isabella Mumford, 6–0 6–1. The runner-up had produced a surprise in the semi-final by ousting Eileen Bennett, 4–6 6–3 6–0. (Lowe and Phyllis Satterthwaite were not available as they travelled over the border to Italy to play in the Bordighera tournament.)

After an unbroken spell of fine weather lasting five weeks, the rain made an appearance on the last day, Sunday, at the Cannes Club, where the Côte d'Azur Championships were being disputed. Cochet was much in a class by himself and consequently won the men's singles title. However, he did manage to drop a set to Brame Hillyard in the semi-final before going through, 6–2 2–6 6–2. The final was played on a rain-sodden court and Cochet, with a sustained onslaught for a set and a half, had Aeschliman on the back foot and he faded, 6–4 6–3 6–0. The Swiss had beaten the Finn, Arne Grahn, in the round before, in an uneven affair, 8–6 8–6.

The ladies' singles final was not played. Owing to the Sunday morning's rain the match between Helen Wills and Joan Ridley was put off to the following day. But this day and the Tuesday also were blank days and then, on the Wednesday, when there was a possibility of play, news came that Joan Ridley had injured her hand in closing the door of her car and was forced to retire, leaving the American the winner, by default. In the semi-final Eileen Bennett did some justice to her natural ability by running Helen Wills to 6–2 6–4, leading in the second set, 4–2. In the other match Joan Ridley beat Yvonne Bourgeois, 7–5 4–6 8–6, which was a titanic up and down struggle. Cochet and Helen Wills won the mixed doubles. This was the American's last tournament of the season. After losing to Suzanne Lenglen at the Carlton Club she had played in five tournaments and won every singles title, plus a handful of doubles events. For the next three weeks Helen Wills toured Italy. She was never to return to the Riviera.

The last important meeting on the Riviera, the Cannes Championships, staged at the Beau Site Hotel had disastrous weather with a succession of storms and only on the ninth day was it possible to finish the two singles events. All other competitions were abandoned.

Aeschliman won the men's singles after a narrow escape against Arne Grahn in the semi-final, when the Finn led 8–6 6–5, but lobbing by the Swiss won the third set with the loss of only one more game. Lowe had no energy left for the final which was immediately put on court following a long struggle with Brame Hillyard, 6–3 3–6 6–4. Aeschliman won by a procession of points, 6–1 6–2. This was the last occasion that Lowe played competitively on the Riviera.

Lili de Alvarez was given a good fight by Honor Woolrych in the ladies' final, driving with vigour to lead 3–0 and within a point of 5–4. However, she tired and could not stay the course – and no wonder, this was her fourth match of the day.

The second Carlton Club meeting began with rain-sodden courts, but ended in sunshine. Aeschliman won another singles title, beating Brame Hillyard in the final, 3–6 6–2 6–3 6–1. For two sets there was nothing between them but from then on Aeschliman's better length controlled the play. Brame Hillyard deserved to reach the last stage, with praiseworthy wins over Salm, 6–4 6–2, and Grahn, 1–6 6–4 6–4.

In the ladies' singles, Dorothy Shepherd-Barron managed to rise to the occasion with the aid of good overhead work to beat Phyllis Satterthwaite in the semi-final, 3–6 6–1 6–4, but against Lili de Alvarez in the final, she could not contain the Spaniard's driving ability, which became the winning factor, 6–2 6–3. Suzanne Lenglen returned from Italy to compete in the doubles with Phyllis Satterthwaite and, as expected, the title was won without any severe opposition in the final against Lili de Alvarez and Dorothy Shepherd-Barron.

Despite the lateness of the season, the third Monte Carlo tournament, commencing on 5th April attracted a good entry. De Morpurgo returned and dictated the run of play against Brame Hillyard in the final, who found difficulty in keeping up the pressure in the third set. The score was 6–4 6–4 6–2. Lili de Alvarez had an easy win in the ladies' singles, particularly as Phyllis Satterthwaite decided to retire from the final without taking the court. Jack Hillyard and de Morpurgo won the doubles, likewise Suzanne Lenglen and Phyllis Satterthwaite, who repeated the victory from a week earlier over Lili de Alvarez and Dorothy Shepherd-Barron in the final. No one present watching this match could possibly envisage that this was the last time that Suzanne Lenglen would play competitively on the Riviera. Within four months she would have withdrawn from Wimbledon and turned professional.

At the Juan-les-Pins Club, the entry was a little on the thin side. Pierre Landry of France beat his fellow countryman, Emmanuel du Plaix in the final of the singles, 6–4 6–3 6–2. Lili de Alvarez opted not to play in the singles, which resulted in Mrs Dorothy Coleman defeating Mrs Young in the final, 6–2 6–1. Landry won two other titles, paired with Aeschliman and Lili de Alvarez. There was no ladies' doubles event.

The last tournament of the season was staged from 19th to 25th April and was the occasion for the inaugural St Raphael meeting. Grahn was successful in winning the men's singles, while Lili de Alvarez was supreme in the ladies' division. She went on to win a second title in the mixed doubles with Pescher.

# 1927
# Henri Cochet's Title Run •
# Many English Ladies Compete

The season opened Christmas week at La Festa Club, Monte Carlo, when the Monaco Championships were at stake and well-supported. Brugnon, the holder, won the men's singles comfortably but he had to go the full course in the final against Erik Worm of Denmark who after losing the opening two sets really produced some fine play. However, Brugnon renewed his volleying attack against a tiring opponent to win, 6–1 6–1 4–6 4–6 6–1. To reach the final, played on Christmas Day, Brugnon easily beat Jack Hillyard, 6–0 6–2, while Worm was taken by René Gallepe of Monaco to 6–4 7–5. Phyllis Satterthwaite, present as usual, strolled through the ladies' singles, but the good form of Miss Madge Slaney in the final pushed her to 6–3 6–4, before taking the title for the fourth time.

Gallepe and Worm scored a decisive win in the doubles final over Brugnon and Myers, 6–3 7–5 6–4. A new event for mixed pairs of the same family was introduced with the winners being Brame Hillyard and his wife. A handsome cup was presented by George Butler.

The meeting which followed at the Beau Site Hotel brought an unexpected success for Alan Behr, an American cousin of Karl Behr, the former player, in the men's singles. He survived quite a large field to defeat Aeschliman with his patience and steadfast retrieval in the final, 6–3 4–6 6–3 6–4. Behr's outstanding achievement was to nullify Mayes' normal effective passing shots in two well-fought sets in the semi-final, 7–5 6–4. In the other half, Aeschliman beat Worm in another tight match, 5–7 6–3 7–5. Some earlier interesting results saw Behr beat Cholmondeley, 6–3 6–0, Worm defeat Brame Hillyard narrowly, 9–7 8–6, and Aeschliman overcome de Stefani, 5–7 6–4 6–2.

Phyllis Satterthwaite was again well in control to retain her singles title, giving no quarter to Mme Taunay in the final, 6–2 6–0. The semi-finalists were Mrs Morris and Domini Crosfield, who both retired without striking a ball. Gallepe and Worm won the doubles for the second week running.

After missing last season the Hyères meeting returned but with a very low key entry. Many of the competitors were not widely known and the two singles titles were won by George Fletcher and Miss Mary Hartland from England. Most of the top players were engaged along the coast, competing in their relative Club Championships.

No less than 26 countries were represented in the lists of the events at the Metropole Hotel tournament, Cannes – a record for the Riviera. Many of the players took part in the handicap events. The outstanding performance of the week was that of Mayes who beat Brugnon in the semi-final of the singles, then ran Cochet to five sets in the final. The first match was close and exciting, with Mayes producing many fine passing shots and lobs and Brugnon playing some exquisite volleys. After falling behind in the second set Mayes let it go, before leading 4–2 in the decider. The Frenchman caught up, but in the 10th game Mayes broke service to win, 6–4 1–6 6–4. Mayes' match against Cochet over five sets was reported as one of the best ever seen on the Riviera. As quite often, the man from Lyons took matters too easily to begin with and stood at 0–6 3–5 before being his true self. Having won the second and third sets, each at 7–5, he led 5–3, but Mayes astonished all present by saving a match point and eventually took the set at 11–9. Cochet, much fresher in the fifth set, commanded the situation by continually volleying to win through 0–6 7–5 7–5 9–11 6–1. There was tremendous applause from the appreciative crowd. Cochet earlier defeated Behr, 6–3 6–2. At the quarter-final stage Behr held on to dismiss de Stefani, 6–8 8–6 6–1, Mayes beat Worm, 6–2 6–0, and Cochet beat Brame Hillyard, 6–1 6–3.

Neither Diddie Vlasto nor Phyllis Satterthwaite were threatened on their way to the final of the ladies' singles, but the match did not take place, as the Englishwoman retired, indisposed, possibly bearing in mind completing other events.

The following week the Carlton Club enjoyed another excellent array of top men playing. Neither Cochet nor Brugnon had an easy passage to the final of the singles, with the former being stretched to overcome de Stefani, 6–4 7–5, and in the semi-final, Worm, 2–6 6–4 6–2. The latter had difficulty in ousting Lester, 6–3 4–6 6–3, but then took his revenge over Mayes for his defeat the previous week by dictating the play from the beginning to triumph, 6–1 6–3, Mayes no doubt still affected by his arduous effort at the Metropole. The final, lasting five sets, was a see-saw effort throughout, with both players alternating hot and cold. However, in the fifth set Cochet gave a superlative exhibition, winning a love set with the loss of very few points. The score in Cochet's favour was 1–6 6–1 6–0 1–6 6–1 – a most unusual sequence.

Henri Cochet was in great form during the early part of the season, winning four singles titles and the Butler Trophy for the first time, paired with Jacques Brugnon.

The ladies' singles title went to Diddie Vlasto who had a one-sided victory over Cristobel Hardie in the final, 6-3 6-1. Eileen Bennett should have beaten the Frenchwoman in the round before, when she led 5-1 in the deciding set. Here she faltered and subsequently missed four match points. Diddie Vlasto, courageous to the end, edged out, 3-6 6-4 9-7. Elizabeth Ryan, having missed the last season, returned. She and Phyllis Satterthwaite withdrew from the singles to concentrate on other events. Together they narrowly defeated Eileen Bennett and Diddie Vlasto in the final, 6-2 8-6, while the American paired with Cochet to win the mixed event.

The second international tournament held at the Cannes New Courts Club was blessed with fine weather, apart from the last Sunday. The sensation of the week was undoubtedly the defeat of Cochet by Brugnon, who probably played the best match of his career, in the men's singles final. He attacked from the start and with Cochet remaining on the baseline, held a strategic advantage to win, 6-2 6-2 6-3. In one part of the duel Brugnon won 17 games out of 21.

Neither semi-final yielded a close match, with Brugnon beating Worm, who was not fully fit, 6-2 6-2, and Cochet having no problem with Behr, 6-3 6-1. There was a notable victory for the young Irishman, George Lyttleton Rogers, who accounted for Lester but then fell to Worm, 4-6 7-5 6-2. In other contests Behr beat Mayes for the second time in the season, 8-6 4-6 6-2, and Brugnon comfortably defeated de Stefani, 6-4 6-2.

Elizabeth Ryan won the ladies' singles title but she did not go through unscathed in her last three matches. Miss Claire Beckingham ran her to 9-7 6-4, then Cristobel Hardie captured a set but fell away, 6-3 3-6 6-1, while in the final, Phyllis Sattherthwaite hitting harder than usual, eventually capitulated 6-3 10-8. Brugnon and Cochet won the men's doubles and Elizabeth Ryan completed a 'triple'.

Rain early in the week and frost later interfered with the programme at the Cannes Gallia meeting and gave Simond a real problem. With only five courts available and a large entry to cope with, he arranged for some of the earlier rounds of the level events and handicaps to be decided on the courts of other clubs in the area. All the level events were completed by the Sunday evening.

Brugnon decided to rest from the men's singles, which left Cochet a free hand to coast through to win the title. He beat Mayes in the last four with something to spare, 6-3 6-4, and in the title round conceded just four games to Behr over three sets. The American tried energetically to break down his opponent's game, but he was playing a man of superior class. Serving with unusual speed, Cochet won 6-2 6-1 6-1. Behr had passed

Worm in the semi-final, adopting a more aggressive play, to register a 6–4 6–4 win.

As expected, Elizabeth Ryan took the honours in the ladies' singles but was given a tough ride in the final by Eileen Bennett. Noticeably improved, the Englishwoman, hitting with confidence, won the opening set but could not sustain her progress. In the third set, a net cord and a disputed point generally sealed her fate, 4–6 6–4 6–3. Cochet and Brugnon decided to split their partnership in the men's doubles, allowing the former to play with Aeschliman, as holders of the Cup. They retained their title with a 12–10 6–2 9–7 victory over Gallepe and Worm.

Cochet duly added another singles title to his tally by winning the first Nice meeting. In the final, played in delightful weather, he beat de Morpurgo in straight sets, 9–7 6–2 6–2. As usual, the Frenchman was slow off the mark, but having seen off an up and down first set, sailed through without any trouble. His victory gave him much pleasure since he had lost to the Italian in the final the year before. Cochet beat de Stefani in the semi-final after again starting slowly, 2–6 6–3 6–3, while de Morpurgo accounted for Brugnon, 7–5 6–2.

With Elizabeth Ryan and Phyllis Satterthwaite not competing in the singles, Eileen Bennett won her first tournament on the Riviera. The four semi-finalists in the event were English. Eileen Bennett overcame the rock-like steadiness of Cristobel Hardie and just survived a fluctuating match, 4–6 6–2 7–5. Her opponent in the final was Miss Betty Nuthall, the British junior champion, and with something in hand won the title, 6–3 6–2. Betty Nuthall, a newcomer to the coast, did well to eliminate Mrs Bramley Moore in the round before, 8–6 6–3. Miss Sylvia Lumley-Ellis figured in the draw. Aeschliman and Cochet were too good for Worm and Gallepe in the men's doubles final, winning 6–4 6–0 6–2.

There was a record entry for the Beaulieu meeting, with over 300 matches being scheduled. The amenities had been improved in many respects, including the provision of new balls for all matches, including the handicaps.

With Brugnon and de Morpurgo not competing in the singles and Cochet withdrawing, the best two players remaining, von Kehrling and Jan Kozeluh, brother of Karel, the professional, met in the semi-final. Early

Although competing the two previous seasons, Eileen Bennett (right) had to wait until the first meeting at Nice to secure her initial singles triumph. In the final she beat Betty Nuthall, a three-times British junior champion.

on the Czech had difficulty in overcoming Aron and Czetwertyski but against von Kehrling his backhand passing shots and volleying were top class to force a 9–7 6–1 victory. In the other semi-final Gallepe surprised Behr, 3–6 6–3 6–3, but he was no match for Kozeluh in the final and, although playing well, went down, 6–4 6–2 6–3.

One match, Behr versus H. Sydow of Austria, is worth recording. Behr won 4–6 6–2 6–1, but the 25 games took three hours and ten minutes, of which the first set lasted one and a quarter hours. The average strokes in a rally were between 30 and 40 and one of 80 was counted.

As expected, Elizabeth Ryan and Phyllis Satterthwaite fought out the final of the ladies' singles, with the former winning 6–4 6–4. In the round before, the American gave Miss Dorothy Shaw, a young lady from Yorkshire, few chances, 6–0 6–2, while Phyllis Satterthwaite's excellent length was the undoing of Cristobel Hardie, 6–2 6–2. Aeschliman and Cochet won the doubles title for the third week running, while Dorothea Chambers and Elizabeth Ryan paired to win the ladies' division.

The main Monte Carlo meeting held on La Festa courts was seriously interrupted by rain after the first few days. When the bad weather started, the firmly established Butler and Beaumont trophies for the international team doubles were well-advanced and accordingly were given precedence over other events. By doing so they were finished on time. As expected the men's doubles was won by Brugnon and Cochet, who beat Worm and Einer Ulrich in the final, 9–7 6–4 6–3, with the match finished just in time for Brugnon to catch his train to Paris en route for America. The Danes had been extremely sporting in agreeing to go on to court immediately following their semi-final encounter.

In the Beaumont Cup there were three British pairs in the semi-final, but the winners of the event were Elizabeth Ryan and Mrs Elizabeth Corbiere representing the USA, who had something in hand in defeating Dorothea Chambers and Betty Nuthall in the final, 6–4 6–2.

In the men's singles the title was retained by von Kehrling, who had successive victories over Pierre Landry, 6–4 6–1, and Sydow, 9–7 6–1, to reach the final, but unfortunately here Worm had a touch of fever and withdrew. The day before, the Dane had beaten Christian Boussus, another Frenchman, visiting for the first time, 6–2 6–2, the latter having achieved a sound win over Behr, 7–5 6–1.

In the ladies' singles, seven of the quarter-finalists were British, but experience shone through and as expected, Elizabeth Ryan's attacking strokes broke down Phyllis Satterthwaite's defence to register a 6–3 6–4 score. This was the American's fourth win in the event since 1922.

The Championships of the Riviera, held on the courts of the Menton Club, were affected by rain and extended for two days. The best match of the meeting was also the last and involved the mixed doubles final in which von Kehrling and Lili de Alvarez faced de Morpurgo and Elizabeth Ryan. The latter pair won the first set 6–4, mainly because the Spaniard was making many costly mistakes. However, all of a sudden she dominated the court and with beautiful strokes her side won the next 10 games. Their opponents never gave up and after a very tight finish, a von Kehrling winning service concluded the struggle at 4–6 6–0 6–4.

The two outstanding men in the singles, von Kehrling and de Morpurgo, fought out the final. This was not a great spectacle for the crowd, but the Italian was worthy of the Cup, probably because of his physical advantage, 6–4 6–3 6–4. In the semi-finals, de Morpurgo beat Worm, 6–2 6–2, and von Kehrling defeated Gallepe, 6–1 7–5.

Elizabeth Ryan won yet another singles title against Dorothy Shaw in the final, using her volleying powers to stretch her to two tight sets, 6–4 7–5. Eileen Bennett was surprisingly eliminated in the quarter-final by Miss N. Hunt, a Shropshire girl, wintering at Bordighera, 6–4 0–6 7–5. Lili de Alvarez retired at the same stage, which left Dorothy Shaw and Miss Hunt as opponents, with the former duly winning, 6–4 2–6 6–1.

In the men's doubles Germany secured her first victory in a French tournament for 14 years when Heinrich Kleinschroth and von Kehrling beat Gallepe and Worm in the final, 6–2 3–6 11–13 6–3 6–4. The Coupe des Nations was won by Frederick Scovel and Elizabeth Ryan.

The South of France Championships at Nice were well supported, despite the attraction of several of the leading players to the Bordighera meeting, held simultaneously. With a break in tradition, the Committee decided that all matches in the men's singles would be best of five sets. Simond did not approve but, nevertheless, carried out the necessary programme. In this event the two Hillyards, Brame and Jack, seemed probable finalists but, although the former had no bother in beating an American, R.M. Archibald, who retired after two sets, 6–1 6–3, the latter was surprisingly downed by Hermann Artens of Austria over five sets, 6–8 6–2 7–5 3–6 6–2. Brame Hillyard, twice the age of Artens, had the stamina to last the full distance in the final and indeed led 5–3 in the fifth set, but the younger man's aggression at this stage gave him the title, 2–6 5–7 6–1 6–3 10–8.

Lili de Alvarez was the new champion and in the final contest, where both players frequently drove out of court, she beat Phyllis Satterthwaite, 6–3 6–3. Betty Nuthall and Cristobel Hardie reached the last four and each pushed her opponent hard. The winner beat Betty Nuthall, 6–4 6–2, and the runner-up passed Cristobel Hardie, 7–5 6–2.

There was an unexpected victory in the ladies' doubles when Miss Elsie Goldsack and Dorothy Shaw, after disposing of Phyllis Satterthwaite

Exciting to watch because of her attacking strokes, Lili de Alvarez of Spain was the No.2 player in the world. During the season she captured four singles titles, at Nice, Cannes Club, Beau Site Hotel and Monte Carlo.

and Betty Nuthall, beat the sisters, Dorothy Coleman and Eden Petchell in the final, 7–5 6–2. The winners had never before played together. Ludwig Salm and Artens won the men's doubles, and the King of Sweden, paired with Cristobel Hardie, captured the handicap mixed doubles.

The Cannes Club tournament, one of the most popular on the Riviera, was favoured by excellent weather conditions. The Championships of the Côte d'Azur were at stake. Most noteworthy was the first appearance in France since the First World War of the famous German player, Otto Froitzheim, but apart from this, the closing stages of the ladies' singles were by far the most engrossing happening.

Thirteen years had elapsed since Froitzheim had reached the final of the All Comers' singles at Wimbledon, but despite being a little heavier the skills were still apparent as he passed Gallepe, du Plaix and Cholmondeley without losing a set. The German had great difficulty in overcoming Aeschliman in the semi-final when he tried his utmost to end the match in two sets, after being 2–5 down in the second, but he had to be satisfied with victory at 6–3 6–8 6–3. In the final Mayes was the other side of the net and there was little between the players. In the end Froitzheim was seized by cramp early in the fifth set and retired with the score at 1–6 6–3 2–6 6–4 2–0 ret'd. Artens was well-beaten by the winner in the semi-final, 6–2 6–0.

In the ladies' singles the obvious finalists were Lili de Alvarez and Elizabeth Ryan, but the American was unexpectedly dispatched by Hélène Contostavlos in the semi-final, 9–7 8–6, the deciding factor being the strength of her driving on both wings. The Spaniard beat Eileen Bennett in a semi-final containing numerous rallies, 6–4 6–3, and went on to beat the lady from Marseilles in the last match, 6–3 6–3. The King of Sweden was in action again, in partnership with Wallis Myers in the handicap doubles.

After the last four years of disappointing weather, the Beau Site meeting for the Cannes Championships encountered pleasing conditions. The courts were reported to be "dusty", due to lack of attention and made worse by the occasional high wind. The main interest centred on the ladies' singles where, after beating Eileen Bennett over the full distance, Helene Contostavlos for the second week running got the better of Elizabeth Ryan by being far too accurate, 6–3 6–2. The result of the final was similar, when Lili de Alvarez's severe attack allowed Hélène Contostavlos just five games, 6–2 6–3.

Mayes notched another title in the singles, clearly performing better than Gallepe in the semi-final, 6–2 6–3. In the final against Aeschliman the Canadian started badly but he found his touch in the second set and from then on the issue was never in doubt, 3–6 6–0 6–3 6–1. Elizabeth Ryan and Worm both won two doubles titles, together and individually with Eileen Bennett and Gallepe, respectively.

The fourth annual tournament conducted by the Juan-les-Pins Club was a great success, helped enormously by the good weather all the week. The entry was not conspicuously strong, as many of the leading players had gone elsewhere, but it was good enough to provide plenty of entertainment for the players and spectators alike. The fact that only three courts existed did not hamper the arrangements. Worm and Phyllis Satterthwaite figured as winners in all finals, but there were many tight encounters. The Dane beat the American, Frederick Scovel, in the semi-final of the singles, 6–4 6–2, and followed with a tough match against Brame Hillyard, 9–7 6–4 6–4. Hillyard had been taken to the limit by Rogers, 3–6 7–5 7–5. Phyllis Satterthwaite had a tremendous struggle in the ladies' final with Sylvia Lafaurie before she claimed the title, 7–5 6–8 7–5. A report mentioned that the tournament was run "by Mr Tinling, a youth of 16 years of age".

## The New La Festa Country Club

Commencing in early summer over 1,500 workmen were employed in the construction of the new club at Monte Carlo. 25,000 metres of earth were cut away from the mountainside to build the several terraces, which had a total of 20 courts.

The clubhouse was designed to have a restaurant which seated 150 people, while the dressing room accommodation was for 700 members. The Monaco Championships, 17th-24th December, 1927 were transferred from the old club because of bad weather. This was the first tournament to be played on the new ground.

This was Mr Teddy Tinling who spent his life associated with the many facets of tennis and who, after the Second World War, became universally famous as the designer of clothes for the leading lady players. In 1924, as a youngster of 13 he lived in Nice and umpired his first of a hundred or so matches for Suzanne Lenglen. He then helped with the programming of matches at the tournament before becoming Simond's assistant, 1927–1930.

Although late in the season, the second St Rafael tournament attracted a good class, if not large, entry. For the second week running, Worm won all three titles, excelling in the singles where he beat Gallepe in the final, 6–4 6–3 8–6. Sylvia Lafaurie brought off a stunning win in the semi-final of the ladies' singles by eliminating Elizabeth Ryan, 6–2 8–6, but she could not quite maintain this form and fell to Phyllis Satterthwaite in the closing match, 7–5 8–6. Elizabeth Ryan had some consolation by winning the doubles with Phyllis Satterthwaite and the mixed with Worm.

Monte Carlo opened the round of tournaments during the season and also drew it to a close. Worm followed up his triple victories at the last two tournaments by winning the singles and the mixed doubles, but failed in the men's doubles, where with Gallepe he lost in the final to Aeschliman and Jack Hillyard, 6–3 6–0 8–6. In the singles the Dane beat Aeschliman comfortably in the final, 6–4 6–1 6–4, but Phyllis Satterthwaite failed to win her third singles title in a row when she was soundly defeated by Lili de Alvarez, 6–0 6–2.

# 1928
# Henri Cochet Returns • Henry Mayes Wins Last Title at 47

The opening of the season on 17th December, with the Monaco Championships in contention, was seriously disrupted by bad weather. In order to conclude the programme many matches were transferred from La Festa to the quick-drying courts of the new La Festa Country Club, due to be officially opened in February.

Mayes was quick off the mark to win the men's singles. Gallepe offered little resistance to his progress in the semi-final, winning just three games in the opening set, while Aeschliman offered nothing in the final, as he withdrew, having used up all his physical reserves in a mixed doubles contest. Earlier, Rogers had a notable win over Jack Hillyard, 7–5 3–6 6–0, but then fell to Aeschliman in the semi-final, 9–7 8–6.

A view of the new La Festa Country Club at Monte Carlo, showing the centre courts and clubhouse, during exhibition matches after the official opening of the grounds by the Duke of Connaught on 27th February. In early 1929 the name of the club was changed to the Monte Carlo Country Club.

The ladies' singles final was also decided by a walkover, when Phyllis Satterthwaite gave the title to Lili de Alvarez. The Spaniard was head and shoulders above the remainder of the players and won through with the loss of just three games in total. By common consent the last match of the meeting was the semi-final of the mixed doubles, in which Myers and Lili de Alvarez eventually beat Aeschliman and Eden Petchell, 8–10 8–6 6–4, after two hours. The men's doubles was unfinished.

The following week the New Year tournament, held at the Beau Site Hotel, was delayed by rain, which was unfortunate since the entry was unusually large. Eskell Andrews of New Zealand made his debut on the Riviera and reached the semi-final of the men's singles. Here his strokes were not sufficiently controlled and he fell to Aeschliman, 6–4 6–2. In the other half of the draw, Mayes had some difficulty with Paul Barrelet de Ricou, before winning, 6–1 11–9. The final, as expected, resulted in the Canadian being triumphant, in three sets, 6–1 6–1 9–7.

Eileen Bennett won the ladies' singles but was given a tremendous struggle by Madge Slaney, with the outcome uncertain until near the end. In the third set, Eileen Bennett led 4–1, but lost the next nine points through over-confidence. However, Madge Slaney was too tired to profit and went down, 4–6 7–5 6–3. Elizabeth Ryan retired from the singles, but pocketed two doubles events.

At Juan-les-Pins, Mayes won his third title is as many weeks. His opponent in the final, Aeschliman, could make little impression on the Canadian, who was far too steady, to end at 6–0 6–3 6–3. These two contenders combined to take the men's doubles, while Elizabeth Ryan, in a class of one, defeated Mrs T. Cazalet in the final of the singles, 6–1 6–1. Tinling was again the Referee.

The outstanding feature of the Cannes New Courts Club week was Eileen Bennett's defeat for the first time of Elizabeth Ryan in the final of the ladies' singles. Her fast service proved destructive but her great asset was to retrieve all the American's shots with purpose and power. Against an opponent, also on top form, she certainly earned her 6–4 6–3 victory. In the semi-finals, Eileen Bennett beat newcomer, Sig.na Lucia Valerio, the Italian champion, by a safe margin, 6–3 6–2, while Elizabeth Ryan was a good deal harassed before seeing off Ermyntrude Harvey, 8–6 6–3.

Brugnon did not defend his singles title and once more Mayes and Aeschliman ended in opposition in the final, with a three set win registered by the former, 8–6 6–3 6–1. Both men passed the semi-final stage with ease, Mayes beating Emmanuel du Plaix, 6–1 7–5, and Aeschliman downing Gallepe, 6–0 6–2. The weather throughout the week was well-favoured.

For the past few seasons the gathering at the Metropole Hotel had suffered from poor weather and this season was no different. On the last

ROGER
BRODERS

# MONTE·CARLO

IMP. MONÉGASQUE À MONTE-CARLO

Friday and Sunday there was incessant rain and on the following days the courts were so saturated that several semi-finals and two finals, the ladies' singles and mixed doubles, were played at other clubs in the area, mostly at the Gallia Club, whose tournament followed on the Monday.

There was little opposition to prevent Cochet, winner of the Wimbledon Singles Championships the previous summer, as he crushed Eric Peters, 6–1 6–1, to reach the final. Here he met Mayes, who had been put to much running by de Stefani in the round before, 8–6 7–5. The last match was played on a soft court, which suited the Canadian. He won the first set and very nearly took the third, but once the Frenchman got past this, he was home and dry, 6–8 6–3 10–8 6–1. Mayes, some twenty years the senior, put up a tremendous fight all the way.

The ladies' singles was not too interesting, with Eileen Bennett and Betty Nuthall deciding to miss the singles event, making Elizabeth Ryan's victory pretty well assured. Phyllis Satterthwaite reached the final after a somewhat curious match which ended, 6–2 0–6 6–0. In the final the Englishwoman could only muster a game in each set, although the play was closer than the score indicated. Lucia Valerio was the other semi-finalist.

Eileen Bennett and Betty Nuthall combined in the doubles but were beaten by Elizabeth Ryan and Phyllis Satterthwaite in the final, 6–2 6–4. Artens and Salm won the men's division.

The Gallia Club meeting had fine weather and a good entry which drew large crowds during the week. The match which everyone wanted to see was the semi-final of the ladies' singles between the two young players from England, Eileen Bennett and Betty Nuthall. There was very little between the two rivals and after a bout lasting two hours, Eileen Bennett just won, 9–7 2–6 12–10 – a total of 46 games, with each taking 23. The deciding set was in doubt until the last shot. The winner had a match point at 5–4 but made a poor return. Betty Nuthall led 7–6 and 8–7 but eventually her opponent reached 11–10 and eased out. Throughout both hit hard and defended well. Elizabeth Ryan reached the final by defeating Hélène Contostavlos, 7–5 10–8, thereby avenging the two defeats of last season. She was somewhat lucky to win the first set at 7–5 and in the second recovered from 4–1 and 5–2 down to end at 10–8. For the second time in a fortnight, Eileen Bennett beat the American to win the title. In the first set, Elizabeth Ryan failed to consolidate a winning lead to allow her opponent through at 8–6. Eileen Bennett then advanced with increasing confidence and stood firm in any crisis to end 8–6 6–3 – certainly a step forward for the young winner.

Cochet won the singles cup outright, although he had a narrow escape against de Stefani in the semi-final before winning, 5–7 7–5 8–6. The Italian was thrice within a stroke of the match. In the other semi-final,

Countess Clara Schulenburg and Count Victor Voss both played during the 1897 season on the Riviera. Over 31 years later, during March, they were married in Berlin.

Mayes defeated Rogers, 6–3 6–8 6–1, but it was no easy passage until the final set. Mayes won the first two sets against Cochet in the final but the Frenchman tightened up and once having won the third set, the result was never in doubt, 2–6 1–6 6–3 6–0 6–3. The winners of the singles combined to win the mixed doubles.

The entry lists at the main Carlton Club tournament were strengthened by the arrival of von Kehrling and Gaslini, but on the down side, Jan Kozeluh failed to appear. Betty Nuthall had returned to England for a fortnight, Eileen Bennett did not play in the singles and Cochet only appeared in the men's doubles.

Von Kehrling was expected to win and did so. He reached the final at the expense of Worm, 6–4 7–5, and Aeschliman, 6–1 6–1, to meet Emmanuel du Plaix, ranked No.15 in France. The wind during this match made play difficult, but the Hungarian's topspin shots gave him an advantage and he won by three sets to one, 6–0 2–6 6–3 6–2. Du Plaix had two good wins on the way, beating de Stefani, 2–6 6–4 6–1 and Salm, 6–0 4–1 ret'd. Peters came close to beating de Stefani earlier, when he led 4–1 in the final set.

Elizabeth Ryan had some close encounters before reaching the singles final where Helene Contostavlos was waiting. After failing against the American's drop shots in the opening set, the Greek lady found a brilliant driving touch in the second but, unfortunately, lapsed again in the third, which the winner took to love – the score was 6–3 1–6 6–0. In the quarter-final, Hélène Contostavlos had a tremendous struggle before passing Lucia Valerio, 12–10 5–7 6–4 – a total of 46 games. Surprisingly Cochet and Mayes lost the doubles final to Gaslini and von Kehrling, 5–7 6–3 6–4 6–2.

There was an excellent entry for the first meeting at Nice where, with plenty of courts available, progress was swift. Cochet returned to singles play and reached the final without much threat, although he was pushed hard by Vladimir Landau, a young Russian player, and dropped the middle set to Rogers before finishing 7–5 2–6 6–2. Von Kehrling had a stiff time reaching the final, just getting the better of Aeschliman, who was on top form, 3–6 6–4 6–4, and Kozeluh in the semi-final, 6–3 6–4. Cochet's defeat of von Kehrling was quite conclusive and he took no chances from start to finish to win, 6–2 6–1 8–6.

In the ladies' singles the two outstanding figures met in the final, with Elizabeth Ryan avenging her two previous defeats by Eileen Bennett. The latter was suffering from a cold and far from her best. She pushed hard at times but generally was not accurate enough. The score of 6–4 6–2 reflected the play. The two players joined forces for the ladies' doubles, an event that was theirs from the beginning. Cochet and Eileen Bennett won another mixed title.

Fortunately the weather was kind at Beaulieu, enabling Simond to deal comfortably with the large and representative entry. The two finalists in the men's singles were von Kehrling and Kozeluh. The Hungarian deserved more than one game in the opening set but was generally too slow in his volleying. After failing to win the second set, his stamina was lacking and he retired in favour of the holder at 6–1 7–5 ret'd. Von Kehrling was earlier hard-pressed by de Stefani, 3–6 6–2 6–4, but passed Rogers comfortably, 6–0 8–6. The Czech beat Gaslini, 6–4 6–2, and then received a walkover from Artens, who reserved himself for the doubles.

There were new faces in the ladies' singles, with Miss Margaret Saunders and Miss Gwen Sterry joining the other British players, Cristobel Hardie, Ermyntrude Harvey and Phyllis Satterthwaite. There was also Frl Cilly Aussem and the first appearance of Miss Kea Bouman of Holland. In the end the final was between the 'regulars' with Elizabeth Ryan once again defeating Phyllis Satterthwaite, who could only muster two games in the opening set. In the quarter-final Peggy Saunders attacked the winner with great zest and excelled in reaching 11–9 6–4. Gwen Sterry beat Ermyntrude Harvey, 4–6 6–2 6–2, but could only prise three games from Elizabeth Ryan. An early round surprise was the defeat of Cilly Aussem by the American, Elizabeth Corbiere, in three sets. Jack Hillyard won both doubles events, pairing with Kozeluh and Elizabeth Ryan.

The Monte Carlo Championships commenced on 27th February to coincide with the official opening of the new La Festa Country Club, situated high up overlooking the sea.

Cochet won the Cup for the first time, but did not show his best form, particularly in the final when von Kehrling won the first two sets and reached 3–all in the third. A net cord lost him the next game and from then on the Frenchman took complete control, although the Hungarian never gave up, 3–6 2–6 6–3 6–3 6–2.

In the semi-final, Cochet was behind again against Kozeluh, but then took the reins to run out quickly, 2–6 6–1 6–2. In the round before, Roderick Menzel, a colleague of Kozeluh and a heavy hitter, pushed Cochet to 4–6 7–5 ret'd.

The outcome of the ladies' singles and other events would probably have been different if Elizabeth Ryan had not, towards the end of the week, pinched the first finger on her right hand in a door. As the singles unravelled, Eileen Bennett came through to play in the final against Cristobel Hardie, who had advanced at the expense of Elizabeth Ryan. Eileen Bennett, who won the first set, 6–3, was then led 5–2, but with a great burst of speed rattled off the next five games for victory, 6–3 7–5. Notable in an earlier round was the performance of Peggy Saunders, who pushed Elizabeth Ryan to the limit at 6–0 4–6 7–5. The Butler Trophy was won by Cochet and René de Buzelet and the Beaumont Cup by Dorothea Chambers and Ermyntrude Harvey. The mixed doubles title was won by Cochet and Eileen Bennett but, because of the bad weather on the Sunday, the match was played at the Menton Club.

The Menton tournament, always very popular with English visitors, was managed for the first time by Simond, upon the retirement of Madge, who had served as Referee for so long.

The surprise of the men's singles was Dr Johann Buss of Germany, who overwhelmed Menzel in the quarter-final, 6–1 6–2, and then proceeded to press hard against von Kehrling to get within two points of the match in straight sets, before eventually losing, 1–6 9–7 6–4. The Hungarian went on to win the title, beating Worm in four sets, 6–1 8–6 1–6 6–3. In the third set, Worm was performing so well that von Kehrling decided to take a breather and renew his energy and this paid off. Worm had a notable win over de Stefani in the last four, 6–3 3–6 6–1. Cochet played only in doubles.

Lili de Alvarez made her first appearance in singles, where a final against Betty Nuthall was anticipated. However, the latter was defeated in the third round by Miss Marjorie Morrill, an American born in Menton in 1910. The victor then fell to Lucia Valerio, 1–6 6–3 6–1, who in turn went on to dismiss Gwen Sterry, 7–5 6–0, to reach the final. Lili de Alvarez's route was via Peggy Saunders, who gave her many anxious moments before winning, 7–5 6–3. In the title round the Spaniard was somewhat handicapped by a sprained ankle but, nevertheless, played sufficiently well against the Italian, 6–4 7–5. Von Kehrling won the doubles with Worm and the mixed doubles with Cilly Aussem, while Dorothea Chambers and Peggy Saunders notched up the ladies' doubles. Cochet and Mlle Paulette Mariollet won the Coupe des Nations Cup for France. When Dorothea Chambers returned home she decided to relinquish her amateur status and take up professional coaching.

The important South of France Championships, held at the Nice Club, did not attract such a high standard of entry as normal, no doubt as this clashed with the Bordighera meeting. Also, several of the top players had concluded their programme for the Riviera at Menton.

Charles Kingsley, making his first visit of the year, had attempted a week or so earlier to be one of the first passengers to make the journey from London to Cannes by aeroplane but, unfortunately, this crashed at Lyons on the way. He was knocked out and suffered several cuts, but later was able to continue by rail. Consequently he was not at his best on the court in the quarter-final of the men's singles and needed five sets to eliminate Stanley Harris, a former rugby international, 5–7 6–3 6–3 3–6 6–0, before bowing to Aeschliman, 6–2 5–7 6–1 6–3. The other semi-finalist was Rogers, who pressed Gallepe in four sets, 6–4 8–6 3–6 8–6. The Swiss was always too good for the Irishman in the final and deserved his success in straight sets, 7–5 9–7 6–3.

The ladies' singles became a contest between America and Germany, both having two players in the semi-finals. Better in health, Cilly Aussem played well to beat Elizabeth Corbiere, 6–1 7–5, but was unexpectedly defeated in the final by Baroness Paula von Reznicek, who was extremely steady in every department and showed good strategy, 6–3 6–2. The winner had little difficulty in passing Mrs Endicott in the semi-final, 6–2 6–0. Betty Nuthall did not compete in the singles. Aeschliman completed a triple. The King of Sweden, despite his seventy years, showed remarkable energy in winning the doubles and mixed doubles events with Vladimir Landau and Cilly Aussem, respectively.

The popular Cannes Club meeting was to a large extent ruined by rain on the Wednesday, Thursday, Friday and Sunday. Several players could not stay for a finish on the Monday and there were some who withdrew due to illness. To counter some of these occurrences, Simond selected the best sixteen men to compete in the Côte d'Azur Championships and put the other entrants into a class 'B' level singles.

The final of the men's singles was never played, as Froitzheim withdrew, having to return to Weisbaden. Cochet, the title winner, beat his doubles partner, Aeschliman, in the semi-final and, as quite often the case, the Frenchman lost the opening set before winning, 3–6 6–3 7–5. Earlier, Froitzheim had won the opening set from Kingsley who withdrew in the course of the following set with a nosebleed. He was still recovering from his recent flying incident.

The feature of the ladies' singles was in the last four when Elizabeth Corbiere eventually overcame Ermyntrude Harvey, 6–1 5–7 7–5. This pitted her against Cilly Aussem but she had the misfortune to eat something which had made her ill. She had recovered to some degree when she took to the court but, although putting up a good show in the opening set, went down 6–3 6–0. The winner had passed Lady Gladys Roundway (Duddell, Colston) 6–3 6–3. Aeschliman won both doubles events.

There was an extremely unusual occurrence at the Beau Site Hotel tournament for the Cannes Championships when Cochet was defaulted to Mayes in the final of the men's singles. The Frenchman was 54 minutes late in arriving and Mayes had already left the ground, so Simond had no option other than to give a walkover. Cochet offered no objection. Prior to this, Cochet was taken to two advantage sets by Cholmondeley, 7–5 7–5, and then in the semi-final met Kingsley who was on top form. The Englishman squared the match at set all after being within one point of losing the match and then was within one point of squaring the deciding set, before falling 6–1 6–8 6–4. Mayes beat Worm and was then pushed hard by Aeschliman prior to winning, 8–6 2–6 6–1.

Elizabeth Ryan met Cilly Aussem for the first time in the final of the singles, but the German could only win two games in the second set. She was uncertain how to tackle the American's drop shots and was always on the defensive. Elizabeth Ryan also won the doubles with Phyllis Satterthwaite and the mixed doubles with Worm.

The second outing of the season at Beaulieu had a relatively small entry, as many of the leading players had left for other destinations. Worm won

After earlier visits to the Riviera in 1924 and 1925 René Lacoste, the world No.1 ranked player, returned to compete at the Monte Carlo Easter meeting. In a very strong field dominated by Australian Davis Cup players he won through to take the singles title.

the men's singles title but was given a good fight in the final by Rogers, who played too much at the back of the court, thereby giving the Dane the volleying advantage. In an interesting encounter the final score was 6–3 2–6 6–0 7–5. Worm had further success in capturing the doubles with Jack Hillyard and the mixed doubles with Phyllis Satterthwaite who also won the ladies' singles title. There was little opposition to her in this event as she comfortably defeated Sra Bella Pons of Spain in the final, 6–0 6–1.

The St Raphael tournament was cancelled and the season was brought to a close with the third meeting at Monte Carlo. This venue attracted a very strong entry with the return of Lacoste and Mayes together with the Australian Davis Cup team, which had just arrived in Europe. Strangely, none of the latter got past the fourth round, with Gerald Patterson falling to Rogers, 6–1 6–4, Harry Hopman downed by Lacoste, 6–3 6–3, and Jack Crawford being passed by Gentien, 4–7 7–5 6–3. Lacoste and Mayes qualified for the final without undue strain, but here the Canadian, conceding 20 years, gave his utmost and was unlucky not to win in a contest lasting 2 hours and 35 minutes. The score to the Frenchman was 5–7 2–6 7–5 6–2 8–6. In the semi-finals Lacoste beat Gentien, 6–3 6–2, and Mayes defeated Enrique Maier of Spain, 6–1 6–0.

Lili de Alvarez, back in the fold, had a comfortable run in the ladies' singles, having beaten Paula von Reznicek, 6–4 6–2, before passing Phyllis Satterthwaite for the title, 6–2 7–5. The Spaniard also won the two doubles events. The men's doubles title went to Crawford and John Hawkes. A welcome competitor in this event was Brookes, who reached the semi-final of the doubles with Mayes. This was the last time Mayes competed on the Riviera. A new event, the Prix de Famille, was introduced and won by F.F. Furnivall and Miss D. Furnivall.

# 1929
# Esna Boyd and Emmanuel du Plaix Dominate • Disastrous Weather

The opening tournament of the season, staged at the Beau Site Hotel, commencing on 17th December, did not attract the very top players. Brame Hillyard, at the age of 52, was remarkable in winning the men's singles, beating Aeschliman in the semi-final, by wisely resting in the middle set, 6–3 0–6 6–4, and then downing his namesake, Jack Hillyard, in the final in three sets, 9–7 6–3 6–2. The winner's vigorous driving often thwarted his opponent's volleying attack. Jack Hillyard reached the last four by ousting de Stefani in a long and fluctuating encounter, 6–1 5–7 7–5.

Visiting for the first time, Miss Esna Boyd of Australia dominated throughout. In the ladies' singles final she proved to be far superior to Sylvia Lafaurie, who mustered only one game, that in the first set. Phyllis Satterthwaite gave the Australian a good fight in the opening set of the semi-final before fading, 7–5 6–2, while the Frenchwoman eventually sailed past Mme Taunay, 5–7 6–0 6–3. Esna Boyd won the doubles with Phyllis Satterthwaite, while Rowley Scovell won the mixed with Sylvia Lafaurie.

There was an unusual occurrence the following week, when the Hyères New Courts Club and the Cannes Club meetings were held concurrently, with the former attracting a stronger entry. Here Brugnon was clearly the favourite to take the men's singles, with de Morpurgo the other likely finalist. But the Italian fell foul in the quarter-final to the Swiss, Hector Chiesa, who in turn succumbed to newcomer Franz Matejka, the Austrian champion, 6–2 6–1. The latter displayed a top class game against Brugnon in the final and led by two sets to love, only to yield at 8–6 in the third and eventually go down 5–7 4–6 8–6 6–4 6–2. Brugnon beat Buss to reach the final, 6–3 6–4.

In the ladies' singles Phyllis Satterthwaite bravely held her own in the final against Esna Boyd up to 6–all in the opening set but having lost

Brame Hillyard brought off a remarkable win at the Beau Site Hotel opening tournament by winning the men's singles with victory over Jack Hillyard in the final. Brame Hillyard was 52 years of age.

the next two games, retired. The Australian went on to capture the two doubles events with Phyllis Satterthwaite and de Morpurgo.

At the Cannes Club, the main interest was centred on the 18 year old Frenchman, Beni Berthet, who reached the final of the men's singles with a victory over Carlos Magrane of Argentina, 7–5 6–4. He then extended de Stefani in two long sets before excelling to capture the third, but then had nothing in reserve to fall, 12–10 9–7 2–6 6–0. Earlier, de Stefani beat Aeschliman 3–6 7–5 6–2. The other finals were concluded but were hampered throughout by wet weather. Sylvia Lafaurie took the ladies' singles from Mme Taunay, 6–1 4–6 6–4, while in the men's doubles Scovel and de Stefani got the better of Aeschliman and Magrane, 1–6 6–4 7–5.

The Metropole Hotel tournament suffered badly from the weather when play was held up for three days, necessitating an extension until the following Tuesday. The men's singles fell to de Morpurgo, the strongest player present, who beat his Davis Cup colleague, de Stefani, in the final. The winner found himself 5–0 down at the start but with a supreme effort saved the set after 24 games and, with his opposition fading, won 13–11 6–4 6–1. De Stefani had previously shone in dispensing with Matejka, 6–4 6–1, while at the same stage de Morpurgo overwhelmed Aeschliman, 6–1 6–1.

Esna Boyd and Phyllis Satterthwaite proved to be the best two ladies and, to form, the Australian took the title without being pressed too hard, 6–2 6–2. She also won the doubles with her singles opponent but the other final in which she was involved, with Matejka versus de Morpurgo and Phyllis Satterthwaite, was abandoned at 6–all in the final set owing to darkness. De Morpurgo and Jack Hillyard won the men's doubles.

The weather continued to play havoc at the newly named Monte Carlo Country Club, the former La Festa Country Club. The frost was so severe that the gallery courts were out of commission for a couple of days, while the less exposed courts were only available at a late hour.

The draw for the men's singles indicated that Brugnon and de Morpurgo would contest the final, but both were threatened on the way. Brugnon was hampered by a blistered hand. He nearly lost a set to the Russian, Mikhailoff, but in the semi-final against Rogers he lost the middle set before giving the Irishman the shortest shrift in the other two sets, 6–0 3–6 6–0. De Morpurgo at times was pushed hard to penetrate the baseline defence of Antoine Gentien, 6–4 6–2. In the final, fought on a damp court, de Morpurgo's victory over Brugnon was quite decisive. The latter's backhand was purely defensive and invited attack. The score was 6–3 6–2 6–2.

Phyllis Covell made a welcome appearance, but her game lacked severity against Phyllis Satterthwaite in the semi-final as she fell, 6–2 6–4. The winner again met Esna Boyd in the final and incurred her fourth consecutive defeat by the Australian, but she struggled hard before losing, 7–5 6–3. Esna Boyd completed the 'triple' in partnership with Phyllis Satterthwaite and Aeschliman. Brugnon and Gentien won the men's doubles but only in the 14th game of the 5th set against Jack Hillyard and de Morpurgo.

There was no let up in the weather the following week when the Cannes New Courts Club held their meeting and play was seriously delayed by frost and snow. The only event actually completed was the men's singles. In this, Yoshiro Ohta, an experienced Japanese Davis Cup player, made his debut on the Riviera. After taking a winning lead in the final set against de Stefani in the fourth round, he eased pressure and paid the penalty. There was another meeting between de Morpurgo and Brugnon in the final, with the match being played on a court that had to be treated with petrol to rid it of snow. The Frenchman failed to reach his best form and was comfortably put aside, 6–3 6–4 6–2. Brugnon had difficulty in beating de Stefani in the semi-final, 6–0 1–6 6–2, and de Morpurgo received a walkover from Gentien, who in the round before defeated Rogers in a very close encounter, 7–5 9–11 9–7.

Phyllis Satterthwaite was surprisingly a victim of Marjorie Morrell in the quarter-final. The winner lost the opening set, 10–8, but won the second after being five times within a stroke of defeat. In the decider, the American's youthful stamina won through to outclass her opponent, 8–10 8–6 6–2. Marjorie Morrell went down to Sylvia Lafaurie in the semi-final, 6–1 9–7, and Esna Boyd dispatched Phyllis Covell, 5–7 6–0 6–1. As the final could not be played due to the weather, Esna Boyd insisted that Sylvia Lafaurie should take the Cup. All other finals were divided.

Another week of inclement weather hit the Riviera and this time the Cannes Gallia Club suffered badly. With only five courts available the decision was taken to concentrate on the two singles events and cancel the remainder.

The final of the men's singles between Cochet, the holder for the past three years, and de Morpurgo provided one of the best matches ever seen on the Riviera. The Italian, who lost the first two sets by a small margin, won the third after a desperate contest and the fourth a little more easily.

Australian Esna Boyd making her second trip to Europe visited the Riviera for the first time. She dominated the ladies' events to win five tournaments in succession before just losing at her last meeting to Eileen Bennett in the final. Esna then left for London to be married.

In the fifth set he stood at 5–3 and 30–love but Cochet escaped. However, de Morpurgo's great chance came in the 12th game when he needed just one point for victory. After pounding Cochet's backhand, a return shot was set for the kill but while smashing he slipped on traces of the earlier frost and put the ball out of court. Cochet won the set in the 16th game,

Frenchman, Emmanuel du Plaix had an excellent season bringing off several surprise wins and at one stage capturing three singles titles in succession.

perhaps a little lucky to do so. The final score was 7–5 6–4 5–7 2–6 9–7. The two semi-final matches were over quickly, with de Morpurgo beating du Plaix, 6–1 6–3, and Cochet defeating de Stefani, 6–2 6–1.

The ladies' singles brought another success for Esna Boyd who had no difficulty in passing Miss Muriel Thomas in the final, 6–1 6–1. The Englishwoman had performed with merit to dispose of Marjorie Morrell in an earlier round, 6–4 6–3.

After several bad weeks of disturbed weather the Carlton Hotel at Cannes enjoyed a good spell of fine sunshine, although it was occasionally cold.

The last eight of the men's singles had a quality representation, with de Morpurgo, Patrick Spence (South Africa), making his debut on the Riviera, Brame Hillyard, Ohta, du Plaix, de Stefani, Alberto del Bono (Italy) and Stanley Harris. Spence pushed de Morpurgo to 7–5 7–5, Harris countered the hard driving of del Bono, while Ohta and de Stefani accounted for Hillyard and du Plaix respectively. In the semi-final, de Stefani just beat Harris, 7–5, in the third set, while Ohta narrowly lost the first set against de Morpurgo and then faded. As expected, de Morpurgo's match against de Stefani for the title was a foregone conclusion and ended, 6–4 6–2 6–4.

There was a great surprise in the final of the ladies' singles when Esna Boyd was beaten by Eileen Bennett, 6–4 5–7 6–4. This was the Australian's first loss in singles since her arrival on the Riviera. This was also her last singles match before her marriage, for which she travelled to London immediately after. Earlier, Esna Boyd had put out Diddie Serpieri (Vlasto) a former holder, 6–2 6–2, but struggled hard to defeat Miss Joan Fry, 7–9 6–4 6–3, in the semi-final, at which stage Eileen Bennett drove well to oust Phyllis Covell, 9–7 6–3. The men's doubles was captured by Aeschliman and Spence and the mixed doubles by de Morpurgo and Diddie Serpieri.

The first Nice tournament, scheduled for 11th to 17th February, was abandoned completely because of snow. There was an irony about this, as this meeting, the first of two held in Nice, had reputedly a minor role while the second normally held in March bore the title of the South of France Championships. However, in the past few years the 'minor' gathering attracted a better entry. Consequently, the Nice Committee decided to transpose the two meetings and attribute the major title to the first. Now the snow had intervened, the title was moved back to the former date after all (11th to 17th March). (This was the first time a tournament on the Riviera had been abandoned completely, without a ball being struck.)

At last the weather changed for the better and the Beaulieu meeting was able to proceed unhindered. The Italians dominated the men's event with de Morpurgo defeating his colleague de Stefani in the final of the Beaulieu Championships and joining del Bono to success in the doubles. De Stefani passed Rogers with little difficulty but in the semi-final against Ohta there was a different story as the Japanese fought tenaciously for each point and actually led 3–1 in the third set. However, the Italian crawled back to win, 4–6 6–3 6–4. Ohta earlier put out Kozeluh, the holder for the previous two years, 6–4 7–5. In the final, de Stefani was within a point of taking de Morpurgo to a fifth set before losing, 8–10 6–2 6–3 7–5. De Morpurgo's route to the final was via du Plaix and Spence in the semi-final, 6–2 1–6 6–3.

English ladies were to the forefront of the singles, with four filling the semi-final spots. Betty Nuthall showed great improvement and deserved to win the title from Joan Fry, who tired from earlier matches, against Cilly Aussem, 4–6 6–3 6–2, and Phyllis Covell, 3–6 6–4 6–3, and could only muster two games in the opening set and one game in the second. Noteworthy was the winner's defeat of Phyllis Satterthwaite by judicious tactics in the semi-final, 6–3 3–6 6–2. Earlier in the week there was a surprise when Phyllis Satterthwaite conquered Eileen Bennett, 6–2 9–7.

In the doubles, the holders, Jack Hillyard and Kozeluh, lost in the final to the Italians, 6–3 6–1 6–4, while in the ladies' doubles, the all-English final resulted in Eileen Bennett and Joan Fry outlasting Betty Nuthall and Phyllis Covell, 6–3 2–6 6–2.

The main Monte Carlo meeting was probably the most successful held so far, as a wealth of top men players from many countries competed, many of them attracted to the now prestigious Butler Trophy. The men's singles final was fought out by Cochet and de Morpurgo and won by the former in three close sets. De Morpurgo should have won the third set when leading 4–1 but this spurred Cochet on to take five games on the trot to win, 8–6 6–4 6–4. De Morpurgo had been pressed hard by Ohta, 7–5 7–5, before dismissing the German veteran, Heinrich Kleinschroth, in the semi-final,

6–2 6–2, while Cochet was given a walkover by Brugnon, who decided to save himself for other events. Early on, Rogers and Wilbur Coen, a youngster from the USA, numbered amongst Kleinschroth's victims.

The final of the ladies' singles resulted in Eileen Bennett losing her title to Betty Nuthall in a very long match, 7–5 5–7 6–4, the winner's improved backhand tipping the balance. After beating Cilly Aussem, Eileen Bennett survived another long, testing contest as she eventually overcame Mme Simone Mathieu of France, 6–4 7–9 8–6, in the semi-final. At the same time, Betty Nuthall received a walkover from Phyllis Covell.

The Butler Trophy had a great entry from which Brugnon and Cochet emerged comfortably as winners. The surprise finalists were the improvised pairing of Rogers and Peters, who beat in turn, Coen and Scovel, de Morpurgo and del Bono and Boussus and Landry. However, in the end they were no match for the Frenchman, who sailed through, 6–3 6–0 6–2.

The Beaumont Cup was won by Phyllis Covell and Betty Nuthall in three sets against Simone Mathieu and Mlle Simone Barbier of France, 4–6 6–2 6–2. The latter pair eliminated Eileen Bennett and Joan Fry in the previous round, 6–4 0–6 6–3. The 'normal' doubles events were won by de Morpurgo and von Kehrling, Marjorie Morrell and Joan Fry and Cochet and Eileen Bennett.

The following week, 4th to 11th March, two tournaments were in progress at the same time, the Menton meeting and the new Miramar gathering at Juan-les-Pins. There could not have been any regulations existing regarding a player competing in two concurrent tournaments as Cochet played in both, although it must be mentioned that he confined himself to the Coupe des Nations event at Menton, of which he was the holder with Paulette Marjollet.

At Menton there was brilliant weather the whole week. Von Kehrling retained his singles title without a serious threat and in the final his shrewd courtcraft was too sound for Matejka by the score, 6–4 7–5 6–1. In the semi-final von Kehrling had two close sets with de Stefani, 6–4 6–4, while Matejka overwhelmed A. Renard, a young Frenchman, 6–3 6–0. The latter had performed with merit to oust Rogers, 6–1 6–3.

Phyllis Covell became the Riviera Championships singles winner by beating two Germans at the closing stage, first narrowly passing Paula von Reznicek, 3–6 6–2 7–5, and in the final, Cilly Aussem in a very close encounter, 6–4 9–7. A feature of the event was the fine play of the young Swiss girl, Miss Lolette Payot, to whom Phyllis Satterthwaite retired when 0–3 down in the final set and who put up a spirited defence to push Cilly Aussem in the semi-final to 2–6 6–2 6–3. In the Coupe des Nations the holders Cochet and Paulette Marjollet were surprisingly knocked out in the semi-final by Rogers and Phyllis Covell, 0–6 6–3 9–7, and the winners

To C. R. CHISMAN, ESQ,
FROM JOHN LAVERY
WITH MANY COMPLIMENTS
1930

went on to further success in the final, downing Jack Hillyard and Phyllis Satterthwaite, 6–3 1–6 6–2. There were four handicap events.

At the Miramar Club, Cochet had a narrow escape from defeat at the hands of Landry, who had two match points against him. Having survived, Cochet went on to beat Edouard Garcia of Brazil in the semi-final, 6–4 8–6, and du Plaix in an uneventful climax, 6–3 6–3 6–4.

In the ladies' division a 17 year old German girl, Frl Annemarie Lowenthal, promised much for the future when she beat Sylvia Lafaurie in the semi-final, 6–3 6–3, and gave Eileen Bennett a good run for her money in the first set of the final, before bowing, 7–5 6–0. A surprise in the final of the men's doubles saw Gallepe and Landry beat Cochet and Aeschliman, 6–2 6–1. As expected, Cochet and Eileen Bennett won the mixed doubles.

The South of France Championships, transferred back from earlier in the season, did not attract as good an entry as normal. Some players had returned home early, while others favoured the Bordighera tournament. The solid defence of du Plaix captured the men's singles, but he was stretched to beat Aeschliman, the holder, in the semi-final, 6–4 3–6 6–3

During his winter sojourn to the Riviera, John Lavery painted his oil on canvas 'Tennis under the Orange Trees at Cannes' in 1929 and dedicated the work to the tournaments held at the Beau Site Hotel. The lady serving is his step-daughter, Alice Trudeau, who was coached for a period by George Lyttleton Rogers.

8–6, and after dropping the opening set to Artens, the 1927 winner, he always had the measure of the Austrian and ran out, 3–6 6–1 6–3 6–0. Artens beat Gallepe in the last four, 6–1 6–4 6–4.

In the final of the ladies' singles, Paula von Reznicek, the holder, avenged her defeat at Menton by Phyllis Covell, 6–8 6–2 6–4. The Englishwoman scored a notable win over Cilly Aussem in the semi-final, 6–2 6–3. Aeschliman and Gallepe won the men's doubles and Phyllis Covell and Muriel Thomas took the ladies' title.

In the absence of Cochet, the holder, France still retained the Côte d'Azur Championship title at the Cannes Club through du Plaix, who in four rounds lost just one set. In the final his tireless driving wore down the courageous effort made by Fritz Kuhlmann of Germany, 8–6 6–2 9–7. Kingsley and Lester, who had just arrived on the Riviera, did not do themselves full justice and departed in the semi-final to Kuhlmann, 3–6 6–4 7–5, and du Plaix, 12–10 6–4, respectively.

The first appearance of the season by Lili de Alvarez created additional interest. In the semi-final of the ladies' singles she was near elimination when Cilly Aussem stood within a stroke of 5–3 in the final set, but with determination she edged out, 6–3 2–6 6–4. After this fine exhibition the final was relatively tame and Paula von Reznicek could only collect five games, 6–4 6–1. The runner-up repeated her victory over Phyllis Covell at Nice, in the semi-final, 6–4 7–5. Aeschliman and Gallepe added one more title to their collection and Phyllis Covell and Sylvia Lafaurie captured the ladies' doubles.

The second Beau Site Hotel meeting for the Cannes Championships was dominated by Frenchmen. Paul Feret, competing in his first tournament since being reinstated as an amateur, had to summon all his powers of defence to shake off Pat Hughes in the semi-final, 4–6 6–1 7–5. At the same time, Kingsley fell in two advantage sets to du Plaix, 8–6 8–6, and the Frenchman went on to conquer Feret in the final, 7–5 6–1 4–6 6–2, to achieve his third tournament win in a row.

Phyllis Satterthwaite produced an excellent win over Cilly Aussem in the semi-final of the ladies' singles, which lasted two hours and could have gone either way. In the final set the German led 5–2, but was pulled back to 3–6 7–5 7–5. However, Phyllis Satterthwaite could make little headway in the final against Sylvia Lafaurie and had to be content with winning only three games in each of the two sets. Du Plaix won a second title in partnership with Coen.

The last of the Monte Carlo tournaments found Worm performing his best by winning the men's singles and doubles titles. In the singles final he was too experienced for Coen and with a continuous net attack achieved a 6–2 6–2 5–7 6–3 victory. The American had performed well in disposing

of Feret and then Aeschliman, in a marathon semi-final, 6–4 7–9 6–4. Worm had progressed at the expense of Lester and Gallepe, 6–1 4–6 6–1.

The ladies' singles final was an all-French affair, with Simone Mathieu defeating Sylvia Lafaurie, 6–3 1–6 6–4. Paula von Reznicek had pushed Simone Mathieu to the limit in the round before, 5–7 7–5 7–5. Elizabeth Ryan and Cilly Aussem were present but did not compete in the singles. This was the American's first tournament of the season, having just returned from India. She paired with Phyllis Satterthwaite to win the doubles comfortably. Gallepe and Worm were the best men's pair.

The St Raphael tournament attracted quite a thin entry with only four events contested, with the normal ladies' singles being omitted. There was a change of fortune in the final of the men's singles when Aeschliman, after dropping the first two sets against du Plaix, pulled back to win, 4–6 3–6 6–4 6–3 6–0. Aeschliman went on to capture two further titles, pairing with du Plaix and Sylvia Lafaurie, the latter also winning the ladies' doubles with Mme Daisy Speranza-Wyns.

Considering the lateness there was a good entry at the Beaulieu Club. Chief interest centred on the ladies' singles event where Lili de Alvarez and Elizabeth Ryan competed, but a final between the two was prevented

The first Davis Cup tie played on the French Riviera was Monaco's first appearance in the competition. They beat Switzerland by three matches to two on the Condamine courts, 29th to 31st March. (Left to right) Charles Aeschliman, René Gallepe, Vladimir Landau and Jean Wuain. The winning pair are in the middle.

when Paula von Reznicek defeated the American in the semi-final, 6–3 6–2. In the final the German put up a stubborn resistence against Lili de Alvarez, who was in brilliant and daring mood to win, 6–3 6–3. Earlier Lili de Alvarez beat Phyllis Satterthwaite, 6–4 6–0. Du Plaix won his fourth singles title in five weeks beating Rogers in the final, 6–3 6–3 6–3, his steadiness of driving being the vital factor. The doubles winners were Jack Hillyard and Worm, Lili de Alvarez and Sylvia Lafaurie, and Worm and Phyllis Satterthwaite.

The last tournament of the season was held at the Juan-les-Pins Club from 15th to 21st April and was generally a low-key affair with a small entry and confining the events to three. Du Plaix won his fifth in six weeks, beating Rowley Scovell of England in the final, 6–2 6–1. The ladies' singles final was close throughout, but in the end Sylvia Lafaurie overcame Daisy Speranza-Wyns, the 15th ranked Frenchwoman, 8–6 6–4. The mixed doubles was won by Scovell and Daisy Speranza-Wyns, the 15th ranked Frenchwoman, who beat du Plaix and Sylvia Lafaurie in the last match, 6–1 6–2.

The first Davis Cup tie to be played on the Riviera took place on 29th–31st March, when Monaco making their debut in the competition, defeated Switzerland by 3 matches to 2 on the Condamine courts.

# 1930
# Bill Tilden's Memorable Visit •
# Elizabeth Ryan Wins Nine Singles Titles

There was a feeling of eagerness in the air to get started with the season when two tournaments were held concurrently over Christmas. Apart from the well-established Beau Site Hotel meeting at Cannes, the New Courts Club at Hyères was staging their second annual tournament.

At the Beau Site Hotel the men's singles was won by the young Frenchman, Paul Barrelet de Ricou, who, playing extremely beautiful tennis, defeated Rogers in the final, 8–6 6–2 6–4. In the round before de Ricou was involved in quite a marathon match with Aeschliman before eventually succeeding, 6–8 6–4 9–7. Rogers' entry to the final came at the expense of Henri Raynaud, 6–3 7–5.

Elizabeth Ryan was an early starter to the season and was rewarded by capturing three titles. In the singles final Sylvia Lafaurie did very well to win the middle set, particularly as she was recuperating after appendicitis, but the American steadied to win 6–3 1–6 6–3. Unfortunately, Sylvia Lafaurie injured her knee in the final of the ladies' doubles and was unable to contest the last match in the mixed doubles.

Over at Hyères, where a good entry was received, Johann Buss won the men's singles title defeating Henri Reynaud in the final, 5–7 6–2 6–4 6–2. In the semi-final, the player from Marseilles beat the Swiss champion, Jean Wuarin, 6–4 5–7 8–6. The ladies' title was claimed by France's most promising player, Mlle Doris Metaxa who, despite losing the middle set to Mlle Regine Vlasto, remained in control to win, 6–3 3–6 6–2.

When the players gathered the following week at the Metropole Hotel at Cannes, de Ricou proved his ability again by defeating Rogers in the men's singles final, 5–7 6–1 6–4 8–6. Elizabeth Ryan met her old rival, Phyllis Satterthwaite, once more in the ladies' singles final, which the American won, 6–2 2–5 ret'd. Rogers won two titles paired with Aeschliman and Elizabeth Ryan and the latter completed a third victory, partnered by the singles' runner up.

Bill Tilden's achievement during his one and only visit to the Riviera was phenomenal as he played continuously, week after week from 6th January to 27th April, entering 15 tournaments. In singles he competed in 14 events and won them all except one when he was unwell.

At the meeting there was considerable discussion with regard to foot-faults, as apparently many players refused to be foot-faulted. Many threatened to retire if the umpire foot-faulted them, so the officials decided not to act.

There was great interest in the first appearance on the Riviera, at the Monaco Championships held at the Condamine Courts, of the world renowned American, William (Bill) Tilden, Wimbledon singles champion in 1920 and 1921 and United States champion from 1920 to 1925. On the way to the singles final he beat Col. Arthur Berger, Landau and then de Ricou, 6–2 6–2 6–4, before taking the title from Rogers, 7–5 6–1 6–8 6–0. Rogers had greatly distinguished himself by capturing the scalps of Kingsley, 6–0 8–10 6–4, and Brugnon 6–2 1–6 6–8 6–4 7–5, both matches played on the same day. His duel against the Frenchman was exciting as he trailed 0–3 in the fifth set before breaking through at 5–4.

Elizabeth Ryan, as expected, won the ladies' singles, again beating Phyllis Satterthwaite in the final, 6–3 6–4. In the semi-final the Englishwoman defeated Mlle Arlette Neufeld, No. 5 in the French ranking, 6–0 6–4, who had passed Madge Slaney, 6–4 6–2. Mlle Ida Adamoff, a Russian ranked No. 8 in France, extended Elizabeth Ryan in the semi-final, 3–6 6–3 6–4. Kingsley combined with Tilden to take the doubles and Elizabeth Ryan and Phyllis Satterthwaite paired to win the ladies' event. John and Elsie Pittman (Goldsack) on honeymoon, entered the Prix de Famille and won the event.

The following week was allocated to the championships of the leading clubs at the various resorts. As usual, membership could be obtained at short notice or even overnight, so that the entry was quite often up to nearly the standard of an open meeting. The Monte Carlo County Club had secured the services of Tilden, who in the final defeated Kingsley, 4–6 6–2 6–3 6–4.

The next gathering in line was the New Courts Club at Cannes where the finals were delayed until the Tuesday, owing to incessant rain for three days. The courts were naturally on the slow side and this enabled Tilden to use his sliced drives and drop shots with deadly effect, allowing de Stefani to win only six games in the final of the men's singles, 6–1 6–4 6–1. On the way to the last match the American accounted for Hunter, Brame Hillyard, Graham, Cholmondeley and in the semi-final, Berthet, 6–2 6–1 6–2. In the other half of the draw, de Stefani eliminated Artens (conqueror of Kingsley, 7–5 6–3) in the semi-final, 6–0 4–6 6–1 6–2.

Elizabeth Ryan was again supreme in the singles but was forced to concede the middle set against Lucia Valerio, before dominating the play, 6–2 2–6 6–0. The American also lost a set against Cilly Aussem in the semi-final, which could have resulted in either player winning – the score was 5–7 6–4 6–3. Lucia Valerio dismissed Joan Ridley 7–5 7–5 before beating Sylvia Lafaurie, 6–3 7–5. Tilden was well supported by Kingsley and Cilly Aussem to win both doubles.

There were quite a number of upsets at the Cannes Gallia Club meeting, where the arrival of de Morpurgo was expected to extend Tilden, but he was beaten by Rogers in five sets. The Irishman then faced another five-set encounter against Artens in the semi-final – a tremendous struggle won by the former, 6–4 7–5 5–7 5–7 6–3. Artens had earlier beaten Brugnon. Tilden, coasting through without any pressure, beat Kingsley, 6–0 6–1 6–1, and Artens, for the title, 6–0 6–2 6–0.

Elizabeth Ryan's victory in the ladies' singles was never threatened, as her way to the final was eased when Ermyntrude Harvey surprisingly eliminated Cilly Aussem, winning the third set, 6–1. The Englishwoman could then do little right, seizing just one game in the second set against Elizabeth Ryan. In the other semi-final Sylvia Lafaurie eventually got the better of Phyllis Satterthwaite, 6–3 3–6 6–3, but in the final, after leading 3–2 in the opening set, she faded badly, 6–3 6–2. The men's doubles final was never put on court as Kingsley injured his hand and with his partner, Tilden, withdrew to Brugnon and Cochet. (The latter pair did not compete in the singles.)

At the Carlton Club tournament there occurred a great upset in the men's singles when Tilden was beaten in the third round by Peters, ranked No.11 in Britain, 9–7 8–6. Peters had not intended to enter the singles but was prevailed upon to do so to replace Aaron, who had withdrawn, and thereby complete the draw. The circumstances surrounding this need to be explained –

the American ate something at dinner the evening before which made him ill. Having spent a disturbed night and eating no breakfast, he went on court late on Wednesday morning and played a game which, to all present, showed that there was something amiss. Only after the match did he inform the referee of the problem and had merely remarked that he did not feel fit. Rain overnight had made the court surface soft and Peters' drop shots and timely advances to the net had their reward, forcing his opponent to yield the opening set. Tilden, towards the conclusion of this set, was a little upset by the umpire, who failed to call a fault and he lost his service in the 16th game. To some degree he regained his composure but found Peters continuing to drive well and pass him when he came up for the volley. Tilden just managed to hold his service from 0–40 to reach 4 all and then Peters fell behind at 4–5. Tilden failed to take advantage and

Eric Peters had the distinction of inflicting the only singles win against Tilden during the season, which occurred in the third round at the Carlton Club tournament when Tilden was unwell. This was the only occasion that Tilden was beaten in his career by an Englishman.

eventually lost his service in the 14th game. (This is the only occasion in his career that Tilden lost to an Englishman.)

Peters lost in the next round to Gaslini, 6–3 8–6, who in turn went down to Artens in the semi-final, 6–1 6–1 8–6. De Morpurgo was expected to at least reach the final but, after accounting for Brame Hillyard, 6–2 6–1, he failed against de Stefani, 6–4 2–6 6–2 6–3. The latter, always with a little in hand, won the title, beating Artens, 6–2 4–6 6–3 6–2. Brugnon entered the lists but was surprisingly ousted by a young Greek, M. Nicolaides, early on.

Elizabeth Ryan won her sixth singles title of the season, easily overcoming Joan Ridley in the semi-final, 6–2 6–1, and then received a walkover in the ultimate match from Sylvia Lafaurie, on account of illness. The latter had passed Phyllis Satterthwaite, 6–1 6–0. Brugnon and Cochet won the doubles, likewise Sylvia Lafaurie and Elizabeth Ryan, but in the mixed event Tilden and Cilly Aussem surprisingly fell to Cochet and Elizabeth Ryan in the final – but it was very close at 12–10 6–3.

Newcomers to the coast were Englishman, Harry Lee (left) and Bunny Austin, who taking advantage of Tilden's non-entry at the Beaulieu Club, contested the final of the singles with Lee surprisingly winning in five sets.

The next stop on the circuit was Nice, where the South of France Championships were decided. Tilden had by no means shaken off the effects of his illness of the week before, but in spite of this he was able to come out on top after two exhausting matches to take the title against opponents who played extremely well. In the semi-final he beat Peters, 4–6 2–6 6–3 6–3 6–3, and then Rogers, 4–6 8–6 6–1 4–6 6–0. De Stefani was tipped to reach the final but, after beating Coen, 5–7 6–3 6–3, was halted at the semi-final by Rogers to the tune of 6–0 6–2 4–6 6–4. None of the leading French players were listed.

Owing to Elizabeth Ryan, Paula von Reznicek and Sylvia Lafaurie scratching, Cilly Aussem, at the top of her form, sailed through to win the singles title, beating Joan Ridley in double quick time, 6–4 6–1, and then Mrs Carolyn Hirsch, the 15th ranked American in 1928, 6–2 6–0. There was an upset in the ladies' doubles final when Phyllis and Nancy Radcliffe just defeated Joan Ridley and Phyllis Satterthwaite in the final, 6–3 3–6 8–6. Tilden and Coen won the doubles but rain prevented the mixed doubles being played.

There was an excellent entry at the Beaulieu meeting including newcomers from England, Henry (Bunny) Austin and Harry Lee, plus

Daniel Prenn from Germany. There was a personal triumph for Lee, who had the satisfaction of overcoming in the last four rounds Davis Cup players, Worm, 1–6 11–9 6–3, von Kehrling, 6–2 9–7, Prenn, 6–3 6–4, and in the final, Austin, 3–6 6–3 6–3 3–6 7–5. He had taken to the prevailing conditions with hardly any trouble and when facing a deficit of 1–3 in the fifth set against Austin, his doggedness carried him home. Austin just beat Coen in the semi-final, 6–0 0–6 8–6, while Lee beat Prenn 6–3 6–4. Tilden decided to rest from the singles, but paired with Coen to win the doubles.

Newly arrived on the coast from England were the honeymoon couple, Llewellyn Owen and his wife Violet. She seemed to have a great chance to win the ladies' singles, when she beat Rosie Berthet, 6–0 6–3, Cilly Aussem, 4–6 7–5 6–4, and Doris Metaxa, 6–1 6–2, to reach the final. However, waiting for her was Joan Ridley who in the end triumphed. The match was divided into two sessions, owing to a heavy shower, when the score stood at 6–3 0–6 to Joan Ridley. After the interval, the latter's leading driving gave her the edge, 6–4. Overall, the ladies' entry had been of excellent class. Hughes and Violet Owen combined well to capture the mixed doubles.

During the past few seasons at the Monte Carlo Country Club, the two international team competitions for the Butler and Beaumont trophies had gained in stature and prestige, with the organisers encouraging leading nations to send teams. This generally meant that competitors would have to undertake more matches than normal throughout the week. Britain had three pairs competing in the Butler Cup, Peters and Rogers, Hughes and Lee and Austin and Kingsley. All achieved some success but the last named pair excelled in defeating the holders, Brugnon and Cochet in the semi-final,

The finalists in the Butler Cup staged at Monte Carlo (left to right) Bunny Austin, Charles Kingsley, Mr George Butler (the donor), Bill Tilden and Wilbur Coen. The Americans won in four sets.

6–3 6–2 5–7 5–7 8–6. However, in the final they were just unable to prevail against Coen and Tilden who won, 6–2 1–6 9–7 6–3. The final of the ladies' cup was an all-French affair with the two Simones, Barbier and Mathieu, beating Doris Metaxa and Mlle Colette Rosambert, 6–1 8–6.

In the men's singles, Tilden had fully recovered his fitness and proceeded in the draw with his usual confidence. Earlier, he beat Brame Hillyard and

Matejka, before passing Kingsley, who took a set from him in the quarter-final, 5–7 6–3 6–1 6–1, and de Morpurgo, 6–2 7–5 6 1, to reach the final. Here, Austin, who put out Prenn in an uphill encounter in the round before, 2–6 3–6 6–2 6–3 6–2, held his own for two sets, without really being within a chance of winning them, before Tilden won convincingly, 6–4 6–4 6–1.

The ladies' singles title went to Cilly Aussem, who in her last three matches passed Phyllis Satterthwaite, 6–4 7–9 6–1, Joan Ridley, 0–6 7–5 6–0, and in the deciding match, Simone Mathieu, rather easily, 6–2 6–1. Simone Mathieu had previously beaten Doris Metaxa, 6–3 6–1, and earlier Joan Ridley did well in disposing of Simone Barbier, 3–6 6–3 7–5.

A week later many of the stars moved along the coast to Menton, on the Italian border, to compete in the Riviera Championships. Brugnon appeared to have lost his confidence a week earlier at Monte Carlo, but all of a sudden he was able to restore his equanimity. In the semi-final of the singles he lost a close first set against Rogers but then left his opponent standing, 4–6 6–1 6–1. In the final he played with the same assurance against Tilden and was able to run the American to five sets, 10–8 7–5 3–6 4–6 6–1. In the last set, Tilden, sensing the position, produced his very best. Austin did not compete in the event but a notable achievement was gained by Brame Hillyard who kept Coen on court for 44 games and only just lost, 12–10 5–7 6–4. The holder of the title, von Kehrling, lost in an early round to Matejka, while the two Englishmen, Hughes and Lee, both fell victim to Rogers.

Cilly Aussem confirmed her previous week's victory over Simone Mathieu in the final of the ladies' singles, 9–7 6–2. Both at times made outstanding recoveries. Returning to the Riviera, Elizabeth Ryan beat Paula von Reznicek, 1–6 7–5 6–1, after being down 1–6 1–5, but then fell to Simone Mathieu, who lost the first 10 games before recovering in the semi-final, 0–6 6–4 6–1. Phyllis Satterthwaite took the opening set from Cilly Aussem before being overwhelmed, 4–6 6–1 6–1. Tilden won the doubles with Coen and the Coupe de Nations with Elizabeth Ryan.

Miss Helen Jacobs, the No.2 American player, had accepted an invitation from the French Tennis Federation to spend several weeks on the Riviera, en route to Paris and London. Unfortunately, she was unwell crossing the Atlantic and when she reached Nice had contracted tonsillitis, later diagnosed as pleurisy. After a few days, although very weary, she competed in the tournament but, under pressure from Tilden, withdrew from her singles semi-final against Simone Mathieu and the doubles, much to the disappointment of the gallery.

Simone Mathieu went on to win the singles title. At the two previous meetings she had lost in the final to Cilly Aussem, but on this occasion the

German decided not to compete and this allowed Elizabeth Ryan through. Good placing and excellent returns of service gave Simone Mathieu the match at 6–4 7–5. In the semi-final Elizabeth Ryan defeated Paula von Reznicek, 6–3 6–1.

As expected, Tilden was triumphant and won all three events without really being closely challenged. In quite a strong field he romped through the singles beating Aeschliman, 6–0 6–3, de Stefani, and in the final, Rogers, 6–2 6–2 6–3, showing an all-round game which was positively compelling. Newcomers, Takeichi Harada and Hyotare Satoh took time to acclimatise, but in the semi-final the former gave Rogers much to think about and only by producing a defensive game towards the end he was able to go through against Harada, 6–1 6–8 6–3 7–5. Earlier, Rogers passed Kingsley, 7–5 6–2. Tilden won the doubles with Coen and the mixed with Cilly Aussem, while Cilly Aussem and Elizabeth Ryan took the doubles.

There was an outstanding English achievement at the Cannes Club tournament when Violet Owen accomplished the downfall of Elizabeth Ryan in the semi-final of the ladies' singles by preventing her opponent from volleying, 8–6 6–1. However, in the final against Cilly Aussem Violet was quite ineffective and won only 18 points in her 6–0 6–0 drubbing. The winner had passed Paula von Reznicek in the previous round, 6–3 6–2. Helen Jacobs did not compete.

Tilden marched on, winning two titles. In the singles he had far too much skill at his command for Matejka, 9–7 7–5, Kingsley, 6–3 6–1 6–0, and de Stefani in the final, 6–4 6–3 6–4. The Italian had earlier performed well by disposing of Satoh and Tamino Abe. Edward Avory, making his initial visit to the Riviera, did well to take a set off Horada. Tilden was not invincible, for with Cilly Aussem he fell at the last stage of the mixed event, for only the second time during the season, to Harada and Elizabeth Ryan, 6–3 3–6 6–1.

There was a very unusual occurrence toward the end of the week at the Beau Site Hotel gathering, in that both singles finals were shared by agreement. The reason given for sharing the Coen and Tilden match was that they were "team mates", while in the case of the

Honeymooning from England were Llewellyn and Violet Owen. Immediately, Violet struck outstanding form at the Beaulieu meeting by beating Rosie Berthet, Cilly Aussem and Doris Metaxa, only to fall in a very tight match to Joan Ridley. She later caused an upset by defeating Elizabeth Ryan at the Cannes Club.

Elizabeth Ryan and Paula von Reznicek contest, the explanation given was to allow the latter to return home to Germany as she was only left in that one event.

Coen played very well throughout and his victims included Kingsley, de Stefani and in the semi-final, Abe, 6–8 11–9 6–1 4–6 6–3. Satoh reached the last four after a close battle with Rogers, but was well beaten, as expected, by Tilden, 6–1 6–2 6–3. The surprise of the ladies' singles was the elimination of Helen Jacobs by Paula von Reznicek at the semi-final stage, 6–2 6–3. The American was in better health but had not recovered her best form. In the other semi-final Elizabeth Ryan gained her revenge over Violet Owen, who had beaten her the week previously. This was a very tight contest which could have gone either way, with the score ending at 4–6 6–3 6–4. The Englishwoman fought really hard.

Coen and Tilden won the doubles by defeating Gallepe and Rogers in the final, 6–4 6–3 6–2. Tilden paired with Cilly Aussem to win the mixed, while Helen Jacobs and Elizabeth Ryan won the ladies' division, but not before overcoming in a tense match, Lili de Alvarez and Violet Owen, 4–6 7–5 6–4.

The St Raphael tournament attracted a good entry, particularly from the men and, as expected, this became another triumph for Tilden. In the semi-final he beat Abe, who had previously accounted for Buss, while Rogers passed Satoh, the conqueror in previous rounds of Brame Hillyard and Gallepe. In the final, Tilden crushed Rogers with unbelievable ease, 6–1 6–0 6–2. Coen decided to opt out of this event.

Elizabeth Ryan also had no bother in winning the ladies' singles, overwhelming Mme Albina Korotvickova of Czechoslovakia in the final, dropping just one game in the second set. Coen and Tilden won the men's doubles, but were give a tough fight by Abe and Satoh in the final, 6–2 3–6 6–3 6–8 6–4. Cilly Aussem joined Tilden to win the mixed event and with Elizabeth Ryan, the ladies' doubles.

The Miramar tournament held at Juan-les-Pins the second week in April was another platform for Tilden to show his brilliance and he did not disappoint. Once again Coen moved through the draw to challenge Tilden in the final and, driving with pace and purpose, managed to win the opening set but thereafter the winner was never in doubt, with the score, 4–6 6–1 6–2 6–3. Elizabeth Ryan avenged previous defeats by Cilly Aussem to win the singles title, 6–2 7–5. The mixed doubles final had a mild upset when Coen and Elizabeth Ryan defeated Tilden and Cilly Aussem in a brilliant match, 1–6 6–3 6–4.

Considering the lateness of the second Beaulieu meeting, the competitors and spectators gave good support. Everything was so easy for Tilden, even to obtaining a walkover in the singles final from Coen, who was unable to compete owing to a strained leg. The semi-finals were also disappointing as Tilden beat Gallepe, 6–0 6–0 6–0, with only four games going to deuce, while Coen had an easy passage after Aeschliman retired at set all and 2–all.

After being given a walkover by Elizabeth Ryan, Phyllis Satterthwaite had one of her outstanding successes of the season when she beat Helen Jacobs in the final of the singles, 2–6 8–6 6–4, after two and a half hours. The rallies were long and mostly dictated by the Englishwoman's continual lobbing campaign. The American had some compensation when partnering Elizabeth Ryan to win the ladies' doubles. Coen and Tilden sailed through the men's doubles and in an interesting contest, Tilden and Elizabeth Ryan won the mixed title. They proved too strong for Coen and Helen Jacobs, 6–1 6–3.

The last meeting of the season was the third at Monte Carlo and concluded on 27th April. (The last scheduled event at Juan-les-Pins was cancelled.) Tilden was again untouchable, beating Frenchman, Jean Lesueur, in the singles final, 6–1 6–3 6–3, and joining Coen and Lili de Alvarez to achieve the 'triple'. Lili de Alvarez, making a welcome reappearance at the meeting, won the ladies' singles with victories over Ida Adamoff, 1–6 6–3 6–4, and in the final, Mlle Josane Sigart of Belgium, 3–6 6–2 7–5. The Prix de Famille was won by M. Sigart and his daughter, Josane. This tournament was part of Helen Jacob's original programme, but after pondering for a couple of days and renewed pressure from Tilden, she decided to withdraw and travel to Paris in preparation for the French Championships.

Tilden never again played on the Riviera. He won his third singles title at Wimbledon in July and turned professional in December.

This was the last season that the Marquess of Cholmondeley competed on the Riviera, having first played as Lord Rocksavage in 1912. He later held the high office of the realm, Lord Great Chamberlain, to King Edward VIII (1936–1937) and Queen Elizabeth (1952–1966). He was an outstanding calligrapher and an expert at polo. He was widely regarded as the best-looking man of his generation. He died on 16th September 1968, aged 85.

This was the last season that Lord George Cholmondeley played on the Riviera. He was a very enthusiastic player who had competed most years since 1912, when he was Lord Rocksavage.

# 1931

# George Lyttleton Rogers and Phyllis Satterthwaite Share Season's Honours

For the first time the Juan-les-Pins Club undertook the organisation of the opening tournament of the season, staged over the Christmas period. Despite the limited number of entries there were good matches to be seen. With competitors adjusting to the conditions there were naturally a few upsets. Of the new English players, Malcolm Young surprised all by eliminating Augustin in the first round, 8–6 6–2, but then fell to Roger George, 6–1 6–3. Miss Susan Noel lost in the opening round of the ladies' singles to Mme René Meunier, who recently achieved first series status in the French ranking, 6–3 6–0. There was indeed a shock in this event when Muriel Thomas won the title with an easy win over Elizabeth Ryan, who was well off form in the final, 6–2 6–1. In the semi-final the winner put out Mlle Cosette Saint Omer Roy, 6–2 6–2.

Aeschliman won a triple crown by beating Worm in the singles final, 6–1 6–2 6–1, and paired with the finalist to easily win the doubles beating Marcel Renault and Marcel Jourdre, 6–3 6–0. Aeschliman's third title came with Muriel Thomas. Besides the level events, two handicap singles were played.

The Beau Site Hotel New Year meeting was, as usual, very successful and the number of participants appreciably up. Rogers won the men's singles title after being morally defeated in the semi-final by Aslangul, who led 5–4 and 40–15 in the third set when he retired owing to another engagement. The Irishman, in good form, went on to win the title from Aeschliman, 8–6 6–1 3–6 7–5. For the fifth time Elizabeth Ryan won the singles title, but this was not achieved without an uphill struggle all the way. She was extended to 39 games by Mme Aimée Charpenel, No.15 in France, 4–6 6–3 11–9, and in the semi-final by Miss Betty Soames, 6–4 4–6 6–4, before clinching the event against Phyllis Satterthwaite, 4–6 8–6 6–1. The runner-up had passed Muriel Thomas, 6–4 7–5.

Seldom had Elizabeth Ryan suffered defeat in two doubles events, but this was the case when, partnered by Phyllis Satterthwaite she lost to Mme Taunay and Muriel Thomas, 8–10 6–2 6–2, and with Rogers to Aeschliman and Muriel Thomas, 4–6 6–3 6–3, both in final matches. This was Simond's 27th year as referee at the tournament.

Cannes was again the scene of action for the second week when the

Metropole Hotel meeting took place. Rogers came out on top in the men's singles, but before clinching the title had to win a five-set final against Feret, 8–10 7–5 4–6 6–4 6–2. The Frenchman was considered to have played exceedingly well, as being the first tournament of the year, he acclimatised quickly to the intense brilliance of the sunlight, which was normally such a handicap to newcomers. Both finalists had easy rides in the semi-finals, Rogers over Worm, 6–3 6–2, and Feret passing Bernard Law, an American, 6–1 6–2. Aeschliman, unfortunately, retired owing to illness in the third round.

There was a noteworthy performance from Mme Hélène Nicolopoulo (Contostavlos), who a few years earlier had been France's leading player before being resident in Greece. In her first tournament of the year she lost just one set in taking the title, beating en route Cosette Saint Omer Roy, 4–6 6–2 6–0, Elizabeth Ryan, 6–3 6–2, and in the last match, Phyllis Satterthwaite, 6–3 6–2.

There was an exciting men's doubles final in which Jack Hillyard and Landau came from behind to beat Feret and Rogers, 5–7 4–6 8–6 6–2 6–4. Elizabeth Ryan won two doubles titles with Phyllis Satterthwaite and Rogers.

At the Cannes New Courts Club, Phyllis Satterthwaite was in dazzling mood to win the ladies' singles title when she beat Lucia Valerio in the final, 6–3 10–8. Her best performance came in the round before when she claimed victory over Hélène Nicolopoulo, who had beaten her at the Metropole Hotel meeting. A lobbing campaign broke up her opponent's all-court game to seal her win at 6–4 6–4. The suprise was the elimination of Elizabeth Ryan at the same stage by the Italian for the loss of just two games, both in the second set. The American was completely out of touch. An unexpected elimination occurred in the second round when Sig.na Elsa Riboli of Italy ousted Muriel Thomas, 6–3 6–1.

Rogers won both the singles and doubles titles, but he had little to spare against Count Oscar de Minerbi, No.7 in the Italian ranking, in the semi-final where he edged out, 9–7 3–6 12–10. Berthet, showing much improvement in his game, defeated Ladislav Hecht, the Czechoslovakian champion, 6–3 9–7, and Aeschliman, 6–4 2–6 6–0, but could not overcome

The season was an outstanding success for Irishman, George Rogers, who won seven singles titles, at the Beau Site Hotel, Metropole Hotel, Cannes New Courts Club, Carlton Club, Nice, Beaulieu and the Cannes Club. His disappointment was to lose the final at Monte Carlo to Henri Cochet. Seen with Rogers is Betty Nuthall after they won the 'Coupe des Nations' at Menton.

Rogers in the final to fall in straight sets, 6–0 6–4 6–4. The men's doubles was taken by Jack Hillyard and Rogers, the ladies' doubles by Elizabeth Ryan and Phyllis Satterthwaite, while the mixed doubles final was divided.

During the week a novel 'mixed singles' event was held between men not better than four-sixths in a first class handicap and ladies who were three-sixths or better, and this proved very popular. In the semi-finals there were three ladies, with Lucia Valerio coming through to defeat M.K. Sweet in the final, 6–4 6–2. A cup was presented by Lord Charles Hope.

Entries at the Gallia Hotel meeting exceeded 100 and included new arrivals Brugnon, du Plaix, Fisher, Salm and Aimée Charpenal. Brugnon was outstanding and won all three titles. In the singles final he defeated Rogers, who for the most part played a sound game, but the Frenchman was decisive at the close to win, 6–8 6–0 6–4 4–6 6–0. De Minerbi unexpectedly beat Aeschliman, who was experimenting with a new grip, 6–3 6–0. At the same time, Rogers beat Hecht, 6–2 7–5. Early on, Brame Hillyard recorded a win against du Plaix who, leading 6–4 5–4, retired with a blistered hand.

Phyllis Satterthwaite repeated her previous week's victory over Lucia Valerio in the final, after an exhausting match lasting two and a half hours and running to 42 games, 5–7 7–5 10–8. The match consisted of long baseline rallies and occasional lobs. In the semi-final Phyllis Satterthwaite beat Aimée Charpenel, 6–0 7–5 and Lucia Valerio defeated Muriel Thomas, 6–2 6–2. Elizabeth Ryan did not compete in the singles, but won the doubles with Lucia Valerio and the mixed with Brugnon, the latter also taking the men's doubles with du Plaix.

After some below par performances over the past few weeks, Elizabeth Ryan recaptured her knack of winning when she claimed the singles title for the seventh time since 1920 at the Carlton Club meeting. Victory over Muriel Thomas in the semi-final, 6–0 6–1, certainly gave her revenge for an earlier failing and she went on to beat old rival, Phyllis Satterthwaite in the final, with much in hand, 6–2 6–4. The runner-up had dismissed the American, Miss Dorothy Andrus, 6–0 6–4. However, just as she was gaining form she contracted influenza and was forced to retire from both finals of the doubles, playing with Cilly Aussem and Jack Hillyard. This was the German's only event.

Cochet, also not too well, withdrew from the men's singles, which left Rogers an easier passage to take the title. He lost a set to Garcia, 7–5 4–6 6–4, a set to du Plaix, 6–3 2–6 6–3, before mastering Hecht in the last round, 6–3 6–3 6–2. The Czech had earlier notable wins over Aeschliman, 6–4 1–6 6–3 and del Bono, 7–5 6–4. Brugnon and Cochet won the doubles after two tough challenges, mainly from Jack Hillyard and Worm, who stood within two points of winning the match. The final against

Aeschliman and Rogers was equally taxing, ending in a 20–game third set.

The South of France Championships at Nice was the scene for Rogers to win his fifth singles title of the season. With the arrival of Boussus it appeared his run of success would end, but where Brugnon had conquered two weeks earlier, Boussus failed in a contest in which endurance was the deciding factor. The Frenchman started well in the final and after 3–4 in the opening set won 11 games in a row to lead 6–4 6–0 2–0. Rogers slowed the pace of the match and with superior stamina edged back and after a tight fourth set won the fifth, 6–0, in ten minutes. The final score was 4–6 0–6 6–4 6–4 6–0. In the semi-finals Boussus dismissed Hecht, 6–2 6–2 6–0, and Rogers after a very long and uninteresting baseline duel, beat du Plaix 7–5 7–5 9–7.

After Elizabeth Ryan retired in the third round, the singles title fell open to Phyllis Satterthwaite. She beat Dorothy Andrus in the semi-final, but not before 42 games had been played over two hours. The American's volleying and ground strokes were supreme but the Englishwoman's steadiness and patience told in the end, 11–9 5–7 6–4. In the final, Phyllis Satterthwaite comfortably strode through, 6–1 6–3, against Paulette Marjolett, who had reached that stage when Ida Adamaoff retired at 2–3, owing to blisters. Boussus and du Plaix won the doubles crown after a long marathon against Aeschliman and Worm, 6–3 1–6 2–6 11–9 6–3.

The following week on the circuit two tournaments were held simultaneously, the well-established one at Beaulieu and at Monte Carlo the new Monegasque Championships, under the auspices of the Monegasque Federation, held on the Condamine courts.

The entry at Beaulieu was not affected and many players competed in both tournaments. The men's singles was strengthened by the inclusion of Lesueur and Kingsley, plus a newcomer from England, John Olliff. Rogers was successful in winning once again but a five set final duel with du Plaix was necessary before the decision. Du Plaix squared the issue after losing the opening two sets and reached 3–1 in the fifth, but the Irishman braced himself to win the next five games and the match, 6–3 10–8 3–6 5–7

For her tenth consecutive season on the Riviera, Phyllis Satterthwaite produced her best ever record. She contested 11 singles finals and won six, at Cannes New Courts Club, Gallia Club, Nice, Beaulieu, Menton and Cannes Club. Seven doubles titles also came her way.

6–3. Olliff acclimatised well and beat Edouard Lotan, 6–1 6–4, to reach the semi-final, but here he could make little impression on Rogers and succumbed, 6–1 6–2. Du Plaix qualified for the final by beating Hecht, 6–3 6–4, despite the latter's fine play at the net. Kingsley was another earlier victim of du Plaix, 6–2 10–8. In early rounds an American, Bernard Law, scored unexpected wins over both Italians, de Minerbi and del Bono.

Phyllis Satterthwaite continued her run of success by winning the ladies' singles from Miss Mary Heeley, newly arrived from England. This was a very lengthy match with rallies lasting up to 50 strokes, but the winner mixing her game with lobs and drop shots made the score, 6–2 6–1. Mary Heeley was judged to have done well in the event when she passed Dorothy Andrus, 6–3 6–1, and Albina Korotvickova in the semi-final, 6–2 9–7. Phyllis Satterthwaite dropped a set to Mlle Leila Claude Anet in reaching the final, 3–6 6–4 6–1.

Two Yugoslavs, Franjo Kukuljevic and Franjo Schaeffer, won the men's doubles beating three strong pairs, del Bono and Gaslini, Jack Hillyard and Worm and in the final, Olliff and Rogers, 6–1 1–6 7–5 3–6 6–1. Elizabeth Ryan and Dorothy Andrus formed a strong partnership to win the ladies' doubles, an event where Mrs Fearnley-Whittingstall (Bennett) and Betty Nuthall made an appearance.

The tournament at the Condamine was held during the latter half of the week. Playing brilliantly, Enrique Maier, the Spanish Davis Cup player, beat Matejka, 6–4 6–1, Lesueur, 6–0 6–3, and in the final, Artens, 6–2 5–7 6–1 6–3, the latter having disposed of von Kehrling , 6–3 6–8 9–7.

The ladies' singles final between Simone Mathieu and Cilly Aussem was a great match which lasted for two hours. The Frenchwoman lost the first five games but won the next seven. She then eased up and lost the next set. There was then a sequence of deuces and Simone Mathieu led 5–2, but the German nearly caught her. In the end, two clever drop shots settled the issue at 7–5 3–6 6–4. Earlier, Simone Mathieu had beaten Ida Adamoff, 6–4 6–2, while Cilly Aussem was extended by Lucia Valerio, 8–6 6–4, and Colette Rosambert, 6–2 6–4. The doubles events were won by Boussus and Lesueur and Cilly Aussem and Lucia Valerio.

As usual the main Monte Carlo meeting attracted a top class entry from countries spread around Europe. The main focus of interest centred on the two international competitions for doubles, which in the case of the Butler Trophy had 23 pairs entered. Although unexpected, Spain's victory by Maier and Francisco Sindreu was well-deserved as they moved round by round to defeat von Kehrling and Emil Gabrowitz in the final, 6–4 6–4 6–2. The runners-up had removed the favourites, Boussus and Cochet, in the round before in five sets, 6–4 4–6 7–5 1–6 6–2, when both their opponents were well below their best. The Hungarians had also eliminated

The finalists of the Beaumont Cup, played at Monte Carlo, were all British, with Muriel Thomas and Mary Heeley (left) losing to Betty Nuthall and Eileen Fearnley Whittingstall in the final. Mrs Beaumont, the donor of the Cup, is in the centre.

Jack Hillyard and Kingsley earlier over five sets. The winners had needed five sets to advance over Olliff and Rogers, 6–2 6–2 3–6 8–10 6–4. Overall there were many long matches. The final of the Beaumont Cup was an all British affair with Betty Nuthall and Eileen Fearnley-Whittingstall comfortably defeating Mary Heeley and Muriel Thomas, 6–2 6–3. The winners were pushed hard by Colette Rosambert and Doris Metaxa in the previous round, 8–6 8–6.

Rogers' run of success came to an end in the final of the men's singles when Cochet made the Prince of Monaco's Shield his own property in recognition of his third win in the event. Rogers had beaten Worm, 6–1 8–6, Maier, 6–3 8–6 and Boussus, to face in the final, Cochet, who was the complete master on the day, and won in straight sets, 7–5 6–2 6–4. However, the Irishman was, to some degree, handicapped by a muscular strain. Cochet had dropped a set to du Plaix, 8–10 8–6 6–3, before beating Artens in the semi-final, 6–3 6–2.

Simone Mathieu won the Duke of Connaught's Vase by ousting Phyllis Satterthwaite in the final of the ladies' singles, but the match was on a knife edge in the deciding set when the Englishwoman was 3–4 and 0–40 down and then recovered to lead 5–4 and 30–15, requiring just two points for victory. However, the wind carried several of her lobs out of court and she yielded the match at 4–6 6–4 7–5. Phyllis Satterthwaite played exceedingly well to eliminate Cilly Aussem in the round before, 6–2 6–4, while Simone

Mathieu took time to defeat Doris Metaxa, 4–6 6–4 6–1. In other finals the winners were von Kehrling and Artens, Phyllis Satterthwaite and Muriel Thomas, and Cochet and Eileen Fearnley-Whittingstall winning for the third time.

The Riviera Championships at Menton were interrupted by rain on the Friday and Saturday and play was finally concluded on the Tuesday. Both the favourites for the singles' honours were beaten, Rogers going down to Garcia in the semi-final of the men's singles, 2–6 6–1 9–7, and Simone Mathieu, surprised by Phyllis Satterthwaite, who continually lobbed, in the final of the ladies' division, 7–5 6–4.

Von Kehrling won the singles title for the third occasion, without losing a set and in the final crushed Garcia by 6–2 6–3 6–1. Artens, who might have extended the winner, withdrew in the semi-final.

Seasoned campaigner, Bela von Kehrling of Hungary, won the Riviera Championships at Menton for the third occasion to retire the Cup. He also won the doubles and mixed doubles for the fourth time.

The holder of the ladies' singles title, Cilly Aussem, fell in a very long quarter-final match lasting two hours to Lucia Valerio, 7–5 5–7 8–6. At that same stage, Phyllis Satterthwaite beat Dorothy Andrus, 3–6 6–4 6–1, Betty Nuthall defeated Ida Adamoff, 4–6 7–5 6–1 and Simone Mathieu ousted Mary Heeley, 6–1 6–3. In the next round Simone Mathieu proved too fluent for Betty Nuthall, 7–5 6–3, and Phyllis Satterthwaite gradually overcame Lucia Valerio, 4–6 6–4 6–1. Von Kehrling completed a 'triple' in the doubles with Rogers and Cilly Aussem. Rogers and Betty Nuthall won the Coupe des Nations event.

After four weeks on the Riviera, Betty Nuthall found her best form at the second Nice tournament when she defeated Simone Mathieu in the final of the ladies' singles, 6–0 3–6 8–6. She won the first seven games but then errors began to creep in to her game and the Frenchwoman evened the match. In the deciding set Betty Nuthall found herself 3–5 and match point down, but her fighting spirit allowed her to draw level and eventually pull the match out of the fire at 6–0 3–6 8–6. In the semi-final, Betty Nuthall beat Ida Adamoff in two love sets, while Simone Mathieu beat Lolette Payot, 7–5 6–2.

The men's singles title was taken by Aslangul who beat Worm, 3–6 6–4 6–2, and then Aeschliman in the final, 0–6 2–6 6–3 6–3 6–2, a notable recovery after a poor start. Elizabeth Ryan played in the two doubles, gaining success with Cilly Aussem but losing with Worm in the quarter-final of the mixed event.

The tournament at the Cannes Club was affected by rain for two days but was successfully concluded by the Tuesday. Rogers was back to his winning ways and captured the Côte d'Azur Championships, but had great difficulty in the final overcoming Aeschliman, who led by 2 sets to 1 and only yielded 9–7 in the fifth set. The final score was 1–6 6–2 4–6 6–1 9–7. Both semi-finals had comfortable wins, Rogers over Ignacy Tloczynski of Poland and Aeschliman passing Landau, 6–4 6–4. All the leading English players had returned home.

Phyllis Satterthwaite won the ladies' singles event without losing a set and so recorded her sixth win of the season. Lolette Payot survived a strenuous match against Muriel Thomas, 5–7 6–1 7–5, before easily losing in the final, 6–2 6–0. Jack Hillyard and Rogers won the men's doubles and Cilly Aussem and Elizabeth Ryan, not entering the singles, comfortably won the ladies' event.

Japanese visitors to the Beau Site Hotel tournament met with remarkable success by winning the men's singles and doubles event. Hyotare Satoh's victory over Rogers in the singles final took most spectators by surprise, but once he had overcome the first set defeat he eased through to win, 3–6 6–4 6–1 8–6. In the semi-finals Satoh beat Tloczynski, 6–3 6–3, while Rogers beat Jean Couiteas of France, 3–6 6–2 6–0, after eliminating the other Japanese competitor, Jiro Satoh.

Phyllis Satterthwaite's long line of singles' successes in the season came to an end when she was beaten by Cilly Aussem in the semi-final of the ladies' singles, 6–1 6–0. Lolette Payot emphasised her advance to the front rank by defeating Helen Nicolopoulo in the other semi-final before losing to Cilly Aussem, 6–3 6–3. Elizabeth Ryan won two doubles events with Cilly Auseem and Rogers.

At the St Raphael tournament, Hyotare Satoh found his form quickly to win the men's singles title, beating Louis Haench of Germany in the final, 6–3 8–6 6–4. In the quarter-final Worm passed Jiro Satoh, 6–2 3–6 6–3, but then fell to Haench, 6–2 6–2. In the other semi-final Hyotare beat André Merlin of France, 6–1 5–7 6–2.

Albina Korotvickova brought off her best win of the season by ousting Helen Nicolopoulo in the semi-final, 6–2 10–8, but could not reach the same heights in the last match against Ida Adamoff and faded, 6–3 6–4. Muriel Thomas had done well to run the eventual winner in the other semi-final, 6–1 5–7 6–2. In the doubles, the two Japanese won the men's event, Elizabeth Ryan and Muriel Thomas the ladies' division and Hyotare Satoh and Muriel Thomas the mixed.

The second Monte Carlo meeting, held at the Country Club early in April, ran smoothly. The men's singles title was taken by Jiro Satoh, who beat the up and coming Frenchman, Marcel Bernard in the final, 6–4

Cilly Aussem, the German No.1 player, making her fourth visit to the Riviera late in the season, won three singles titles, Beau Site Hotel, Miramar Club and the Easter meeting at Monte Carlo. Just under three months later she became Wimbledon singles champion.

6–2 6–2. Unfortunately, Bernard had just completed a five set final in an under-21 event and was, naturally, a little weary.

Cilly Aussem, playing her best tennis for some time, lost only five games to Lili de Alvarez in the final of the ladies' singles, 6–1 6–4, the latter being the holder. Phyllis Satterthwaite, not in the singles draw, won the doubles with Mme Sylvia Henrotin (Jung- Lafaurie), but lost in the final of the mixed doubles with Jack Hillyard. Lesueur and Gentien were doubles winners. The Prix de Famille was won by Beni and Rosie Berthet.

Cilly Aussem followed up her success of a week earlier by winning the Mirimar Club gathering by beating Sylvia Henrotin in the final,

6–2 6–0. The winner had just previously beaten Muriel Thomas, 4–6 6–2 6–2, while Sylvia Henrotin had recorded a score of 4–0 ret'd against Frl. E. Sander of Germany.

Hyotare Satoh beat his namesake Jiro in the men's final, 6–3 6–2 5–7 3–6 6–3. To reach the final, Hyotare beat Minoru Kawachi, 6–1 6–2, while Jiro beat Lesueur, 6–1 6–0. Earlier Kawachi had passed Aeschliman, 6–4 6–3, and Hyotare had the better of Kukuljevic, 6–2 6–4.

Sylvia Henrotin won the two doubles, with Cilly Aussem and Worm, while Hyotare and Kawachi took the men's division after a strenuous battle against Aeschliman and Jack Hillyard in the final, 9–11 6–4 6–4 6–4. A couple of months later Cilly Aussem reached the pinnacle of her career by winning the ladies' singles title at Wimbledon.

The last tournament of the season took place at the Beaulieu Club from 20th to 26th April, when France won both the singles titles. Lesueur won the men's competition, defeating Law in the final, 6–4 7–5 6–3, while Sylvia Henrotin broke up Phyllis Satterthwaite's baseline defence by a judicious net attack to claim the ladies' title, 7–5 6–2. Together the finalists won the ladies' doubles, but a big surprise came when Kukuljevic and Mme Bruyn Kops won the mixed title after beating the well-tried pair, Jack Hillyard and Phyllis Satterthwaite in the semi-final and Schaeffer and Muriel Thomas in the last match, 6–2 4–6 6–3.

At a meeting of the Tennis Regional Commission of the Côte d'Azur a resolution was carried that all Clubs on the Riviera adopt the same price entry for open tournaments – 35FF per player for each championship event and 25FF per player for handicap events.

# 1932
# Dearth of English Competitors

The season began in a moderate way with a Christmas tournament staged at the Juan-les-Pins Club. The entry was small and confined to two open events and two handicap singles. Worm had matters well in hand in winning the men's singles, despite dropping the opening set in the final to John Leader, an English schoolboy from Tiverton, 4–6 6–2 6–4, after a win over Magrane in the round before, 6–0 6–1. Leader had advanced with a surprise win over Aeschliman, 6–4 3–6 6–2, while good volleying saw him through against an American, Warwick, in the semi-final, 6–4 6–3. Aeschliman and Worm comfortably captured the doubles. On Christmas Day an exhibition match was arranged in which Aeschliman and Muriel Thomas beat Worm and Cosette Saint Omer Roy, 6–2 6–2.

At the New Year meeting, held at the Beau Site Hotel, Miss Sheila Hewitt, the British junior champion, put up a very creditable performance in winning the ladies' singles title, particularly as she was not acclimatised to the conditions present on the Riviera. In the final she lost a close first set to Muriel Thomas, before gaining control to lose just three further games to win, 8–10, 6–2 6–1. Her driving was her best weapon. In the semi-final she was given a walkover by Phyllis Satterthwaite, who was suffering from a heel injury, but in the round before she had disposed of Cosette Saint Omer Roy, 6–0 4–6 6–3.

Rogers retained the men's singles title by beating Worm comfortably in the final, 6–1 6–2 11–9. Earlier the Irishman was extended to 34 games by Warwick, 7–5 5–7 6–4, before disposing of Leader, 6–3 6–3. Worm had passed Aeschliman to reach the last round, 6–4 6–0. Rogers won a second title with Landau, while Muriel Thomas notched up two wins with Phyllis Satterthwaite and Aeschliman.

The second Monegasque Championships, held on the Condamine Courts, were held up by rain for three days but, nevertheless, the meeting was brought to a successful conclusion by the Sunday as the entry was quite small. Rogers pursued a leisurely path through the men's singles, but dropped a set to Andrea de Ahmerar of France, 5–7 6–3 6–4. In the semi-final he defeated Warwick, 6–4 7–5, before winning the title from Max Ellmer in four sets, 6–4 2–6 9–7 6–2.

From an entry of 13, Elizabeth Ryan and Phyllis Satterthwaite met across the net in the final of the singles, with the unexpected outcome of the

American having it all her own way, 6–1 6–3. There was no ladies' doubles event but in the two competitions played, the victors were Aeschliman and Worm and Rogers and Elizabeth Ryan.

The first of the Cannes big three meetings at the New Courts LTC followed, where the five events carried for the first time the title of Mediterranean Championships.

Rogers won another singles title after a series of prolonged matches, eliminating Paul Jourde of France, 8–6 5–5 ret'd, Lotan, 4–6 7–5 7–5, and Ellmer, 7–5 4–6 6–0, ahead of reaching the final. Here he met du Plaix, who had received a walkover from Aeschliman and he had to battle long and hard to survive at 5–7 6–3 6–4 5–7 6–3.

Sheila Hewitt distinguished herself once more by reaching the semi-final of the singles and pushing Lucia Valerio to two twelve-game sets. In the final the indefatigable Italian outlasted Ida Adamoff in three long sets, 7–5 4–6 6–4. Rogers, in great form, won a triple with Alberto del Bono and Elizabeth Ryan. The latter, who did not compete in the singles, also won the mixed doubles with Muriel Thomas.

Unusually, by the end of January, not so many English competitors had arrived on the Riviera but, to make amends, some prominent entries were received from other countries to make a total of around 80 competing at the Gallia Club tournament.

Brugnon and Elizabeth Ryan were back in singles competition. The Frenchman and Rogers were the outstanding players in the men's division but unfortunately the Irishman was compelled to withdraw from the final without taking the court, due to illness. In the semi-final Brugnon comfortably passed Ellmer, 6–2 6–3, while the Irishman took a similar path against du Plaix, 6–2 6–4.

Lucia Valerio repeated her win of the previous week over Ida Adamoff, 6–4 6–2, to reach the final but, as expected, Elizabeth Ryan's volleys were too accurate as she recorded a straightforward victory, her fifth at the tournament, 6–3 6–3. Muriel Thomas excelled in taking a set from the American, 7–5 4–6 6–4. Elizabeth Ryan won both doubles events, in partnership with Muriel Thomas and Rogers.

A week later at the Carlton Club the outstanding feature was the semi-final singles match between Sheila Hewitt and Elizabeth Ryan. The English girl drove with great accuracy, particularly on the forehand side, to take the opening set, 11–9, but the American readjusted her game to run out, 6–3

Elizabeth Ryan set a formidable record by winning the Carlton Club singles title for the eighth time since 1920. In the final she beat Elsa Riboli of Italy, a newcomer to the scene.

6–4. Sheila Hewitt showed her class earlier by eliminating two Americans, Elizabeth Corbiere, 6–3 6–2, and Mrs Dorothy Burke (Andrus), 6–3 6–1. There was great interest in this event by the first appearance this season of the Italian No.3, Elsa Riboli. She beat Phyllis Satterthwaite in the semi-final, 4–6 6–1 6–4, but could only collect three games against Elizabeth Ryan, 6–2 6–1. This was the American's eighth singles win at the Carlton Club since 1920.

Brugnon and Rogers duly reached their anticipated final of the singles, but the Frenchman was badly off form and lost in three sets, 6–1 8–6 9–7. In the last four, Brugnon defeated Aeschliman, 6–4 7–5, and Rogers passed du Plaix, 6–2 6–3. Rogers and Elizabeth both won two doubles titles.

The South of France Championships, now established as the first meeting held at Nice during February were, as usual, very successful. The topic of conversation was Rogers' first singles defeat of the season when he fell to Brugnon after five sets in the final. The Irishman's steady play enabled him to lead by two sets to one but after the interval was hustled off his game, mainly by Brugnon mixing the pace of his shots with a great deal of spin, 6–2 3–6 2–6 6–3 6–2. In the semi-final the winner raced through Aeschliman, 6–1 6–0 6–3, whereas Rogers dropped a set before seeing off del Bono, 6–2 2–6 6–2 6–2.

Sheila Hewitt again showed her great potential in passing Elsie Haycroft, 6–1 4–6 6–2, and Mlle Edith Belliard of France, 6–3 6–1, but was halted in the semi-final by Phyllis Satterthwaite's determination and guile. After losing the opening set, 1–6, the youngster led 4–1, only to be caught eventually at 5 all. Games went with service until 11-all, when Phyllis improved her control to edge out 13–11. Elizabeth Ryan reached the final without losing a set, beating Elsa Riboli quite easily, 6–4 6–1, but then found Phyllis in great resistive mood and lobbing well, which required her to display her best to triumph, 6–3 1–6 6–2.

Unusually, Rogers failed to win a doubles title, with the spoils going to Aeschliman and Lotan, Elizabeth Ryan and Muriel Thomas, their fifth success on the circuit, and Brugnon and Phyllis Satterthwaite.

Beaulieu attracted the best entry of the season, where many European male players were anxious to test their skills before the following week's tournament at Monte Carlo, which staged the now prestigious international doubles event.

The list included Artens, Jaime Durrall (Spain), von Kehrling, Gabrowitz, Maier, Kukuljevic, Forenc Marsalek (Czechoslovakia), Hecht and many others. Irrespective, Rogers was installed as favourite for the singles title, but von Kehrling had other ideas and showing his very best form eliminated the Irishman in the semi-final, 7–9 6–1 6–3. Rogers was erratic at times. Maier's rapid rise in the game showed as he moved steadily

# Carlton Tennis Club

### ORDRE DES JEUX POUR AUJOURD'HUI SAMEDI

—::—

**9 heures 45.** — Batmanoff c. Mins (H.) ; Crandell c. de Miramon (H.) ; Mlle Moreau c. Mme de Tuckary (H.) ; Mrs Smallwood c. Mlle E. Thomasson (H.) ; Capt. Cole et Aeschliman c. Castori et Kuhn (H.).

**10 heures 30.** — **Finale Championnat Double Messieurs :** Jacques Brugnon et Emmanuel du Plaix c. G. Lyttelton Rogers et Worm ; **Demi-Finale Championnat Simple Dames :** Mrs Satterthwaite c. Mlle Riboli (C.) ; Mme Garcia c. Comtesse de la Rochefoucauld ou Mlle Vogel (H.) ; Dr Warden et de Miramon c. Blondeau et Durenne (H.) ; Castori c. Batmanoff ou Mins (H.).

**11 heures 15.** — Miss Ryan et Miss Thomas c. Mrs Walter Burke et Mrs Corbiere (C.).

**11 heures 30.** — Marquise du Crozet c. Mme Garcia ou gagnante (H.) ; Breitenter et Landell c. Castori et Kuhn ou Capt. Cole et Aeschliman (H.) ; Miss Platt et Sir Albert Stern c. Mlle Thomasson et Mathieu (H.).

**14 heures.** — Mlle Adamoff et Brugnon c. Miss Thomas et du Plaix ou Mrs Satterthwaite et Worm (C.) ; Mlle Moreau ou Mme de Tuckary c. Mrs Smallwood ou Mlle E. Thomasson (H.) ; Finale handicap double messieurs.

**14 heures 45.** — Miss Ryan et Rogers c. Miss Hewitt et Aeschliman (C.) ; Finale handicap simple messieurs ; Mrs Smallwood et Dr Warden c. Mme de Tuckary et Batmanoff (H.).

GRUVES & Cⁱᵉ - CANNES

The programme of matches at the Carlton Club for Saturday, 6th February. There are many famous names listed.

through the draw, beating Leader, 7–5 6–1, and Hecht, 6–2 6–3, to reach the semi-final where he overcame du Plaix, 6–3 3–6 6–0. In the final von Kehrling contested the first two sets on level terms, attacking Maier's weaker backhand to advantage, but he was unable to maintain this pace and when the Spaniard launched a net attack in the fourth set he was forced to yield, 6–4 7–9 6–1 6–1. The event contained many good matches, including Leader beating del Bono, 6–1 7–9 6–3.

There was not much doubt about the finalists in the ladies' singles, with Elizabeth Ryan facing Phyllis Satterthwaite. The match was not close and the American won with great ease, 6–0 6–1. The runner-up's contest in the round before intrigued the gallery when Mlle Jadwiga Jedrzejowska of Poland, playing her first meeting of the season, took the first set, running for everything, but she then became a victim of her opponent's lobbing campaign to go down, 5–7 6–2 6–3. In the doubles, Elizabeth Ryan and Muriel Thomas were invincible once more.

The Monte Carlo Country Club, hosting the Monte Carlo Championships plus the Butler and Beaumont trophies, was now well-established as the main tournament attraction on the Riviera each season. Certainly the two international doubles competitions had increased the prestige of the week with many of Europe's leading players anxious to take part. The patronage of the Grimaldi family was also a telling factor.

Roderick Menzel of Czechoslovakia, making his first appearance of the year at an open tournament, was in great form winning the Monte Carlo singles by defeating four Davis Cup players. The following week at Menton he was in superb form again to win the singles title.

France excelled at the meeting by winning four out of the seven main events. Cochet did not defend the men's singles title, which he had won for the third consecutive time the previous year, reserving his energies for the doubles. In the Butler Trophy, Brugnon and Cochet were the outstanding pair, losing one set only in final to Marsalek and Menzel, 3–6 6–2 6–4 6–2. Cochet thus recorded his fourth victory in this event in seven years and his third with Brugnon. The trophy attracted 21 pairs and with the quality available, some exciting matches took place.

The Beaumont Cup was also a triumph for France, with Simone Mathieu and Colette Rosembert just getting the better of the American pair, Dorothy Burke and Elizabeth Ryan in the final, 8–6 1–6 6–3. The best British pair, Sheila Hewitt and Muriel Thomas, put up a tremendous fight against the winners in the semi-final, losing in two advantage sets, 12–10 7–5. At the same stage the Americans saw off Elsa Riboli and Lucia Valerio, 6–3 6–3.

In the men's singles, Roderick Menzel, making his first appearance in open tournament play this season, thoroughly deserved his victory by beating four Davis Cup players, Gabrowitz, 6–2 6–2, Artens, 6–4 6–3, von

Kehrling, 10–8 7–5, Peters, 4–6 6–4 6–3, and then Rogers in the final, 6–4 7–5 6–2. The Czechoslovakian played cleverly into the strong wind during the last match as his opponent struggled to keep him from the net. Rogers played well to defeat Maier in the semi-final, 6–4 1–6 6–4.

Sheila Hewitt proved she was capable of performing to the highest standard on the big occasion in beating Jadwiga Jedrzejowska in a long baseline duel, 6–4 7–5, outdriving Lolette Payot, 6–4 6–4, and Ida Adamoff, 6–4 6–2, to reach the final. Simone Mathieu, defending her title, reached the last stage comfortably, her best win being over Lucia Valerio, 6–3 6–4. In the final, the determined French lady had too much experience but, nevertheless, was given a good fight by her opponent before winning at 6–1 6–4. The winners of the doubles were Brugnon and Maier, Dorothy Burke and Lucia Valerio and Cochet and Colette Rosambert.

The singles winners the week before at Monte Carlo continued their domination at the Riviera Championships held at the Menton Club. Neither was extended as previously, as Maier, Peters and Hecht dropped out of the men's events and Elizabeth Ryan, Sheila Hewitt and Leila Claude Anet from the ladies.

The big surprise of the meeting was the defeat of Rogers by André Merlin in the semi-final of the singles, 6–0 2–6 8–6. The Frenchman led 5–1 in the deciding set before Rogers fought back to 5–all. Merlin found difficulty in assuming the attack against Menzel in the final and could only win three games in the first two sets. Menzel eased up in the third but came back with renewed energy after the interval to win, 6–3 6–0 4–6 6–4. He was not under any pressure to beat Schaeffer in the semi-final, 6–1 6–3.

Simone Mathieu was far too good for the other ladies and her powerful drive from both sides kept Lucia Valerio on the run in the final. The latter tried to break up the French lady's game by lobbing, but to no avail and the score of 6–2 6–3 summed up the situation. Sheila Hewitt rested from the singles, where Colette Rosambert had a notable win over Phyllis Satterthwaite, while another surprise was the defeat of Lolette Payot by Ada Adamoff, 6–3 6–1. In the last four, Simone Mathieu beat Ida Adamoff, 6–1 6–2, while Lucia Valerio defeated Colette Rosambert.

Simone Mathieu won three other titles, the doubles with Colette Rosambert, the mixed doubles and the 'Coupe de Nations' international event, both with André Martin-Legeay. The King of Sweden took part in the handicap events. Towards the end of the week rain interfered with the play, which was concluded on the Monday. This was said to be the first time a tournament had overrun during the season.

The second Nice tournament, held at the Parc Imperial, obtained a far weaker entry than the week before and provided forecasters with a more certain bet. De Stefani, making his first visit of the season to the coast, used the week as practice for his forthcoming Davis Cup matches but, as the opposition was not too compelling, he generally sailed through to win the men's singles title. He did drop a set to Lotan in the semifinal, 6–0 6–4 3–6 6–2, but was never really concerned and in the final was extended only slightly at the start by the rapidly improving Tloczynski, 7–5 6–0 6–2. The Pole had played well against Martin-Legeay, who won the first set by installing himself at the net, but thereafter the Pole took control, 4–6 6–2 7–5 6–4.

Much of the interest in the ladies' singles was the continued improvement of Colette Rosambert who beat Phyllis Satterthwaite for a second time in as many weeks, 6–0 7–5, to reach the final. Simone Mathieu was given a hard match by the rising Rosie Berthet, However, in the final, Simone's well-balanced game and powerful drives pushed Colette into many errors for a 6–3 6–3 victory. Switzerland won the men's and mixed doubles, with Hector Fisher being the prime reason. His superior volleying combined well with Aeschliman and Lolette Payot. The strong combination of Phyllis Satterthwaite and Muriel Thomas won the ladies' doubles with a noteworthy victory over Simone Mathieu and Colette Rosambert in the final, 6–4 2–6 6–2.

There was a very disappointing conclusion to the Cannes Club meeting for the Côte d'Azur Championships when rain towards the end of the week obliged de Stefani to withdraw from the final of the men's singles and doubles finals in order to return to Rome and Davis Cup commitments. Tloczynski, therefore, received a walkover in both events. He had performed well to pass de Bono, 6– 3 6–4, and his colleague, Maks Stolarow, 6–2 4–6 6–1.

Jadwiga Jedrzejowska gave Poland a third title by winning the ladies' singles, her first singles of importance outside her own country, by achieving fine wins over Ida Adamoff, 4–6 6–2 6–3, and in the final, Muriel Thomas, 6–3 6–2. The runner-up did well in eliminating Lolette Payot, 6–4 6–2. Aeschliman and Lolette Payot always had the edge in capturing the mixed doubles.

Rogers returned to competition on the Riviera to win the Cannes Championship for the first time at the Beau Site Hotel, towards the end of March. His task was far from simple as he was fully extended in the final by Haersch, who carried him to 55 games. The Irishman had to be at his best to come back from a deficit of 2 sets to 1 and then find his way through two long advantage sets. The German set the mood by defeating Tloczynski in the round before, 9–7 6–1, while Rogers with great confidence outplayed Stolarow, 6–4 6–3. Gerbeault made a welcome appearance after many years, enjoying the pleasures of yachting, to beat Leader, 4–6 6–4 7–5, before falling to Haersch, 6–1 6–1.

# SAINT-RAPHAËL

## VALESCURE
## BOULOURIS
## LE TRAYAS
## ANTHÉOR
## AGAY

J. Munier

MOULLOT, MARSEILLE

Jadwiga Jedrzejowska met Lolette Payot for the first time ever in the final of the ladies' singles and a long and close match resulted, both trying to force and win points with aggressive forehand drives. In the end, Lolette Payot won, 9–7 7–5. The winner had accounted for Muriel Thomas, 6–4 6–1, and the runner-up, Dorothy Burke, 7–5 2–6 6–2. Aeschliman won two doubles titles with Lotan and Lolette Payot and in a tremendous struggle for the ladies' doubles crown, Dorothy Burke and Muriel Thomas eventually put aside Ida Adamoff and Jacqueline Goldschmidt, 6–3 16–18 6–2 – the highest number of games played in a set during the season.

There were shocks in both singles events at the Beausoleil Championships staged at Monte Carlo. Rogers was beaten in the final of the men's by the French No.12 player, Beni Berthet. The Irishman led by 2 sets to 1 but could not thwart the net attack of his young opponent, to lose in five sets, 4–6 6–1 1–6 6–4 6–4. Berthet beat Martin-Legeay in the semi-final, 6–3 4–6 7–5, the latter having surprisingly disposed of Paul Feret, 6–2 6–1.

Simone Mathieu suffered her first singles reverse at the hands of Lolette Payot in the final. The Frenchwoman showed poor form whereas the winner, losing a close opening set, allowed just a further six games to be taken from her, 5–7 6–4 6–2. In earlier contests, Rosie Berthet narrowly passed Lucia Valerio, 6–4 2–6 7–5, and Lolette beat Dorothy Burke, 6–3 4–6 6–1. Winners of the doubles were Feret and Rogers, Simone Mathieu and Colette Rosambert and Martin-Legeay and Simone Mathieu. The Prix de Famille event was taken by Berthet and Rosie Berthet.

The Cannes New Courts Club held a second meeting early in April but, as expected at that time of the season, the number of entries was down.

Jiro Satoh and Sylvia Henrotin each recorded three victories. The Japanese defeated Aeschliman in the final of the singles, 6–3 10–8 6–2, and paired with Rogers to win the doubles. Sylvia's victim in the singles final was Ida Adamoff, who was ranked one place above her in France, 6–2 6–3, and joined with Muriel Thomas to take the doubles from Ida Adamoff and Rosie Berthet, 3–6 6–0 6–2. In the final of the mixed doubles, the combination of both singles winners received a walkover.

The last tournament of the season at the Juan-les-Pins Club featured another Japanese player, Hyotare Satoh who, returning from India, soon acclimatised to the conditions to capture the singles title from Rogers in the final, 6–4 4–6 6–1. On the way he beat Gittings, 6–3 6–3, and H. Uthmoller of Germany, 6–4 6–2, the latter responsible for eliminating Aeschliman, 8–6 6–4. Rogers was given a tough outing by Garcia, 11–9 4–6 6–1.

Ida Adamoff won the singles final overcoming Muriel Thomas, 6–4 7–5, the loser bringing off a notable win over Sylvia Henrotin in the round before, 5–7 6–2 6–4. Muriel won two doubles titles with Aeschliman and

Sylvia. Unusually, the Beaulieu Club was scheduled to hold a tournament on the same dates as the Juan-les-Pins meeting, but this was cancelled, as was the Miramar Club gathering arranged for 11th–17th April.

Sometime after the conclusion of the season a report was issued mentioning that the Riviera suffered from a dearth of visiting players through the acute financial depression and the majority of those who attended were French. This was certainly the case regarding English players of which there was an unusual shortage, so different from a couple or so years earlier when the majority of the top-ranked or up-and-coming players were present for a few weeks.

Reference was also made to the 1932/33 season when it was anticipated that larger entries would be received in spite of the counter-diaries of the Italian Riviera and a movement to promote a series of tournaments in Spain during February and March by a Mr Ernest Willy, who was known as the 'godfather of tennis' in Spain.

At the beginning of the season the last French Professional Championships was played at the Beaulieu Club on 7th to 10th January, with the singles being won by Karel Kozeluh. The event was subsequently transferred to Paris.

# 1933
# Five Singles to Lolette Payot,
# Four to Sheila Hewitt

For the first time the round of tournaments for the season commenced at the Provencal Club at Antibes during the Christmas week. There was a surprise result on the last day when Ellmer beat Rogers in the final of the singles, 6–4 6–4, but mention must be made that the Irishman appeared to be affected by a fall when he met Aeschliman during the semi-final.

Two French ladies fought out the singles final with Paulette de Saint Ferréol, a highly ranked second series player, defeating Cosette Saint Omer Roy, 6–3 6–4. There was no men's doubles contest, but Rogers teamed up with Muriel Thomas to take the mixed title.

The following meeting, held on the courts of the Beau Site Hotel, was postponed for a day by bad weather and only completed by the second Wednesday. Rogers avenged his defeat the week before by Ellmer in the singles final, where he required a total of 59 games. The Swiss led by 2 sets to 1 and in the fifth set reached 6–5 and 30 love before Rogers, who displayed better stamina, rallied to win the last three games, saving a match point on the way, 5–7 6–2 3–6 10–8 7–5. Rogers was involved in another long match in the semi-final in dispatching Aeschliman, 8–6 1–6 8–6, where the loser actually won more games. The fitness of Rogers was a key factor which he attributed to a recent course of physical training.

The surprise match of the gathering was the defeat of Aeschliman and Cochet in the final of the doubles by Lotan and Rogers, 1–6 1–6 6–4 7–5 6–4. Everyone watching expected to see Cochet assert himself in the final set, but it was not to be. The Frenchman did not contest any other event, being busy at the Monte Carlo Country Club making a film demonstrating the strokes of the game.

Phyllis Sattherthwaite proved to be by far the strongest lady competitor and won the singles with ease, beating Cosette Saint Omer Roy in the final, 6–3 6–1, and joining with Muriel Thomas to win the doubles. The latter, with Rogers, were the best mixed pair.

The Juan-les-Pins tournament was cancelled so the next meeting on the list was the third Monegasque Championships played on the Condamine Courts. The winner of the men's singles was Vladimir Landau, who beat Jack Hillyard, one of the few Englishmen competing, in the semi-final,

8–6 6–2, and was then given the title when Lotan retired from the final. The latter had beaten d'Adhemar, 6–1 6–4.

Phyllis Satterthwaite had only one testing contest in the ladies' singles, being extended by Edith Belliard in the final, 6–4 7–5. There was a very strange score for a final, when Aeschliman and Lotan beat Jean Rouillot of France and John Gittings (USA), 6–0 6–0 6–0. The reason for this was difficult to explain except that the losing pair had won a very strenuous encounter in the morning by disposing of Hillyard and Landau, 9–7 6–3 6–4. Elizabeth Ryan made her first appearance of the season taking part with Hillyard to annex the mixed doubles.

Sheila Hewitt opened her Riviera campaign in grand style by winning the ladies' singles at the Cannes New Courts LTC. After a couple of days practice at Nice, without dropping a set, she brought off three good victories in succession, Dorothy Burke, 8–6 6–2, Phyllis Satterthwaite, 6–4 6–4 and in the final, Muriel Thomas, 6–4 6–3. The runner-up had beaten Edith Belliard in the round before, 6–3 6–2. Elizabeth Ryan stood out.

Rogers reached his fourth singles final in a row and confirmed his Beau Site Hotel victory over Aeschliman, this time by a wider margin, 3–6 6–4 6–4 6–2. Rogers and Elizabeth Ryan both won two doubles titles.

Brugnon made his first trip to the Riviera for the season at the Gallia Club and in good form won the cup for the third year in a row, beating Aeschliman and Ellmer in the two concluding rounds. The former pressed him hard, particularly in the opening set, before losing, 7–5 6–2, while the latter made openings from his back court play, but quite often failed to take advantage. The final score was 6–3 1–6 7–5 6–3. Ellmer beat Rogers for the second time this season in the semi-final, 6–2 7–5.

Sheila Hewitt was not extended in winning the ladies' singles title. She did not drop a set and her hardest match was defeating Annemarie Lowenthal in the semi-final, 7–5 6–3, while in the final she overwhelmed Muriel Thomas by the speed of her driving, 6–4 6–0. Cilly Aussem made her first appearance on the coast this year and paired with Elizabeth Ryan, but they were unexpectedly beaten in the final by Dorothy Burke and Muriel Thomas, 6–3 3–6 6–4. The losers did not compete in the singles.

Sheila Hewitt won her third singles title in as many weeks by beating Cilly Aussem in the final of the Cannes Carlton Club tournament. This was the best win of her career, a feature being the manner in which she fought back to win the third set. After losing the opening two games,

After creating a good impression in her first visit to the coast the year before, Sheila Hewitt returned to reach quite an extraordinary level of play as she entered four tournaments and won the singles at each. In the finals she defeated Muriel Thomas at the Cannes New Courts Club and Gallia Club and Cilly Aussem at the Carlton Club and Nice.

Sheila won the next nine, but at this stage she began to waver and was caught at 3 all. Eventually the set went to the German, 8–7, after Sheila had forfeited a match point on a net cord. In the last set, Cilly came within two points of victory at 6–5, before her opponent won the next three games by a wide margin. The tense battle had lasted 90 minutes. Apparently, Cilly had been well prepared, having practised for some weeks beforehand and then competing at the Gallia meeting.

Earlier in the day the men's singles title was decided and this brought a shock result when Aeschliman overcame Brugnon in three sets, 7–5 6–2 6–4. The Swiss player's unorthodox shots were under perfect control, which seemed to disturb his opponent. Rogers was surprisingly dismissed in the quarter-final by an 18-year old Dutchman, Willem Karsten, whose chopped backhand and effective volleying worried the Irishman, who in the end was narrowly beaten, 6–4 2–6 7–5. In the semi-final, Aeschliman mastered Karsten, 7–5 8–6. Cilly Aussem again paired with Elizabeth Ryan but for the second week failed to withstand Dorothy Burke and Muriel Thomas in the final, 7–5 2–6 7–5.

Sheila Hewitt scored her second singles victory over Cilly Aussem in the South of France Championships staged at the Nice Club. This was her fourth singles title since the start of the season. This was a very conclusive two set performance, dominating play and forcing her opponent on the defensive throughout. The first set was close but in the second set Cilly made many errors, served double faults and hit easy returns into the net. Sheila's well placed drives and great ball control gave her the match, 6–4 6–3. As expected this contest drew a good audience, but not as vast as the day before in the semi-final when Sheila met Miss Margaret (Peggy) Scriven, fresh out from England and making her debut on the coast. It was recorded that their encounter attracted the largest Riviera gallery since the Lenglen-Wills match in 1926. Peggy performed creditably in extending the match to 29 games, lasting 90 minutes. In the first set her spinning drives puzzled her opponent and prevented her normal attacking drives. However, Sheila refused to be dominated and squared the match. After an early lead in the deciding set, Peggy showed signs of fatigue and lost the next five out of six games. The final score was 4–6 6–4 6–3. Elizabeth Ryan played singles for the first time and gave good resistance to Cilly Aussem in the other semi-final, but after holding a point for the first set, faded quickly, 8–6 6–1. Another English newcomer was Miss Mary Hardwick, who lost to Dorothy Burke, 7–5 6–2.

In the men's final, Rogers obtained revenge for an earlier defeat by Ellmer. The battle was long and only achieved by the Irishman in the 14th game of the fifth set, 6–3 4–6 6–4 4–6 8–6. Brugnon was unable to sustain any form and was well beaten by Ellmer in the semi-final, 6–1 7–9

6–1 6–1, while at the same stage Rogers, in commanding style, crushed Aeschliman, 6–2 6–0 6–3.

Aeschliman had some consolation in winning the doubles with Lotan, after losing twice during the past weeks. Cilly Aussem and Elizabeth Ryan at last achieved a victory over Dorothy Burke and Muriel Thomas.

With the staging of the Beaulieu Club tournament at the end of February there were new arrivals to the scene, including Austin, Olliff, Maier, von Kehrling, Hector Fisher, Heinrich Kleinschroth and, for the first time, the No.2 German player, Gottfried von Cramm. Among the ladies, Simone Mathieu and Sheila Hewitt decided to compete in the doubles only. The meeting was serious affected by rain and frosty courts, which often prevented early morning play. Nevertheless, three of the five open events were completed by the Sunday and the other two on the following day.

Von Cramm scored an impressive victory over von Kehrling in the final of the men's singles. His excellent form wore down the resistance of his 50-year old opponent by outstanding tactical skill, 6–3 6–3 3–6 8–6. The German thereby emulated the feat of Friedrich Rahe 20 years earlier by winning the title for his country. Austin advanced to the semi-final without effort to meet von Kehrling on a very slow court. The Englishman drove well in the opening set but von Kehrling showed good speed around the court to square the match and then ran his opponent about to win the match, 2–6 6–3 6–2. Olliff played well in the other semi-final, but the German held most of the cards to win, 6–4 6–3.

Peggy Scriven won her first title of the year, but needed all her courage and fighting spirit to achieve her goal. She first beat Cilly Aussem in the

Due to an unprecedented week of rain, the meeting at the Monte Carlo Country Club was forced to abandon many events. However, Bunny Austin was able to secure the singles title, beating Henk Timmer and then George Rogers in the final, both matches played in the same afternoon.

semi-final after a duel of 32 games, in which she overcame losing the middle set to force the issue with her cross–court drives to get home at 6–4 5–7 6–4. The final against Elizabeth Ryan was also a very long drawn out contest, this time of 43 games, but again Peggy, with great resolution, won through, 6–3 11–13 6–4. Earlier, Elizabeth as expected, beat Phyllis Satterthwaite, 6–3 6–4.

Dorothy Burke and Muriel Thomas won another doubles title by beating Simone Mathieu and Elizabeth Ryan in the final, 6–2 6–2. The losers had eliminated Sheila Hewitt and Peggy Scriven in the semi-final with complete ease, 6–1 6–0. The men's doubles title was taken by Maier and Durrall.

A very bad spell of rain, almost unprecedented in its persistence for the time of year, caused the main Monte Carlo Country Club meeting to be seriously interrupted for five consecutive days. The tournament was, consequently, extended into the second week and the open doubles and all handicap events abandoned. Remaining were the two open singles and the two international cup events. (The average number of days on which rain had fallen on the Riviera over the previous 50 years was given as 51, slightly less than one day a week.)

In an extremely high level entry, containing many leading players from the Continent, Austin won the men's singles title. To his immense credit he won the semi-final and final both in the same afternoon. In the first match he won ten of the first 12 games against Henk Timmer, to hold a lead of a set and 4–1, but the Dutchman rallied to win the second set before fading, 6–1 4–6 6–3. Austin went on to beat Rogers in straight sets and would have won more easily than 11–9 6–3 7–5, but for cramp, which attacked him when leading 2–0 in the third set. At 5–all Austin had another attack but after receiving massage recovered and won the next two games for the match. One of the favourites for the title was von Cramm, but he was eliminated by Rogers in the semi-final, 6–1 6–4. Earlier, Timmer beat von Kehrling, 7–5 6–2, and Rogers defeated Maier, 6–2 4–6 6–3.

Lolette Payot captured the ladies' singles. She came through the easier half of the draw, which contained Sheila Hewitt, who unfortunately was forced to withdraw having contracted influenza. To reach the final the Swiss player defeated Ida Adamoff, 6–2 6–4, and Simone Barbier, 6–2 6–1. Peggy Scriven scored a fine victory over Cilly Aussem in the quarter-final by maintaining a vigorous attack for the first nine games to eventually win, 6–0 6–2. She then faced Simone Mathieu in the semi-final and looked like nearing the end of the match when leading 3–1 in the deciding set, but the Frenchwoman had other ideas and driving with relentless pressure won the next five games, 4–6 6–2 6–3. Reacting after this long struggle, Simone

Four years after making her debut on the Riviera, Lolette Payot from Switzerland returned in great style to win five singles titles. Her first victory was at Monte Carlo followed by four in succession at Nice, Cannes Club, Beau Site Hotel and Cannes New Courts Club.

offered little resistance the next day when the final match was played at the Menton Club and submitted at 6–0 6–4.

The Butler Trophy was won by Roland Journu and Martin-Legeay, who beat another French pair, Boussus and Lesueur in the final, 4–6 6–3 6–4 7–5. The winners deserved their triumph as in the previous match they eliminated the holders, Brugnon and Cochet, in five sets after their victims held several match points. In the Beaumont Cup, Simone Mathieu and Colette Rosambert lost their title to Dorothy Burke and Elizabeth

Ryan in the final, 7–5 6–2. The English pair, Phyllis Satterthwaite and Muriel Thomas, lost in the semi-final to the runners-up, 3–6 7–5 8–6.

Martin-Legeay played exceptionally well throughout the week at Menton where the Riviera Championships were being decided. He won the men's singles title with wins over Gabrowitz, 7–5 6–2, von Kehrling, 5–7 6–2 10–8, and then in the final, von Cramm, 4–6 7–5 6–4 6–4.

In the ladies' singles the two prominent players were Simone Mathieu and Peggy Scriven. In the semi-final the latter rallied well to beat Ida Adamoff from a set and 4–2 down, 2–6 7–5 6–3, but in the final she found Simone in faultless mood and mustered just five games, 6–3 6–2. Leading to the final, Phyllis Satterthwaite did well to extend the ultimate winner, 6–3 4–6 6–3.

Martin-Legeay continued to shine and retained two titles, the men's doubles with new partner Lesueur, and the international competition, Coupe des Nations, with Simone Mathieu. The ladies' doubles was again a battle in the final between Simone Mathieu and Elizabeth Ryan versus Dorothy Burke and Muriel Thomas, the former winning, 8–6 6–3.

The following tournament staged on the Parc Imperial courts at Nice from 13th to 19th March, experienced competition from the Bordighera gathering in Italy, where most of the leading players opted to compete.

The men's singles title ended with Tloczynski, who after an uncertain start in the final, gained control over Ellmer, 2–6 6–2 6–2 6–1. The Pole was given an early passage in the round before by Journu, who fell at 6–3 6–1 6–1, but at the same stage Ellmer was taken the full distance by Josef Hebda, 3–6 6–3 6–1 3–6 6–4.

The ladies' singles event did not include outstanding names and Lolette Payot was able to cruise through and take the final from Frau Grete Deutsch of Czechoslovakia, 6–1 6–2. The Swiss won the mixed doubles title with Aeschliman, who also captured the men's doubles with Journu. The King of Sweden was present during the week, competing in the handicap doubles events with Aeschliman and Lolette Payot, the latter winning the mixed title. The weather throughout was fine.

For the second week running the Riviera had to share a tennis week with its counterpart in Italy. On this occasion it was the Cannes Club with San Remo. The distribution of players was similar to the week before, with the majority of the better players opting to play over the border.

At Cannes, Tloczynski, the holder of the men's singles title and winner from the previous week, had to submit in the final to his Davis Cup colleague, Hebda, who after losing the opening set to love steadily took control to win 0–6 6–4 6–3 6–3. This gave him the Côte d'Azur Championship. Both players dropped a set in the round before, Hebda to Ellmer, 4–6 6–2 6–2, and Tloczynski to Karsten, 6–3 3–6 6–1.

Lolette Payot had little opposition in the ladies' singles and beat Grete Deutsch in the final, 6–2 6–3. She also had success in the mixed doubles with Aeschliman, and notched up her third consecutive win. Aeschliman also won the men's doubles with Gittings. The King of Sweden took part in the handicap events.

The Cannes Championship, staged at the Beau Site Hotel, attracted a good entry, particularly in the ladies' singles, where Lolette Payot came out on top in the final after a very close match with Simone Mathieu. She led 5–0 in the third set and only just managed to get home at 6–3 4–6 6–4. The semi-final between Cilly Aussem and Simone Mathieu was quite a remarkable match, lasting two and a half hours, where the Frenchwoman won 10–8 in the final set after surviving three match points when 7–8 down. The final score was 6–2 2–6 10–8. In the other half, Lolette Payot advanced at the expense of Frau Liesl Herbst of Austria, 6–3 6–3.

Matejka was in great form to beat Ellmer in the semi-final, 6–2 8–6, and then trailing by 2 sets to 1, steadied to overcome Rogers for the title, 8–6 3–6 2–6 6–3 6–4, after a contest lasting well over two and a half hours. Cilly Aussem won the two doubles titles, pairing with Rogers and Lolette Payot, while Rogers and Matejka were too strong for Aeschliman and Gittings in the men's division.

A week later at the Cannes New Courts Club meeting, Matejka continued in his winning vein to comfortably win the singles title from Karsten in the final, 6–3 6–2 6–3, having passed Aeschliman with ease, 6–3 6–1. The runner-up was the surprise winner over Ellmer in the semi-final, 7–5 2–6 8–6.

Lolette Payot won the fourth title in as many weeks, firstly receiving a walkover from Jacqueline Goldschmidt and then easing past Muriel Thomas in the final, 6–2 6–2. Muriel played well to dismiss Grete Deutsch, 6–3 6–0. Aeschliman was outstanding in the doubles, winning with Lotan and Lolette Payot. There was no ladies' doubles event.

The Japanese Davis Cup team who were touring Europe contested the Miramar Club meeting at Juan-les-Pins and came away with three titles. Jiro Satoh got the better of his fellow countryman, Ryosuke Nunoi in the final of the men's singles, 7–5 4–6 6–3 9–7. In the semi-final Satoh beat Erkishi Itoh, 6–1 6–1, and Nunoi defeated Aeschliman, 6–2 7–5. Nunoi and Itoh won the men's doubles title but progress was difficult due to the

During the season the men's singles at tournaments were well shared but Franz Matejka, the top ranked Austrian player, managed to string together two titles, at the Beau Site Hotel and Cannes New Courts Club.

resistance given by Aeschliman and Lotan in the final to the tune of 7–9 6–4 7–5 6–1.

Dorothy Burke deserved to win the ladies' singles title, displaying a controlled game to defeat Muriel Thomas in the final, 6–2 6–2. The pair combined to win the ladies' doubles title, but they needed much perseverance and determination before winning, after the deficit of the first set, 5–7 6–0 6–3. Satoh and Dorothy won the mixed doubles, just beating Aeschliman and Muriel in the last match, 1–6 7–5 7–5.

The Japanese team moved on the following week to enter at Easter the third Monte Carlo meeting of the season, challenging for the Beausoleil Championships. For the second time Jiri Satoh played Nunoi in the final of the singles, with the outcome again going to the former, but on this occasion the battle was over five sets, 0–6 6–4 4–6 6–3 6–4. Japan also won the men's doubles crown but to the disappointment of the crowd, Itoh and Ryuki Miki withdrew from the final, leaving Nunoi and Sotah the victors.

There was a surprise in the ladies' singles when Sylvia Henrotin beat Cilly Aussem after a strenuous encounter in the final, 6–2 8–10 6–3. Another upset occurred in the ladies' doubles final when Sylvia Henrotin and Simone Barbier beat the well-tried combination of Dorothy Burke and Muriel Thomas, 5–7 6–3 6–1. Aeschliman and Muriel won the mixed doubles. The 'Prix de Famille' was won by Fernand and Sylvia Henrotin.

The last tournament of the season, held at the Provençal Club, Antibes, from 24th to 30th April, was successful and comprised many players of good standard. Unfortunately, the men's singles final was abandoned owing to rain when Aeschliman was leading Lotan, 1–6 6–3 6–4 2–5, forcing the title to be divided. The other four finals were concluded with the ladies' singles being won by Sylvia Henrotin who beat Dorothy Burke in the final, 6–4 6–2. In the semi-final the winner beat Edith Belliard, 6–2 6–3, and the runner-up defeated Cosette Saint Omer Roy, 6–3 8–6. Aeschliman and Lotan won the men's doubles and Dorothy Burke and Muriel Thomas the ladies' division. Aeschliman and Muriel won the mixed title.

During the season, Gem Hoahing, a 12-year old girl of Chinese descent from the West Twickenham LTC in London, made the first of many visits to the Riviera. Accompanied by her parents she stayed at the Hotel Beaulieu, which was situated high above Cannes, overlooking the Mediterranean. The Proprietor of the hotel was Aeschliman, who arranged the daily transport of the players to the tournaments. Gem Hoahing played in some handicap events.

The second Davis Cup tie played on the Riviera took place during August, when Monaco lost to Switzerland by 4 matches to 1, on the Condamine courts, as a qualifying competition for 1934.

# 1934
# Georgio de Stefani Wins Six Titles •
# The Ladies Share

The first tournament of the season took place at the Provençal Club, Antibes, just prior to Christmas. Frost-bound courts delayed the start for three days but, as the entry was comparatively small, the later stages were played off on time by Christmas Eve.

Roger George, No.14 in France, claimed the men's singles title with victories over Lotan, 4–6 6–3 6–0, and Aeschliman in the final, 7–5 9–7 6–0. Muriel Thomas proved to be the best lady present by taking the singles title, overcoming Mrs Smallwood, 6–1 7–5, and Cosette Saint Omer Roy, 6–3 7–5. Aeschliman and Mrs Smallwood paired to win the mixed doubles beating George and Cosette Saint Omer Roy in the final, 2–6 8–6 6–4. The men's and ladies' doubles events were not scheduled.

The Christmas meeting which followed was staged at the Beau Site Hotel, where the entry was again small. For two days, bad weather interrupted progress but the finals were eventually completed. George won the men's singles for the second week running, defeating Ellmer quite easily in the final, 6–2 6–3. George was too strong for Aeschliman in the semi-final, 6–3 6–4, while at the same point, Ellmer beat Journu, 6–0 6–3.

Because of walkovers, Cosette Saint Omer Roy was required to play just one match to win the singles title, that against Mlle Alice Weiwers of Luxembourg, 6–2 6–2. George won a second title when paired with Jack Hillyard, but they had to fight all the way in the final to beat Aeschliman and Lotan, 8–6 7–5 7–5. Muriel Thomas also won two titles, the ladies' doubles with Phyllis Satterthwaite and the mixed with Aeschliman.

There was a very restricted entry for the Juan-les-Pins meeting during the first week of January. Alice Weiwers brought off two excellent wins over Grete Deutsch, 6–0 6–1, and Mme Aimée Charpenel-Cochet, 7–9 6–4 10–8, but was probably a little tired in the final against Cosette Saint Omer Roy, who won the title 6–2 6–3.

Aeschliman had a notable success in the men's singles, defeating André Jacquement of France and Pereux with only the loss of four games to each, to win the event. There appears to be no record of any doubles event being played.

The fourth Monegasque Championships, held on the Condamine Courts, allowed Aeschliman and Cosette Saint Omer Roy to follow up

Cosette Saint Omer Roy had a tremendous start to the season by winning four singles titles in as many weeks at the Beau Site Hotel, Juan-les-Pins, Monaco Championships and the Cannes New Courts Club.

their success of the previous week. The Swiss was extended by Monaco's Gaston Medecin, 8–6 7–5, before beating Landau in the final, 6–4 6–0 6–4. Landau's victim in the round before was the American, Wilmer Hines, 6–1 6–4. The ladies' singles entry was very weak and Cosette Saint Omer Roy coasted through to the title. Probably the best performance of the week was the victory of Aeschliman and Hines over Jack Hillyard and Landau in the final of the doubles, 6–3 6–0 7–5. The mixed title was won by Landau and Paulette de Saint Ferréol. There was no ladies' doubles event.

Fine weather and the largest entry of the season so far, marked the Cannes New Courts Club tournament. Arriving from St Moritz, de Stefani was generally in great form to capture the singles title, although he was taken the full distance in the final by Ellmer, before edging out, 3–6 6–3 6–3 3–6 6–4. In the semi-finals, Ellmer beat Hines, 6–4 6–1, while de Stefani crushed another American, Henry Culley, without the loss of a game. Culley had earlier brought off a notable win over Karsten, 9–7 8–10 6–1.

The ladies' singles attracted several English players, of whom Miss Joan Ingram did well to beat two strong competitors, Alice Weiwers, 6–2 6–2 and Mrs Gladys Clarke-Jerroise of England before falling to Cosette Saint Omer Roy in the final, 3–6 6–1 8–6. Aeschliman and Lotan showed their class to beat Culley and Hines in the final of the doubles, 7–5 6–4 6–1. Elizabeth Ryan won both the ladies and mixed doubles, in partnership with Muriel Thomas and Hines.

Over 60 players competed at the Gallia Club gathering. The presence of Brugnon increased the strength of the men's entry but unfortunately he opted only for the doubles. The men's singles final was a repetition of the week earlier, when Ellmer again put up tremendous resistance before losing to de Stefani after four sets and 48 games, 6–4 6–2 8–10 7–5. The winner had the measure of Hines in the semi-final, 6–4 6–0, while Ellmer did well to suppress Gentien, 8–6 6–3.

Joan Ingram again shone, beating Paulette de Saint Ferréol in the last four, 3–6 8–6 6–2, and taking the middle set from Muriel Thomas in the final. She led 2–0 in the deciding set, but then lost six of the next seven games, 6–0 4–6 6–3. Muriel Thomas had passed Countess Gabriele Szapary of Austria, 6–3 6–2. Brugnon won the two doubles titles with Gentien and Elizabeth Ryan, the latter also cruised through the ladies' division with Muriel Thomas.

The week at the Carlton Club meeting was very successful and attracted an entry of over 80 players. After taking the singles at the last two tournaments, de Stefani looked certain to notch up the third, but Aeschliman had other ideas. After passing Artens in the quarter-final, 6–3 6–1, he brought off the surprise of the week by ousting the Italian, 6–0 7–5. He successfully managed to break up the ambidextrous player's sound game by varying the length of his returns and so getting his opponent out of position. In the final, Aeschliman was able to win the first set against Gentien, who then volleyed his way to the title, 4–6 6–3 6–2 6–1. The Swiss had run out of steam. Hines gave the Frenchman a good run in the semi-final, before going down, 6–4 6–2.

Muriel Thomas repeated her success of the previous week by comfortably taking the singles title. She was not pressed throughout and the final against Cosette Saint Omer Roy was easy going at 6–2 6–2. The one competitor who could have given her problems, Joan Ingram, fell unexpectedly to Miss Betty Hobson of England in the third round, 6–4 6–4.

Brugnon did not contest the singles and, as expected, won the two doubles, the men's with Gentien and the mixed with Elizabeth Ryan, the latter also winning the ladies' doubles with Muriel Thomas. Miss Adeline (Billie) Yorke made her first appearance on the Riviera but confined herself to the doubles, having recently recovered from an illness.

The following week at the Parc Imperial, Nice, Muriel Thomas won the South of France Championships singles, for her third title in as many weeks, beating toward the end, Countess Szapary, 2 sets to 1, Miss J. McAlpine, 6–2 6–0, and in the final, Miss Mary Hardwick, 6–1 6–0, tired after playing matches earlier in the day. Miss McAlpine and Mary, both from England, were making their debut on the coast. Miss McAlpine indicated to all the improvement she had made in the game, by beating Joan Ingram, 6–4 6–1, and Billie Yorke, 6–3 5–7 7–5. Mary Hardwick beat Sylvia Henrotin in the semi-final, 6–3 6–3.

Rogers was back in contention for the first time during the season and duly won the men's singles by overcoming Gentien in the semi-final, 4–6 6–2 6–4 6–4, but was then very hard pushed to eliminate Artens in the last encounter, 2–6 6–3 2–6 6–3 6–2.

Cully and Hines showed their improvement by winning the men's doubles. Hines was also in great form when combining with Muriel Thomas to beat Aeschliman and Elizabeth Ryan in the mixed doubles final, 6–2 6–3. Muriel Thomas listed a 'triple' in combination with Elizabeth Ryan, while the King of Sweden won the mixed handicap with Mary Hardwick.

Austin's initial challenge of the season was made at the Beaulieu Club, where he completely dominated the men's singles. He just advanced through his five matches without losing a set, casting aside Hines, 6–0 6–4, Ellmer, 6–4 6–2, Gabrowitz, 6–3 6–0, and in the final, Jourdu, who failed to win a game until the score stood at 6–0 6–0 5–0 against him. Austin was finding the lines at will and on the day seemed unbeatable. However, Journu had brought credit to his country having passed Rogers, 6–4 7–5, de Stefani, 7–5 6–4, and Hecht, 6–2 6–4. This was really a very top class field.

Billie Yorke's win in the ladies' singles was quite unexpected. Normally recognised as a doubles player, she was forced to fight hard in the four matches necessary to capture the title, first Countess Szapary, 6–1 5–7 7–5, then Phyllis Satterthwaite, 3–6 6–0 6–4, Dorothy Andrus (reverting to her maiden name from Burke), 10–12 6–2 7–5, and in the final, Syliva Henrotin, 6–1 4–6 6–4. There is no doubt that the winner's stamina at the end of long and exhausting matches was the principal factor of her success. In earlier contests Dorothy Andrus beat Joan Ridley, 6–4 6–4, Sylvia Henrotin defeated Joan Ingram 6–1 6–0, and Lucia Valerio beat Mary Hardwick, 3–6 6–4 6–3. Like the men, the ladies' singles was of the highest quality.

Brugnon, not playing singles paired with Journu to win the doubles, while Elizabeth Ryan won two titles with Sylvia Henrotin and von Cramm – the latter a new combination.

Austin carried on where he had finished the week before, dominating the men's singles at the Monaco Championships, held at the Monte Carlo Country Club. He was never really extended, beating in the last three rounds, Brugnon, 6–3 6–3, Menzel, 6–4 6–2 2–1 ret'd, and de Stefani 6–1 8–6 6–4. As soon as Austin had overcome Menzel's whirlwind opening, he was master of the situation. When led 2–1 in the third set, Menzel retired having several doubles matches to play. In the final, versus de Stefani, the second set was the crucial one, when the Italian broke through to lead 6–5, but Austin braced himself to win the next seven points and eventually the set at 8–6. The third set was a foregone conclusion. Austin's domination over the past two weeks was worth noting. He had played 10 matches, without losing a set and won 136 games to 40. Von Cramm was expected to be a finalist, but he fell to Hecht in the third round, 0–6 7–5 6–4. Hecht then lost to Artens, 12–10 6–3, who then in turn lost to de Stefani, 6–0 6–1 ret'd.

Muriel Thomas was the only surviving English player to reach the semi-final of the singles, with Joan Ridley, Billie Yorke and Phyllis Satterthwaite falling in the round before. She then defeated Countess Szapary after quite a struggle, 4–6 7–5 6–2, before deciding to retire from the final against Sylvia Henrotin, preferring to save herself for the doubles. In the semi-final, Sylvia beat Lucia Valerio, 6–4 6–2.

Czechoslovakia won the Butler Trophy for the first time, through Hecht and Menzel, who beat the holders, Journu and Martin-Legeay, in the semi-final, after five gruelling sets, 12–10 5–7 3–6 6–2 6–3. They went on to beat Brugnon and Lesueur, 6–3 2–6 6–4 6–2. Austin paired with Jack Lysaght, but were well beaten by Brugnon and Lesueur, 6–1 6–4 6–4. England captured the Beaumont Cup for the fourth occasion, when Muriel Thomas and Billie Yorke defeated Dorothy Andrus and Elizabeth Ryan in the final, 3–6 6–4 6–3. In the semi-finals, the winners beat Sylvia Henrotin and Colette Rosambert, 3–6 6–3 6–3, and the runners-up accounted for Mary Hardwick and Joan Ingram, 6–1 6–2. In the 'ordinary' doubles finals, Austin and Rogers beat Artens and Menzel, 6–2 4–6 6–4 6–2, Elizabeth Ryan and Muriel Thomas beat Sylvia Henrotin and Joan Ingram, 6–4 6–4, and von Cramm and Elizabeth Ryan beat Menzel and Sylvia Henrotin, 6–4 6–1.

After the hustle and bustle of the Monte Carlo meeting, the gathering at the Menton Club was a more leisurely affair. The majority of the English players had left for other places. Rain interfered during the second half of the week, but the programme was completed.

The men's singles event for the Riviera Championships was won by de Stefani, who defeated the holder Martin-Legeay in the final, 8–6 6–2 6–2. His well-judged lobs were quite often a telling factor. In the semi-final the Italian lost just five games to Lesueur, 6–2 6–3, but Martin-Legeay had to wage a two hour battle before he could subjugate Journu. After losing the first set he managed to square the match but still faced two match balls before eventually going through, 5–7 12–10 8–6. Journu was a victim of cramp.

Sylvia Henrotin continued to demonstrate a high quality of play to capture the ladies' singles with the loss of one set, that to Lucia Valerio in the final 3–6 6–3 6–0. The runner-up narrowly survived a 22 game final set against Dorothy Andrus in the semi-final, 6–4 4–6 12–10, while the winner had firm control all the way against Countess Szapary, 6–3 6–1. Earlier, Joan Ridley lost to Sylvia Henrotin, 6–1 6–3. The doubles titles were well shared with, as expected, Muriel Thomas and Elizabeth Ryan completely dominating their division. Von Kehrling and Gabrowitz just won the men's doubles, lasting the better against Lesueur and Martin-Legeay, 2–6 6–1 6–1 7–9 6–2.

Georgio de Stefani was the star of the season, consistently in form at the nine tournaments in which he took part. He won six singles titles at the Cannes New Courts Club, Gallia Club, Menton, Nice, Cannes Club and the Beau Site Hotel. There was, however, a surprise when he fell to Charles Aeschliman in the final at the Carlton Club.

The Coupe des Nations was won for the third year running by Martin-Legeay, but on this occasion he shared the court with Sylvia Henrotin. The victors at one stage were 3–1 down in the deciding set to Hines and Elizabeth Ryan, before winning the next five games, 13–11 2–6 6–3.

As expected, the second Nice meeting did not feature the same quantity or quality of the players as the first meeting. Nevertheless the week was most enjoyable, with the visitors enjoying the facilities of the Parc Imperial Club.

For the second week running de Stefani took the honours in the men's singles but was carried to a vantage third set by Ellmer, the runner-up from the year before, 6–1 6–3 9–7. De Stefani beat Lotan in the semi-final, 6–3 6–2 8–6, while Ellmer was pushed to four sets by Artens, 6–2 4–6 6–0 6–4.

The ladies' singles was not of a very high quality, which allowed Phyllis Satterthwaite to stroll through and win the final against Miss Mona Riddell of Somerset, 6–2 6–0. The latter had produced an excellent win over Paulette de Saint Ferréol, 6–2 6–1. De Stefani won a second title, paired with Jack Hillyard, who in the men's doubles final just defeated Lotan and Aeschliman, 2–6 8–6 7–5. Phyllis Satterthwaite and Paulette de Saint-Ferréol failed to win the ladies' event, losing in the final to Grete Deutsch and Frl Totta Zenden of Germany, 8–6 4–6 6–4.

Competing on the Riviera for the first time, England's Miss Nancy Lyle made a tremendous impact by winning the ladies' singles at the Cannes Club, by registering a victory over Simone Mathieu, making her first visit of the year, in the final. She proved her fighting qualities in the semi-final when Muriel Thomas won the first set and led 5–2 in the second. On a very damp court, Nancy Lyle fought back every inch of the way and, after surviving three match points, took the set 9–7. After a stoppage she returned to secure the final set and the match, 4–6 9–7 6–3. Simone Mathieu defeated Grete Deutsch, 7–5 6–2, to reach the final, where she found her opponent's steadiness and ability to draw her from the baseline, difficult to overcome and was beaten, 6–4 6–4.

De Stefani won his third singles title in a row, beating Matejka in the final after dropping the third set when leading 5–4, but then making good, 6–1 6–1 5–7 6–3. In the semi-finals, de Stefani beat du Plaix, 6–4 6–3, and Matejka overcame Ellmer, 4–6 6–2 6–2. Muriel Thomas won two doubles titles, with Simone Mathieu and Hector Fisher. This time, Aeschliman and Lotan had the upper hand against de Stefani and Jack Hillyard in the doubles final.

A feature of the week was the fine performance of Gem Hoahing who won the ladies' handicap singles by beating Totta Zenden in the final, 6–3 6–1. Gem showed great ability in returning the widest shots from the baseline.

At the Beau Site Hotel meeting, where the Cannes Championships were decided, a return match between Nancy Lyle and Simone Mathieu was expected. But this was not to be as Jacqueline Goldschmidt, No.4 in France, beat both players to capture the title. In the semi-final, Nancy Lyle could not counter her opponent's steady driving and after saving several match points fell at 6–1 8–6. In the final, Simone lost the opening set but appeared to gain control when leading 4–1 in the second, but Jacqueline Goldschmidt, with fine courage, reduced the lead and staved off four set points to win the close fight, 6–4 11–9.

De Stefani won his fourth consecutive singles victory, beating Ellmer in the final, 3–6 6–1 7–5 6–2. This was a long match in which the Swiss could have won the third set and affect the match outcome. His display signalled recent improvement in his game, as shown by his semi-final win over Matejka, 6–4 6–0. In the other match, de Stefani had no problem with Artens, who retired after the first set, 6–1.

Muriel Thomas won both doubles, with Nancy Lyle and Hector Fisher, while the men's doubles was captured by Artens and Matejka. There was some notable competition in the handicap events, which attracted much attention. In the mixed doubles, Princess Ingrid of Sweden partnered Count Szapary and lost to Dr Warden and Grete Deutsch and the King of Sweden with Nancy Lyle lost to Lysaght and Gem Hoahing.

Gem Hoahing, the 13-year old girl from West Twickenham, had the honour of playing against King Gustav of Sweden in the mixed doubles handicap at the Beau Site Hotel. Pairing with Jack Lysaght she beat the King and Nancy Lyle. The week before at the Cannes Club, Gem defeated Totta Zenden of Germany in the final of the handicap singles, 6–3 6–1.

In the previous few weeks, Hines had shown great improvement in his play and this culminated in him winning the men's singles at the third Monte Carlo meeting for the Beausoleil Championships. In the semi-final he beat Lotan, conqueror of Aeschliman, 6–4 6–4, before producing his best to beat Ellmer in straight sets, 6–4 6–4 7–5. Hines was also a finalist in the two doubles events and winner of the Macomber Cup for under-21s.

Sylvia Henrotin reached three finals, winning the singles with a seesaw match against Grete Deutsch in the semi-final, 6–3 4–6 6–4, but then taking the title with an easy win over Dorothy Andrus, 6–1 6–1. The two finalists paired to win the doubles, beating Grete Deutsch and Totta Zenden in the final, 8–6 7–5. Hector Fisher and Dorothy Andrus won the mixed event. The Prix de Famille was won by Max Ellmer and Mlle Ellmer. In the junior singles, Gem Hoahing beat a boy named Campbell in the final, 6–1 6–1.

Aeschliman was the outstanding player at the Provençal Club tournament, by winning three events. Reaching the final of the men's singles, untroubled, he was then given a walkover by Lotan. Aeschliman paired with Wolff to win the doubles and with Sylvia Henrotin to take the mixed event.

Sylvia Henrotin was pushed to the limit by Dorothy Andrus in the final of the singles 5–7 8–6 6–4. In the round before, the winner eliminated Mlle Jacqueline Horner, 6–4 3–6 6–2, while the American was too good for Paulette de Saint-Ferréol, 6–4 6–1.

The last two tournaments of the season, the Cannes New Courts Club and the Miramar at Juan-les-Pins, were cancelled.

This was the last season that Elizabeth Ryan competed on the Riviera, having first appeared in 1913. At the end of 1934, she turned professional.

# 1935
# Simone Mathieu's Phenomenal Season

The opening of the season was held at the Miramar Club, Juan-les-Pins, just prior to Christmas and consisted of only two events.

Lotan, an Englishman who lived in Nice, proved to be in excellent form throughout. In the singles he beat Ken Warden, 6–0 6–3, Jacquemet, 6–2 2–6 6–1, and in the final, knocked out with ease, Gabriel Mercier, the 4th ranked Swiss, 6–1 6–0. Later in the day the two finalists paired to capture the doubles title, overcoming Landau and Medecin, 2–6 7–5 6–1.

The Christmas tournament, which was held at the Beau Site Hotel, did not contain a large entry or many players of high-standing, but nevertheless the outcome was that Ellmer proved his status by winning the men's singles without conceding a set. Not being pressed, he defeated Jacquemet, 6–2 6–1, before entering the final, where he dominated Medecin from start to finish, 6–1 6–1 6–1. The loser had beaten Mercier, 7–5 6–2.

Simone Mathieu, starting her campaign earlier than usual, showed her class by winning the ladies' title, although she was extended to an advantage set in the last two rounds by Alice Weiwers, 6–1 8–6, and Muriel Thomas, 6–2 7–5. The latter had passed Cosette Saint Omer Roy in the semi-final, 6–3 6–1. The surprise of the meeting was the defeat of Simone Mathieu and Muriel Thomas in the final of the ladies' doubles by Cosette Saint Omer Roy and Alice Weiwers, 6–2 8–6. Jacquemet and Lotan were the outstanding pair in the men's doubles, likewise Landau and Simone Mathieu in the mixed. Jacques Bonte, a first series French player from Paris, won the men's singles at the first tournament of the season at the Monte Carlo Country Club, but was given a hard match in the final by Landau, which lasted 42 games over four sets, 7–5 2–6 7–5 6–4. In the round before, Bonte defeated Medecin, 6–1 6–3, while Landau accounted for Lotan, 6–2 6–1.

Simone Mathieu won the ladies' division, but was well held in the second set by Phyllis Satterthwaite before going through, 6–2 6–4. The round before saw the Frenchwoman beat Jeannette Poncelet by walkover and Phyllis pass Mrs Olga Haycraft, 6–2 6–0. Jacquemet and Lotan won the doubles final from Bonte and Medecin, 6–4 4–6 6–1 6–3. Ladies' and mixed doubles were not played.

The Condamine courts at Monte Carlo were the scene of the 5th Monegasque Championships, held the second week in January. Landau, the winner in 1933, regained his title by beating a young Monegasque player, Aleco Noghes, 6–2 6–2, as a preliminary to receiving stern opposition in the final from Mercier, who started well but gradually faded, 5–7 6–3 6–0 6–4. As expected, Simone Mathieu was not threatened and gained easy victories over Mme Louvean and Paulette de Saint Ferréol, 6–0 6–2. Landau and Medecin took the men's doubles title, while Landau won a 'triple' in partnership with Simone Mathieu.

Another low-key affair with a small entry at the Provencal LTC, enabled Culley to give good account of himself in the men's singles by dismissing Mercier in the last four, 6–4 5–7 6–2, and then extending Landau to 40 games in the final, 6–2 4–6 6–4 7–5. The winner had the measure over Jacquemet earlier, 6–4 6–0.

Simone Mathieu won three events. She was not pressed in the singles final by Cosette Saint Omer Roy, 6–1 6–3, and later paired with Phyllis Satterthwaite to win the doubles and Landau to take the mixed doubles. There was no men's doubles event.

The tennis scene moved back to Cannes where the Gallia meeting was being held. Gentien appeared to quickly reach his best form to capture the men's singles title as he edged his way past Jacquemet, 6–4 6–4, and Hines, 2–6 6–4 8–6 6–3, the latter having dismissed Lotan earlier, 6–4 4–6 6–3.

Full of confidence, Simone Mathieu won three titles. In the singles she was pushed very hard in the final by the holder, Muriel Thomas, who had the opportunity to win the second set before falling at 6–3 8–6. In the semi-final, Simone was in a different class to Frl Irmgard Rost, the No.2 ranked German, and advanced without losing a game, while Muriel held the reins throughout to beat Alice Weiwers, 6–4 6–3. Culley and Hines as a pair were too strong for Jacquemet and Lotan in the doubles final, recording a 6–1 6–4 6–3 score. Simone paired with Muriel and Gentien to win the other two doubles events.

A week later at the Carlton Club, Gentien continued in great shape to retain his singles title, beating Hines in the final, 3–6 0–6 6–4 6–3 6–4. In the semi-final, Hines beat Jacquemet, 3–6 6–4 6–3, while Gentien beat del Frate, 2–6 6–4 6–3.

Simone Mathieu had an easy passage to the ladies' final in defeating Countess Szapary, 6–1 6–1, but in the deciding round was given a hard time by Muriel Thomas, 6–3 8–6. The runner-up had passed Edith Belliard, 8–6 6–2. Culley and Hines won the men's doubles and Simone and Muriel the ladies' doubles. Hines won a second title, pairing with Phyllis Satterthwaite in the mixed.

The South of France Championships, held at Nice, attracted the best entry of the season. Simone Mathieu won the ladies' singles title for the first time, but her unbeaten record over the past few weeks came as near as possible to being broken. She reached the final without effort, winning 12 games in succession from Phyllis Satterthwaite, but in the final she came within a stroke of defeat at the hands of Edith Belliard. Refusing to be overcome by her opponent's shrewd tactics, Edith took the first set of 22 games and reached match point in the second. However, failing to clinch the point, her resistance weakened and she eventually lost, 10–12 7–5 6–3. Edith Belliard beat the holder, Muriel Thomas in the quarter-final, 6–2 6–3, and was forced to produce her best in the next round against Gem Hoahing, before winning, 6–3 6–3. The 14-year old had earlier beaten Mrs Weeta Crawshay Williams, 6–2 6–4. Also, Phyllis Satterthwaite had two good wins against Countess Szapary, 6–2 6–3, and Jeannette Poncelet, 7–5 6–4.

Improving round-by-round, Hines brought off a mild surprise by winning the men's singles, disposing of Martin-Legeay in erratic form in the semi-final, 6–2 7–5 6–3, and then playing an enterprising game to overcome Ellmer for the title, 6–2 3–6 6–1 6–4. Ellmer narrowly beat Culley in the other semi-final, 2–6 6–1 7–5 6–8 6–1.

Billie Yorke made her first appearance of the season but played doubles only. Pairing with Phyllis Satterthwaite, they gained a creditable victory over Simone Mathieu and Muriel Thomas in the final of the doubles, 6–0 8–10 6–4. Boussus and Brugnon beat Lesueur and Martin-Legeay in the final of the men's doubles, 9–7 7–5 2–6 2–6 6–3. Lesueur and Countess Szapary won the mixed doubles and in the final of the ladies' singles handicap, Gem Hoahing defeated Olga Haycraft, 4–6 6–3, 6–4.

The Beaulieu Championships, held at the Beaulieu Club, attracted the strongest entry of the season so far, particularly in the men's division where ten players of Davis Cup status competed as well as Giovanni Palmieri, a former Italian champion, who was barred from the competition, having been a professional at one period.

Austin returned to the fray hoping to retain his singles title, but the windy conditions in the semi-final against Palmieri prevented his volleying

Simone Mathieu began her astonishing, and indeed unique, record of winning consecutive singles titles on the Riviera. During the season she entered 16 tournaments and won them all. The following season was another golden run when she won 14 titles, added to which she claimed a further six in 1937 before withdrawing. Her record of 36 consecutive singles titles will stand forever.

being as sharp as usual and he was subsequently unable to tempt his opponent from the baseline. After losing the opening set, Austin recovered to set all but the Italian built on a 3–0 lead in the deciding set, which was sufficient for him to win, 6–4 4–6 6–3. Von Cramm, making his first visit of the year, in the other half of the draw had to wage an anxious match to pass Hebda in two tight sets, 7–5 8–6. In the final, played under calm conditions, he dominated Palmier to win the title, 6–2 6–4 6–3. Some earlier notable results saw Hebda defeat Ellmer, 7–5 6–3, Landau beat Artens, 2–6 6–0 6–2, and Palmieri defeat Martin-Legeay, surprisingly, 6–0 6–0.

Simone Mathieu, well in command, as usual, during the present season, deprived Billie Yorke of her title. The Englishwoman held her rival well, particularly in the opening set, but her resistance then declined and the match ended at 6–4 6–2. Billie Yorke beat Muriel Thomas in the semi-final, 6–2 7–9 ret'd, and Simone Mathieu defeated Lucia Valerio at the same stage, 6–2 6–4. Gem Hoahing added to her reputation by winning a set from the 7th ranked Italian, Giuliana Grioni in the opening round, 4–6 6–4 6–2. Muriel Thomas won two doubles titles, the ladies' with Simone Mathieu and the mixed with von Cramm. Martin-Legeay and Lesueur won the men's doubles final after a tremendous struggle against Culley and Hines, 11–9 6–8 6–3 5–7 6–2.

Now regarded as the prime attraction on the Riviera circuit, the Monte Carlo Country Club tournament lived up to expectations and produced some skilful and attractive matches, especially those featuring the men.

In the men's singles, Austin had to surrender his title to Palmieri in the final. Initially the Englishman could do little right, with the steadiness of the Italian allowing him only four of the first 21 games. He survived a match point at 2–5 in the third set and did well to reach 5 all but then his touch deserted him and he was well-beaten, 6–1 6–1 7–5. Palmieri, long-known as one of the best Continental players, surprised most by beating von Cramm in the semi-final after five sets and 50 games. He was near defeat in the fourth set and recovered well from 0–2 to 5–6 in the 5th set before a run of three games gave him the match, 6–4 0–6 2–6 7–5 8–6. Hines, by beating Boussus, 3–6 6–3 6–4, faced Austin in the semi-final, where he gave good account of himself before going down, 6–3 7–5 6–3. Some of the other highlights included von Cramm's defeat of Brugnon, 7–5 7–5, and Hebda, 6–4 6–2. Other excellent matches saw Hines beat Artens, 6–4 7–5, and Lesueur defeat Ellmer, 2–6 6–3 6–3.

By comparison the ladies' singles was quite straightforward, with Simone Mathieu going through without losing a set, her last three scores being against Countess Szapary, 6–2 6–1, Grete Deutsch, 6–0 7–5, and in the final, Lucia Valerio, 6–2 6–4. Susan Noel, returning to the circuit, did well to eliminate Edith Belliard after 34 games, 8–6 2–6 7–5, and

then extend Lucia Valerio to 6–4 6–3. Gem Hoahing played in the singles proper but lost to the Countess, 6–4 6–0. The young girl had consolation by winning the ladies' singles handicap event, beating Miss Iris Hutchings in the final. The King of Sweden paired with Lucia Valerio in the mixed doubles handicap.

The Butler Trophy was well contested and resulted in Martin-Legeay and Lesueur beating Boussus and Brugnon in the final, 2–6 6–1 6–3 6–2. Muriel Thomas and Billie Yorke were too good on the day for Simone Barbier and Simone Mathieu in the last match for the Beaumont Cup, 6–3 6–4. As this was Muriel Thomas' third win in the event, she retired the trophy. In the 'ordinary' doubles, Josef Caska, Czechoslovakia, and Palmieri won the men's event, Simone Mathieu and Muriel Thomas the ladies' event and Austin and Billie Yorke, the mixed.

The departure of a number of leading players from the Riviera weakened the entry at the Menton Club meeting, but nevertheless there were sufficient numbers of international class remaining to maintain interest. Undoubtedly, the most notable feature of the week was success of

The Menton Club which had 12 courts annually staged the Riviera Championships. The winners of the singles events during the season were Josef Caska (left), a 19-year old Czech, who impressed everyone, and Simone Mathieu.

19-year old Caska, who beat Brugnon, 6–0 6–3, and Hines, 3–6 6–4 6–2 6–2, to take the title. Against Hines, once he settled down, there was only one winner. Hines did well to beat Lesueur in the semi-final, 6–3 6–4. Both semi-finals were played during falling snow.

There was never much doubt that Simone Mathieu would continue her conquests. Earlier in the season, Edith Belliard had a match point against her, but this time in the final she made no mistake and romped home, 6–2 6–1. Susan Noel impressed all by reaching the semi-final where she fell to Edith, 6–3 6–2, while at the same time, Simone Mathieu had no problem in ousting Grete Deutsch, 6–0 6–1.

Culley and Hines were in the driving seat to win the men's doubles final over Caska and Richard von Planner of Austria, 6–3 6–4 1–6 6–4, while Edith Belliard and Simone Mathieu were too good for Susan Noel and Countess Szapary, 6–1 7–5. Hines and Simone won the mixed doubles and Brugnon and Edith were successful in the Coupe des Nations.

The entry for the Côte d'Azur Championships at the Cannes Club was, to some degree, weakened by the counter attraction of San Remo on the Italian Riviera, to which many of the leading exponents had departed. However, there were still enough talented players available to extend the favourites and create interest.

Simone Mathieu was once again successful in winning the ladies' singles, but for the second occasion during the season she was forced to drop a set. This was during the final against Kay Stammers of England, competing on the Riviera for the first time. Kay had spent some time practising with Edmund Burke and was familiar with the conditions. After two sets the struggle was even, but in the decider the Frenchwoman's superiority was clear as she won six games in a row and the match, 6–1 2–6 6–0. In the semi-final she surprisingly lost five games to Alice Weiwers, 6–2 6–3, and again Kay Stammers played well to dispose of Grete Deutsch, 6–1 7–5.

Brugnon, entering singles for the first time during the season, overcame four long matches before facing Ellmer in the final. He needed five sets to take the title and after leading 4–2 in the final set was caught at 5 all before eventually winning, 6–3 6–4 0–6 2–6 9–7. Both semi-finals went to three sets, Brugnon beating Matejka, 7–5 5–7 6–2, and Ellmer passing Lotan, 6–0 4–6 6–2.

The finalists of the ladies' singles, Simone Mathieu and Kay Stammers, combined to win the doubles, while the Frenchwoman and Brugnon won the mixed event. The latter also won the men's doubles paired with William Robertson of the United States.

The week following the Cannes tournament was unusual in that no meeting was scheduled for the Riviera. Consequently, the Bordighera meeting, just over the Italian border, attracted one or two of the leading players. Simone Mathieu entered and won the singles title with victory over Cilly Aussem in the final, 6–3 6–2. She also won the ladies' doubles paired with Muriel Thomas and the mixed with Lesueur.

Back in France the schedule continued with the gathering at the Beau Site Hotel, where the Cannes Championships were at stake. Simone Mathieu was in great form and defeated Kay Stammers in three finals. The latter did well in the singles, passing Jacqueline Goldschmidt in the semi-final, 6–3 6–4, but in the final against Simone she produced a very disappointing display and went down, 6–3 6–3. Simone's other titles were achieved in final partnerships with Muriel Thomas against Jacqueline Goldschmidt and Kay Stammers, 6–1 7–5, and with Lotan over Matejka and Kay Stammers, 6–3 8–6.

In the men's singles, Ellmer was not pressed throughout the final by Matejka and the score of 6–2 6–1 6–3 tells the story. However, he was pushed hard reaching the last match by Lotan who ran him to 7–5 7–5. The men's doubles title was won by Ellmer and Matejka.

Simone Mathieu's performance at the second Nice Meeting was a mirror image of the Beau Site Hotel meeting, as she won the ladies' singles and then the two doubles with the same partners, Muriel Thomas and Lotan. In the singles, Frau Paula von Stuck did what few other players had achieved during the season in extending Simone to an advantage set in the semi-final, 9–7, and then, surprisingly, retired, possibly because of her long match in the previous round against Susan Noel, 6–3 2–6 6–4. Edith Belliard reached the final when Jacqueline Horner also retired, but could make no headway against Simone Mathieu, to the tune of 6–2 6–2.

Karel Pachovsky, the 9th ranked Czechoslovakian, brought off his best performance in international competitions by winning the men's singles title, beating Landau in the final, 6–1 1–6 6–3 6–3. He also had notable wins over Medecin, 6–3 6–3, and Lotan, 6–2 6–3 3–1 ret'd. Jacquemet and Lotan won the men's doubles.

The following week, in a less representative field at the Provençal LTC, Pachovsky and Simone Mathieu stood out among the rest of the competitors. The Frenchwoman, after passing Jeannette Poncelet in the semi-final, 6–2 6–0, had a straight-forward win over Jacqueline Goldschmidt, 6–3 6–3, the latter having dismissed Paula von Stuck, 7–5 6–1. Pachovsky had a struggle to beat the German, Dr Herbert Tuebben, in the final, 6–1 7–5 4–6 6–3. In the round before, Pachovsky easily conquered Englishman, George Godsell, 6–1 6–0. Landau and Simone Mathieu won the mixed doubles. No ladies' doubles event took place.

With many of the international players gone elsewhere at this time of the season, the entry at the late Cannes Club meeting attracted few men players of international level. Godsell produced an excellent result in winning the men's singles, beating England's Alan Hornsby Wright, 6–2 6–3, and Lotan in the final, 6–3 1–6 6–3.

Simone Mathieu, won yet another singles title with ease, defeating Paula von Stuck in the final, 6–4 6–2. Lotan and Simone Mathieu won the mixed event beating Godsell and Alice Weiwers, 6–3 6–3.

The last tournament of the year was held over Easter at the Monte Carlo Country Club from 22nd to 28th April and attracted quite an outstanding entry. The presence of the Australian Davis Cup team raised significantly the standard of the men's events, where in the singles Jack Crawford beat Donald Turnbull, 6–3 6–2, and Vivian McGrath defeated Adrian Quist, 7–5 4–6 6–2. The final was quite extraordinary with play lasting over three hours and 55 games, when Crawford and Quist decided to agree to share the title.

The last tournament of the season at the Monte Carlo Easter meeting had an outstanding entry from the men, including the Australian Davis Cup team. *Left to right:* Jack Crawford, Vivian McGrath, Donald Turnbull and Adrian Quist. In the final of the singles, Crawford met Quist but after 55 games lasting three hours they decided to share the title.

Lili de Alvarez made a reappearance, after a long absence, beating Edith Belliard, 6–1 1–6 8–6, before facing Simone Mathieu in the final and going down 6–4 6–1. Culley and Hines excelled in the men's doubles, accounting for Crawford and McGrath, 7–5 6–4, and Marcel Bernard from France and Harry Hopman of Australia, 2–6 8–6 7–5 2–6 6–4. Simone Mathieu won the ladies' doubles with Edith Belliard and the mixed with Hopman.

So ended an extraordinary season for Simone Mathieu, who entered 16 tournaments on the French Riviera and won all the 16 singles titles and only twice did she lose a set. To this record may be added the 12 doubles and 11 mixed doubles title she also captured. Besides the foregoing, she also won a 'triple' at Bordighera and a 'triple' at the Cannes Club Members' tournament (not open).

# 1936
## Simone Mathieu Again Supreme •
## Fred Perry's Two Week Visit

The start of the new season was plagued by bad weather, with persistent rain forcing the abandonment of the opening tournament at the Monte Carlo Country Club, scheduled for 23rd -29th December.

The Beau Site Hotel New Year Meeting which followed was also affected by rain and had to run into a second week for completion. This gathering did not attract a large field, although many of the regular supporters returned to compete. The men's singles title was won for the first time by Landau, who defeated another Riviera resident, Lotan, in the final, 6–4 6–3 6–3. Landau reached the two doubles finals, but lost both.

Simone Mathieu began where she left off the previous season by comfortably winning the ladies' singles by beating Phyllis Satterthwaite in the final, 6–0 6–2. The Englishwoman played well in the previous round to dismiss Cosette Saint Omer Roy, 6–2 6–1, while Simone Mathieu received a walkover. The feature of the meeting was the victory of Cosette Saint Omer Roy and Alice Weiwers over Simone Mathieu and Phyllis Satterthwaite in the final of the ladies' doubles, 6–1 6–2, the winners securing the event for the second year.

There was a surprise at the Monegasque Championships, held on the Condamine courts at Monte Carlo, when Medecin was victorious in the men's singles with an excellent win over his Davis Cup colleague, Landau, in the final, 8–10 6–4 6–4 2–6 6–2. The winner also had a notable win over Jacquemet in the semi-final, 6–2 6–2, while Landau lost the opening four games against Noghes, but then won the next 12.

Simone Mathieu's path to winning the ladies' singles title was without obstruction as she crushed Iris Hutchings in the final, 6–1 6–0. Jack Hillyard and Jacquemet won the men's doubles and Landau and Simone Mathieu the mixed event for the second year. No ladies' doubles was played.

A late scheduled tournament was held the following week at the Monte Carlo Country Club, but was restricted to three events. Lotan was successful in the men's singles, overcoming Noghes, 0–6 6–4 6–1, before defeating Medecin in the final, 6–4 6–0 6–1. The Prince of Cutch fell to Medecin, 6–1 6–2.

Simone Mathieu was again in devastating form, beating Phyllis Satterthwaite in the last match of the singles, 6–0 6–0. In the semi-final, she beat Olga Haycraft, 6–1 6–0, while Phyllis passed Paulette de Saint Ferréol, 6–3 6–3. The winners of the singles paired to beat Landau and Phyllis in the final, 6–3 6–8 6–3.

The Gallia Club tournament attracted quite a number of international players, which boosted the entry. Brugnon made a welcome return but experienced many anxious moments before capturing the men's singles. He was two points from defeat at the hands of Jacquemet in the semi-final, 8–6 2–6 7–5, but overcame Artens, impressively, in the final, 6–2 6–1, to register his fourth win in the event. Aron had put up a great fight before losing to Artens, 9–7 4–6 6–2.

The ladies' singles final was full of interest. Susan Noel was 6–1 and 4–0 down against Simone Mathieu in the final, but having pulled up to within a point of 4 all and running forward to a dropshot, fractured her left wrist and was forced to retire. Two sisters, the Misses Pat and Dawn Owen, making their debut on the circuit, did quite well, particularly Pat, who defeated Cosette Saint Omer Roy, 6–4 8–6, before putting up a spirited fight against Susan Noel, 6–0 7–5. As expected, Simone Mathieu won two doubles titles, with Phyllis Satterthwaite and Martin-Legeay, while the latter took the men's doubles with Brugnon.

Martin-Legeay won the men's singles title at the Carlton Club meeting by employing a series of lobs against a tiring Brugnon in the fifth set of the final, to edge through, 2–6 6–2 6–2 2–0 6–4. Brugnon had a comfortable ride over Aron in the semi-final, but a young American, Norcross Tilney, extended him in the earlier round, to lead 6–5 in the deciding set, but the Frenchman's greater experience drew errors from his opponent to win, 6–4 3–6 8–6. Martin-Legeay strolled past Karsten in the last four, 6–2 6–2.

There was no stopping Simone Mathieu who won her fifth singles title of the season by overwhelming Phyllis Satterthwaite in the final for the third time, 6–1 6–1. Leading up to the last match, Simone Mathieu beat Paulette de Saint-Ferréol, 6–1 6–0, and Phyllis Satterthwaite defeated Cosette Saint Omer Roy, 6–4 6–3. Simone remained unbeaten at the meeting, winning the ladies' doubles with Phyllis and the mixed with Martin-Legeay. Brugnon paired with Robertson to claim the men's division.

The South of France Championships at Nice followed and was a triumph for Lesueur, who pocketed the men's singles crown. Unexpected was the downfall of Martin-Legeay by Roberston, to enter the semi-final, 6–4 6–3. Here the American beat Karsten in a long tussle. The Dutchman did not realise that he was playing the best of five sets and having gained the third set, extended his hand to receive his opponent's congratulations. This upset his concentration and he only won three more games, 4–6 6–3 4–6 6–3 6–0. In the meantime, Lesueur beat Brugnon in three ten game

BEAULIEU s/ MER

IMP.MOULLOT. MARSEILLE

Edité par la Municipalité

sets before setting a volleying attack to outpace Robertson in the final, 6–4 6–4 3–6 6–3.

Simone Mathieu went happily on her way, once again defeating Phyllis Satterthwaite in the final of the ladies' singles, 6–1 6–1, and so retained the title. After winning a first round match, Gem Hoahing could only muster two games in the second set against Olga Haycraft, who eventually fell to the champion, 6–4 6–2. Phyllis Satterthwaite had the better of Paulette de Saint Ferréoll, 6–2 6–4. Simone paired with Kay Stammers, who did not play singles, to gain the doubles and with Martin-Legeay the mixed. Lesueur and Martin-Legeay clinched the men's doubles event.

The Beaulieu Championships, played at the Beaulieu Club, adjacent to the Bristol Hotel, had a cosmopolitan entry. A number of international players were testing the local conditions for the first time, but most failed to produce their best and the honours fell chiefly to the French.

Brugnon, playing well at times, won the men's singles for the first time. Henner Henkel from Germany went down to him after winning the opening eight games in the third round, a result which revealed the Frenchman's tenacity and skill to fight back, 0–6 7–5 6–3. Camille Malfroy of New Zealand went out against Martin-Legeay in the second round, 7–5 6–3, and Ference Puncec of Yugoslavia was beaten by Ellmer in three sets, 6–3 4–6 6–2. The Swiss met his match against Lesueur in the semi-final and was well-beaten, 7–5 6–1 6–3.

Simone Mathieu retained her singles title, but in the semi-final Phyllis Satterthwaite gave her a good run in the first set, before collapsing 6–4 6–0. In the final, Simone was in command from start to finish against Billie Yorke, 6–0 6–2, but the latter's duel with Kay Stammers in the round before was the match of the event, which ended 8–6 2–6 6–3. The men's doubles final was an all-French affair with Martin-Legeay and Lesueur defeating Brugnon and Boussus, who did not play singles, 6–4 8–6 6–4. Simone Mathieu won the doubles with Kay Stammers, who also took the mixed title with Lesueur.

The steady increase in prestige over the past few years of the Monte Carlo Championships, held at the Monte Carlo Country Club, made the event the principal tournament of the season. The standard of the men was exceptional. In the singles event, fourteen of the 'last sixteen' were of Davis Cup standard, with countries such as Germany, Italy, France, Yugoslavia etc to the fore.

Von Cramm, on his first visit to the area this season, was in confident mood throughout and after defeating de Stefani in the semi-final with the loss of a set, 6–0 3–6 6–1 6–3, he overcame his compatriot, Henner Henkel, in the final by 4–6 4–6 7–5 6–4 7–5. This was a battle royal, which lasted two and a half hours and consisted of 54 games. Henkel actually led

5–3 in the third set. He gained worthy victories in the earlier rounds, as he accounted for Ellmer, 6–4 6–2, Boussus, 6–0 4–6 6–3, before crushing Palmieri in the semi-final, 2–6 6–0 6–0 6–2. There were many other outstanding contests.

Simone Mathieu continued her domination to win the title for the fourth occasion, without dropping a set. Jadwiga Jedrzejowska put up a good fight in the second set of the final, but the result was never in question, to the tune of 6–0 6–4. There was a terrific struggle in the quarter-final, by Mme Josane de Meulemeester (Sigart), who eventually beat Billie Yorke, 4–6 6–1 9–7, but the Englishwoman had several chances in the deciding set when she led at 5–3 and 6–5, but failed to take the advantage. The winner then lost to Simone Mathieu, 6–2 6–0. Kay Stammers lost to the Pole in the other semi-final, 6–4 6–0, after being well-extended by Gem Hoahing, 7–5 6–4.

The Butler Trophy was won by Martin-Legeay and Lesueur, beating Brugnon and Boussus in the final, 3–6 6–2 6–1 6–3, while the Beaumont Cup was taken by another French pair, Simone Mathieu and Edith Belliard, who easily beat Phyllis Satterthwaite and Billie Yorke in the last match, 6–4 6–2. The Championship doubles events were won by Boussus and Lesueur, Josane de Meulemeester and Simone Mathieu and Martin-Legeay and Simone Mathieu.

The departure of the German team naturally weakened the entry at the Menton Club, but nevertheless there were many first-class players competing, led by the French who won three of the six level events.

Although the holder of the ladies' singles title, Simone Mathieu, feeling the strain of her recent matches, decided to take a rest from the singles but she continued to be a force in the doubles. In her place Jadwiga Jedrzejowska won the title, beating Edith Belliard in the final without difficulty, 6–2 6–1. However, the Pole was given a hard match in the round before by Kay Stammers, who fought through 28 games before her dismissal, 6–4 8–6, while at the same stage, Edith Belliard had an easy victory over Mlle Emilie d'Hannoncelles of France, 6–0 6–2.

The consistent form of Tilney was probably the feature of the week. With a series of good wins he put behind him Kai Lund (Germany) 6–3 6–3, Kazimierz Tarlowski (Poland), 6–3 6–2, and Landau, 6–4 6–1, to reach the final and face Lesueur. Here the Frenchman won the first two sets

Jean Lesueur, recently promoted from No.6 to No.3 in the French ranking lists, won two singles titles, first the South of France Championships at Nice, beating William Robertson in the final, and at Menton, overcoming Norcross Tilney in five sets. The latter gave his prize voucher to the poor of Menton. Lesueur also won the two doubles at the meeting as well as the 'Coupe des Nations Cup' with Simone Mathieu.

and led 5–3 and 40–15 in the third, but Tilney made a fantastic recovery before eventually capitulating in the fifth set, 6–2 6–1 5–7 5–7 6–1. He gave his voucher prize to the poor of Menton. Lesueur had struggled to overcome Puncec in the last four, 6–2 5–7 6–4. Brugnon retired from the event, suffering from tennis elbow.

Susan Noel's wrist had mended sufficiently for her to partner Jadwiga Jedrzejowska to victory in the ladies' doubles final over Simone Mathieu and Edith Belliard, 6–3 6–3. Brugnon and Lesueur comfortably won the men's doubles, with the latter successful in the mixed event with Kay Stammers. Lesueur also won a fourth title with Simone Mathieu in capturing the Coupe des Nations trophy. The King of Sweden participated in the handicap events.

A week later at the Cannes Club, Simone Mathieu was back to register her ninth singles victory of the season – but only just! She was certainly given a stern challenge in the final by Jadwiga Jedrzejowska, who saved three match points in the second set and led by 5–4 30–15 in the deciding set. The Frenchwomen's sound defence just prevailed, 6–0 5–7 7–5. Kay Stammers reached the semi-final but suffered her third defeat of the tour at the hands of Jadwiga, 6–4 6–4. Earlier, Alice Weiwers had eliminated Susan Noel, 9–7 6–4, before bowing to Simone, 6–0 6–3.

Josef Siba of Czechoslovakia played some of the best tennis of his career to defeat Puncec, 6–1 6–1, Lesueur, 6–4 9–7 6–1, and in the final, Boussus, 6–3 6–8 6–2 ret'd. Apparently, the Frenchman was suffering from exhaustion. Another fine run was recorded by Robertson, who accounted for Tarlowski, 6–4 3–6 6–1, Ellmer, 6–3 6–2, and Matjka, 6–3 6–1, before he fell to Boussus, 7–5 6–1 6–2.

Lesueur won the men's doubles with Boussus and the mixed with Kay Stammers, but there was a surprise in the final of the ladies' doubles when Edith Belliard and Kay beat Simone Mathieu and Susan Noel, 2–6 6–3 6–2.

Siba followed up his success of a week earlier by reaching the final of the men's singles at the Provençal Club, with a straightforward win over Matejka, 6–2 6–1, but unfortunately the match against Josef Malacek of Czechoslovakia for the title could not be decided, owing to continuous rain. Malacek had narrowly passed Ellmer in the other semi-final, 6–2 6–1.

Simone Mathieu and Kay Stammers met for the first time during the season in the final of the ladies' singles. The Englishwoman threw away her chance of taking the second set when leading 5–2 by serving double faults and making other unforced errors, which allowed Simone to draw level. Kay was ahead again at 6–5, but Simone, a determined fighter, won the next three games for 6–2 8–6. There were easy wins in the semi-final,

There was much local interest when Fred Perry visited the Riviera for two weeks at the end of March. Due to injury he had not played for six months. He competed at the Beau Site Hotel and Cannes Club and captured both singles, defeating Max Ellmer in the finals. He also won both doubles at each venue and played with the King of Sweden in the doubles handicap. Later in the year Fred won his third singles crown at Wimbledon.

where Simone beat Grete Deutsch, 6–1 6–0, and Kay Stammers defeated Susan Noel, 6–0 6–2.

The ladies' doubles final between Simone Mathieu and Pat Owen versus Kay Stammers and Susan Noel was abandoned at 7 all in the opening set, because of rain. Malacek and Siba claimed the men's doubles and Filmer Sankey and Kay Stammers the mixed title.

A view of the Beau Site Hotel courts where the Cannes Championships were staged in March. There were six courts available.

There was great local interest when Englishman, Fred Perry, made his debut on the Riviera at the Beau Site Hotel during the last week in March. Perry, the 1934 and 1935 Wimbledon singles champion was competing in his first tournament since an injury sustained at the American Championships, six months earlier. The incident occurred in the sixth game of the singles semi-final against the American, Wilmer Allison, when Perry slipped on a damp court and fell heavily. Later doctors revealed that Perry's right kidney was severely swollen, causing much pain.

At the Beau Site Hotel, Perry won the three Cannes Championships without really exerting himself and in the singles sailed through to meet Ellmer in the final. Perry had two match points in the third set, of which he failed to take advantage. However, he was in no danger and ran out, 6–2 6–4 6–8 6–3. Perry linked up Matejka to take the men's doubles title and Simone Mathieu to capture the mixed.

Simone Mathieu continued her victory trail but there was disappointment that Susan Noel was not her adversary in the final. Paulette de Saint Ferréol had other ideas and defeated her in the semi-final, 7–5 ret'd, through indisposition. Simone won the final, 6–3 6–1. The Frenchwoman won a third title paired with Susan Noel.

The second Cannes Club meeting which followed was again dominated by Perry, who took home the three titles. By coincidence Perry faced Ellmer in the final and again the Swiss won the third set. This Perry conceded in a light-hearted mood, but his speed of foot on the baseline in the fourth set was too great for the Swiss, who was beaten, 10–8 6–2 4–6 6–3.

Perry went on to win the doubles with Ellmer and the mixed with Simone Mathieu. Added to which, he joined with the King of Sweden to win the doubles handicap event. Perry left the Riviera after two weeks, unbeaten. In July he won his third successive singles crown at Wimbledon and later in the year turned professional.

Simone Mathieu was unstoppable and had no difficulty in crushing Susan Noel in the singles final, 6–1 6–2. The Frenchwoman beat Cosette Saint Omer Roy in the semi-final, 6–1 6–1, and Susan Noel accounted for Alice Weiwers, 6–2 6–1. The two finalists lined up to win the ladies' doubles.

With the end of the season nigh, a few of the regular competitors left for other venues, but at the second Nice meeting two Frenchmen endeavoured to go through to the final of the men's singles, with Bernard Destremau launching an early attack to break Feret's defence to win, 6–1 7–5 6–2. The semi-finals were both settled in straight sets, with Destremau beating Lotan, 6–1 6–2, and Feret overcoming Ellmer, 9–7 6–1.

Simone Mathieu retained her singles title with her usual confidence, dropping three games to Jacqueline Horner, 6–1 6–2, and four games to Grete Deutsch in the final, 6–0 6–4. Destremau and Feret won the men's doubles title, while Simone achieved a 'triple' in partnership with Edith Belliard and Feret.

The last meeting of the season, held at the Monte Carlo Club from 13th to 19th April, produced some surprise results in the men's singles, with Henkel going down to Vanni Canapele, Destremau to newcomer Valentino Taroni of Italy, and Bernard to Lotan – all before the semi-final. In the end, Taroni defeated Feret in the final over five sets, 6–2 5–7 8–6 2–6 7–5.

Simone Mathieu remained unbeaten in singles during the season by winning her 14th successive title, beating Edith Belliard in the final, 6–4 6–1. The two then paired to win the ladies' doubles, while Bernard and Feret won the men's division. Simone won the mixed with Bernard.

The third Davis Cup tie played on the Riviera took place on 1st to 3rd May, when the Netherlands beat Monaco by 3 matches to 2 on the Condamine courts.

# 1937
# Simone Mathieu's Run Ends •
# Kho Sin Kie Wins Five Singles

Tennis clubs on the Riviera prepared to look forward to a very promising season, in the light of a recent devaluation of the franc, giving a consequent advantage of about 33% to British people over the previous season's exchange rate, which ensured a greater influx of visitors to the area. The pound bought 105 francs instead of 75. The leading hotels announced there would be no increase in their charges, likewise the tennis clubs. Some, indeed, such as the Menton Club, reduced their annual subscription from 500 to 400 francs. Also, many clubs spent considerable money in re-laying courts and providing extra facilities.

There was a very gentle start to the season with the New Year meeting, held at the Beau Site Hotel. Making his debut on the Riviera, the Chinese champion, Kho Sin Kie, gave an excellent display in beating Landau in a protracted final lasting five sets, 4–6 6–4 7–5 5–7 6–0. As indicated by the score, Kie showed how well he had come to terms with the local conditions. The two finalists in partnership won the men's doubles title.

Simone Mathieu pocketed the ladies' singles title for the third successive year, but was given a fierce challenge in the semi-final by Alice Weiwers, who won the long opening set before fading 8–10 6–2 6–2. In the final, Cosette Saint Omer Roy similarly put up a strong fight at the start but subsequently fell at 8–6 6–3. The latter had accounted for Iris Hutchings, 7–5 6–1. Simone joined Susan Noel (not playing singles) to win the doubles and Landau the mixed event.

Kho Sin Kie continued his good form the following week when he captured the men's singles at the 7th Monegasque Championships, held at the Condamine Courts. In the final he dictated the play from start to finish, to defeat Medecin, 6–3 6–2 6–3.

Simone Mathieu's progress to winning the singles title was not hampered, as she eased by Miss Nancy Liebert, without the loss of a game and then cruised past Iris Hutchings in the last match, 6–1 6–3. The mixed doubles final was an extended affair, with Gallepe and Simone Mathieu eventually winning, 8–6 9–7, against Kho Sin Kie and Nancy Liebert. Gallepe and Medecin won the men's doubles, but there was no ladies' doubles competition.

Normally, the Tennis Regional Commission for the Côte d'Azur each year arranged for a week's break in the tournament schedule, to allow clubs to play their championships, but this year, two weeks were allocated for club championships and inter-club matches. The circuit returned to normal for the Gallia Club meeting. Familiar with the conditions, Kho Sin Kie beat the holder, Brugnon, in the men's singles final without the loss of a set, 6–4 6–3 6–4. The Frenchman was unable to find the form he displayed a day earlier, when he passed Diederik Teschmacher, the Dutchman, 6–3 6–1. At the same stage, Karsen fought well against the Chinese player, but only achieved a 6–2 6–3 scoreline.

Simone Mathieu was again invincible in the ladies' singles, passing Iris Hutchings, 6–4 6–3, and Alice Weiwers, 6–2 6–2, to claim the title. Earlier, Alice Weiwers held control throughout by defeating Paulette de Saint Ferréol, 6–2 6–3. Brugnon won two doubles titles, pairing with Robertson and Simone Mathieu. No ladies' doubles was played.

At the Carlton Club, there was much interest centred on the first appearance on the Riviera of Sta Anita Lizana from Chile, particularly when she reached the final of the ladies' singles, to face Simone Mathieu. In very windy conditions, the Chilean recovered from a poor start, winning four games from 1–4. She was then outplayed by the driving ability of Simone, who won the next nine games for 7–5 6–0. A very large crowd watched the contest. In the semi-finals, Simone Mathieu crushed Nancy Liebert, 6–0 6–0, while Anita Lizana eased past Cosette Saint Omer Roy, 6–1 6–3.

Making his debut on the Riviera, the Chinese champion, Kho Sin Kie won five singles titles at the Beau Site Hotel, Monaco Championships, Gallia Club, the South of France Championships at Nice and later in the season, Nice again.

Kho Sin Kie suffered his first defeat of the season, being well beaten in the quarter-final, 6–3 6–1, by the Czechoslovakian, Eugene Ambros, who went on to pass Robertson, 6–3 6–4, to reach the final, but then lost to his compatriot, Vojtech Vodicka, 6–2 6–1 6–2. Brugnon fell to Vodicka in the semi-final, 6–2 6–1. Simone Mathieu won the ladies' doubles event with Anita Lizana and achieved a third success with Brugnon in the mixed.

Another week and the action moved along the coast to the Nice Club at the Parc Imperial, where the South of France titles were up for contention.

The enthusiasts were hoping for the ladies' singles event to conclude with a rousing final between Simone Mathieu and Anita Lizana – and they were far from being disappointed. Compared to the week before, the match was on a knife-edge throughout. Starting erratically, the Chilean lost the opening set but played herself in and led 2–1 in the final set. The Frenchwoman's steadiness and general courtcraft allowed her to reach 5–2. Anita saved a match point and fought back to 5 all, but here Simone's

Anita Lizana from Chile made an impressive start when she visited the coast for the first time and took Simone Mathieu to an advantage set at the Carlton Club. She lost again to her the following week but later acclimatised to the local conditions and swept to victory at Menton and the Cannes Club, beating on both occasions Jadwiga Jedrzejowska, another first time visitor.

experience and greater consistency prevailed as she won the next two games and the match, 6–3 2–6 7–5. The winner was not threatened on the way to the final, easily putting aside Paulette de Saint Ferréol, 6–0 6–0, but the Chilean was given a strong tussle by Mary Hardwick, when her overall control gave her a victory at 6–4 6–2.

Kho Sin Kie won his fourth title of the season, displaying form which to some degree had deserted him the week before. In the quarter-final he passed Karl Schroder of Sweden, 6–0 6–4, then Brugnon, 6–1 1–6 6 4 6–3, and in the final, Lesueur, the holder, 13–11 6–3 4–6 6–3. The Chinese won the men's doubles with Brugnon and Simone Mathieu and Joan Ingram took the ladies' event, the latter winning the mixed with Lesueur. The King of Sweden participated in handicap events.

The entry at the Beaulieu Club was of very high quality, with many of the matches being outstanding. In the men's singles final, Henkel attacking with his service and formidable on the volley, gained his first victory over his fellow countryman, von Cramm, 5–7 6–2 6–3. Neither German lost a set on the way to the final, with Henkel defeating Pierre Geelhand of Belgium, 6–2 8–6, and Vodicka, 6–1 6–2, and von Cramm passing Robertson, 6–3 6–3, and Hecht, 6–3 6–3. There were two Englishmen making their debut. Charles Hare shone in ousting Sven Nystrom of Sweden, 6–0 6–1, and Frantisek Cejnar, 6–3 1–6 6–2, but fell to Vodicka in the fourth round, 6–1 6–3. Don Butler was no match for Schroder, 6–3 6–2. Kho Sin Kie left the scene early on, dispatched by Vodicka, 6–4 6–4.

Simone Mathieu won the cup outright by beating newcomer Frau Hilde Sperling of Denmark, formerly of Germany, in the final, 7–5 6–1. It was the Dane's first defeat on hard courts for two years. The match was remarkable for the length of some of the rallies, which at times reached 70 strokes. Simone Mathieu was 5–2 down in the first set before winning 11 of the next 12 games – she was so determined to win. In the semi-final, Simone, in a tight match, beat Anita Lizana, 6–2 7–5, but Hilde Sperling showed no mercy to Mary Hardwick, 6–0 6–1. As expected, Henkel and von Cramm were too good for all in the men's doubles. Hilde Sperling won the doubles with Simone Mathieu and the mixed in tandem with Pat Hughes.

Once again a first-class entry was assembled at the Monte Carlo Country Club for the Monte Carlo Championships and the international doubles trophies. In an exceptionally strong field, von Cramm retained the men's singles title, overcoming Boussus in the final. The German appeared to have something in hand when he led by 2 sets to 1, but Boussus, in fighting mood, took the fourth set and led 2–0 in the fifth. Von Cramm drew on his resources to triumph, 6–2 3–6 6–2 2–6 6–3. Von Cramm had forfeited a set to Vodicka, 4–6 6–2 6–4, but outplayed Palmieri, in the semi-final, 6–0 8–6 6–2. Boussus also showed good form, passing through the draw to defeat Kho Sin Kie, 1–6 6–0 6–4, and Henkel, for a place in the final, 3–6 1–6 6–3 6–4 6–2.

The ladies' singles event created much interest with Simone Mathieu and Hilde Sperling reaching the final without the loss of a set. When rain stopped play in this match, the French woman led 6–5 in the opening set. However, on resumption the following day, Hilde won the next three games for the set and at this stage, Simone, rather surprisingly, retired, preferring to reserve herself for her doubles matches. In the semi-final, Hilde Sperling had beaten Anita Lizana, 6–0 6–4, while Simone Mathieu comfortably defeated Mme Colette Boegner (Rosambert), 6–0 6–4. The latter had earlier notched up a good win over Jadwiga Jedrzejowska, 6–2 1–6 7–5.

Simone Mathieu's loss in the singles brought to an end an unprecedented run of success on the French Riviera, in which she captured 36 consecutive titles, 16 in 1935, 14 in 1936 and 6 in 1937.

Von Cramm and Henkel won the Butler Trophy beating Hare and Hughes in the final, 7–5 6–3 6–3. There was a strange score in the semi-final when the Germans disposed of Boussus and Brugnon, 6–1 1–6 6–0

Another first-timer to the Riviera was Denmark's Hilde Sperling, formerly Krahwinkel, who lost in her initial outing to Simone Mathieu at Beaulieu. However, a week later at Monte Carlo the roles were reversed when the Frenchwoman withdrew during the final bringing to a close her 36 consecutive title run.

6–0. Simone Mathieu and Colette Boegner retained the Beaumont Cup after a very tight struggle in the final versus Joan Ingram and Billie Yorke, 6–3 6–8 6–3.

The Monte Carlo doubles championships were won by Butler and Hughes, Simone Mathieu and Hilde Sperling, while the mixed event was divided at the semi-final stage, due to rain – the first for a month.

With the Germans having moved on elsewhere, the singles titles for the Riviera Championships at Menton Club were won by two hitherto unsuccessful competitors on the Riviera. Schroder, in much better form than in earlier meetings, won through to win the singles title without the loss of a set. In sequence he beat d'Adhemar, 6–3 6–2, Vodica, 6–4 6–1, then the two Poles, Tloczyski, and in the title round, Kazimieriz Tarlowski, 8–6 6–2 6–4. For his part the latter had the better of Cenjar, 6–2 6–4, and Hebda, 6–4 6–4. Earlier, Tloczyski accounted for Kho Sin Kie, 6–8 6–4 6–2.

Anita Lizana won her first singles title on the Riviera by securing victory over Jadwiga Jedrzejowska in a very hard-fought match which, unfortunately, did not go the full distance. Capturing the opening set at 8–6, the Chilean might have won the contest when she led 5–2 in the second, but she faltered and allowed her opponent to run out at 8–6. In the third set the Pole fell in the third game and was forced to retire, due to cramp, leaving the score at 6–8 8–6 1–1 ret'd. Both finalists were given much to think about in the semi-final, with the winner edging past Alice Weiwers, 8–6 6–4, and the runner-up passing Miss Penny Weekes of England, 6–1 7–5.

Due to continuous rain, neither of the three doubles events could be finalised after reaching the semi-final stage. Fortunately, the international contest for the Coupe des Nations was completed, which allowed Brugnon and Paulette de Saint Ferréol to defeat Schroder and Miss Gull Roberg of Sweden in the final, 6–3 6–4. The King of Sweden paired with Schroder to win the handicap doubles.

Continuing in a winning vein, Anita Lizana won the singles for the second week running at the Cannes Club, ending with victory again over Jadwiga Jedrzejowska in the final. The Chilean had many chances to win the Côte d'Azur Championships in two sets, as she led 5–1 in the first and second sets. She won the first set 7–5, but was overtaken in the next by the same score. In the decider she took control to dominate the play to win the match, lasting just over two hours, 7–5 5–7 6–1. Both finalists had been hard-pushed in the round before, Anita by Mlle Simone Iribarne, France's No.2 player, 3–6 6–0 6–3, and Jadwiga Jedrzejowska by Alice Weiwers, 6–1 5–7 6–4. Joan Ingram had fallen victim to the Chilean in the quarter-final, 6–2 7–5.

At the Monte Carlo Country Club an exceptionally strong entry was achieved in the men's singles, the outcome being that Gottfried von Cramm (left) retained his title, beating Christian Boussus in the final over five sets.

The men's singles final was the reverse of the week earlier, when Tarlowski overcame Schroder in four sets, 6–2 3–6 9–7 6–4. Count Adam Baworowski of Austria, who lost to Tarlowski in the semi-final, 6–3 6–3, had two excellent wins, first over Merlin, 6–3 6–3, and then Ellmer, 6–4 7–9 6–3. Tarlowski was given a walkover to the final, when Georg von Metaxa of Austria retired.

Simone Iribarne won the ladies' doubles with Jacqueline Goldschmidt in a surprising win in the final over Anita Lizana and Jadwiga Jedrzejowska, 3–6 6–4 6–4. Brugnon, playing just doubles, paired with Schroder to win the men's division, while Baworowski and Simone Iribarne won the mixed.

Kho Sin Kie, who earlier won the South of France Championships at the Nice Club, repeated his success at the second meeting. Showing great control, he defeated Ellmer, 6–3 6–3, before dominating Baworowski in the final in straight sets, 6–4 6–0 6–4. Probably the outstanding match of the event took place in a duel to reach the final, where Baworowski eventually downed Merlin, after saving a match point in the third set, 6–4 6–8 9–7.

Jacqueline Goldschmidt did well to win the ladies' title on her first singles appearance of the season, beating a much-improved Alice Weiwers in the final, 6–3 1–6 6–3. The winner was not in danger, beating England's Miss Denise Huntbach in the semi-final, 6–1 6–4, but Alice Weiwers was pushed to the limit by Grete Deutsch, 11–9 4–6 6–3. Earlier, Joan Ingram was ousted by Alice Weiwers, 6–2 6–3, and Denise Huntbach accounted for Nancy Liebert, 7–5 8–10 7–5, and Paulette de Saint Ferréol, 1–6 6–4 6–0. The doubles winners were Baworowski and von Metaxa, Joan Ingram and Cosette Saint Omer Roy, while the mixed doubles was divided between Merlin and Joan Ingram and Ellmer and Alice Weiwers.

After being within one game of defeat in the final of the men's singles, Baworowski came from behind to win the Cannes Championships, held at the Beau Site Hotel. He trailed Ellmer by 2 sets to 1 and 4–5 in the third, before recovering to lose only one more game and eventually to triumph, 5–7 5–7 7–5 6–0 6–1. The Austrian had played a clever match to eliminate newcomer Daniel Prenn of Germany in the semi-final, 7–5 6–4, while in the other half of the draw, Ellmer beat von Metaxa, 6–2 6–4. Earlier, Boworowski defeated Karsten, 6–3 6–3.

Alice Weiwers won her first singles title during the season with great ease from Grete Deutsch, 6–0 6–1. A surprise semi-finalist was Miss Mary Norman from Staffordshire, who did well in stretching Alice Weiwers to 6–4 6–2. Earlier, she had produced a shock in eliminating Joan Ingram, 1–6 6–1 6–4. Grete Deutsch beat Cosette Saint Omer Roy, 6–3 6–3.

Muriel Thomas returned to tournament play and with Grete Deutsch won the ladies' doubles title. Baworowski and von Metaxa took the men's doubles and Prenn and Joan Ingram the mixed event.

The winners of the previous week's tournament were again successful at the Monte Carlo second gathering, held over the Easter weekend. Baworowski, who received a walkover from von Metaxa in the semi-final, was forced to come from behind to claim the singles title, after being led by 2 sets to 1 by Bernard. The final score was 6–2 3–6 5–7 7–5 6–3. Bernard reached the final via Prenn, 6–3 7–5.

Alice Weiwers had one of the best successes of her career when she beat Colette Boegner in the singles final, 8–6 6–1. In the semi-final the winner was given a walkover by Cosette Saint Omer Roy and Colette Boegner, the runner-up was given a good game by Mary Norman, 6–1 6–4. Baworowski and von Metaxa repeated their doubles win and Joan Ingram gained two doubles events, paired with Phyllis Satterthwaite and von Metaxa.

Despite many of the leading players having deserted the scene, the Provençal Club held a successful meeting, attracting familiar names, particularly among the ladies. The men's singles title was won by a Parisien,

Christian de Galea, who defeated Noghes in an excellent match for the title, 10–8 6–4. Noghes had reached this stage by overcoming Max Belhommet of France.

Undoubtedly, the best lady present was Alice Weiwers, who in the semi-final of the ladies' singles beat Mary Norman, the early conqueror of Paulette de Saint Ferréol, before comfortably winning the title from Susan Noel, 6–3 6–4. The Englishwoman had eliminated Jacqueline Horner in the round before. In the ladies' doubles final, there was a mild surprise when Jacqueline Horner and Susan Noel beat Cosette Saint Omer Roy and Alice Weiwers, 11–9 6–3. The men's doubles was captured by de Galea and Noghes, while Max Belmommet paired with Alice Weiwers to take the mixed title.

The last tournament of the season was held at the Miramar Club at Juan-les-Pins from 12th to 18th April and consisted of just three events. Lotan was successful in the men's singles, defeating Edmond Rivoire in the final, 6–3 6–2 6–4. Susan Noel won the ladies' singles, but was given a hard fight by Frl Stein in the final, 6–3 3–6 7–5. The men's doubles final was won by Rivoire and Phillipe Ville of France over Lotan and Fernand d'Ainvelle, 6–1 1–6 5–4, abandoned.

At the beginning of the year, a testimonial was organised for George Simond, who had refereed some 35 years on the Riviera. He was 70 years of age and it was felt a fitting opportunity for those who had derived so much pleasure from competition in the tournament under his control, to recognise the fine service he had rendered to the game. A committee was set up consisting of the Marquis and Marchioness of Cholmondeley, Lord and Lady Roundway, Lord Charles Hope, Sir Arthur and Lady Crosfield, Jean Borotra, Wallis Myers and Brame Hillyard.

Over the next couple of months, over 400 people from all walks of life, involved one way or another with tennis on the Riviera contributed, with the list being headed by the King of Sweden, the Duke of Connaught and other notable personalities.

As a mark of appreciation a testimonial was organised for George Simond who had practically refereed every tournament on the Riviera since the turn of the century. With him is Phyllis Satterthwaite.

# 1938
# Eastern Europeans Excel • Five Singles to Jadwiga Jedrzejowska and Alice Weiwers

Following the usual pattern, the New Year meeting opened the proceedings of the season at the Beau Site Hotel, from 27th December to 2nd January.

From a good class entry Rogers won through the men's singles to capture the title from Kho Sin Kie, 1–6 6–4 6–2. To reach this last stage, the Irishman had to overcome Ellmer in a tight struggle, 6–8 6–3 7–5. In the other semi-final, the Chinese player was not worried throughout by Jacquemet, to win, 6–2 6–4.

Old opponents, Alice Weiwers and Cosette Saint Omer Roy, met in the final of the ladies' singles with the former coming out on top, 3–6 6–4 6–4. The men's doubles was taken by Ellmer and Rogers and, as anticipated, the ladies' event was won by Cosette Saint Omer Roy and Alice Weiwers. The mixed doubles was one of the most interesting events of the tournament, with Rogers and Muriel Thomas eventually beating Ellmer and Alice Weiwers, 5–7 7–5 7–5.

Kho Sin Kie retained his men's singles title at the 8th Monegasque Championships held, as usual, at the Condamine courts, by overcoming all the local players without difficulty. In the last two rounds he accounted for Noghes, 6–0 3–0 ret'd and Medecin, 6–1 6–0 6–3. Earlier, Medecin beat Gallepe, 6–3 6–3. Rogers did not play in the singles but paired with Kho Sin Kie to win the doubles from Gallepe and Landau, 6–1 6–4 3–6 6–4.

Jeannette Poncelet, from Nice, dominated the ladies' singles, although she dropped a set in the final to Iris Hutchings, 2–6 6–3 6–0. Kho Sin Kie teamed with Nancy Liebert to beat Gallepe and Jeannette Poncelet in the final of the mixed, 6–3 3–6 7–5. A ladies' doubles event was not played.

The season's first visit to the Monte Carlo Country Club recorded that Kho Sin Kie took his revenge for recent defeats by Rogers, by capturing the men's singles final in a well-fought match over four sets, 6–0 6–4 4–6. 8–6. The field was not particularly strong and the finalists passed opponents in the semi-finals, Kho Sin Kie beating Medecin, 6–1 6–2, and Rogers losing the middle set to d'Adhemar, 6–0 6–8 6–4.

Alice Weiwers again showed outstanding form as she moved through the ladies' singles without dropping a set. She beat Iris Hutchings, 6–4 7–5, and then Billie Yorke to win the title, 6–2 6–4. The latter had difficulty in passing Cosette Saint Omer Roy, 7–5 7–5. There was a surprise in the final of the men's doubles when Medecin and Noghes beat Kho Sin Kie and Rogers, 7–5 10–8 7–5. Simone Mathieu made an appearance in the ladies' doubles with newcomer from England, Miss Valerie Scott, but they retired in the final. Kho Sin Kie and Nancy Liebert won the mixed competition.

The next tournament centred on the Gallia Club at Cannes, where Robertson distinguished himself by producing an outstanding performance to win the men's singles title. Passing du Plaix without a problem in the semi-final, 6–2 6–0, he then took advantage of a slow court to ease through against Rogers in the final, 6–1 6–3 7–5. The day before, the latter produced his best to eliminate Brugnon, 6–3 6–3. Kho Sin Kie did not compete in the event.

Alice Weiwers maintained her early promise to win the first prize in the ladies' singles. In the semi-final she defeated Billie Yorke, 6–2 6–1, in advance of taking the title with her steady play against Miss Gracyn Wheeler, No.5 in America, making her debut on the Riviera, 3–6 6–3 6–0. The American had quite a fight on her hands in disposing of Valerie Scott, 7–5 7–5. A close quarter-final contest resulted in Valerie beating Susan Noel, 7–5 4–6 6–3. In the finals of the doubles, Kho Sin Kie and Rogers beat Brugnon and Robertson, 6–4 8–6, and Alice Weiwers and Cosette Saint Omer Roy beat Valerie Scott and Muriel Thomas, 7–5 6–4. The mixed event was unfinished.

Alice Weiwers continued to dominate the ladies' play by winning her fourth singles title of the season at the Carlton Club. In the last two rounds she defeated Valerie Scott, 6–4 2–6 6–3, and in a repeat of the week before, Gracyn Wheeler, 6–3 6–1. The latter had earlier beaten Cosette Saint Omer Roy, 6–0 3–6 6–4. Unusually, there were two walkovers in the quarter-final, Valerie Scott passing Susan Noel and Cosette Saint Omer Roy defeating Billie Yorke.

The anticipated men's singles final between Kho Sin Kie and Rogers did not materialise, as the Irishman arrived at the ground too late for his quarter-final match against Martin-Legeay, who was given a walkover. In the semi-final, Kho Sin Kie beat Ellmer, 6–2 3–6 7–5, and took the title, beating Robertson in a long series of rallies, 6–3 6–1 6–3. The latter passed Martin-Legeay in the semi-final, 6–3 6–1.

Kho Sin Kie and Rogers continued their successful doubles partnership by winning the title over Brugnon and Martin-Legeay. This was a long match in which the French pair were 0–4 down in the fifth set and managed to recover, but eventually lost in the 24th game. The final score was 10–8 1–6 6–2 3–6 13–11. Alice Weiwers also won the doubles with Cosette Saint Omer Roy, beating Simone Mathieu and Gracyn Wheeler in the final, 6–2 4–6 6–1, and was successful in the mixed event with Kho Sin Kie.

Spectators attending the South of France Championships staged at the Nice Club were richly rewarded by viewing some very exciting matches. Without doubt, the most fascinating contest of the week occurred in the quarter-final of the ladies' singles, where Gem Hoahing, aged 17, making her first competitive play of the year, brought off the best win of her burgeoning career by eventually defeating Simone Mathieu. This confrontation lasted for two hours and reached a climax in the third set when the Chinese girl saved two match points at 4–5, before reaching 7–6 and match point. She faltered, but eventually won in the 24th game. The final score was 6–4 1–6 13–11. Simone Mathieu played well, but was not up to her best as she was still convalescing after a recent illness. Gem went on to beat Valeric Scott, coming from behind at 1–5 in the opening set, to win 8–6 6–3, but then in the final could not counter Gracyn Wheeler's service and attack and was beaten, 6–4 6–2. The American defeated Alice Weiwers in the semi-final, 6–4 2–6 6–4. Billie Yorke did not compete.

Kho Sin Kie won the men's singles championship, attacking severely in the final, versus Ellmer, 6–1 2–6 6–0 8–6. Both finalists reached the title round in straight sets, Kho Sin Kie beating Robertson, 6–2 6–1 6–3, and Ellmer dismissing Medecin, 6–2 6–4 6–1. The latter surprised Rogers early on, 8–6 4–6 6–3.

At Nice, during the South of France Championships, there was a memorable encounter when 17-year old Gem Hoahing brought off one of the best wins of her career by beating Simone Mathieu after two hours 6–4 1–6 11–9. During this, Gem saved two match points. She went on to lose to the American, Gracyn Wheeler in the final.

Austin was on the ground, but only competed in the doubles, in partnership with Rogers. They reached the final but lost to Brugnon and Kho Sin Kie after five sets, 6–2 6–3 3–6 1–6 6–2. Jadwiga Jedrzejowska won both doubles, in tandem with Simone Mathieu and Brugnon.

The meeting at the Beaulieu Club attracted a very high-level entry, with several of England's leading players taking part, as well as 15 players of Davis Cup status and some ladies who were holders of national championships. The weather was fine all the week. Throughout the men's singles there were many fine contests involving mid-European players, which led to Puncec winning the title by overcoming Cejnar in a very long affair, 6–8 6–3 0–6 6–4 6–3. Puncec came through the field at the expense of Czeslaw Spychala of Poland, 6–1 8–6, Richard Ritchie (son of Major Ritchie), 6–2 6–3, Dragutin Mitic (Yugoslavia), 6–1 6–3, and to some degree surprisingly, Austin in the semi-final, 7–5 6–4 . On his part, Cejnar accounted for Hughes, 1–6 6–3 6–3, Hecht by walkover and Boussus, 6–0 3–6 6–1. Earlier, Hebda put out Rogers, 6–4 6–4, before losing to Mitic, 6–1 6–4, and in all English encounters, Peters beat Butler, 6–0 6–4, before falling to Austin, 6–3 6–2.

Returning to the Riviera, Peggy Scriven produced excellent form from the start and in the end regained the title she won in 1933. Her hardest match was against Billie Yorke in the quarter-final, which took over two hours to decide. She led by a set and 5–2, but allowed herself to be caught before eventually settling the matter, 6–3 5–7 6–4. From there she proceeded to pass Gracyn Wheeler, 6–3 6–4, and in the final, Jadwiga Jedrzejowska, 5–7 6–1 6–3. Seven of the last 16 were English contenders. Austin and Hughes combined well to beat Kho Sin Kie and Rogers in the doubles final, 6–2 5–7 13–15 6–3 6–3. Jadwiga Jedrzejowska and Muriel Thomas won the ladies' doubles and Henri Bolelli (France) paired with the Pole to take the mixed event.

As expected, the tournament for the Monte Carlo Championships, held at the Monte Carlo Country Club, featured the best entry of the season and included the majority of the players from the previous week at Beaulieu. In a large draw for the men's singles, Puncec was in irresistible form once again, to capture the title, so much so that, after passing Hecht in three sets, 6–4 6–2 6–3, he crushed Boussus in the final, 6–0 6–1 6–1, winning the first 11 games. The Frenchman had played brilliantly to dispose of Bolelli in the semi-final, 7–5 6–0 6–2, following a tight match against Kho Sin Kie, 2–6 6–4 10–8. In the quarter-finals, Bolelli beat Cejnar, 2–6 6–0 6–3, Puncec beat Peters, 6–3 6–2, and Hecht beat Ronald Shayes of England, 6–0 3–6 8–6. Other notable encounters were Ellmer's defeat of Rogers, 6–4 3–6 6–4, before losing to Hecht, 6–3 12–10, and the major upset of the week, when Bolelli ousted Austin in his first match, 6–4 6–3. The Englishman was seeded No.1 and exempted from the earlier rounds.

Jadwiga Jedrzejowska avenged her previous week's defeat at the hands of Peggy Scriven, by her straightforward victory in the final, 6–4 6–3. Peggy had quite a struggle to dismiss Gracyn Wheeler in the semi-final, 4–6 6–2 6–3, while the winner eased through against Alice Weiwers, 6–4 6–1. The four losers in the quarter-final were all English players, Olga Haycraft, Effie Peters, Rita Jarvis and Patricia O'Connell, the last two making their debut. Simone Mathieu did not compete.

The Butler Trophy was won by Bolelli and Pierre Pellizza, who put out another French pair in the final, Boussus and Brugnon, 7–5 6–3 4–6 7–5. Austin and Hughes reached the semi-final, but lost to the runners-up, 4–6 6–3 1–6 6–0 6–2. Simone Mathieu and Colette Boegner retained the Beaumont Cup with victory in the final over Betty Nuthall and Billie Yorke, 6–4 6–0. The winners had passed Susan Noel and Peggy Scriven without too much difficulty in the semi-final, 7–5 6–1, while the runners-up defeated Valerie Scott and Muriel Thomas at the same stage, 6–4 1–6 6–4. The winners of the Monte Carlo Championships were Kho Sin Kie and Rogers, Jadwiga Jedrzejowska and Muriel Thomas, and Hebda and Jadwiga Jedrzejowska. The King of Sweden, at 80, took part in the handicap events.

After the hustle and bustle of Monte Carlo, the Menton Club meeting was a quieter affair but, nevertheless, a very successful competition. Schroder retained the Riviera Championships men's singles title in the face of strong opposition from the Central European players. In the final, he faced Taroni, back on the circuit after missing a year, who had made a good impression in passing Spyschala, 6–2 5–7 6–1, Rogers, 6–1 3–6 6–1, and Pachowski, 3–6 7–5 6–1, to reach that stage. However, the Swede's game, to some degree, overwhelmed him and he went down, 6–3 6–2 6–1. The winner had experienced an anxious time in defeating Baworowski in the semi-final, 3–6 7–5 6–1. Earlier, Pachowski had impressed, with victories over Butler, 7–5 5–7 6–1, and Lesueur, the winner of the title in 1936, 10–8 6–4. Shayes fell to Spychala in a tough match, 3–6 7–5 7–5.

There was quite an upset in the ladies' singles semi-final when Mlle Hella Kovac, Yugoslavia's leading player, eliminated Peggy Scriven, 1–6 6–2 6–1, following the exit of two other English players, Rita Jarvis, 7–5 6–4, and Valerie Scott, 9–7 6–4. However, Hella managed to hold Jadwiga Jedrzejowska on level terms for two sets in the final, but the Pole's experience and patience won in the end, 4–6 6–4 6–2. In the round before, the winner had beaten Mary Whitmarsh, a young Englishwoman, making her debut, 6–2 6–1. Bolelli and Lesueur won the men's doubles and Rita Jarvis and Valerie Scott took the ladies' division, while Bolelli won a second title with Jadwiga Jedrzejowska. There was a very impressive performance by Shayes, linking up with Peggy Scriven to win the Coupe des Nations.

Regaining the form she displayed last summer, Jadwiga Jedrzejowska won all three events at the Côte d'Azur Championships, held at the Cannes Club. In the final of the singles she defeated Alice Weiwers, who confirmed the advance she had made in the game, after a close struggle, 6–2 5–7 6–4. The winner passed Grete Deutsch in the semi-final, 6–2 6–0, and Alice Weiwers struggled past Susan Noel, 9–7 7–5. The Pole won the ladies' doubles with Muriel Thomas, defeating the well-tried pair of Cosette Saint Omer Roy and Alice Weiwers in the final, 6–4 6–4, and joined Brugnon to take the mixed event from Hebda and Muriel Thomas, 6–4 1–6 6–2.

Schroder was surprisingly beaten in the final of the men's singles by Baworowski in five sets, 2–6 6–3 3–6 1–6 6–3. The Austrian's steady play earned him the deciding set against an opponent who all through the match did not serve up to his usual standard. The Swede beat Tloczynski in the round before, 6–4 6–1, while Baworowski was given a walkover by Hebda. Shayes lost to Owen Anderson from America in the third round, 6–4 6–4. Brugnon and Schroder won the men's doubles.

The following week, the circuit moved east along the coast to the Provençal Club. In contrast to the past few weeks, the men's standard was considerably lower and allowed Constantin Tanacescu from Romania to win his first singles event of the season. After beating Penth Forsmann of Finland in the semi-final, 6–0 6–3, he moved on to victory over Ake Wallen from Sweden in the final, 6–3 6–3 6–1. The Romanian did not drop a set in the event.

Jadwiga Jedrzejowska was not extended in capturing the ladies' singles and had a straightforward win over Grete Deutsch in the last match, 6–3 6–4. The winner accounted for Paulette de Saint Ferréol in the semi-final, 6–0 6–2. Schroder, who did not play singles, won the men's doubles with Wallen and the mixed doubles with Jadwiga Jedrzejowska.

Rogers returned to competition play at the Beau Site Hotel, where the Cannes Championships were contested. He was in good form, beating in turn, Jacquemet, 7–5 6–1, Ellmer, 6–0 6–4, to reach the final where he comfortably beat Schroder, 6–4 6–3 6–3. In this last match, the Irishman maintained his attack throughout, preventing his Swedish opponent from using his volleying skill. For his part, Schroder had the better of du Plaix, 6–4 6–3, and the winner from the previous week, Tanacescu, 6–3 6–2.

Jadwiga Jedrzejowska beat Alice Weiwers for the third time in the season, capturing the final of the Cannes Championship, 6–1 8–6. This was her fifth title in as many weeks. The Pole eased past Cosette Saint Omer Roy, 6–2 6–2 in the semi-final, while Alice Weiwers was too good for Susan Noel, 6–3 7–5.

Simone Mathieu reappeared in competitive play in the doubles events, but was eliminated in both at the semi-final stage. Success in the doubles events was achieved by Ellmer and Rogers, Jadwiga Jedrzejowska and Muriel Thomas and Ellmer and Alice Weiwers.

The gathering at the Miramar Club at Juan-les-Pins was well-supported by the players, considering the season was drawing to a close. Lesueur was in dazzling form to take the men's title, winning in straight sets over Tanacescu in the final, 6–3 6–2 6–1. He was also quite severe in disposing of M. Badin of Romania, 6–2 6–2, in the semi-final, where Jacquemet fell to the runner-up 6–0 6–4.

Jedwiga Jedrzejowska struck a 'purple patch' mid-season by capturing five singles titles in as many weeks. Her outstanding forehand drive served her well to win at Monte Carlo, Menton, Cannes Club, Provençal Club and the Beau Site Hotel.

In March the International Club of Great Britain with the King of Sweden as part of the team, played the IC of Monaco. Left to right: Monaco – Vladimir Landau, Christian Jaffredy, Christian de la Plane, P. Nicorini, Maurice Schlegel, Gaston Medecin. GB – The King, Jacques Brugnon, Kho Sin Kie, Eric Peters, Bunny Austin and Wallis Myers. In between the teams is Princess Antoinette of Monaco. Myers was responsible for the founding of the IC of GB.

Alice Weiwers continued her great run of success to take the ladies' singles, but she was forced to drop a set to Jacqueline Goldschmidt in the final, 6–3 2–6 6–2. Alice beat Paulette de Saint Ferréol in the round before, 6–0 6–2, while the runner-up was pushed hard to oust Jacqueline Horner, 6–3 9–7.

Simone Mathieu chose not to play singles but, as usual, was dominant in the doubles. She registered two victories in the ladies' class, with Muriel Thomas, beating Cosette Saint Omer Roy and Alice Weiwers in the final, 6–4 6–4, and with Lesueur in the mixed final, accounting for Tanacescu and Cosette Saint Omer Roy, 6–1 6–3.

Destremau reappeared in singles play, to win the second Nice Club tournament at the Parc Imperial, recovering from losing the opening two sets to defeat Lesueur in the singles final, 2–6 4–6 9–7 6–3 6–3. Destremau had beaten Tanacescu, 1–6 7–5 6–1, and Lesueur defeated Jacquemet, 6–0 6–2, in the semi-finals. The latter had produced the shock of the event by ousting Kho Sin Kie in the quarter-final, 6–3 6–3.

Simone Mathieu won the ladies' singles without conceding a set. She comfortably passed Cosette Saint Omer Roy in the semi-final, 6–2 6–4, before defeating Alice Weiwers, 7–5 6–3. Jeannette Poncelet had a notable win over Jacqueline Horner, 6–1 6–4, prior to losing to Alice Weiwers, 6–1 6–0. The winners of the doubles were Lesueur and Kho Sin Kie, Cosette Saint Omer Roy and Alice Weiwers and Destremau and Mme Arlette Halff of France. There were four handicap events, in which the King of Sweden played with Lesueur and Simone Mathieu.

The Monte Carlo Country Club was the venue for the concluding tournament of the season, held over Easter, 18th to 24th April. The entry was comparatively small, with the major honours being achieved by French players.

Destremau continued to produce his best in winning the men's singles, easing through the field to beat fellow Frenchman, René Jamain, in the final, 6–4 6–2 6–1. Deciding to play singles, Simone Mathieu coasted through, and well in control defeated Alice Weiwers in the last match, 6–4 6–0. There was an interesting contest in the men's doubles final, when Destremau and Antoine Gentien (France) beat Landry and Tanacescu in four sets, 3–6 6–2 6–4 6–2. The ladies' doubles title went to Cosette Saint Omer Roy and Alice Weiwers, and the mixed to Gentien and Simone Mathieu.

# 1939

# Six Singles to Simone Mathieu, Five to Alice Weiwers, Four to Constantin Tanacescu

The season began, as usual, with the New Year meeting, held at the Beau Site Hotel at Cannes. Two Romanians took a prominent part in the proceedings, when Tanacescu and newcomer, M. Badin contested the men's singles final, with the former winning, 1–6 6–0 7–5 6–4. They paired for the men's doubles but, after a two hour struggle, were beaten in the final by the Monagasquians, Gallepe and Medecin, 10–8 8–6 5–7 6–1.

Alice Weiwers proved her worth by taking the ladies' singles title, beating her old foe, Cosette Saint Omer Roy in the final, 7–5 7–5. In the semi-finals, Alice Weiwers beat Mme Emmanuelli, 8–6 6–2, and Cosette Saint Omer Roy defeated Princess Anne d'Orléans (Orbrag), 6–1 6–1. In the mixed doubles final, Gallepe and Cosette Saint Omer Roy defeated Tanacescu and Alice Weiwers, 6–4 6–4. There was no ladies' doubles event.

Borotra made his first appearance on the Riviera since 1926, when he competed in the Monegasque Championships, held on the Condamine Courts. He took matters in his stride up to the semi-final where he beat Badin, 7–5 6–1, before proceeding to overcome some resistance from Tanacescu in the final, 6–3 11–9.

Alice Weiwers, who had recently been added to the French ranking lists at No.4, eased past Iris Hutchings in the singles final, 6–0 6–3, and then won a second title, capturing the mixed doubles in partnership with Tanacescu over Christian de la Plane and Iris Hutchings, 6–1 6–3. Badin and Tanacescu combined to bring off a surprise win in the final of the men's doubles, over Borotra and Medecin, 6–4 6–1. There was no ladies' doubles event.

After a two week break, the circuit resumed at the Monte Carlo Country Club. The big upset of the meeting was the defeat of Simone Mathieu in the final of the ladies' singles by Alice Weiwers, 6–4 4–6 7–5. The Frenchwoman was not able to reproduce her usual remorseless type of tennis so soon after competing on wood in Paris. Alice Weiwers' improvement had been noticeable for some time and she gained her just reward. She had confidently beaten Iris Hutchings in the round before, 6–1 6–1, while Simone Mathieu had likewise accounted for Weeta Crawshay Williams, 6–2 6–1.

For the second year running, Alice Weiwers from Luxembourg dominated the early season's play, resulting in her winning five singles titles. Her partnership with Cosette Saint Omer Roy brought them a total of 14 titles on the Riviera.

Tanacescu impressed those present with his all-round ability and he was rewarded by winning the men's singles title by beating Rogers in the final, 6–3 7–5, following his easy win over Medecin in the round before, 6–2 6–1. Rogers passed Badin at the same time, 6–0 6–4. Another win was achieved by the Irishman in the quarter-final, when he defeated de Morpurgo, who had recently returned to tournament play, 6–4 7–5. As expected, Kho Sin Kie and Rogers won the men's doubles from Tanacescu and Badin, 6–3 6–4, and Cosette Saint Omer Roy beat Simone Mathieu and Phyllis Satterthwaite in the last match, 6–2 6–4. Rogers and Simone won the mixed doubles.

The Gallia Club, enjoying good weather, had excellent entertainment during the week by a strong class of entry who provided a series of closely contested matches, particularly in the later rounds. The tall Gracyn Wheeler won the ladies' singles title, but she had to spend much time on court to fulfil this achievement. In the semi-final, her match against Alice Weiwers lasted over three hours. The latter won the opening set from 5–2 down and held three match points in the second set. Gracyn rallied well and eventually struggled home at 11–13 11–9 7–5, after again being behind at 4–5 in the third set. The 56 game match was recorded as the longest ladies' singles match ever played on the Riviera at that time. Gracyn Wheeler pursued her all-round tactics to defeat Simone Mathieu in the final. She started badly, but clearly dominated the third set of the contest to win, 1–6 6–3 6–4. The runner-up had passed Hella Kovac, with much to spare, 6–0 6–2. The Czech had eliminated Mrs Nancy Glover (Lyle), 0–6 6–4 6–4.

Kho Sin Kie and Rogers met in the final of the men's singles, with the outcome following the usual pattern of the Chinese player, with his superior ball control, winning 6–4 7–5 6–2. The runner-up reversed the result of a week earlier against Tanacescu in the semi-final, after not scoring a game in the first set, 0–6 6–4 6–3. Kho Sin Kie dropped a set to Badin, before completely controlling the play, 2–6 6–1 6–3. Dennis Coombe from New Zealand was an earlier victim of Badin, 4–6 6–1 6–3. Medecin captured the scalp of Brugnon in the third round, 5–7 8–6 7–5.

Brugnon and Kho Sin Kie were too strong for Coombe and Englishman, Murray Deloford, in the final of the doubles, 6–3 5–7 6–1 6–2, while Cosette Saint Omer Roy and Alice Weiwers added yet another win to their tally in the ladies' event, but not before overcoming, in a marathon match, Simone Mathieu and Gracyn Wheeler, 22–20 6–4.

The Carlton Club tournament followed and for the third time of the season, Simone Mathieu was beaten in a final of the ladies' singles, losing to Alice Weiwers, her conqueror at Monte Carlo earlier, whose all-court attack and greater severity gained her a 6–3 6–3 victory. The winner was stretched to the full reaching the semi-final by Miss Klara Somogyi, Hungary's top player, 4–6 6–0 6–4, while Simone Mathieu, having won a tight first set, sailed past Hella Kovac, 7–5 6–0. Gracyn Wheeler retired at the quarter-final stage.

The method for drawing the men's singles event was amended to allow four seeded players to be exempted in the early rounds. Kho Sin Kie preserved his unbeaten singles record in retaining the event. In a moderately strong entry he was never extended to a deciding set, overcoming Tanacescu, 6–3

6–4, and then Rogers in the final, 6–3 6–4 6–0. In the quarter-final, two notable encounters saw Rogers beat Martin-Legeay, 6–4 4–6 ret'd, and Lesueur defeat Badin, 4–6 6–3 6–0. Coombe was a victim of the former, 6–3 6–3.

Simone Mathieu, paired with Gracyn Wheeler, reversed their defeat by Cosette Saint Omer Roy and Alice Weiwers of the week before, winning the doubles final, 6–3 5–7 6–1. Kho Sin Kie and Brugnon were easily the best doubles pair, but needed a five set fight to overcome Lesueur and Martin-Legeay, 6–4 3–6 6–3 4–6 6–2. The mixed doubles were not concluded, due to lack of time. During a week of fine weather, the King and Queen of Denmark watched the play, while the King of Sweden took part in two handicap events.

The South of France Championships at Nice drew the strongest entry of the season so far, with over 140 competitors, with some notable names joining the fray.

In the men's singles, eight players were seeded and exempt from playing in the early rounds. Kho Sin Kie required one more win in the singles and doubles events to gain possession of both cups. However, he was overcome with cramp, within sight of victory over Tanacescu in the singles final and lost in five sets, 2–6 6–2 3–6 6–4 6–1, and later retired with Brugnon from the men's doubles final, which was claimed by Caska and Hecht as a walkover. There were some tough encounters earlier in the singles, when Lesueur beat Brugnon, 2–6 6–4 6–2, and Kho Sin Kie defeated Martin-Legeay, 7–5 6–1. Later Tanacescu overcame Hecht, 6–0 6–3 6–4, and Kho Sin Kie beat Lesueur, 6–3 6–2 6–3, in the semi-finals.

Making his second visit to the Riviera, Constantin Tanacescu, Romania's leading player took home four singles titles, with two victories each over Kho Sin Kie and George Rogers.

Simone Mathieu found her best form at last and, avenging her earlier defeat by Gracyn Wheeler, won the final by the convincing score of 6–0 6–2. The champion defeated Hella Kovac, 6–3 6–2, and Gracyn overcame Klara Somogyi, 6–2 6–8 6–2, in the round before. Sylvia Henrotin appeared in the draw, but fell to Klara in the quarter-final. In the same round, Simone Mathieu disposed of Cosette Saint Omer Roy, 6–2 6–1. Cosette and Alice Weiwers beat Simone and Gracyn in the last encounter in the doubles, 6–8 6–4 6–4. Henkel played only in the mixed doubles and in a very competitive draw partnered Gracyn to victory over Lesueur and Simone in the final, 4–6 6–3 8–6.

The presence of many leading continental players and several top English competitors ensured entertaining matches at the Beaulieu Club. The men's singles had several new faces in a very strong entry, from which Tanacescu repeated his singles victory of a week before. He was one of eight contestants who were seeded and joined the draw at the last 16. The Romanian reached the final over Hans van Swol (Netherlands), 7–5 6–4, Mitic, 6–1 6–0, and Pierre Pellizza of France, 6–1 7–5, and then outlasted Caska by the quality of his returns and mobility to win the five set final, 7–5 3–6 2–6 6–1 6–3. Caska had accounted for the Hungarian, Jozsef Asboth, 6–2 4–6 6–3, and Yvon Petra of France, 6–8 6–4 6–2, leading up to the final. Other notable victories included Brugnon dispatching two Englishmen, Henry Billington, 6–1 6–2, and Deloford, 6–3 6–3, while a third, Laurie Shaffi, had the satisfaction of defeating Henkel, 6–4 6–4. Kho Sin Kie fell to Petra in the quarter-final, 6–3 6–4.

Hilde Sperling returned to the scene and captured the ladies' title. She allowed Iris Hutchings just one game in the semi-final, but was forced to concede the opening set to Alice Weiwers in the final, 4–6 6–0 6–1. Alice Weiwers reached the last round by ousting Gracyn Wheeler, 6–0 6–1, and defeating Mme Simone Laffargue (Iribarne), 6–3 6–1. The latter had played exceedingly well earlier, beating Kay Stammers, playing in her first match of the year, 7–5 7–5. There was an all-French men's doubles final, in which Lesueur and Petra beat Martin-Legeay and Pellizza, 8–6 3–6 4–6 6–1 7–5. Billington and Hughes were knocked out in the quarter-final by Caska and Hecht, 6–3 6–3. Simone Mathieu and Gracyn beat Simone Laffargue and Hilde Sperling in the final of the ladies' doubles, 4–6 6–2 9–7, and Kho Sin Kie and Alice Weiwers won the mixed event from Pellizza and Sylvia Henrotin, 6–3 6–2. As usual, the King of Sweden took part in the handicap events.

The Monte Carlo Championships, staged at the Monte Carlo Country Club had become the premier tournament on the Riviera. There was a formidable entry of European talent with the men containing most continental Davis Cup teams, but none of them could prevent the singles semi-final company of three French players, of whom two contended the final.

Pellizza produced a fine performance in winning the championship. Although he dropped sets to Billington, 6–3 3–6 6–1, and Mitic, 7–5 3–6 6–1, he allowed Henkel just two games in each set before achieving a relatively easy semi-final against Bolelli, 8–6 6–0 6–0. Pellizza's opponent in the final was Petra and this match developed into a spectacular duel with perhaps the winner's powerful service the telling factor, 6–8 6–3 6–4 6–2. Petra's path to the final was via Malfroy, 6–4 6–3, Caska 7–5 6–2, and Tanacescu, 3–6 9–7 6–1 6–3. Earlier, Bolelli beat Hecht, 6–3 6–3.

Hilde Sperling confirmed her reputation as Europe's leading player by winning the ladies' singles without losing a set. She beat Sylvia Henrotin, 6–3 ret'd, Simone Laffargue , 6–2 6–4, before overcoming Simone Mathieu, 8–6 6–3. Simone Laffargue had passed Alice Weiwers in the quarter-final, 6–4 6–2, at which stage Simone Mathieu crushed Iris Hutchings, 6–0 6–0, before being far too good for Kay Stammers, 6–3 6–0.

The Butler Trophy draw was of the highest standard and was resolved when in all-French final, Lesueur and Petra beat Bolelli and Pellizza, 8–6 6–2 6–1 2–6 6–1. There was a new cup for the ladies' doubles, presented by Lord Iliffe. Simone Mathieu, who won the Beaumont Cup outright the previous year, retained her title, in partnership with Mme Nelly Landry, beating Miss Evelyn Dearman of England and Kay Stammers in a tough match, 12–10 6–3. The Monte Carlo Championships men's doubles was won by Pellizza and Petra and the ladies' doubles by Simone Mathieu and Hilde Sperling. The mixed was abandoned at the semi-final stage.

Puncec made his first appearance of the season at the Menton Club and, as anticipated, won the Riviera Championship singles. As ever, he was ruthless from the back of the court and got the better of Hans Redl of Germany, formerly of Austria, in the final, after his opponent held points for the first set. The Yugoslav later coasted through to victory, 11–9 6–2 6–0. There was surprise that Redl reached the final, but he certainly deserved this position, having beaten Tloczynski, 6–4 6–4, and Caska, 6–0

At the Monte Carlo Championships, the Beaumont Cup for the ladies' international team event was replaced by a new cup donated by Lord Iliffe. The new winners were Simone Mathieu and Nelly Landry of France (left) with the runner-up from England, Kay Stammers and Evelyn Dearman. In the middle is Princess Antoinette of Monaco.

6–1. Puncec was always in control over Martin-Legeay in the semi-final, 6–1 6–4.

Simone Laffargue's improvement was well demonstrated as she captured the ladies' singles title. In sequence, she downed Klara Somogyi, 7–5 ret'd, Sylvia Henrotin, 4–6 6–0 6–3, and Alice Weiwers, 6–2 6–1, before bringing off one of the best victories of her career by defeating Simone Mathieu in the final, after losing the opening set, 2–6 6–4 6–3.

In earlier rounds, Miss Nina Brown of England beat Miss Susie Kormoczy (Hungary), 6–2 6–0, but Evelyn Dearman and Miss Dorothy Holman of England, both fell to Mlle Eva Porakova of Czechoslovakia. Kay Stammers was beaten in the quarter-final by Simone Mathieu, 6–3 6–2.

Lesueur and Petra took the men's doubles title, while Evelyn Dearman and Kay Stammers won the ladies' event, surprising Cosette Saint Omer Roy and Alice Weiwers on the way. Petra and Simone Mathieu were the mixed champions and Petra and Sylvia Henrotin claimed the Coupe des Nations.

Petra returned to singles competition at the Cannes Club, where he won the Côte d'Azur singles championship. There were many continental players in the draw, but the English contingent had returned home to prepare for the hard court season. Petra won the title without losing a set. In excellent form, he passed Tanacescu, 6–2 9–7, and Robert Abdesselam of France, 6–2 9–7, to reach the final, where his net-storming campaign proved too much for Baworowski, 7–5 7–5 6–2. The latter, then playing under the colours of Poland, had brought off some of his best victories of the season in passing Martin-Legeay, 6–3 6–3, Pellizza, 6–4 6–3, and Boussus, 6–1 5–7 6–2, a fine run. Schroder, far from his best, lost to Hebda, who then capitulated to Boussus, 6–4 6–1.

Simone Mathieu and Simone Laffargue met in the final of the ladies' singles for the second week in succession and the former reversed the result after a long struggle, 8–6 6–3. The winner had passed Mme Marguerite Lebailly (France), 7–5 6–2, while Simone Laffargue won a long battle against Alice Weiwers, 1–6 6–1 6–4. Jadwiga Jedrzejowska did not participate in the event.

Lesueur and Petra won their fifth title of the season and Pellizza and Simone Mathieu captured the mixed doubles. The latter, with Jadwiga Jedrzejowska, were beaten in the ladies' doubles final by Cosette Saint Omer Roy and Alice Weiwers, 2–6 6–4 6–1.

The entry at the Miramar meeting, held at Juan-les-Pins, was far from large but, nevertheless, contained notable names, resulting in many interesting contests. After beating Schroder, 6–3 6–3, Baworowski won the singles final against Abdesselam, 6–2 12–10 6–3. The Frenchman then lost

Poland was to the fore for three weeks as Adam Baworowski captured the singles titles at the Miramar Club, Beau Site Hotel and the second meeting at Nice, beating in the finals Robert Abdesslam, Karl Schroder and Antoine Gentien, respectively.

a second final, when paired with Boussus, to Landau and Schroder, 6–4 6–4. Alice Weiwers won the ladies' singles event and paired with Boussus to take the mixed.

Baworowski continued to impress the following week by winning the Cannes Championships at the Beau Site Hotel. In the singles final he was forced to recover from 2 sets to 1 down, before gaining complete control against Schroder, 7–5 6–1. Surprisingly, von Metaxa fell to Coombe in the quarter-final, 6–1 6–2.

Simone Mathieu, head and shoulders above the ladies, had the singles title in hand throughout, beating Jeannette Poncelet in the semi-final, 6–1 6–1, and Frl Elfriede Kriegs Au, born in Austria but ranked as Germany's tenth player, in the last match, 6–1 6–2. Jeannette Poncelet had a fine win against Jacqueline Horner earlier, 6–4 6–2. The men's doubles was won by Lesueur and Schroder, who beat Baworowski and von Metaxa for the title, 1–6 1–6 6–4 7–5 6–4. The ladies' doubles was decided when Jacqueline Horner and Simone Mathieu beat Jadwiga Jedrzejowska and Muriel Thomas in a tight fight, 6–2 2–6 9–7. Simone won a third title with Schroder.

No-one present on the last day at the Beau Site Hotel could have envisaged that this would be the last international tournament ever played at this legendary site.

Baworowski increased his tally to three singles titles in three weeks by winning the Nice Championships at the Parc Imperial, overcoming Gentien in an interesting match, 4–6 6–3 6–3 8–6. The winner mastered Schroder in the last four, 4–6 6–3 6–2, and Gentien did similarly against Destremau, 6–4 6–3.

For the second week running, Simone Mathieu had complete control over Elfriede Kriegs Au in the final of the ladies' singles, 6–1 6–0. The champion allowed Paulette de Saint Ferréol four games in the semi-final, 6–3 6–1, while Elfriede accounted for Jacqueline Goldschmidt, 6–2 8–6. Simone Mathieu also won the ladies' doubles with Jacqueline Horner, and the mixed with Gentien. The men's division was won by Feret and Schoder, who beat Baworowski and Lesueur in a marathon match, 3–6 6–3 3–6 6–4 9–7. Aslangul and Aeschliman made an appearance during the week to dispute the men's veterans' singles final, with the Frenchman winning, 4–6 6–3 6–3. The King of Sweden paired with Baworowski to win the men's doubles handicap event.

The Monte Carlo Easter meeting was, as usual, very successful and despite being towards the end of the season attracted many top players. France dominated the five events, winning four and sharing the other. Feret was outstanding among the men, capturing three titles. In the men's singles he beat his compatriot, Destremau, for the title in straight sets, with only the third being close, 6–1 6–3 8–6. In the semi-final he was given strong opposition by Peters, before going through, 6–3 8–6, while Destremau beat another Frenchman, Jacques Sanglier, 6–4 6–2.

Simone Mathieu had relatively little to do to win the singles title and, after passing Elfriede Kriegs Au in the semi-final, 6–3 6–1, completely overwhelmed Iris Hutchings in the final without conceding a game, 6–0

6–0. The runner-up had played well to down Effie Peters, 6–2 7–5.

Feret, with Abdesselam at his side, formed a formidable partnership to win the men's doubles, being too strong for Landau and Peters, 6–0 6–1, and the French pair, Roger Dubuc and Sanglier in the final, 6–2 6–2. Feret won his third event in partnership with Elfriede Kries Au, causing quite a shock by beating Gentien and Simone Mathieu in the final of the mixed doubles, 6–4 6–2. The Cosette Saint Omer Roy and Alice Weiwers combination had a very close match against Simone Mathieu and Paulette de Saint Ferréol, but after squeezing past a 16 game second set, took the next six games, 2–6 9–7 6–0.

The last tournament of the season was played during the week of 17th to 23rd April at the Provençal Club. The proceedings were under the control of Col. Hartman, who had assembled a good representation from several countries, with over 50 players participating.

Simone Mathieu ended her visit to the coast in top form, defeating in the singles, old foes, Cosette Saint Omer Roy in the semi-final, 6–3 6–3, and Alice Weiwers in the deciding round, 6–3 6–0. The runner-up had disposed of Jeannette Poncelet, 6–3 6–3.

Gentien seemed well equipped to claim the men's singles title but, sensationally, he was eliminated in the quarter-final by relatively unknown Norwegian, A. Smedsrud, after quite a tussle, 8–6 3–6 7–5. In the semi-final, Smedsrud beat Dennis Slack of England, 3–6 6–3 12–10, but fell to Jacquemet in the final, 6–2 3–6 6–0. The winner had beaten Jean Mariani of France, 6–4 6–4.

There was a further upset in the mixed doubles event when Gentien and Simone Mathieu were eliminated in the semi-final by Gilberto Pentecorvo of Italy and Alice Weiwers, 7–5 6–4. The winners went on to beat Jacquemet and Jeannette Poncelet in the final, 6–4 6–4. Gentien and Jacquemet won the men's doubles beating Aeschliman and Lotan in the final, 6–4 6–3, while Cosette Saint Omer Roy and Alice Weiwers overcame Simone Mathieu and Miss Violet Lermitte in the final, 6–2 6–3. This was the winning pair's 14th doubles title on the Riviera.

*"When I was 12, I went with my mother and father to the Riviera. We got the train from Paris in 1933. It was a great thrill – I had barely ever been on a train. We stayed at Charlie Aeschliman's hotel in Cannes. Mother was recuperating after an operation and we spent three weeks there. It was the first time I'd seen orange trees – growing at the side of the courts. I remember that it was always sunny. It was the tail end of the Halcyon days. The early thirties were the best years – the Duke of Westminster and Coco Chanel were there …. Times were changing. The Prince of Wales and Mountbatten were there. It was all short skirts and the Charleston".*

GEM HOAHING, 2013

# The Summer Seasons

Ever since he middle of the 19th century wealthy people from the northern parts of Europe, particularly those Londoners suffering from the cold, damp and foggy winter conditions, had been attracted to the generally delightful weather on the French Riviera. The introduction of the train made the effort of the long journey relatively comfortable.

As the number of visitors increased, so did the number of hotels etc to provide suitable accommodation. However, the area was regarded as a winter resort and when the summer months arrived, the majority of the hotels closed. Tennis followed the same pattern and usually the schedule of tournaments ended around late April.

By the 1930s hoteliers realised that trade was possible all the year and on 2nd August the leading managers met and decided that henceforth they would not close their establishments during the summer.

This gave thought to tennis clubs to also stage tournaments during this period, no doubt hoping that the extra visitors would achieve support from the public as spectators. In 1928 three clubs, Gallia LTC, Juan-les-Pins LTC and Miramar LTC, had taken an early plunge and staged meetings during August. In the main, the standard of competitors was below that expected on the winter/spring circuit and quite often the entry was made up of local players, while the top stars were attracted to the regular tournaments throughout Europe. There is mention that the Juan-les-Pins LTC held a tournament in 1924.

Gradually other clubs tried their hand and the schedule rose to a peak of 10 gatherings in 1932 and 1933, but settled down to half a dozen up to 1939. Those involved were Cannes LTC, Cannes New Courts Club, Gallia LTC, Juan-les-Pins LTC, Menton LTC, Metropole LTC, Miramar LTC, Monte Carlo, Provençal LTC and Val d'Esquières LTC.

# Epilogue

In July 1939 the scheduled tournament list for the 1940 winter/spring programme on the Riviera was issued and generally followed previous years, beginning with the Beau Site Hotel New Year meeting and concluding around mid-April. The 1939 summer tournaments had got underway, but were played under the shadow of war with Germany. Come August the threat loomed closer with some players, particularly the French, being called to their regiments. At the conclusion of the Provençal Club meeting on 13th August, the remainder of the schedule was cancelled and on the fateful day, 3rd September, Britain declared war on Germany and France quickly followed.

For several months life on the Riviera continued as before but there were no international tournaments, just a few local gatherings. There was soon a shortage of balls and equipment. Everything changed when Italy declared war on Britain and France on 10th June 1940. Immediately thousands of English residents and visitors scurried to leave the area. With German forces advancing at an alarming rate in the north, the French Premier resigned on 16th June and Marshal Pétain took over. The armistice was signed on 22nd June and within a few days France was divided in two, the north under the direct control of the Germans and the south, including the Riviera, under the Pétain government.

For a year or so there was little competition tennis but in 1941 the French Tennis Federation organised an official tournament in both zones, with the best players having a play-off, subsequently, in Paris. Later, those in the unoccupied zone were able to stage a few tournaments from time to time in the Cannes and Nice areas.

In July 1943 the Allied Forces based in the Mediterranean made their first assault on southern Europe by landing in Sicily and the Germans, realising the vulnerability of the Riviera coast, took over the unoccupied zone on 8th September and immediately set about fortifying the area. On 15th August 1944 American and French forces landed at Agay, five miles east of St Raphael and by the first week of September the coast was again under French control.

The war had changed many things but great strides were made to get back to normality as quickly as possible. As in the First World War, the United States Army staged a very successful Forces European Inter-Theatre Championships held at the Parc Imperial, Nice from 10th to 15th September in which Private Budge Patty, the 1950 Wimbledon champion-to-be, won the singles title before a crowd of 5,000, beating Captain James Wade in the final, 6–3 6–0 6–4. His prize was a wrist watch.

In March 1946 three international tournaments were held, the first at Monte Carlo Country Club from 11th to 19th March, followed by Nice and the Cannes Club. In 1947 there were seven official tournaments scheduled and by 1950 the number had settled to around 15. Most of the Clubs had survived but the legendary Beau Site Hotel tournaments did not reappear as the hotel had been converted into apartments. The Menton Club, badly damaged, did not stage an international meeting until 1951. Four clubs entered the arena for the first time, one at Cannes Montfleury and three at Nice: Cimiez, Méditerranée and Olympic Gymnaste.

In the first couple of years some players from the previous era returned, among whom were Alice Weiwers, Cosette Saint Omer Roy, Billie Yorke, Kay Menzies (Stammers), Henri Cochet, Pierre Pellizza and Paul Feret.

During the fifties and sixties the entries at the tournaments, particularly those held in March/April, included many top players, not only from the usual countries, but also from Australia and the USA, preparing for the European summer season. The expansion of air travel was a contributory factor.

As before, the main Monte Carlo Country Club tournament was the highlight of the season, with the Butler Trophy and Iliff Cup creating much interest. Also, at that time the circuit attracted young teams of players from several countries who used the visits to gain experience and training.

The introduction of Open tennis into the game in 1968 brought about the rapid decline of the tournament scene on the Riviera. Players gradually went elsewhere and competed in point-linked circuits, earning prize money for the first time. Overnight the game had gone from a pastime to outright professionalism. By the late 1970s all venues had ceased to conduct international tournaments, bar Monte Carlo and Nice.

Monte Carlo began Open Championships in 1969 and Nice in 1971, both offering cash prizes. With ladies not competing after 1987, Nice continued up to 1995 and then re-emerged in 2010. Monte Carlo continued annually with men only after 1980. This meeting with its spectacular setting, overlooking the Mediterranean, with the ability to hold over 10,000 spectators, is undoubtedly one of the world's greatest tournaments – very different from the old days at the Hotel de Paris.

# The Blue Train

After four years of the horrid First World War, the majority of people looked forward to a better life. The number of rich and famous who visited the Riviera in the period heading up to the War had steadily grown each year and with conditions soon back to normal, they were eager to resume their accepted lifestyle. Near to top of their list was the ability to be able to travel to the Continent once again and escape the cold and foggy winters of the cities for the delightful weather on the French Riviera.

The hotels were quick to open their doors again, despite many establishments converting from being hospitals and convalescent homes for the armed forces. The momentum of people visiting grew quickly and by the mid 1920s had reached a peak. This was quite obvious from the space given each mid-December by the London 'Times', which devoted a whole column to the 'Calendar of Social and Sporting Events' for the Riviera

A train for the Riviera leaves Calais-Maritime in the mid-1920s. The grand station building was bombed during the Second World War in 1944 and never completely restored.

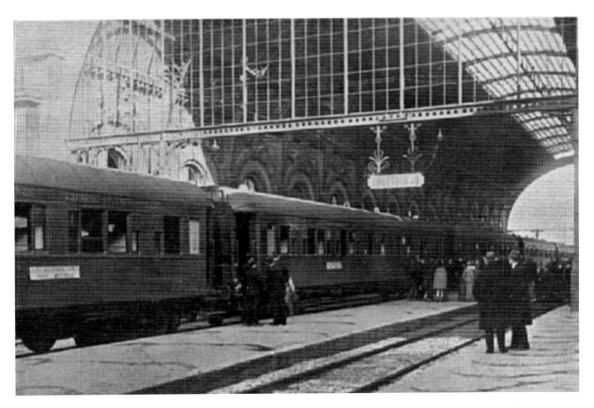

One of the new Calais-Mediterranean Express trains with all-steel carriages painted dark blue arriving at Nice Railway Station in 1922.

season at Cannes, Beaulieu, Hyères, Monte Carlo, Menton, Nice and St. Raphael. Then, starting a month later, a regular weekly column gave the listing of all the comings and goings of Royalty, Lords and Ladies and other dignitaries to the same resorts.

The train service to the South of France was soon restored after the War, but a need grew from the wealthy for a new standard of luxury overnight travel from London and Paris and this was quickly met by a private French railway company, the Chemins de Fer de Paris à Lyon et à la Mediterranée, or PLM, who commenced a service on the 8th December 1922 and continued each year from November to April.

The 'Blue Train' as it was known, departed from Gare Maritime at Calais at 1pm, having picked up passengers crossing the Channel from London. The train headed for the Gard du Nord in Paris, allowing passengers on and off, then having circulated around Paris, arrived at Gare de Lyon, where additional passengers and coaches were picked up, before setting off early evening to the south.

The train stopped at Dijon, Chalons and Lyon, reaching the Mediterranean at Marseille in the morning, before finally heading east along the coast, calling at St. Raphael, Juan-les-Pins, Antibes, Cannes, Nice, Monaco and terminating at Menton on the Italian border. The journey from Paris to Cannes took 12 hours.

A typical dining car – 'Wagon Restaurant'.

A spring morning in 1935 at Cannes Railway Station as the horse-drawn and motor vehicles await the arrival of the overnight Blue Train passengers from Paris. Note the prominence of the Carlton Hotel service.

It was exclusively first class, having steel sleeping cars, operated by the Compagnie Internationale des Wagons-Lits, plus a dining car, renowned for providing a really top class menu. The sleeping cars were painted blue with gold trim and each had 10 sleeping compartments, served by an attendant.

In 1936 the French Government introduced a paid two week holiday for French workers. This gave the opportunity for middle and working class people to be able to afford a vacation on the Riviera and consequently second and third class sleeping cars were added to the Blue Train. The railway was nationalised in 1938 and from then on the SNCF ran the service as an ordinary night train.

The train did not run during the Second World War but resumed after. When regular airline services began between Paris and the south of France in 1945, many of the wealthy switched from the train. In 1978 couchettes were introduced to attract a wider range of passengers. By 1980 the night trains were gradually replaced by high-speed TGV trains which cut the length of the journey from Paris to Cannes from twenty hours to five and this finally ended the overnight travel.

# History of Clubs Staging International Tournaments

## ANTIBES

### Provençal Lawn Tennis Club

The Provençal Club was founded in 1932, with six courts laid down along the Route de Littoral, Antibes. The first international tournament took place that year from 19th to 25th December, when the winners of the singles were Max Ellmer and Paulette de Saint Ferréol.

Two meetings a year took place until 1936 when they became annual up until the Second World War in 1939. The Club also began a summer meeting in 1933, generally held in August, up to 1939.

The Club managed to survive the War and promptly resumed, holding tournaments up to 1965.

## BEAULIEU

### Beaulieu Lawn Tennis Club

Although associated with the Bristol Hotel, the Beaulieu Lawn Tennis Club, opened in late 1912, was separately constituted, having three excellent tennis courts, situated in beautiful gardens adjoining the premises, across the narrow Avenue Bristol. The courts were well-spaced, with a run back at each end of 26 feet and a side division of 16 feet between courts. Additionally, the backgrounds to the courts were perfect. The Club attracted a large and expanding membership.

The hotel was a magnificent six-storey building, designed by Danish architect, Hans-Georg Tersling and erected for Sir Blundell Maple, the London furniture maker. The hotel, opened on 1st January 1899, was located between the station and the sea, and at that time was one of the largest and most luxurious palaces on the Riviera. There were 300 rooms, several libraries and huge pavilions at each end to accommodate concerts and plays. The imposing entrance hall connected the

The Beaulieu Club courts with the imposing Bristol Hotel in the background.

five floors, each having 60 rooms, while the top floor housed the staff. The imposing large gardens on the south side were planted with flowers, orange trees and palm trees.

In 1904 a Rotunda was constructed adjacent to the hotel to accommodate additional dining space. Now owned by the Municipality the building is listed as an historic monument.

During the late evening of 28th March 1911 a fire, aided by a strong wind, swept through the upper part of the hotel and completely destroyed the third storey. The fire was under control by early the next morning, when reports confirmed that there was no loss of life. The damage was estimated to be around several million francs.

Due to economic restraints the hotel was sold in 1954 and became a luxury condominium, still retaining the magnificent lobby.

The Club's first open tournament began on 3rd February 1913 and inaugurated the year's series of Riviera tournaments. The event attracted many leading players and support from the public was excellent. George Simond was referee and Tom Fleming was engaged as the Club's professional.

Towards the end of 1924 four new En-Tout-Cas courts were added to the grounds and the existing three courts re-dressed with the same composition. The intention was to hold their first winter tournament, commencing on 22nd December, but the courts were deemed not ready, so the meeting was transferred to the Hotel Metropole at Cannes.

# CANNES

**Beau Site Hotel** (see page 19)
**Cannes Lawn Tennis Club**

The Croquet and Lawn Tennis Club, situated in Rue Lacour, was opened on 21st February 1908 by the Grand Duchess Anastasia of Mecklenburg-Schwerin, Honorary President of the Club. Mr Charles Letts, the President, warmly welcomed the Duchess, while Lord Brougham presented her with a memento of the occasion, an inscribed tennis racket. The Mayor of Cannes also spoke. Afterwards, the Grand Duchess paired with Reggie Doherty, played an exhibition match against George Simond and Countess Clara Schulenburg for two sets, which ended all square. Other royalty present at the opening were the Grand Duke and Grand Duchess Cyril Vladimirovich, Grand Duke and Grand Duchess George Mikhailovich, Princess Stephanie (Countess Lonyay), Grand Duke Michael Mikhailovich and Countess Anastasia Torby. Tea and refreshments were served and the municipal band played various airs.

The first open tournament staged by the Club commenced on 21st March 1910 after being put back for five days because of a clash with the Beau Site tournament. Many well-known players were attracted to the

A bird's-eye view of the courts at the Beau Site Hotel during the spring of 1933. There was a total of six courts.

Having tea in front of the Cannes Club clubhouse, known as the Cottage, in between watching the matches, 1923.

programme of four events. Unusually, no handicap events were staged. There were five courts available for play and the referee was Capt. Dawson.

The following year the tournament started on 27th March and was played under the title of 'Championships of the Côte d'Azur'. There were many alterations to the grounds and buildings of the Club. The dressing rooms were greatly enlarged, a new Committee room was built and the front was expanded with a spacious glass verandah. An imposing main entrance to the Club at the corner of Rue d'Antibes and Rue Latour was established, sufficiently large enough for the admission of cars and carriages. Two more courts were added, bringing the total to seven. All these improvements encouraged the membership to expand rapidly.

A view of the main court at the Cannes Club, early 1930s.

This trend continued to grow after the First World War when the first international tournament was staged in March 1920 and by the end of the year 12 courts were in use. For the 1924 season a further two courts were laid down, bringing the total to 14, the number existing in 1939.

### Carlton Lawn Tennis Club (Carlton Hotel)

The rapid rise in popularity of lawn tennis along the Riviera in the years leading up to the First World War, doubtless justified the decision to form the Carlton Lawn Tennis Club and construct five courts adjacent to the newly built Carlton Hotel.

The hotel, with the brick and white stone façade, rising above the Boulevard la Croisette, magnificently overlooking the blue waters of the Mediterranean, was built for Swiss hotelier Henri Ruhl, who commissioned Charles Dalmas as architect. Work started on the building in 1909 and within two years the doors were opened to the many visiting British and Russian nobility. Success was immediate and the hotel acquired the neighbouring de la Plage Hotel, which was demolished and rebuilt as part of the Carlton Hotel. Fully opened in 1913, the building had seven floors, over 300 rooms and the outstanding feature of an extravagant dome at each end of the roof at the front.

The tennis courts were at the side of the hotel, on the Rue Oustinoff, now known as Rue de Canada. Although always associated with the Carlton Hotel, the tennis club became privately owned by the Burke family, Thomas and his three sons, Tommy, Albert and Edmond. Thomas, an Irishman, was one of the game's first qualified professionals, attached to the Fitzwilliam Club in Dublin at a time when the leading Irish players, Hamilton, Pim, Mahony, Stoker etc ranked highly. He was a very competent coach and always in great demand. He twice won the World's Professional Championship, in 1898 and 1902.

Towards the end of the 1890s, when there was a slump in English tennis, Burke decided that there was more scope for coaching in France and after a spell in Paris he married a Frenchwoman, settled down in Cannes and became quite prosperous. Tommy, not always in good health,

Looking along the Boulevard de la Croisette from the beach at the Carlton Hotel in 1919, where the first regular tournament after the First World War was played on the Riviera in February.

A view of the main court at the Carlton Club during the 'match of the century', between Suzanne Lenglen and Helen Wills in February 1926. Every available space for watching the match was taken up, with people even looking from the windows of the east side of the Carlton Hotel.

generally confined himself to coaching, whereas the other brothers often competed in professional tournaments.

The first tournament was originally scheduled to commence on 22nd December 1913, but was postponed until 5th January. This international meeting was very successful, partly due to the presence of Tony Wilding, the Wimbledon champion, also the up and coming French star, Suzanne Lenglen, who each won their singles titles. On the crest of a wave, the management decided to hold a second tournament starting on 6th April. This exercise was just as rewarding, with hundreds of spectators watching the men's final. Wilding and Suzanne Lenglen repeated their domination.

Unfortunately, within a few months, the First World War brought down the curtain on the international tournament scene. During the conflict, from 1917, part of the hotel was used as a hospital for soldiers sent from the front to recuperate. A little later the hotel lost much of the Russian clientele, due to the turn of events in their homeland.

Following the cessation of hostilities the Club had the honour of staging the first open international tournament on the Riviera from 24th February to 2nd March 1919. A large entry was secured, from which Captain Douglas Watters of the American Army won the singles title, while Suzanne Lenglen coasted through her events.

However, a week earlier the American Expeditionary Force held an American Officers' Tennis Championship at Cannes. With the vast

number of competitors at 181 contesting the singles and doubles events, the organisers readily accepted the offer from the Carlton Club and Cannes Club to put their combined 13 courts at their disposal, so essential to enable the early rounds to be completed in an acceptable time. The venture was extremely successful and concluded with Lieut. Richard Williams winning the singles and doubles titles. All personnel were accommodated at the Carlton Hotel.

The magnificent Carlton Hotel in 1930. Opened in 1912, the building had 300 rooms over seven floors. In 1972 the decision was taken to cease providing the famous tennis courts and convert the land into residential accommodation.

That same year, business was so bad that the hotel was put up for sale at a million francs, which was not even sufficient to pay off the management's debts. The situation was gradually overcome, assisted by the hotel being completely requisitioned in January 1922 to hold the United Nations Security Council Conference. Floors and parts of floors were allocated to the different governments, with the USA on the top floor, British on the fourth floor, the French on the third floor etc etc. The great prestige gained from this conference allowed the hotel to regain its old aura and attract the world's top celebrities for years to come, many of whom spent much time on the courts.

The international tournament held regularly in February for many years was always a success, with many outstanding players from Europe participating. The meeting in 1926 attracted unprecedented worldwide press coverage when the idol of the courts, Suzanne Lenglen, defeated the young 18 year-old prodigy, Helen Wills from California, in the final. This was a dramatic match from beginning to end, which the Frenchwoman narrowly won. The content has been acclaimed by many as the "Match of the Century". In the late 1920s a further two courts were added to the Club, making a total of seven.

Although Italian troops occupied Cannes during the Second World War in June 1940, life was little affected and the hotel remained open and became the hub for spies and agents. In 1944 the hotel closed but relief was at hand as the American forces landed in August and soon the hotel was running normally. For some time, two floors were made available to the officers of the American general staff. Soon the world's most famous personalities, from all walks of life, returned.

In 1939 the first International Film Festival was due to be held in Cannes during September, with the hotel as the central attraction, but the intervention of the War forced the event to be cancelled. The Festival was revived in 1946 since when, every year, the world's top movie stars have featured, of course, the personalities changing with the mood of the times.

For nearly 60 years lawn tennis tournaments were staged, but with changes brought about by the introduction of open tennis in 1968, the players were attracted elsewhere and in 1972 the decision was taken to sell off the 4,000 square metres occupied by the courts and construct on the site a residential building. Sadly, no courts now exist at the hotel.

A little over a decade ago the Carlton Hotel became part of the Intercontinental Hotel Group and all suites and bedrooms underwent a complete refurbishment, including the provision of seven new sumptuous panoramic suites on the seventh floor and the restoration of the hotel's magnificent façade to its former glory. This legendary, luxury hotel is listed by the French Government as a National Historical Building.

### Gallia Lawn Tennis Club (Gallia Hotel)

In late 1922 five new courts were constructed and a Club formed adjacent to the Gallia Hotel, once the Casino of Cannes, in a very natural setting along the Boulevard de Strasbourg. The courts were of a different substance to any on the Côte d'Azur, the material coming from Paris. Although on the slow side, having a superior porous quality, the surface of the courts dried rapidly.

The first open tournament, held in 1924, commenced on 21st January and was a great success with Suzanne Lenglen competing in two events. George Simond was due to referee the meeting, but because of illness was replaced by G.A. Sautter.

A successful international meeting was held annually each March up to 1939. After the Second World War the tournament was re-established in 1950 and continued each year until 1967. There were also four winter tournaments staged in January between 1954 and 1959. President of the Club from 1963 was Henri Salfati, father of Monique, the French No.2 player in 1968. In 1960 a company purchased the Gallia Hotel and transformed the building into apartments.

In 1993 the Gallia Tennis Club was completely refurbished and became the Lucien Barrière Club.

Two views of the Gallia Club at Cannes. *Left:* 1924; a general view of the courts with the majestic Gallia Hotel in the background. *Below:* 1930; a doubles match in progress on one of the principle courts.

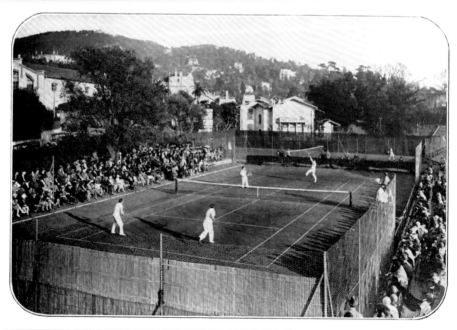

### Metropole Hotel

A building constructed in 1883 became the Metropole Hotel, a luxury establishment situated between Cannes and the Golfe-Juan, when officially opened on 14th January 1890.

The first tournament played on three new courts at the Metropole Hotel began on 16th February 1891 and lasted for five days. Although

The main court in the foreground of the Metropole Hotel, 1908.

nominated as 'open', the two events, the men's singles and doubles, were strictly handicap. A good entry of 16 was attained for the singles, which was eventually won by Harry Grove, who beat H. Wright in the final, 6–3 2–6 7–5. B. Miller and Wright won the doubles. The courts were reported to be 'fiery', owing to a continuous drought. The first prize, a handsome pin, was presented by the Grand Duke Michael of Russia, while the others were subscribed by the residents of the hotel.

The next tournament held by the hotel appears to be many years later in 1904, commencing on 23rd March. The open singles title was won by Major Ritchie, with victory over E. Gwynne-Evans in the last match, 6–2 6–3 8–6. There were five other events, all handicaps. The prizes were presented by the Grand Duke of Mecklenburg-Schwerin and his fiancée, Princess Alexandra of Cumberland. The management hoped that the tournament would be held in the future and called upon hotel residents to respond more liberally to the prize fund, so that better prizes could be given. Unfortunately, their optimism did not materialise and no tournaments were held in 1905 and 1906. However, from then on, apart from 1911 and 1912, an event was staged each year.

During the First World War the hotel became a hospital but soon after hostilities had ceased, returned as a hotel. In 1920 the annual tournament was successfully re-established and in 1924 three further courts were added, making six in all, described as very dark in colour. In the winter of 1931 the last tournament took place, for soon after, the Bishop of Nice purchased the premises for conversion into a seminary for priests. Finally in 1970 the building became the 'Residence du St Paul', a block of luxury flats with two associated courts provided for the occupants.

## New Courts Club

The New Courts Club was founded in 1924, along the Boulevard Eugene in Tripet, under the patronage of Frank Jay Gould. Initially there were 11 courts and within a few years there were over 300 members.

The top court at the Cannes New Courts Club in April 1933, where the winners of the singles titles were Franz Matejka and Lolette Payot. There was a total of 11 courts available.

The first international tournament was held from 11th–17th January 1926, when Henri Cochet and Phyllis Satterthwaite won the singles titles. Suzanne Lenglen gave her support but only in the two doubles events. Starting in 1932 the Club decided to stage two tournaments annually, one in January and the other in April, the first of which was given the title of Mediterranean Championships. In 1934 the second meeting was cancelled owing to disaffiliation from the French Federation and from then on the Club ceased to hold international meetings.

## HYÈRES

### Hyères Lawn Tennis Club (Golf Hotel)

The earliest report of lawn tennis being played at Hyères was in 1882, when a mixed doubles event was held on 6th, 7th and 9th–11th January. The winners were Mr Coombe-Williams and Miss Gibbs, who defeated Mr New and Miss Golding in the final. No details regarding the venue or scores are recorded.

The first open tournament staged at Hyères, described at the time as the beautiful town of palms and one of the gems of the Côte d'Azur, commenced on 31st March 1910 on the pretty grounds of the Golf Hotel, which was situated east of the town in the Gapeau Valley. Described as a sumptuous palace, the hotel had 300 rooms for guests, including 60 with a bath. There was a good entry for the three open and four handicap events, which were played on the four courts. Mr T. Zick, the proprietor of the hotel, provided two challenge cups to the value of 1,400 francs, while the town of Hyères gave a challenge cup for the men's singles, won by Dr John Flavelle, and the local golf club presented a similar one for the Ladies' Singles, captured by Mme Regine Vlasto. The referee was T.H. Oyler.

The management was keen for play to keep to schedule. After a tropical shower had flooded the lower court, they poured petrol on the wettest parts and set light to it. This proved to be only partially successful! Apparently the competitors who were eliminated early were easily able to console themselves with other sports, as within eighty yards of the courts were four croquet lawns and a first-class eighteen-hole golf course.

The hotel ran a very successful tournament up until 1928, when the number of competitors declined. The neighbouring club, the Hyères New Courts, took over for a couple of years before also losing support.

The Golf Hotel became a casualty of the Second World War, when destroyed during the liberation of the South of France in 1944 and was never rebuilt.

### New Courts Club

The New Courts Club was founded in 1928 at the Avenue Beauregard, with 3 courts being available. An international tournament was held in 1929 and 1930.

A view of two of the five courts at the Hyères New Courts Club in 1930.

## JUAN-LES-PINS

### Juan-les-Pins Lawn Tennis Club

The Juan-les-Pins Lawn Tennis Club located at the Chemin de Sables, was opened in 1923, with three courts being available. When the first international tournament was held the following year from 14th–18th

A view of the principal court at the Juan-les-Pins Club during the late 1920s. The club had four courts.

April, the courts were reported to be in excellent condition, but the space around them was deficient, with the only accommodation for spectators being a slightly raised terrace running parallel to the premier court, which was just wide enough to hold three rows of chairs.

Dressing room facilities were furnished in the shape of a dozen 'bathing boxes', just outside the confines of the ground itself and therefore far from convenient. At that time, the possibility to expand the grounds did not seem feasible. The tournament attracted competitors of a good standard, with David Morgan and Sylvia Lafaurie winning the singles titles. Suzanne Lenglen gave support by entering the ladies' doubles. Aided by very acceptable weather the meeting was enjoyed by all.

By the 1930s the Club had added another court and in 1932 became the first Club in the South of France to erect a covered court. After the 1934 meeting the Committee decided not to stage further international tournaments.

### Miramar Lawn Tennis Club

The Miramar Lawn Tennis Club was founded in 1928 at the Avenue de Vilmorin at Juan-les-Pins, with three courts available. Between 1929 and 1939 an international meeting was staged each year.

The Miramar Club at Juan-les-Pins in March 1939. The winners of the tournament were Adam Baworowski and Alice Weiwers.

# MENTON

## Menton Lawn Tennis Club

Menton, the most easterly town on the Côte d'Azur, bordering on Italy, has always attracted a large English community since the latter half of the 19th century, particularly with the arrival of the railway in 1881, allowing the journey between London and Menton to be achieved in 32 hours.

Englishmen, some resident, others winter visitors, were mainly responsible for the formation of the Menton Lawn Tennis and Croquet Club in Avenue Edouard VII. Following the announcement in December 1898 the process took nearly three years before the Club was officially inaugurated on Tuesday, 10th December 1901. Notable among those involved were M. R. de Bourbel, for many years the President, Dr. D.W. Samways, Stewart B. Binny, the Honorary Secretary and A.E. Madge. There were two sand lawn tennis courts and four croquet lawns.

On the day in question there was fear that the matches arranged for the opening ceremony would have to be cancelled, due to the wind blowing a full gale. However, the position of the tennis courts was somewhat sheltered from the south-west and some excellent play was possible.

A number of players travelled over from Nice for the occasion and the best match of the day was a doubles between the Lemaire brothers and J.R. Hay Gordon and Routledge, the latter pair winning after a hard tussle.

An aerial view of the Menton courts with the Clubhouse in the background.

Others who demonstrated their skills were de Bourbel, Andrie and Mlle Chalier and Miss Mildred Brooksmith. At the conclusion of play lunch, provided by Capt. Claremont, was taken at the International Club. The initial membership of the Club totalled 92.

A few weeks later the decision was taken to stage a small handicap tournament, supported by the two players from Monte Carlo, Scott Griffin and A. Cragnon. The Belgian, Willie Lemaire, who resided in Menton, comfortably won the singles event.

Encouraged by this success, the Committee decided to embark upon their first open international meeting in March 1902, after agreeing dates with the Monte Carlo and Nice tournaments. A.E. Madge became the Honorary Referee, a position he held until the mid 1920s. The exercise was most successful, with many well-known players competing, namely the Allen twins, Charles and Roy, Lemaire, Basil de Garmendia (USA) and V. Ker Seymer. In the final of the open singles, Lemaire beat Charles Allen, 3–6 6–2 6–4 7–5, while Miss V. Henshaw won the ladies' singles, defeating Miss Tomer in the final, 6–3 6–1. The doubles handicap event was secured by Charles Allen and de Garmendia. The tournament quickly grew in stature and soon attained the title 'The Riviera Championships'. Another court was laid down in 1904.

In 1906 a new drainage system put down at the Club proved very favourable and with the re-laying of the south court made the courts, as a whole, second to none.

The spring of 1907 was a memorable time for the Club, who were able to ensure their future by purchasing the freehold of their picturesque ground of over 2½ acres for £10,000. The following March a new stand was erected for £100 in time for the international tournament. The Club continued to flourish, with a court being added in both 1910 and 1911 and by 1913 there were a total of six courts available.

During the First World War tennis competitions were suspended but the Club continued to function. In common with other towns on the Côte d'Azur, hotels were requisitioned for convalescing soliders, many of whom were invited to play at the Club. With the war over, a further two courts were installed and accommodation in the stand increased. A year later the Club put down another court, provided a new reading room and enlarged the two dressing rooms. Late in 1923 several plots of land, adjacent to the existing ground, were purchased and by the following season, three more courts were provided, bringing the total available to 12.

In early 1932 the Club premises were sold to the Menton municipality for two million francs, with the town leasing the grounds back to the Club for 50,000 francs per year. However, in the following two years the Club had financial difficulties and only paid 20,000 francs rent, therefore still

A close-up view of the Menton Clubhouse and the top two courts, early 1920s.

owing 80,000 francs. Fortunately the Mayor of Menton and councillors were very considerate to the serious situation of the Club and agreed to allow it to continue to use the grounds at a nominal rent of 10 francs for a further period of 18 months. In late 1934 a further agreement with the town council enabled the Club to continue. At the start of the 1935 season the Club possessed 12 courts and four croquet lawns.

For over eight months, following the outbreak of the Second World War in September 1939, a strange and uneasy tranquillity existed along the Côte d'Azur. Those who were able left the area, but tennis continued to be played in many clubs, although the schedule of international tournaments had been well put aside. The relative peace was shattered on 11th June 1940, when Italy declared war. On 20th June the Italians attacked and Menton and Cap Martin suffered intense bombardment for the next five days. Menton town was severely damaged, as was the Menton Tennis Club building and grounds, made worse by the looting which followed.

Nine years had elapsed when in 1949 the first move was made to restore the Club's premises. This was eventually achieved when a new Clubhouse and grounds were opened in October 1952, following the restoration of the annual international tournament the previous year. Unfortunately, with the changing times, the meeting ceased after 1979. During the period the Club also organised a winter international tournament, held during January 1953–1956 and 1961. In 1956 an annual veterans' tournament was first staged and this has continued to be very successful.

When the Club was reinstated after the Second World War, in 1952, there were only about 50 members. This grew steadily until a peak of 600 was reached in 1987. Nowadays the figure is around 500. There are eight tennis courts available, but no croquet lawns exist.

## Monte Carlo

The first appearance of lawn tennis in the Principality was in January 1880, when a court with a covering of lime was laid down on the lawn of the pigeon-shooting range at the rear of the Hotel de Paris. This situation continued for some 12 years during which time the names of players do not appear to have been recorded, except on one occasion in 1886 when a group travelled over from Cannes on 16th January and formally opened the courts for the season. In these matches, Ernest Renshaw and Harry Grove beat James Dwight and Richard Sears 6–4 8–6 6–2 and in a singles, Grove beat Renshaw, heavily handicapped, 6–4 3–6 7–5. In April 1892 Prince Charles III of Monaco approved a proposal from Comte Bertora, the administrator of the Société des Bains de Mer (SBM), the local authority, for the installation of two permanent clay courts and a croquet lawn, at the total cost of 15,000 francs. During May, work began on levelling the land and there was local speculation that the hotel was expanding or a villa was being built. The area was not of great beauty and was actually the roof of the hotel cellars, showing ugly ventilation chimneys. The work was delayed because the hotel managers were concerned over the storage of

The Monte Carlo Hotel de Paris, 1902.

their wine but eventually, after 11 months, the two courts were completed. On 2nd April 1893 there was an official opening in the presence of many Monaco dignitaries, also some English personalities. Ernest Renshaw and Harry Bacon came over from Cannes and played an exhibition match.

The first tournament was held from 23rd to 29th March 1896 and consisted of four open and other handicap events. The men's open singles was won by George Hillyard of England. The following year began the start of the great days of the tournament, supported for a decade by the Doherty brothers. As regards entries, play and attendance, it eclipsed anything seen there. No less than 226 entries were obtained for the various events and 95 players from all over competed.

However, immediately after the March 1905 meeting, the SBM decided that the two courts at the rear of the Hotel de Paris would be taken over for the construction of an annex to the hotel. The management of the Monte Carlo tournament were given 3,000 francs to transfer the Club to new premises. So, in good time for the 1906 meeting, three new courts were laid down by the sea in Boulevard de la Condamine, midway between the two railway stations. A fourth court was added in 1907.

Many people expressed regret at the passing of the hotel courts, which were the scene of so many exciting matches and featured the domination of the Doherty brothers, Laurie and Reggie, who between them captured all the major titles each year from 1897. The change of venue saw the resignation of Charles Voigt, a man of unique reputation, as referee and

The Monte Carlo Condamine courts, 1907.

organiser and his being replaced by M. Maquet as Secretary and George Simond as referee.

For nine years, up to 1914, the courts at the Condamine were used to stage the Monte Carlo Championships, but after the First World War these were not available for 1919 and were supplanted by the newly provided La Festa courts. The official opening of this club took place on 28th January 1921, when the occasion was celebrated by a number of leading players taking part in exhibition matches, including Suzanne Lenglen pairing with Gordon Lowe against Alain Gerbault and Wallis Myers and winning 6–3 6–1, with admission being 50FF.

In a new centralized and elevated position, above the Casino Gardens, the site was a great improvement on the old quarters at the Condamine. Instead of a place used alternatively for exhibitions of tennis, boxing and flowers, three permanent superior surface courts were laid down, with well-screened backgrounds. The first court accommodated over a thousand spectators. However, there was always a drawback with the position of the courts, when the afternoon sun had a blinding effect on one side, making volleying and smashing almost a lottery.

The courts were built on the roof of a large garage 'Auto Riviera', holding some 300 cars. Facing the courts was a capacious restaurant, while the dressing room accommodation was generous, providing ultra–modern facilities. There were also two 'knock–up' walls for practice.

The complex, designed by an Englishman, was to a standard second to none on the Riviera, at a cost of £10,000. Marble tablets recording the names of past winners of the Monte Carlo Championships were taken

The Monte Carlo La Festa courts, 1921.

down from the previous site and erected in the new Clubhouse. The first international tournament held at the Club commenced on the 28th February 1921. In 1924 six new courts were provided.

In 1925 George Butler, a wealthy patron of the game donated the Butler Trophy for a special men's doubles competition for pairs of the same nationality. A year later, Commander Louis Beaumont, also an American, donated the Beaumont Cup for a similar event for ladies' pairs.

In 1928 the La Festa Club was completely transformed by the construction of new premises. Since the previous late summer, 1,500 workmen were employed on the enormous task, which initially entailed 25,000 cubic metres of earth being cut away from the mountainside to enable the several terraces to be built from the seashore up to the main road between Monaco and Menton.

The Club was designed by Charles Letrasne and built on an entirely new style. On each terrace there were two or three courts separated by tiny lawns, dotted with small cypresses and ponds,

La Festa/Monte Carlo Country Club, 1928/29.

MONTE-CARLO BEACH. — Les Tennis et vue sur Monte-Carlo

Monte Carlo Country Club, 1939.

with steps leading up through the courts. In total 20 courts were provided, twelve initially allocated for international competition. The Clubhouse contained a fine restaurant, seating 150 people and the dressing rooms provided accommodation for 700 members.

The first international tournament held on the new ground, known as La Festa Country Club, was the Monaco Championships played on 17th-24th December 1927. The courts were officially opened on 27th February 1928 by the Duke of Connaught, who threw the first tennis ball onto the courts from a terrace above. Exhibition matches followed before a start was made to the annual tournament for the Monte Carlo Championships. Early in 1929 the Club was renamed the Monte Carlo Country Club.

This breathtaking venue became the top attraction for tennis on the Riviera until the Second World War, when Monaco was occupied by the Italians, followed by the Germans. After the War the first international tournament staged was the Monte Carlo Championships, commencing on 11th March 1946. Only six courts were playable.

Soon matters returned to normal and Mrs Butler and her daughter, Gloria, returned to Monaco from the United States in 1947, to resume their patronage of the tournament, which was quickly established as the premier meeting each season, attracting the top players. So this position continued for many years. When 'open' tennis was introduced in 1968, which led to the downfall of the Riviera circuit, the Monte Carlo meeting survived by accepting sponsorship. Until 1980 ladies were part of the scene, but since then the annual tournament has been restricted to men's singles and doubles.

The present layout and setting of the Club, having 21 clay courts with a stadium seating over 10,000, up high, overlooking the blue waters of the Mediterranean, is undoubtedly one of the most spectacular tennis complexes in the world.

## NICE

### Nice Lawn Tennis Club

The Nice Lawn Tennis Club was founded in 1890 at the suggestion of Ashmore Noakes. A plot of ground, situated in the Platz Mozart was placed at the disposal of the Club by the municipal authorities for the nominal rent of 100 francs per annum. Four fine sand courts were constructed, with a pavilion containing a reading and writing room and men's and ladies' dressing rooms as well as a restaurant. The annual subscription for members was fixed at 60 francs and for monthly visitors at 30 francs, which fees practically covered everything, including balls and the services of ball boys but, of course, not refreshments. Originally there were 28 members.

The courts at the first Nice Club in the Platz Mozart around the start of the 20th century.

A continuous influx of new members over the next few years ensured the Club was firmly established. This success allowed the Committee, supported by the local municipality, to stage their first international lawn tennis tournament on the club grounds, from 11th to 14th March 1895. There were four events – an open Gentlemen's singles and three handicap competitions, a Gentlemen's singles and doubles and a mixed doubles. For the first event the winner received a handsome silver challenge cup, which immediately became his property.

The Club had hoped that a number of leading players staying in neighbouring Cannes would compete, but their non-participation was disappointing. However, several well-known players took part, including Count Victor Voss, S. Blacker-Douglas and L.L. Whiteway, as well as a few top players from Marseilles. The Nice Cup for the Gentlemen's singles was won by a Mr Thomas (Marseilles), who defeated Voss in the final. Third prize went to L. Hitchcock (Marseilles) and fourth prize to Whiteway (Nice LTC). The handicap prizes awarded were – Gentlemen's doubles: first – Thomas and Hitchcock (Marseilles), second – Capt. Warde and Carnegie-Cheales (Nice LTC). Mixed doubles: first – Blacker-Douglas and Mrs Booth, second – J.R. Hay-Gordon and Miss Coster, third – Whiteway and Miss Founde-Bellow.

Gentlemen's singles: first – J. Fall (Weymouth), second – Whiteway (Nice LTC), third – O. Synnett.

The meeting was enjoyed by all and the Committee promised to undertake a more important exercise the following year. This they did and within two years the tournament was widely recognised, attracting top class British players, including Reggie Doherty, Ernest Renshaw and Miss Ruth Dyas, and bearing the title 'The South of France Championships'. By then, the Club had 150 playing and non-playing members.

Vast changes took place at the Club during the summer of 1900 under the guidance of a newly appointed Hon. Secretary, A.G. Morganstern, an American who settled in Nice with his family six years earlier. The Pavilion was enlarged to practically a new building. Two new Club rooms were

A view of the No.1 Court at Parc Imperial, with the hotel in the background, 1924.

provided, prettily decorated and furnished, one in green and the other in red. The south room, which had a large fan window, was used as a lounge, while the other was given over for the Secretary's office and Committee meetings. In front of the two rooms was a large verandah, allowing a fine view over the courts, which had one half covered in glass as a shelter against the wind in the winter. To the north were the dressing rooms, a large area for the men containing a shower and tall lockers designed to hold the long blanket coats, which had become a great fashion. Equally, the ladies were well provided for. An opening on to both the verandah and the Club rooms was the buffet, which provided afternoon tea and other drinks.

In the spring of 1901 the fourth court, which ran north to south at the side of the Pavilion, was entirely rebuilt. At the same time new fencing was erected around the grounds, higher than before and with iron supports set in concrete. Another dozen lockers were installed in the men's dressing room and drying facilities made available. The trees around the courts were cut lower to improve the light for the players. At the request of a number of the French resident members, the Club was kept open during the summer for the first time. Even in the heat of August there was not a day where at least some of the courts were being used during the afternoon. There was always great difficulty in obtaining a court in the mornings between 10am and noon.

In the autumn of 1902 the courts were completely overhauled. Hitherto they were not made using the same earth throughout, but more of a clayey earth, top dressed with fine sand and lacked drainage. The new courts were made of one material, a sort of disintegrated porphyry rock, dark brown in colour, which was laid to a thickness of five inches on the old foundation. The result was said to be marvellous, surpassing the courts at the Beau Site in as much as the drainage was better.

In 1906 Mr Morganstern retired as Honorary Secretary and returned with his family to New York, after residing at Nice for 12 years. His place was taken by Alvarado Rice, who successfully steered the Club for many years.

During the First World War the courts were kept open and often used by service personnel, either on leave from the front or convalescing. With the War over the committee realised that the immediate growth of international tournaments along the Riviera, made the Platz Mozart site, with only four courts, quite inadequate and so decided to move to the spacious grounds of the Parc Imperial in early 1922. 17 courts were constructed over gravel soil on high ground, which dried very quickly after rain. Play was possible within half an hour following a heavy downpour. Subsequently, Platz Mozart became a public garden, with a car park underneath.

The first tournament staged on the new venue was the Club Members' Championship during January 1922, followed by the South of France Championships held from 13th–19th March. The latter was a dazzling success, with by far the majority of the players declaring themselves delighted with the courts. The Duke of Connaught visited on several occasions and expressed his approval. There was talk that the unique setting of the Parc Imperial would allow the Club to develop over the next few years. This was so, because when the 1924 Championships were held from 10th–16th March the pavilion had been extended to include luxurious dressing rooms, a fine restaurant, a dancing saloon, plus roof accommodation for many spectators. Another six courts had been provided, bringing the total to 21. Attached to each court was a nameplate. No.1 Court was 'Suzanne Lenglen', No.2,

'A.F. Wilding', No.3, 'Georges Gault', No.4, 'Lieut St Cyr' and so on, all except the first, paying tribute to a hero of the First World War.

The adjoining huge Parc Imperial Hotel, built in 1899, the imposing background to the Club, was constructed in the Bernond Gardens as a luxury establishment for holidaying Heads of State and nobility. During the First World War the hotel was used as a hospital for the troops and in the winter of 1925/1926 the hotel was acquired by the Nice Municipal Council and transformed into an educational facility.

After the Second World War the annual international tournament was revived in 1946 and continued until the early 1970s. From 1971 to 1987 an open meeting was staged for men and ladies and then from 1988 to 1995 restricted to men. From 2010 an annual open tournament for men was reinstated.

## ST RAPHAEL

### St Raphael Lawn Tennis Club

The Club, formed in 1925, housed four courts along the Avenue de Valescure. The first international tournament took place in April 1926, with the winners of the singles events being Arne Grahn of Finland and Lili de Alvarez of Spain. After 1931 the Club decided to discontinue international meetings.

Finals day at the St Raphael Club, 1930.

# VAL D'ESQUIÈRES

### Val d'Esquières Tennis Club

The Val d'Esquières Tennis Club, as part of the Athletic Club was founded in 1935 within the grounds of the Hotel de la Résidence, Val d'Esquières, and had four courts.

The Club never staged winter/spring international tournaments but held summer meetings during July and August from 1935 to 1939.

# The Principal Characters

### The Renshaw Twins

Four years after the inaugural Lawn Tennis Championship at Wimbledon in 1877, two brothers, William Charles and Ernest James Renshaw from Cheltenham, began their domination of the game, which lasted throughout the 1880s. Their mode of play completely transformed the game from being a pastime to a competitive sport. They quickly became household names, attracting people to flock to Wimbledon to witness the revelation. They were legendary.

The brothers were twins born on 3rd January 1861 at Leamington Spa, Warwickshire, with Ernest the elder by 25 minutes.

The season of 1881 saw the start of William's six year domination of the game, when

*Left:* Ernest Renshaw with (inset) William Renshaw

he won The Championships singles at Wimbledon. In the Challenge Round he crushed the holder, the Reverend John Hartley, 6–0 6–1 6–1, in 37 minutes.

In 1887 he unfortunately suffered an arm injury, commonly known as 'tennis elbow', which forced him to withdraw. The following year, William, fit again, challenged at Wimbledon, but lost in the third round. Ernest, upholding the family honour attained his one and only singles victory at that venue. William regained The Championship in 1889, when he beat Ernest in the last match. This really signalled the end of the Renshaw era.

As a doubles pair, the brothers seldom lowered their colours. Their list of successes in major events reads as follows: Oxford, 1880, 1881, The Championships, Wimbledon, 1884–1886, 1888, 1889, Irish Championships, 1881, 1883–1885, Northern Championships 1882–1886, 1888, South of England Championships, 1884, 1885, 1889.

The brothers were of very similar build, both being approximately 5 feet 10 inches tall and 10st 9lbs in weight. William possessed more powerful attacking shots, was more daring and cooler in judgment. He had the outstanding ability to take the ball very early on the rise, thereby allowing his opponent little time to recover. Ernest's defensive ability was outstanding, with his shots from the baseline near perfection. He was very quick around the court and his lobbing had no equal. Both brothers served, volleyed and smashed well.

For some 16 seasons or so there was a Renshaw twin present on the Riviera, the last being Ernest in early 1899. Ernest died on 2nd September 1899, aged 38 and William passed away on 12th August 1904, aged 43 – neither married.

**The Doherty Brothers**

When the reign of the Renshaw twins came to an end in 1890, the game tended to slow down for a short period, with no appreciable increase in the number of people taking up the racket or indeed giving support as a spectator. Then another two brothers, Reggie and Laurie Doherty emerged into the limelight and tennis took on a new lease of life. Their supremacy lasted ten years, from 1897 to 1906, during which period they completely dominated the sport, at home and abroad, with their graceful and outstanding stroke play and, at the same time, setting an example of conduct and demeanour off court for all to admire and copy. Reginald Frank and Hugh Laurence Doherty were born on 14th October 1872 and 8th October 1875, respectively, at Wimbledon.

Reggie first entered The Championships at Wimbledon in 1894, but not until 1897 did he triumph as champion by defeating Harold Mahony in the Challenge Round. He then defended successfully for the next three

years . His match with Laurie in 1898 was the only time the brothers ever contested a singles match in a tournament. He competed on the Riviera, 1897–1906 and 1908 and won a total of 29 titles – 8 singles, 15 doubles and 6 mixed doubles.

Laurie competed for five years in the singles at Wimbledon, 1896–1898, 1900 and 1901, before he upheld the family honour to win the 1902 Challenge Round and then retained his crown for four years. He competed on the Riviera in 1898 and 1900–1909 and won a total of 41 titles – 15 singles, 17 doubles and 9 mixed doubles.

As a doubles pair, Laurie and Reggie were in a class of their own. Their major triumphs were at Wimbledon where they won a record eight times, 1897–1901, 1903–1905.

During 1900 in Paris, Laurie won the Olympic gold medal for singles and together, the brothers won the doubles event. Both Laurie and Reggie visited the USA in 1902 and 1903 as part of the British Isles Davis Cup team.

Reggie, known as "Big Do", tall and thin, was a natural stylist who possessed a magnificent all-court game, with an outstanding backhand and marvellous power of anticipation. Laurie, known as "Little Do", sturdier than his brother was a great tactician who would play to the needs of the occasion. His wonderful volleying and smashing were exceptional.

Reggie died on 29th December 1910, aged 38, and Laurie passed away on 21st August 1919, aged 43 – neither married.

## Major Ritchie

Ritchie competed on the Riviera over a period of 21 years, 1902–1911, 1920 and 1923. Doubtless there has never been a player so keen to compete

and in the process he captured hundreds of titles from all over – too many to record here. He enjoyed himself and gave pleasure to countless admiring spectators.

After his spell on the Riviera most years, he generally would return to England for the early season and Wimbledon and then week after week tour Europe. Mention a place name and the chances were that he had played there! Probably the highlights of his career came in 1908 when he won the Olympic gold medal for singles in London and a year later reached the Challenge Round of the singles at Wimbledon where he lost to Arthur Gore, after winning the opening two sets. (In 1902–1904 he was runner-up in the All Comers' Singles.) As consolation he won the doubles title twice, in 1908 and 1910, both times with Anthony Wilding. On the Riviera he won a total of 41 titles, 16 singles, 20 doubles and 5 mixed doubles.

Ritchie's name will confuse future historians. His full name was Major Joshua George Ritchie, but the forename Major had nothing to do with the military or rank. That was his first forename and that is what he was always known as and called by. He married Ethel Slattery at Brighton, Sussex, on the 18th October 1909 and they spent their honeymoon touring Devon in an "automobile".

He was born in London on 18th October 1870 and died at Ashford, Middlesex, England on 28th February 1955, aged 84.

## Henry Mayes

Lt. Col. Henry George Mayes, born in England but who spent his early life in Canada, was an outstanding athlete, numbering football, rugby, golf and squash as his accomplishments. He was chosen by Canada to be a reserve in their Davis Cup team in 1914, but did not reach his peak in lawn tennis until he settled in England after the First World War in 1920 and concentrated on the game.

As a soldier he served in the South African War and afterwards made his mark in that country as a games player. He was always devoted to

physical fitness and during the First World War was in charge of training for the Canadian Army. He also advised the American and British Armies and in 1919 the Greek Government.

He was a top class player if not a great player, who possessed that little extra, doubtless adopting the motto "patience and perseverance". He did not have at his command a severe service and his volleying was comparatively poor, but his play off the ground was a model of consistency. His passing shots against an incoming volley were nearly always winners.

If an opponent had a weakness he was sure to realise this and take full advantage.

Mayes did not excel on grass, as his record at Wimbledon shows, but he was unquestionably at his best on the courts of the Riviera, where he played from 1921 to 1928. During this period he won 21 singles title, 7 doubles and 6 mixed, including six singles titles in 1925. He won the Beau Site Hotel singles three years in a row, 1924–1926.

His sudden death due to blood poisoning occurred at Highgate, London on 4th December 1928. He was 47.

### Gordon Lowe

Sir Francis Gordon Lowe had a very distinguished tennis career for 25 years, before and after the First World War, during which time he won countless tournaments at home and abroad. He was part of the British Isles team which brought back the Davis Cup Trophy to England from Australia in 1912. He also played in the competition in 1921, 1922 and 1925.

He competed at Wimbledon from 1906 to 1926 and reached the All Comers' singles semi-final in 1911, the doubles final in 1921 with his brother Arthur and the Championship singles semi-final in 1923. In 1915 at Brisbane he became the first Englishman to win the Australian singles crown and in 1912 and 1920 also competed in the Olympic Games.

An outstanding baseline player, he possessed one of the finest backhand drives down the line. Early on he was inclined to lose his form at crucial moments, but as time went on he was able to overcome this to become a top class performer.

He played on the Riviera in 1907, 1909, 1911, 1913, 1914, 1920, 1921, 1923–1926 and captured a total of 33 titles, 23 in singles (three times at Carlton, Hyères and Monte Carlo), 7 doubles and 3 mixed doubles.

He was the author of several books on the game and edited his Annual, 1932–1936. Lowe served from 1916–1919 in the First World War, rising to Captain and being mentioned in dispatches. He married twice, Margaret Laverton in 1914 and Honor Woolrych in 1926 and succeeded his father to the baronetcy in 1929.

He was born in Edgbaston on 21st June 1884 and died in London on 17th May 1972, aged 87.

## Charles Aeschliman

Charles Aeschliman was one of the Riviera's staunchest tennis supporters, who competed each year from 1921 to 1934 and 1939. His success was predominantly achieved in doubles but there were many times that he was able to rise to the occasion and capture singles titles. On top form he could beat anyone.

He stood 6 feet 2 inches tall. He excelled at the net, with his volleying and anticipation skills. His smashing was excellent, while his play from the back of the court was sometimes suspect.

On the Riviera he won 103 titles, 15 in singles, 55 in doubles and 33 in mixed doubles. He played at Wimbledon between 1926 and 1938. He represented Switzerland in the Davis Cup from 1923 to 1932 and 1934, when he played 50 matches, winning 15 from 32 singles and 9 from 18 doubles.

After earlier schooling in Switzerland, he spent five years in England at public school in Birkenhead. For years he assisted in managing the Beaulieu Hotel at Cannes, of which his father, Otto, was the proprietor. Charles would arrange accommodation and transport to the various tournaments during the tennis season for the players. Generally called 'Charlie', he was very popular with the players.

Aeschliman was born at Cannes on 28th February 1897 and died at Montreux, Switzerland on 5th May 1952. He married American tennis player, Leslie Bancroft, at Brookline, Massachusetts, USA on 16th December 1924. They had two children, Roger and Alice.

## Henri Cochet

Henri Jean Cochet was one of the greatest French players of all time and one of the famous 'Four Musketeers'. He won the Wimbledon singles twice, 1927, 1929, and the doubles twice, 1926, 1928. At the French Championships he won the singles 4 times, 1926, 1928, 1930, 1932, the doubles 3 times, 1927, 1930, 1932, and the mixed doubles twice, 1928, 1929. At the US Championships he captured the singles in 1928 and the mixed in 1927. He represented France in the Davis Cup in 1924, 1926–1933, during which period his country won the Trophy from 1927 to 1932.

He was a very artistic player who possessed a superb half volley and a deadly smash. Also, his ability to return the hardest hit of services and his knowledge of angles were top class. Often at the beginning of a match he gave the impression that he was uninterested but excelled in being able to recover from a normally hopeless position.

Henri Cochet and (far right) Jacques Brugnon.

On the Riviera he generally played for a few weeks each year from 1922 to 1932 and captured a total of 64 titles, 20 singles titles, 23 doubles and 21 mixed doubles.

He was born at Lyon, France on 14th December 1901 and died in Paris, France on 1st April 1987 aged 86. He married Germaine Desthieux on 16th April, 1926.

### Jacques Brugnon

Jacques (Toto) Brugnon was one of the four famous 'French Musketeers' who won the Davis Cup for their country from 1927 to 1932. He played in the competition from 1921 to 1927 and 1930 to 1934.

Although a top class singles player, his forte was undoubtedly doubles, in which he captured the Wimbledon crown four times – 1926, 1928, 1932, 1933, the French title five times – 1926, 1928, 1930, 1932, 1934, and the Australian title in 1928.

Brugnon possessed a magnificent top spin return of service and lob plus an outstanding volley. His smash was good but not decisive. He was very popular.

He was strongly attracted to the Riviera, which he visited each year for a week or two, sometimes twice, from 1926 to 1939. During this period he won a total of 58 titles, 12 in singles, 32 doubles and 14 mixed doubles.

He was born in Paris, France on 11th May 1895 and died in Paris on 20th March 1978, aged 82.

## George Rogers

George Lyttleton Rogers was the outstanding Irish player of the 1930s. As a youngster he played the game in Dublin, but when his father died the family moved to Nice. Here he practised for six hours a day which, besides improving his play, gave him the advantage of familiarity with the local courts and conditions.

He competed on the Riviera from 1927 to 1934, 1938 and 1939. Three of those years, 1931–1933, he reached his peak by winning 42 titles, 15 in singles, 14 doubles and 13 mixed doubles. Overall, his record was 57 titles, 18 in singles, 22 doubles and 17 mixed doubles.

He represented his country in the Davis Cup every year from 1929 to 1939 and played 49 matches in 17 ties, winning 18 from 33 singles and 6 from 16 doubles. He competed at Wimbledon from 1928 to 1939, with his best achievement reaching the fourth round in 1933. He travelled extensively and won many tournaments. He turned professional in 1945.

Rogers was a big man, whose height of 6 feet 7 inches allowed him to serve at great speed. He was basically a baseline player who moved uncomfortably in the forecourt. His forehand drive was well hit and his overhead work was good. On top form he could beat anyone.

He was born at Athy, Ireland on 10th July 1906 and died at Los Angeles, USA on 19th November 1962, aged 56. He married three times.

## Bill Tilden

William Tatem Tilden is generally accepted as one of the greatest ever players of the game. For much of the 1920s he was the world's top ranked player, during which period he won the Wimbledon singles 3 times, 1920, 1921, 1930, and the doubles, 1927. At US Championships he was singles champion 7 times, 1920–1925, 1929, and doubles 4 times 1918, 1921–1923.

In Davis Cup he led the US for 11 years, 1920–1930, when his country won the trophy 7 occasions in succession, 1920–1926.

He possessed an all-round game, spearheaded by a very powerful service. A great tactical ability was matched by a fine temperament. He was a prolific writer of books.

Tilden visited the Riviera just one season, in 1930, and produced a record of play beyond reproach. His achievement was phenomenal. Unlike any other competitor he played throughout from 6th January to 27th April and entered 15 consecutive international tournaments. He captured 13 singles titles (lost one whilst ill and one when resting), 13 doubles titles (in two cases injured, causing retirement) and 8 mixed doubles titles. In addition he competed in the Monte Carlo Club championship and won all three events. That year he went on to win the singles title at Wimbledon and in December turned professional.

He was born at Philadelphia, USA, on 10th February 1893 and died at Los Angeles, USA, on 5th June 1953 aged 60. He never married.

## Wallis Myers

Undoubtedly, the outstanding lawn tennis writer of the first half of the 20th century was Arthur Wallis Myers, whose whole life was devoted to the sport. Many of the dozen or so books he published contained an abundance of facts and were rich in narratives of the expanding tennis history, mostly assembled from his personal experiences over the years.

His first book, published in 1903, 'Lawn Tennis at Home and Abroad', was well before its time and contained over 300 pages packed with information on play and players from around the world, plus an amazing collection of some 220 photographs. The books which followed were just as informative and fascinating.

He first reported tennis from the Riviera for *The Field* in 1902 and six years later took up the appointment as Correspondent for the *London Daily Telegraph*, a post he held until his death. Each winter/spring he would travel south and capture the flavour of the area in contrast to the dark, damp days at home. When time permitted he would compete in the tennis tournaments. He was far from being in the top echelon as a singles player but his enthusiasm made him a good doubles competitor, of sufficient standard to win many titles. His partnership with Jessie Tripp was feared by all.

His other achievements were numerous. Yearly from 1908 to 1938 he produced the 'Ayres Lawn Tennis Almanack' (the Wisden of tennis). In 1924 he founded the International Club of Great Britain (followed by nearly every other nation). He travelled abroad extensively often organising and captaining teams to promote relationships.

During the First World War he worked for the War Office and other Government departments, for which he was awarded the CBE.

He was born at Kettering, Northamptonshire, 24th July 1878 and died at Epsom, Surrey on 16th June 1939, aged 60.

### George Simond

George Mieville Simond was the Referee and handicapper at virtually every tournament on the Riviera from 1903 to the late 1930s. Every week during the season he would move along the coast to the various meetings

and then, when concluded, toured around Europe for the summer carrying out similar duties. This was his life – he did little else. Players admired his conscientious attention to every detail, his fairness to all and great tact in handling competitors in very different circumstances and varying weather.

In his younger days he was one of England's leading players and won a number of tournaments but he gradually specialised in doubles. At Wimbledon he was an All Comers' finalist with Roper Barrett in 1901 and Clement Cazalet in 1906. He also played much on the Continent where he captured many titles, particularly in France and Switzerland. Before the First World War, as well as carrying out his official duties on the Riviera, he would often compete successfully. He normally resided at the Metropole Hotel in Monte Carlo.

The eldest of four playing brothers, Simond was born in London on 23rd January 1867 and died in London on 8th April 1941, aged 74.

### Suzanne Lenglen

For eight years after the First World War, Suzanne Lenglen, the legendary French tennis player completely dominated the scene with a game that had been tuned to perfection.

She spent her childhood winters with her parents in Nice, where she made her home for the next fifteen years before settling back in Paris. Suzanne's father was her mentor and trainer and undoubtedly was responsible for her great success. She immediately shot to fame in 1919 when, playing on grass for the first time at Wimbledon, she defeated the seven times champions, Dorothea Chambers in an exciting Challenge Round.

She played two other unforgettable matches. In 1921 during her opening match at the United States Women's Championships she defaulted to Molla Mallory after losing the opening set on account of being unwell. In 1926 at the Carlton Club at Cannes she beat Helen Wills in a dramatic contest, often known as the 'Match of the Century'.

Most of Suzanne's opponents measured their success in singles by the number of points they won. If they played extremely well they would count the number of games. Three were able to claim a set, but only one a match. Nine times Suzanne won a singles title at a tournament without dropping a game.

At Wimbledon she won 6 singles and 6 doubles titles, 1919–1923, 1925, and 3 mixed doubles, 1920, 1922, 1925. At the French Championships she captured 6 singles and 6 doubles titles, 1920–1923, 1925, 1926 and 7 mixed doubles, 1914, 1920–1923, 1925, 1926. At the 1920 Olympic Games she became singles and mixed doubles champion.

During her career Suzanne won 250 titles. On the Riviera her tally was 118 – 34 singles, 41 doubles and 43 mixed doubles.

She withdrew from Wimbledon in 1926 following a misunderstanding and decided not to grace the courts again. Within a month or so she had signed a professional contract and relinquished her amateur status.

Suzanne Lenglen was born in Paris, France on 24th May 1899 and died in Paris on 4th July 1938, aged 39. She never married.

## Elizabeth Ryan

There is no question that Elizabeth Montague Ryan was one of the finest doubles exponents the game has ever known. If the number of titles she won in a career is the deciding factor, then she stands alone.

At Wimbledon she won 19 doubles titles, 12 ladies' doubles, 1914, 1919–1923, 1925–1927, 1930, 1933 and 1934, and 7 in mixed, 1919, 1921, 1923, 1927, 1928, 1930 and 1932. At the French Championships she captured 4 doubles titles, 1930, 1932–1934, and at the US Championships, 1 doubles, 1926. Her partnership with Suzanne Lenglen over the early part of the 1920's was unbeaten.

Despite her outstanding prowess in singles, which she won in abundance, she never won a major championship. At Wimbledon in 1921 and 1930 she was the runner up.

She possessed a powerful service and smash, plus a dynamic chopped forehand which, coupled with her great stamina and determination made her a formidable opponent.

On the Riviera she played in 1913, 1914, 1920–1925, 1927–1934 and amassed a total of 251 titles, 73 in singles, 99 in doubles and 79 in mixed doubles – a feat completely overwhelming to all other competitors.

Born at Anaheim, California on 5th February 1892, she died at Wimbledon, London on 6th July 1979, aged 87. She never married.

### Phyllis Satterthwaite

Phyllis Helen Satterthwaite (nèe Carr) was completely devoted to the game and sought to play most weeks of her life. She was never able to win a major singles or doubles title but nevertheless was at times a formidable player who, in her day, could beat anyone. She was runner up of the All Comers' singles at Wimbledon in 1912 and 1921.

She was firmly attached to playing each year on the Riviera, where she was employed by a chain of large hotels. This amounted to a total of 19 years, 1921–1939. During this period she amassed 118 titles, 31 in singles, 61 in doubles and 26 in mixed doubles. In 1931, at the age of 45, she reached the final of 11 singles events and captured 6 of the titles (plus winning the Members' tournament at Monte Carlo), beating such players as Cilly Aussem, Betty Nuthall, Lucia Valerio, Simone Mathieu, Hélène Nicolopoulo, Mary Heeley and Dorothy Burke – all top class performers.

Phyllis, tall and slim, played her game from the baseline but she often resorted to clever lobs and drop shots to upset the rhythm of her opponent's play with great success. Often her matches lasted a long time, as one incident shows. During 1930 in a match against Lucia Valerio at Bordighera in Italy, a total of 419 strokes were played over 19 and a half minutes.

She was born at Kensington, London on 26th January 1886 and died at Kensington, London on 20th January 1962, aged 75. She married Clement Satterthwaite at Chiswick, Middlesex on 13th April 1912.

### Helen Wills

Helen Newington Wills was the world's outstanding player from the mid 1920s and 1930s, winning dozens of major titles. At Wimbledon she won 8 singles titles, 1927–1930, 1932, 1933, 1935, 1938, 3 doubles and 1 mixed doubles. At the US Championships she captured 7 singles titles, 1923–1925, 1927–1929, 1931, 3 doubles and 2 mixed doubles. At the French Championships her tally was 4 singles titles, 1928–1930, 1932, and 2 doubles. She was also Olympic singles and doubles champion in 1924.

Normally emotionless and deadly on court she possessed an accurate and persistent drive, which was seldom mastered by her opponents.

*Above:* Helen Wiils.
*Centre:* Lili de Alvarez.
*Right:* Simone Mathieu.

The only year she visited the Riviera was in 1926, when she lost in an epic singles final against Suzanne Lenglen at the Cannes Carlton Club. Other than this setback, her tour was exceptional as she earlier defeated all her singles opponents to capture 7 titles at the Metropole Hotel, Gallia Hotel, Beaulieu, Monte Carlo, Menton, Nice and the Cannes Club. She also won a number of doubles titles.

Helen Wills was born at Centerville, USA on 6th October 1905 and died at Carmel, USA on 1st January 1998, aged 92. She married Frederick Moody at Berkeley, USA on 23rd December 1929 and Aidan Roark at Las Vegas, USA on 28th October 1939.

### Lili de Alvarez

Lili de Alvarez was the first world class Spanish lady player. She was exciting to watch play, with her range of attacking strokes. Her half volley was outstanding, but her service and lobbing were ordinary. She was best remembered for being runner-up in the singles at Wimbledon three consecutive years, 1926–1928, the first against Mrs Kathleen Godfree and the other two facing Helen Wills. At the French Championships she was never able to pass the semi-final of the singles, despite reaching that stage four times, 1930, 1931, 1936, 1937. She took the doubles title in 1929. However, she won numerous titles on the Continent and was ranked No.2 in the world, 1927, 1928.

Her other sporting activities were golf, cycling, skating, skiing, swimming, riding and mountaineering.

Lili played on the Riviera for a few weeks each year from 1923 to 1930 and 1937, during which period she won a total of 34 titles, 19 singles, 7 doubles and 8 mixed doubles.

She was born in Paris, France on 9th May 1905 and died in Madrid, Spain on 8th July 1998, aged 93. She married Count Jean de Gilliard Valdene in Madrid, Spain on 14th November 1935.

## Simone Mathieu

Simone Mathieu (née Passemard) was France's No.1 player from 1928 to 1939, during which period she travelled widely and competed in many tournaments.

At Wimbledon she reached the semi-final of the singles 4 times, 1931, 1932, 1934, 1936, and won the doubles crown 3 times, 1933, 1934, 1937. At the French Championships she reached the singles final 5 times, 1932, 1933, 1935–1937 and won the title twice, 1938, 1939. She also captured 6 doubles titles, 1933, 1934, 1936–1939 and two mixed doubles, 1937, 1938.

A resolute baseliner, she played with great steadiness and determination, quite often in long drawn-out matches. She had an outstanding forehand drive and was a natural doubles competitor.

She excelled on the clay courts of the Riviera, which she visited each year from 1929 to 1939. In 1935 and 1936 she set up records which will never be broken. In the former she entered 16 tournaments and won every singles title (in addition, she won a 'triple' at Bordighera, Italy, and at the Cannes LTC Members' tournament). In the following year she entered 14 tournaments and again won all singles titles (plus the Cannes LTC Members' tournament). In addition she won the first six singles titles in 1937. During the same period, numerous doubles and mixed doubles were captured.

In total on the Riviera she won 138 titles, 52 in singles, 43 in doubles and 43 in mixed doubles.

She was born at Neuilly-sur-Seine, France on 31st January 1908 and died in Paris on 7th January 1980 aged 71. She married René Mathieu at St Cloud, Paris on 14th October 1925.

## Winter/Spring Tournament Venues 1895–1939

| *Towns* | *Venues* | *Tournaments* | *Years* |
|---|---|---|---|
| ANTIBES | Provençal LTC | International tournaments | 1933–1939 |
| BEAULIEU | Beaulieu LTC (Bristol Hotel) | Beaulieu Championships | 1913–1939 |
| | | Other tournaments | 1928–1932 |
| CANNES | Beau Site Hotel | Cannes Championships | 1897–1939 |
| | | New Year tournaments | 1913–1939 |
| | | Other tournaments | 1919–1920 |
| CANNES | Cannes LTC | Côte d'Azur Championships | 1910–1939 |
| | | Other tournaments | 1921–1936 |
| CANNES | Carlton LTC (Carlton Hotel) | International tournaments | 1914–1939 |
| | | New Year tournaments | 1914–1925 |
| | | Other tournaments | 1920–1926 |
| CANNES | Gallia LTC | International tournaments | 1924–1939 |
| CANNES | Metropole LTC (Metropole Hotel) | International tournaments | 1904–1931 |
| | | Other tournaments | 1925 |
| CANNES | New Courts Club | International tournaments | 1926–1934 |
| | | Other tournaments | 1932–1934 |
| HYÈRES | Hyères LTC (Golf Hotel) | International tournaments | 1910–1928 |
| HYÈRES | New Courts Club | International tournaments | 1929–1930 |
| JUAN-LES-PINS | Juan-les-Pins LTC | International tournaments | 1924–1934 |
| JUAN-LES-PINS | Miramar LTC | International tournaments | 1929–1939 |
| MENTON | Menton LTC | Riviera Championships | 1902–1939 |
| | | International Mixed Doubles | 1924–1930 |
| | | Other tournaments | 1922 |
| MONTE CARLO | Hotel de Paris, Condamine, La Festa, La Festa Country Club, Monte Carlo Country Club | Monte Carlo Championships | 1896–1939 |
| | | Butler Trophy | 1925–1939 |
| | | Beaumont Cup | 1925–1938 |
| | | Iliffe Trophy | 1939 |
| | | Easter tournaments | 1919–1939 |
| | | Prix de Famille | 1928–1932 |
| MONTE CARLO | La Festa, La Festa Country Club, Monte Carlo Country Club | Monaco Championships | 1922–1930 |
| | | Prix de Famille | 1927–1930 |
| MONTE CARLO | Condamine | Monagasque Championships | 1931–1939 |
| MONTE CARLO | Monte Carlo Country Club | Other tournaments | 1935–1939 |
| NICE | Nice LTC, Platz Mozart, Parc Imperial | South of France Championships | 1895–1939 |
| | | Other tournaments | 1920–1939 |
| NICE | Nice Country Club | International tournaments | 1914 |
| ST RAPHAEL | St Raphael LTC | International tournaments | 1926–1931 |

# Winter/Spring Tournament Schedule 1895–1939

**1895**
March 11-14         Nice, Nice LTC, Platz Mozart

**1896**
                      Nice, Nice LTC, Platz Mozart
March 23-29        Monte Carlo, Hotel de Paris

**1897**
January 15-21      Cannes, Beau Site Hotel
March 15-21        Nice, Nice LTC, Platz Mozart
March 22-30        Monte Carlo, Hotel de Paris

**1898**
March 7-16         Nice, Nice LTC, Platz Mozart
March 15-21        Monte Carlo, Hotel de Paris

**1899**
February 20- 26    Cannes, Beau Site Hotel (H)
March 13-19        Nice, Nice LTC, Platz Mozart (South of France Championships)
April 4-10          Monte Carlo, Hotel de Paris

**1900**
February            Cannes, Beau Site Hotel (H)
March 19-31        Nice, Nice LTC, Platz Mozart (South of France Championships)

**1901**
March 1-8          Cannes, Beau Site Hotel
March 8-18         Monte Carlo, Hotel de Paris
March 18-24        Nice, Nice LTC, Platz Mozart (South of France Championships)

**1902**
March 1-8          Monte Carlo, Hotel de Paris
March 10-18        Nice, Nice LTC, Platz Mozart (South of France Championships)
March 22-29        Menton, Menton LTC

(H) = Handicap events only

## 1903

| | |
|---|---|
| March 1-8 | Monte Carlo, Hotel de Paris |
| March 9-22 | Nice, Nice LTC, Platz Mozart (South of France Championships) |
| March 23-30 | Cannes, Beau Site Hotel (H) |
| | Menton, Menton LTC (Riviera Championships) |

## 1904

| | |
|---|---|
| February 18-25 | Menton, Menton LTC (Riviera Championships) |
| February 26-March 6 | Monte Carlo, Hotel de Paris |
| March 7-17 | Nice, Nice LTC, Platz Mozart (South of France Championships) |
| March 15-22 | Cannes, Beau Site Hotel (Cannes Championships) |
| March 23-28 | Cannes, Metropole Hotel |

## 1905

| | |
|---|---|
| February 23-28 | Menton, Menton LTC (Riviera Championships) |
| March 3-11 | Monte Carlo, Hotel de Paris |
| March 13-25 | Nice, Nice LTC, Platz Mozart (South of France Championships) |
| March 21-26 | Cannes, Beau Site Hotel, (Cannes Championships) |

## 1906

| | |
|---|---|
| February 22-28 | Monte Carlo, Condamine |
| March 5-9 | Menton, Menton LTC (Riviera Championships) |
| March 12-19 | Nice, Nice LTC, Platz Mozart (South of France Championships) |
| March 20-25 | Cannes, Beau Site Hotel, (Cannes Championships) |

## 1907

| | |
|---|---|
| February 25-March 3 | Menton, Menton LTC (Riviera Championships) |
| March 4-10 | Monte Carlo, Condamine |
| March 11-17 | Nice, Nice LTC, Platz Mozart (South of France Championships) |
| March 19-26 | Cannes, Beau Site Hotel (Cannes Championships) |
| March 25-31 | Cannes, Metropole Hotel |

## 1908

| | |
|---|---|
| February 24-March 1 | Monte Carlo, Condamine |
| March 2-9 | Menton, Menton LTC (Riviera Championships) |
| March 9-18 | Nice, Nice LTC, Platz Mozart (South of France Championships) |
| March 18-26 | Cannes, Beau Site Hotel, (Cannes Championships) |
| March 30-April 6 | Cannes, Metropole Hotel |

## 1909

| | |
|---|---|
| February 22-27 | Monte Carlo, Condamine |
| March 1-7 | Menton, Menton LTC (Riviera Championships) |
| March 8-15 | Nice, Nice LTC, Platz Mozart (South of France Championships) |
| March 17-24 | Cannes, Beau Site Hotel (Cannes Championships) |
| March 27-April 3 | Cannes, Metropole Hotel |

## 1910

| | |
|---|---|
| February 21-26 | Monte Carlo, Condamine |
| March 1-7 | Menton, Menton LTC (Riviera Championships) |
| March 10-15 | Nice, Nice LTC, Platz Mozart (South of France Championships) |
| March 16-20 | Cannes, Beau Site Hotel (Cannes Championships) |
| March 21-24 | Cannes, Cannes Croquet & LTC |
| March 24-30 | Cannes, Metropole Hotel |
| March 31-April 5 | Hyères, Hyères LTC |

## 1911

| | |
|---|---|
| February 27-March 5 | Monte Carlo, Condamine (Monte Carlo Championships) |
| March 6-12 | Menton, Menton LTC (Riviera Championships) |
| March 13-19 | Nice, Nice LTC, Platz Mozart (South of France Championships) |
| March 20-26 | Cannes, Beau Site Hotel (Cannes Championships) |
| March 27-April 2 | Cannes, Cannes Croquet & LTC (Cote d'Azur Championships) |
| April 3-9 | Hyères, Hyères LTC |

## 1912

| | |
|---|---|
| February 12-18 | Monte Carlo, Condamine (Monte Carlo Championships) |
| February 25-March 3 | Menton, Menton LTC (Riviera Championships) |
| March 4-10 | Nice, Nice LTC, Platz Mozart (South of France Championships) |
| March 11-17 | Cannes, Beau Site Hotel (Cannes Championships) |
| March 18-24 | Cannes, Cannes Croquet & LTC (Cote d'Azur Championships) |
| March 25-April 1 | Hyères, Hyères LTC |

## 1913

| | |
|---|---|
| December 30-January 5 | Cannes, Beau Site Hotel |
| February 3-10 | Beaulieu, Beaulieu LTC |
| February 14-15 | Cannes, Cannes Croquet & LTC (Cote d'Azur Championships) |
| February 24-March 1 | Monte Carlo, Condamine (Monte Carlo Championships) |
| March 3-9 | Menton, Menton LTC (Riviera Championships) |
| March 10-17 | Nice, Nice LTC, Platz Mozart (South of France Championships) |
| March 17-23 | Cannes, Metropole Hotel |

| | |
|---|---|
| March 24-30 | Cannes, Beau Site Hotel (Cannes Championships) |
| March 31-April 5 | Hyères, Hyères LTC |

## 1914

| | |
|---|---|
| December 29- January 4 | Cannes, Beau Site Hotel |
| January 5-11 | Cannes, Carlton LTC |
| February 2-8 | Hyères, Hyères LTC |
| February 9-15 | Beaulieu, Beaulieu LTC |
| February 16-22 | Cannes, Cannes Croquet & LTC (Cote d'Azur Championships) |
| February 23-March 3 | Monte Carlo, Condamine (Monte Carlo Championships) |
| March 2-8 | Menton, Menton LTC (Riviera Championships) |
| March 9-15 | Nice, Nice LTC, Platz Mozart (South of France Championships) |
| March 16-26 | Nice, Nice Country Club, Parc Imperial |
| March 23-30 | Cannes, Beau Site Hotel (Cannes Championships) |
| March 31-April 5 | Cannes, Metropole Hotel |
| April 6-12 | Cannes, Carlton LTC |

## 1915-1918

| | |
|---|---|
| | First World War – no tournaments |

## 1919

| | |
|---|---|
| February 24-March 2 | Cannes, Carlton LTC |
| March 3-9 | Monte Carlo, La Festa, (Monte Carlo Championships) |
| March 10-16 | Menton, Menton LTC (Riviera Championships) |
| March 17-25 | Nice, Nice LTC, Platz Mozart (South of France Championships) |
| March 26-April 1 | Cannes, Beau Site Hotel (Cannes Championships) |
| April 21-26 | Monte Carlo, La Festa |
| May 5-11 | Cannes, Beau Site Hotel |

## 1920

| | |
|---|---|
| January 5-11 | Cannes, Beau Site Hotel |
| January 12-18 | Cannes, Carlton LTC |
| February 9-15 | Hyères, Hyères LTC |
| February 16-22 | Cannes, Carlton LTC |
| February 23-28 | Beaulieu, Beaulieu LTC (Beaulieu Championships) |
| March 1-7 | Monte Carlo, Condamine  (Monte Carlo Championships) |
| March 8-14 | Menton, Menton LTC (Riviera Championships) |
| March 15-21 | Nice, Nice LTC, Platz Mozart (South of France Championships) |
| March 22-28 | Cannes, Cannes LTC (Côte d'Azur Championships) |
| March 29-April 4 | Cannes, Beau Site Hotel (Cannes Championships) |
| April 5-11 | Cannes, Metropole Hotel |
| April 12-18 | Cannes, Carlton LTC |
| April 19-25 | Nice, Nice LTC, Platz Mozart |
| April 26-May 2 | Cannes, Beau Site Hotel |
| May 3-9 | Monte Carlo, La Festa - CANCELLED |

## 1921

| | |
|---|---|
| January 3-9 | Cannes, Beau Site Hotel |
| January 10-16 | Cannes, Carlton LTC |
| January 17-23 | Cannes, Cannes LTC |
| January 31-February 6 | Hyères, Hyères LTC |
| February 7-13 | Nice, Nice LTC, Platz Mozart |
| February 14-20 | Cannes, Carlton LTC |
| February 21-27 | Beaulieu, Beaulieu LTC (Beaulieu Championships) |
| February 28-March 6 | Monte Carlo, La Festa (Monte Carlo Championships) |
| March 7-13 | Menton, Menton LTC (Riviera Championships) |
| March 14-20 | Nice, Nice LTC, Platz Mozart (South of France Championships) |
| March 21-27 | Cannes, Cannes LTC (Côte d'Azur Championships) |
| March 28-April 3 | Cannes, Beau Site Hotel (Cannes Championships) |
| April 4-10 | Cannes, Metropole Hotel |
| April 11-17 | Cannes, Carlton LTC |
| April 18-24 | Monte Carlo, La Festa |

## 1922

| | |
|---|---|
| December 26-January 2 | Monte Carlo, La Festa (Monaco Championships) |
| January 2-8 | Cannes, Beau Site Hotel |
| January 9-15 | Cannes, Carlton LTC |
| January 16-22 | Cannes, Cannes LTC |
| January 23-29 | Menton, Menton LTC |
| January 30-February 5 | Hyères, Hyères LTC |
| February 6-12 | Nice, Nice LTC, Platz Mozart |
| February 13-19 | Cannes, Carlton LTC |
| February 20-26 | Beaulieu, Beaulieu LTC (Beaulieu Championships) |
| February 27-March 5 | Monte Carlo, La Festa (Monte Carlo Championships) |
| March 6-12 | Menton, Menton LTC (Riviera Championships) |
| March 13-19 | Nice, Nice LTC, Parc Imperial (South of France Championships) |
| March 20-26 | Cannes, Cannes LTC (Côte d'Azur Championships) |
| March 27-April 2 | Cannes, Beau Site Hotel (Cannes Championships) |
| April 3-9 | Cannes, Metropole Hotel |
| April 10-16 | Cannes, Carlton LTC |
| April 17-23 | Monte Carlo, La Festa |

## 1923

| | |
|---|---|
| December 25-31 | Monte Carlo, La Festa (Monaco Championships) |
| January 1-7 | Cannes, Beau Site Hotel |
| January 8-14 | Cannes, Carlton LTC |
| January 29-February 4 | Hyères, Hyères LTC |
| February 5-11 | Nice, Nice LTC, Parc Imperial |
| February 12-18 | Cannes, Carlton LTC |
| February 19-25 | Beaulieu, Beaulieu LTC (Beaulieu Championships) |
| February 26-March 4 | Monte Carlo, La Festa (Monte Carlo Championships) |

| March 5-11 | Menton, Menton LTC (Riviera Championships) |
| March 12-18 | Nice, Nice LTC, Parc Imperial (South of France Championships) |
| March 19-25 | Cannes, Cannes LTC (Côte d'Azur Championships) |
| March 26-April 1 | Cannes, Beau Site (Cannes Championships) |
| April 2-8 | Cannes, Metropole Hotel |
| April 9-15 | Monte Carlo, La Festa |

## 1924

| December 24-30 | Monte Carlo, La Festa (Monaco Championships) |
| December 31-January 6 | Cannes, Beau Site Hotel |
| January 7-13 | Cannes, Carlton LTC |
| January 21-27 | Cannes, Gallia LTC |
| January 28-February 3 | Hyères, Hyères LTC |
| February 4-10 | Nice, Nice LTC, Parc Imperial |
| February 11-17 | Cannes, Carlton LTC |
| February 18-24 | Beaulieu, Beaulieu LTC (Beaulieu Championships) |
| February 25-March 2 | Monte Carlo, La Festa (Monte Carlo Championships) |
| March 3-9 | Menton, Menton LTC (Riviera Championships) |
| March 10-16 | Nice, Nice LTC, Parc Imperial (South of France Championships) |
| March 17-23 | Cannes, Cannes LTC (Côte d'Azur Championships) |
| March 24-30 | Cannes, Beau Site Hotel (Cannes Championships) |
| March 31-April 6 | Cannes, Metropole Hotel |
| April 7-13 | Monte Carlo, La Festa |
| April 14-20 | Juan-les-Pins, Juan-les-Pins LTC |

## 1925

| December 8-14 | Nice, Nice LTC, Parc Imperial |
| December 15-21 | Monte Carlo, La Festa (Monaco Championships) |
| December 22-28 | Beaulieu LTC (Courts not ready – transferred to Cannes, Metropole LTC) |
| December 29-January 4 | Cannes, Beau Site Hotel |
| January 5-11 | Cannes, Carlton LTC |
| January 12-18 | Hyères, Hyères LTC |
| January 19-25 | Cannes, Gallia LTC |
| January 26-February 1 | Cannes, Metropole Hotel |
| February 2-8 | Nice, Nice LTC, Parc Imperial |
| February 9-15 | Cannes, Carlton LTC |
| February 16-22 | Beaulieu, Beaulieu LTC (Beaulieu Championships) |
| February 23-March 1 | Monte Carlo, La Festa (Monte Carlo Championships) |
| March 2-8 | Menton, Menton LTC (Riviera Championships) |
| March 9-15 | Nice, Nice LTC, Parc Imperial (South of France Championships) |
| March 16-22 | Cannes, Cannes LTC (Côte d'Azur Championships) |
| March 23-29 | Cannes, Beau Site Hotel (Cannes Championships) |
| March 30-April 5 | Juan-les-Pins, Juan-les-Pins LTC |
| April 6-12 | Monte Carlo, La Festa |

## 1926

| | |
|---|---|
| December 14-20 | Monte Carlo, La Festa (Monaco Championships) |
| December 28-January 3 | Cannes, Beau Site Hotel |
| January 4-10 | Hyères, Hyères LTC – Abandoned, bad weather prevented courts being available |
| January 11-17 | Cannes, New Courts Club |
| January 18-24 | Cannes, Metropole Hotel |
| January 25-31 | Cannes, Gallia LTC |
| February 1-7 | Nice, Nice LTC, Parc Imperial |
| February 8-14 | Cannes, Carlton LTC |
| February 15-21 | Beaulieu, Beaulieu LTC (Beaulieu Championships) |
| February 22-28 | Monte Carlo, La Festa (Monte Carlo Championships) |
| March 1-7 | Menton, Menton LTC (Riviera Championships) |
| March 8-14 | Nice, Nice LTC, Parc Imperial (South of France Championships) |
| March 15-21 | Cannes, Cannes LTC (Côte d'Azur Championships) |
| March 22-28 | Cannes, Beau Site Hotel (Cannes Championships) |
| March 29-April 4 | Cannes, Carlton LTC |
| April 5-11 | Monte Carlo, La Festa |
| April 12-18 | Juan-les-Pins, Juan-les-Pins LTC |
| April 19-25 | St Raphael, St Raphael LTC |

## 1927

| | |
|---|---|
| December 20-26 | Monte Carlo, La Festa (Monaco Championships) |
| December 27-January 2 | Cannes, Beau Site Hotel |
| January 3-9 | Hyères, Hyères LTC |
| January 10-16 | Cannes, Metropole Hotel |
| January 17-23 | Cannes, Carlton LTC |
| January 24-30 | Cannes, New Courts Club |
| January 31-February 6 | Cannes, Gallia LTC |
| February 7-13 | Nice, Nice LTC, Parc Imperial |
| February 14-20 | Beaulieu, Beaulieu LTC (Beaulieu Championships) |
| February 21-27 | Monte Carlo, La Festa (Monte Carlo Championships) |
| February 28-March 6 | Menton, Menton LTC (Riviera Championships) |
| March 7-13 | Nice, Nice LTC, Parc Imperial (South of France Championships) |
| March 14-20 | Cannes, Cannes LTC (Côte d'Azur Championships) |
| March 21-27 | Cannes, Beau Site Hotel (Cannes Championships) |
| March 28-April 3 | Juan-les-Pins, Juan-les -Pins LTC |
| April 4-10 | St Raphael, St Raphael LTC |
| April 11-17 | Monte Carlo, La Festa |

## 1928

| | |
|---|---|
| December 17-24 | Monte Carlo, La Festa (Monaco Championships) |
| December 26-January 1 | Cannes, Beau Site Hotel |
| January 2-8 | Juan-les-Pins, Juan-les-Pins LTC |
| January 16-22 | Cannes, New Courts Club |
| January 23-29 | Cannes, Metropole Hotel |

| | |
|---|---|
| January 30-February 5 | Cannes, Gallia LTC |
| February 6-12 | Cannes, Carlton LTC |
| February 13-19 | Nice, Nice LTC, Parc Imperial |
| February 20-26 | Beaulieu, Beaulieu LTC (Beaulieu Championships) |
| February 27-March 4 | Monte Carlo, La Festa Country Club (Monte Carlo Championships) |
| March 5-11 | Menton, Menton LTC (Riviera Championships) |
| March 12-18 | Nice, Nice LTC, Parc Imperial (South of France Championships) |
| March 19-25 | Cannes, Cannes LTC (Côte d'Azur Championships) |
| March 26-April 1 | Cannes, Beau Site Hotel (Cannes Championships) |
| April 2-8 | Beaulieu, Beaulieu LTC |
| April 2-8 | St Raphael, St Raphael LTC - CANCELLED |
| April 9-15 | Monte Carlo, La Festa Country Club |

## 1929

| | |
|---|---|
| December 17-23 | Cannes, Beau Site Hotel |
| December 24-30 | Hyères, New Courts LTC |
| December 24-30 | Cannes, Cannes LTC |
| December 31-January 6 | Cannes, Metropole Hotel |
| January 14-20 | Monte Carlo, Country Club (Monaco Championships) |
| January 21-27 | Cannes, New Courts Club |
| January 28-February 3 | Cannes, Gallia LTC |
| February 4-10 | Cannes, Carlton LTC |
| February 11-17 | Nice, Nice LTC, Parc Imperial (South of France Championships)cancelled-snow, transferred to March 11-17 |
| February 18-24 | Beaulieu, Beaulieu LTC (Beaulieu Championships) |
| February 25-March 3 | Monte Carlo County Club (Monte Carlo Championships) |
| March 4-10 | Menton, Menton LTC (Riviera Championships) |
| March 4-10 | Juan-les-Pins, Miramar LTC |
| March 11-17 | Nice, Nice LTC, Parc Imperial (South of France Championships) |
| March 18-24 | Cannes, Cannes LTC (Côte d'Azur Championships) |
| March 25-31 | Cannes, Beau Site Hotel (Cannes Championships) |
| April 1-7 | Monte Carlo Country Club |
| April 1-7 | St Raphael, St Raphael LTC |
| April 8-14 | Beaulieu, Beaulieu LTC |
| April 15-21 | Juan-les-Pins, Juan-les-Pins LTC |

## 1930

| | |
|---|---|
| December 23-29 | Cannes, Beau Site Hotel |
| December 23-29 | Hyères, New Courts LTC |
| December 30-January 5 | Cannes, Metropole Hotel |
| January 6-12 | Monte Carlo Country Club (Monaco Championships) |
| January 20-28 | Cannes, New Courts Club |
| January 27-February 2 | Cannes, Gallia LTC |
| February 3-9 | Cannes, Carlton LTC |
| February 10-16 | Nice, Nice LTC, Parc Imperial (South of France Championships) |

| February 17-23 | Beaulieu, Beaulieu LTC (Beaulieu Championships) |
| February 24-March 2 | Monte Carlo Country Club (Monte Carlo Championships) |
| March 3-9 | Menton, Menton LTC (Riviera Championships) |
| March 10-16 | Nice, Nice LTC, Parc Imperial |
| March 17-23 | Cannes, Cannes, LTC (Côte d'Azur Championships) |
| March 24-30 | Cannes, Beau Site Hotel (Cannes Championships) |
| March 31-April 6 | St Raphael, St Raphael LTC |
| April 7-13 | Juan-les-Pins, Miramar LTC |
| April 14-20 | Beaulieu, Beaulieu LTC |
| April 21-27 | Monte Carlo Country Club |
| May 4-10 | Juan-les-Pins, Juan-les-Pins LTC - CANCELLED |

## 1931

| December 22-28 | Juan-les-Pins, Juan-les-Pins LTC |
| December 29-January 4 | Cannes, Beau Site Hotel |
| January 5-11 | Cannes, Metropole Hotel |
| January 19-25 | Cannes, New Courts Club |
| January 26-February 1 | Cannes, Gallia LTC |
| February 2-8 | Cannes, Carlton LTC |
| February 9-15 | Nice, Nice LTC, Parc Imperial (South of France Championships) |
| February 16-22 | Beaulieu, Beaulieu LTC (Beaulieu Championships) |
| February 16-23 | Monte Carlo, Condamine (Monegasque Championships) |
| February 23-March 1 | Monte Carlo Country Club (Monte Carlo Championships) |
| March 2-8 | Menton, Menton LTC (Riviera Championships) |
| March 9-15 | Nice, Nice LTC, Parc Imperial |
| March 16-22 | Cannes, Cannes LTC (Côte d'Azur Championships) |
| March 23-29 | Cannes, Beau Site Hotel (Cannes Championships) |
| March 30-April 5 | St Raphael, St Raphael LTC |
| April 5-12 | Monte Carlo Country Club |
| April 13-19 | Juan-les-Pins, Miramar LTC |
| April 20-26 | Beaulieu, Beaulieu LTC |

## 1932

| December 21-27 | Juan-les-Pins, Juan-les-Pins LTC |
| December 28-January 3 | Cannes, Beau Site Hotel |
| January 11-17 | Monte Carlo, Condamine (Monegasque Championships) |
| January 18-24 | Cannes, New Courts Club (Mediterranean Championships) |
| January 25-31 | Cannes, Gallia LTC |
| February 1-7 | Cannes, Carlton LTC |
| February 8-14 | Nice, Nice LTC, Parc Imperial (South of France Championships) |
| February 15-21 | Beaulieu, Beaulieu LTC (Beaulieu Championships) |
| February 22-28 | Monte Carlo Country Club (Monte Carlo Championships) |
| February 29-March 6 | Menton, Menton LTC (Riviera Championships) |
| March 7-13 | Nice, Nice LTC, Parc Imperial |
| March 14-20 | Cannes, Cannes LTC (Côte d'Azur Championships) |
| March 21-27 | Cannes, Beau Site Hotel (Cannes Championships) |

| March 28-April 3 | Monte Carlo Country Club (Beausoleil Championships) |
| April 4-10 | Juan-les-Pins, Juan-les-Pins LTC |
| April 11-17 | Cannes, New Courts Club |
| April 11-17 | Beaulieu, Beaulieu LTC – CANCELLED |
| April 18-22 | Juan-les-Pins, Miramar LTC - CANCELLED |

## 1933

| December 19-25 | Antibes, Provençal LTC |
| December 27-January 4 | Cannes, Beau Site Hotel |
| January 2-8 | Juan-les-Pins, Juan-les-Pins LTC - CANCELLED |
| January 9-15 | Monte Carlo, Condamine (Monegasque Championships) |
| January 23-29 | Cannes, New Courts Club (Mediterranean Championships) |
| January 30-February 5 | Cannes, Gallia LTC |
| February 6-12 | Cannes, Carlton LTC |
| February 13-19 | Nice, Nice LTC, Parc Imperial (South of France Championships) |
| February 20-26 | Beaulieu, Beaulieu LTC (Beaulieu Championships) |
| February 27-March 5 | Monte Carlo Country Club (Monte Carlo Championships) |
| March 6-12 | Menton, Menton (Riviera Championships) |
| March 13-19 | Nice, Nice LTC, Parc Imperial (Nice Championships) |
| March 20-26 | Cannes, Cannes LTC (Côte d'Azur Championships) |
| March 27-April 2 | Cannes, Beau Site Hotel (Cannes Championships) |
| April 3-8 | Cannes, New Courts Club |
| April 10-16 | Juan-les-Pins, Miramar LTC |
| April 17-23 | Monte Carlo Country Club (Beausoleil Championships) |
| April 24-30 | Antibes, Provençal LTC |

## 1934

| December 18-24 | Antibes, Provençal LTC |
| December 25-31 | Cannes, Beau Site Hotel |
| January 1-7 | Juan-les-Pins, Juan-les-Pins LTC |
| January 8-14 | Monte Carlo, Condamine (Monegasque Championships) |
| January 22-28 | Cannes, New Courts Club (Mediterranean Championships) |
| January 29-February 4 | Cannes, Gallia LTC |
| February 5-11 | Cannes, Carlton LTC |
| February 12-18 | Nice, Nice LTC, Parc Imperial (South of France Championships) |
| February 19-25 | Beaulieu, Beaulieu LTC (Beaulieu Championships) |
| February 26-March 6 | Monte Carlo Country Club (Monte Carlo Championships) |
| March 7-12 | Menton, Menton LTC (Riviera Championships) |
| March 13-18 | Nice, Nice LTC, Parc Imperial (Nice Championships) |
| March 19-25 | Cannes, Cannes LTC (Côte d'Azur Championships) |
| March 26-April 1 | Cannes, Beau Site Hotel (Cannes Championships) |
| April 2-8 | Monte Carlo Country Club (Beausoleil Championships) |
| April 9-15 | Antibes, Provençal LTC |
| April 9-15 | Cannes, New Courts Club – CANCELLED |
| April 16-22 | Juan-les-Pins, Miramar LTC – CANCELLED |

## 1935

| | |
|---|---|
| December 17-23 | Juan-les-Pins, Miramar LTC |
| December 24-30 | Cannes, Beau Site Hotel |
| December 31-January 6 | Monte Carlo Country Club |
| January 7-13 | Monte Carlo, Condamine (Monegasque Championships) |
| January 21-27 | Antibes, Provençal LTC |
| January 28-February 3 | Cannes, Gallia LTC |
| February 4-10 | Cannes, Carlton LTC |
| February 11-17 | Nice, Nice LTC, Parc Imperial (South of France Championships) |
| February 18-24 | Beaulieu, Beaulieu LTC (Beaulieu Championships) |
| February 25-March 4 | Monte Carlo Country Club (Monte Carlo Championships |
| March 5-10 | Menton, Menton LTC (Riviera Championships) |
| March 11-17 | Cannes, Cannes LTC (Côte d'Azur Championships) |
| March 25-31 | Cannes, Beau Site (Cannes Championships) |
| April 1-7 | Nice, Nice LTC, Parc Imperial (Nice Championships) |
| April 8-14 | Antibes, Provençal LTC |
| April 15-21 | Cannes, Cannes LTC |
| April 22-28 | Monte Carlo Country Club |

## 1936

| | |
|---|---|
| December 23-29 | Monte Carlo Country Club – ABANDONED, RAIN |
| December 30-January 5 | Cannes, Beau Site Hotel |
| January 6-12 | Monte Carlo, Condamine (Monegasque Championships) |
| January 12-18 | Monte Carlo Country Club |
| January 27-February 2 | Cannes, Gallia LTC |
| February 3-9 | Cannes, Carlton LTC |
| February 10-16 | Nice, Nice LTC, Parc Imperial (South of France Championships) |
| February 17-23 | Beaulieu, Beaulieu LTC (Beaulieu Championships) |
| February 24-March 1 | Monte Carlo Country Club (Monte Carlo Championships) |
| March 2-8 | Menton, Menton LTC (Riviera Championships) |
| March 9-15 | Cannes, Cannes LTC (Côte d'Azur Championships) |
| March 16-22 | Antibes, Provençal LTC |
| March 23-29 | Cannes, Beau Site Hotel (Cannes Championships) |
| March 30-April 5 | Cannes, Cannes LTC |
| April 6-12 | Nice, Nice LTC, Parc Imperial (Nice Championships) |
| April 13-19 | Monte Carlo Country Club |

## 1937

| | |
|---|---|
| December 28-January 3 | Cannes, Beau Site Hotel |
| January 4-10 | Monte Carlo, Condamine (Monegasque Championships) |
| January 25-31 | Cannes, Gallia LTC |
| February 1-7 | Cannes, Carlton LTC |
| February 8-14 | Nice, Nice LTC, Parc Imperial (South of France Championships) |
| February 15-21 | Beaulieu, Beaulieu LTC (Beaulieu Championships) |
| February 22-28 | Monte Carlo Country Club (Monte Carlo Championships) |

| March 1-7 | Menton, Menton LTC (Riviera Championships) |
| March 8-14 | Cannes, Cannes LTC (Côte d'Azur Championships) |
| March 15-21 | Nice, Nice LTC, Parc Imperial (Nice Championships) |
| March 22-28 | Cannes, Beau Site Hotel (Cannes Championships) |
| March 30-April 4 | Monte Carlo Country Club |
| April 5-11 | Antibes, Provençal LTC |
| April 12-18 | Juan-les-Pins, Miramar LTC |

## 1938

| December 27-January 2 | Cannes, Beau Site Hotel |
| January 17-23 | Monte Carlo, Condamine (Monegasque Championships) |
| January 24-30 | Monte Carlo Country Club |
| January 31-February 6 | Cannes, Gallia LTC |
| February 7-13 | Cannes, Carlton LTC |
| February 14-20 | Nice, Nice LTC, Parc Imperial (South of France Championships) |
| February 21-27 | Beaulieu, Beaulieu LTC (Beaulieu Championships) |
| February 28-March 6 | Monte Carlo Country Club (Monte Carlo Championships) |
| March 7-13 | Menton, Menton LTC (Riviera Championships) |
| March 14-20 | Cannes, Cannes LTC (Côte d'Azur Championships) |
| March 21-27 | Antibes, Provençal Club |
| March 28-April 3 | Cannes, Beau Site Hotel (Cannes Championships) |
| April 4-10 | Juan-les-Pins, Miramar LTC |
| April 11-17 | Nice, Nice LTC, Parc Imperial (Nice Championships) |
| April 18-24 | Monte Carlo, Country Club |

## 1939

| December 26-January 1 | Cannes, Beau Site Hotel |
| January 2-7 | Monte Carlo, Condamine (Monegasque Championships) |
| January 23-29 | Monte Carlo Country Club |
| January 30-February 5 | Cannes, Gallia LTC |
| February 6-12 | Cannes, Carlton LTC |
| February 13-19 | Nice, Nice LTC, Parc Imperial (South of France Championships) |
| February 20-26 | Beaulieu, Beaulieu LTC (Beaulieu Championships) |
| February 27-March 5 | Monte Carlo Country Club (Monte Carlo Championships) |
| March 6-12 | Menton, Menton LTC (Riviera Championships) |
| March 13-19 | Cannes, Cannes LTC (Côte d'Azur Championships) |
| March 20-26 | Juan-les-Pins, Miramar LTC |
| March 27-April 2 | Cannes, Beau Site Hotel (Cannes Championships) |
| April 3-9 | Nice, Nice LTC, Parc Imperial (Nice Championships) |
| April 10-16 | Monte Carlo Country Club |
| April 17-23 | Antibes, Provençal LTC |

## 1940 Tournament schedule abandoned

| January 1-7 | Cannes, Beau Site Hotel |
| January 22-28 | Juan-les-Pins, Miramar LTC |
| January 29-February 4 | Cannes, Gallia LTC |

| | |
|---|---|
| February 5-11 | Cannes, Carlton LTC |
| February 12-18 | Nice, Nice LTC, Parc Imperial (South of France Championships) |
| February 19-25 | Beaulieu, Beaulieu LTC (Beaulieu Championships) |
| February 25- March 4 | Monte Carlo Country Club (Monte Carlo Championships) |
| March 4-10 | Menton, Menton LTC (Riviera Championships) |
| March 11-17 | Cannes, Cannes LTC (Côte d'Azur Championships) |
| March 18-24 | Cannes, Beau Site Hotel (Cannes Championships) |
| March 25-31 | Monte Carlo Country Club |
| April 1-7 | Nice, Nice LTC, Parc Imperial |
| April 8-14 | Antibes, Provençal LTC |

**1940-1945** Second World War – no tournaments

# Tournament Winners Winter/Spring 1895-1939

## ANTIBES   Provençal LTC   International Tournaments

| Year | Date | Men's Singles | Ladies' Singles |
|------|------|---------------|-----------------|
| 1933 | 19-25 December (1932) | Max Ellmer (SUI) | *Paulette de St Ferréol* (FRA) |
| 1933 | 24-30 April | *Divided – unfd, rain* Charles Aeschliman (SUI) Edouard Lotan (FRA) | *Sylvia Henrotin* (FRA) |
| 1934 | 18-24 December (1933) | Roger George (FRA) | Muriel Thomas (GBR) |
| 1934 | 9-15 April | Charles Aeschliman (SUI) | *Sylvia Henrotin* (FRA) |
| 1935 | 21-27 January | Vladımir Landau (MON) | *Simone Mathieu* (FRA) |
| 1935 | 8-14 April | Karel Pachovsky (TCH) | *Simone Mathieu* (FRA) |
| 1936 | 16-22 March | *Divided – rain* Josef Siba (TCH) Josef Malacek (TCH) | *Simone Mathieu* (FRA) |
| 1937 | 5-11 April | Christian de Galea (FRA) | Alice Weiwers (FRA) |
| 1938 | 21-27 March | Constantin Tanacescu (ROM) | Jadwiga Jedrzejowska (POL) |
| 1939 | 17-23 April | André Jacquemet (FRA) | *Simone Mathieu* (FRA) |

Note: married ladies are shown in *italics*

| Men's Doubles | Ladies' Doubles | Mixed Doubles |
|---|---|---|
| — | Eden Chew (GBR) | George Rogers (IRL) |
| | Dorothy Winterbottom (GBR) | Muriel Thomas (GBR) |
| harles Aeschliman (SUI) | Dorothy Burke (USA) | Charles Aeschliman (SUI) |
| douard Lotan (FRA) | Muriel Thomas (GBR) | Muriel Thomas (GBR) |
| — | — | Charles Aeschliman (SUI) |
| | | Mrs Smallwood (GBR) |
| harles Aeschliman (SUI) | — | Charles Aeschliman (SUI) |
| olff (LUX) | | Sylvia Henrotin (FRA) |
| — | Simone Mathieu (FRA) | Vladimir Landau (MON) |
| | Phyllis Satterthwaite (GBR) | Simone Mathieu (FRA) |
| eorge Godsell (GBR) | — | Vladimir Landau (MON) |
| chard Turnbull (GBR) | | Simone Mathieu (FRA) |
| sef Siba (TCH) | Divided – unfd rain | William Filmer-Sankey (GBR) |
| ef Malacek (TCH) | Simone Mathieu (FRA) | Kay Stammers (GBR) |
| | Pat Owen (GBR)/ | |
| | Kay Stammers (GBR) | |
| | Susan Noel (GBR) | |
| ristian de Galea (FRA) | Susan Noel (GBR) | Max Belhommet (FRA) |
| eco Noghes (MON) | Jacqueline Horner (FRA) | Alice Weiwers (LUX) |
| rl Schroder (SWE) | — | Karl Schroder (SWE) |
| e Wallen (SWE) | | Jadwiga Jedrzejowska (POL) |
| toine Gentien (FRA) | Alice Weiwers (LUX) | Gilberto Pontecorvo (ITA) |
| dré Jacquemet (FRA) | Cosette Saint Omer Roy (FRA) | Alice Weiwers (LUX) |

## BEAULIEU   Beaulieu LTC (Bristol Hotel)   Beaulieu Championships

| Year | Date | Men's Singles | Ladies' Singles |
|------|------|---------------|-----------------|
| 1913 | 3-10 February | Friederich Rahe (GER) | Elizabeth Ryan (USA) |
| 1914 | 9-15 February | Anthony Wilding (NZL) | Jessie Tripp (BRI) |
| 1920 | 23-28 February | Major Ritchie (BRI) | Suzanne Lenglen (FRA) |
| 1921 | 21-27 February | Algernon Kingscote (BRI) | Elizabeth Ryan (USA) |
| 1922 | 20-26 February | Count Mimo Balbi (ITA) | Elizabeth Ryan (USA) |
| 1923 | 19-25 February | Gordon Lowe (GBR) | *Winifred Beamish* (GBR) |
| 1924 | 18-24 February | Jack Hillyard (GBR) | Elizabeth Ryan (USA) |
| 1925 | 16-22 February | Gordon Lowe (GBR) | Elizabeth Ryan (USA) |
| 1926 | 15-21 February | Bela von Kehrling (HUN) | Helen Wills (USA) |
| 1927 | 14-20 February | Jan Kozeluh (TCH) | Elizabeth Ryan (USA) |
| 1928 | 20-26 February | Jan Kozeluh (TCH) | Elizabeth Ryan (USA) |
| 1929 | 18-24 February | Uberto de Morpurgo (ITA) | Betty Nuthall (GBR) |
| 1930 | 17-23 February | Harold Lee (GBR) | Joan Ridley (GBR) |
| 1931 | 16-22 February | George Rogers (IRL) | *Phyllis Satterthwaite* (GBR) |
| 1932 | 15-21 February | Enrique Maier (ESP) | Elizabeth Ryan (USA) |
| 1933 | 20-26 February | Gottfried von Cramm (GER) | Margaret Scriven (GBR) |
| 1934 | 19-25 February | Henry Austin (GBR) | Adeline Yorke (GBR) |

Note: married ladies are shown in *italics*

| Men's Doubles | Ladies' Doubles | Mixed Doubles |
|---|---|---|
| Heinrich Kleinschroth (GER)<br>Friederich Rahe (GER) | — | Count Ludwig Salm (GER)<br>Elizabeth Ryan (USA) |
| Craig Biddle (USA)<br>Anthony Wilding (NZL) | — | Gordon Lowe (BRI)<br>Jessie Tripp (BRI) |
| Pierre Albarran (FRA)<br>Alain Gerbault (FRA) | — | Major Ritchie (BRI)<br>Suzanne Lenglen (FRA) |
| Felix Poulin (FRA)<br>John Rendall (BRI) | Suzanne Lenglen (FRA)<br>Elizabeth Ryan (USA) | Algernon Kingscote (BRI)<br>Suzanne Lenglen (FRA) |
| Jack Hillyard (BRI)<br>Ernest Lamb (BRI) | Elizabeth Ryan (USA)<br>*Phyllis Satterthwaite* (BRI) | Rupert Wertheim (AUS)<br>Elizabeth Ryan (USA) |
| Uberto de Morpurgo (ITA)<br>Erik Tegner (DEN) | Suzanne Lenglen (FRA)<br>Elizabeth Ryan (USA) | *Divided – rain*<br>Uberto de Morpurgo (ITA)<br>Elizabeth Ryan (USA)/<br>Alain Gerbault (FRA)<br>*Dorothea Chambers* (GBR) |
| Leonce Aslangul (FRA)<br>Uberto de Morpurgo (ITA) | Elizabeth Ryan (USA)<br>*Phyllis Satterthwaite* (GBR) | Leonce Aslangul (FRA)<br>Elizabeth Ryan (USA) |
| Randolph Lycett (GBR)<br>Uberto de Morpurgo (ITA) | Suzanne Lenglen (FRA)<br>Elizabeth Ryan (USA) | Henry Mayes (CAN)<br>Elizabeth Ryan (USA) |
| Bela von Kehrling (HUN)<br>Gordon Lowe (GBR) | *Dorothea Chambers* (GBR)<br>Ermyntrude Harvey (GBR) | Charles Kingsley (GBR)<br>Helen Wills (USA) |
| Charles Aeschliman (SUI)<br>Henri Cochet (FRA) | *Dorothea Chambers* (GBR)<br>Elizabeth Ryan (USA) | Henri Cochet (FRA)<br>Betty Nuthall (GBR) |
| Jack Hillyard (GBR)<br>Jan Kozeluh (TCH) | Elizabeth Ryan (USA)<br>Gwen Sterry (GBR) | Jack Hillyard (GBR)<br>Elizabeth Ryan (USA) |
| Uberto del Bono (ITA)<br>Uberto de Morpurgo (ITA) | Eileen Bennett (GBR)<br>Joan Fry (GBR) | Patrick Spence (RSA)<br>Betty Nuthall (GBR) |
| Wilbur Coen (USA)<br>William Tilden (USA) | Joan Ridley (GBR)<br>*Phyllis Satterthwaite* (GBR) | Patrick Hughes (GBR)<br>*Violet Owen* (GBR) |
| Franjo Kukuljevic (YUG)<br>Franio Schaeffer (YUG) | Dorothy Andrus (USA)<br>Elizabeth Ryan (USA) | Jack Hillyard (GBR)<br>Mary Heeley (GBR) |
| Jaime Durall (ESP)<br>Enrique Maier (ESP) | Elizabeth Ryan (USA)<br>Muriel Thomas (GBR) | Bela von Kehrling (HUN)<br>Elizabeth Ryan (USA) |
| Jaime Durall (ESP)<br>Enrique Maier (ESP) | *Dorothy Burke* (USA)<br>Muriel Thomas (GBR) | Enrique Maier (ESP)<br>Elizabeth Ryan (USA) |
| Jacques Brugnon (FRA)<br>Roland Journu (FRA) | *Sylvia Henrotin* (FRA)<br>Elizabeth Ryan (USA) | Gottfried von Cramm (GER)<br>Elizabeth Ryan (USA) |

## BEAULIEU  Beaulieu LTC (Bristol Hotel)  Beaulieu Championships

| Year | Date | Men's Singles | Ladies' Singles |
|------|------|---------------|-----------------|
| 1935 | 18-24 February | Gottfried von Cramm (GER) | *Simone Mathieu (FRA)* |
| 1936 | 17-23 February | Jacques Brugnon (FRA) | *Simone Mathieu (FRA)* |
| 1937 | 15-21 February | Heiner Henkel (GER) | *Simone Mathieu (FRA)* |
| 1938 | 21-27 February | Ferenc Puncec (YUG) | Margaret Scriven (GBR) |
| 1939 | 20-26 February | Constantin Tanacescu (ROM) | *Hilde Sperling (DEN)* |

## BEAULIEU  Beaulieu LTC (Bristol Hotel)  Other tournaments

| Year | Date | Men's Singles | Ladies' Singles |
|------|------|---------------|-----------------|
| 1928 | 2-8 April | Erik Worm (DEN) | *Phyllis Satterthwaite (GBR)* |
| 1929 | 8-14 April | Emmanuel Du Plaix (FRA) | Lili de Alvarez (ESP) |
| 1930 | 14-20 April | William Tilden (USA) | *Phyllis Satterthwaite (GBR)* |
| 1931 | 20-26 April | Jean Lesueur (FRA) | *Sylvia Henrotin (FRA)* |
| 1932 | 11-17 April | TOURNAMENT SCHEDULED BUT CANCELLED | |

## CANNES  Beau Site Hotel  Cannes Championships★

| Year | Date | Men's Singles | Ladies' Singles |
|------|------|---------------|-----------------|
| 1897 | 15-21 January | Reginald Doherty (BRI) | |
| 1898 | TOURNAMENT NOT SCHEDULED | | |
| 1899(H) | 20-26 February | Reginald Doherty (BRI) | Edith Riseley (BRI) |
| 1900(H) | February | Count Victor Voss (GER) | *Countess Clara Schulenburg (GE* |
| 1901 | 1-8 March | Laurence Doherty (BRI) | *Blanche Hillyard (BRI)* |

Note: married ladies are shown in *italics*
★Cannes Championships from 1904
(H) = International Handicap events only

| Men's Doubles | Ladies' Doubles | Mixed Doubles |
|---|---|---|
| André Martin-Legeay (FRA)<br>Jean Lesueur (FRA) | *Simone Mathieu* (FRA)<br>Muriel Thomas (GBR) | Gottfried von Cramm (GER)<br>Muriel Thomas (GBR) |
| André Martin-Legeay (FRA)<br>Jean Lesueur (FRA) | *Simone Mathieu* (FRA)<br>Kay Stammers (GBR) | Jean Lesueur (FRA)<br>Kay Stammers (GBR) |
| Gottfried von Cramm (GER)<br>Henner Henkel (GER) | *Simone Mathieu* (FRA)<br>*Hilde Sperling* (DEN)) | Patrick Hughes (GBR)<br>*Hilde Sperling* (DEN) |
| Henry Austin (GBR)<br>Patrick Hughes (GBR) | Jadwiga Jedrzejowska (POL)<br>Muriel Thomas (GBR) | Henri Bolelli (FRA)<br>Jadwiga Jedrzejowska (POL) |
| Jean Lesueur (FRA)<br>Yvon Petra (FRA) | *Simone Mathieu* (FRA)<br>Gracyn Wheeler (USA) | Kho Sin Kie (CHN)<br>Alice Weiwers (LUX) |

| Men's Doubles | Ladies' Doubles | Mixed Doubles |
|---|---|---|
| ...ck Hillyard (GBR)<br>...rik Worm (DEN) | Eden Petchell (GBR)<br>*Phyllis Satterthwaite* (GBR) | Erik Worm (DEN)<br>*Phyllis Satterthwaite* (GBR) |
| ...ck Hillyard (GBR)<br>...rik Worm (DEN) | *Sylvia Lafaurie* (FRA)<br>Lili de Alvarez (ESP) | Erik Worm (DEN)<br>*Phyllis Satterthwaite* (GBR) |
| ...Wilbur Coen (USA)<br>...William Tilden (USA) | Helen Jacobs (USA)<br>Elizabeth Ryan (USA) | William Tilden (USA)<br>Elizabeth Ryan (USA) |
| ...ck Hillyard (GBR)<br>...an Lesueur (FRA) | *Sylvia Henrotin* (FRA)<br>*Phyllis Satterthwaite* (GBR) | Franjo Kukuljevic (YUG)<br>*Bruyn Kops* (HOL) |

| Men's Doubles | Ladies' Doubles | Mixed Doubles |
|---|---|---|
| ...eginald Doherty (BRI)<br>...unt Victor Voss (GER) | Helen Pillans (BRI)<br>Kate Pillans (BRI) | Reginald Doherty (BRI)<br>*R.P. Williams* (BRI) |
| ...arence Doherty (BRI)<br>...ward Ditson (USA) | — | Clarence Hobart (USA)<br>*Augusta Hobart* (USA) |
| | — | — |

**CANNES** Beau Site Hotel **Cannes Championships*****

| Year | Date | Men's Singles | Ladies' Singles |
|------|------|---------------|-----------------|
| 1902 | TOURNAMENT NOT SCHEDULED | | |
| 1903 (H) | 23-30 March | George Hillyard (BRI) | — |
| 1904 | 15-22 March | Laurence Doherty (BRI) | *Ruth Winch* (BRI) |
| 1905 | 21-26 March | Major Ritchie (BRI) | Constance Wilson (BRI) |
| 1906 | 20-25 March | Anthony Wilding (NZL) | Toupie Lowther (BRI) |
| 1907 | 19-26 March | Major Ritchie (BRI) | *Ruth Winch* (BRI) |
| 1908 | 18-26 March | Anthony Wilding (NZL) | *Dorothea Chambers* (BRI) |
| 1909 | 17-24 March | Major Ritchie (BRI) | *Countess Clara Schulenburg* (GER) |
| 1910 | 16-20 March | Major Ritchie (BRI) | Rosamund Salusbury (BRI) |
| 1911 | 20-26 March | Anthony Wilding (NZL) | *Hedwig Neresheimer* (GER) |
| 1912 | 11-17 March | Max Decugis (FRA) | Jessie Tripp (BRI) |
| 1913 | 24-30 March | Freidrich Rahe (GER) | Jessie Tripp (BRI) |
| 1914 | 23-30 March | Anthony Wilding (NZL) | Elizabeth Ryan (USA) |
| 1919 | 26 March-1 April | Nicholas Mishu (ROM) | Suzanne Lenglen (FRA) |
| 1920 | 29 March-4 April | Lewis Barclay (BRI) | Elizabeth Ryan (USA) |
| 1921 | 28 March-3 April | Count Mimo Balbi (ITA) | Phyllis Howkins (BRI) |
| 1922 | 27 March-2 April | Jean Borotra (FRA) | Elizabeth Ryan (USA) |
| 1923 | 26 March-1 April | Henry Mayes (CAN) | Kathleen McKane (GBR) |
| 1924 | 24-30 March | Henri Cochet (FRA) | Elizabeth Ryan (USA) |
| | | (Because of the rain the men's singles final was decided at the Gallia Club) | |

Note: married ladies are shown in *italics*
*Cannes Championships from 1904
(H) = International Handicap events only

| Men's Doubles | Ladies' Doubles | Mixed Doubles |
|---|---|---|
| — | — | — |
| Laurence Doherty (BRI) Reginald Doherty (BRI) | — | — |
| Laurence Doherty (BRI) Reginald Doherty (BRI) | — | Reginald Doherty (BRI) *Countess Clara Schulenburg* (GER) |
| Major Ritchie (BRI) Anthony Wilding (NZL) | — | Wilberforce Eaves (AUS) *Ruth Winch* (BRI) |
| Major Ritchie (BRI) Anthony Wilding (NZL) | — | Laurence Doherty (BRI) *Countess Clara Schulenburg* (GER) |
| Major Ritchie (BRI) Anthony Wilding (NZL) | — | Laurence Doherty (BRI) *Countess Clara Schulenburg* (GER) |
| Gordon Lowe (BRI) Robert Powell (CAN) | — | Laurence Doherty (BRI) *Countess Clara Schulenburg* (GER) |
| Maxime Decugis (FRA) Major Ritchie (BRI) | — | Heinrich Kleinschroth (GER) *Hedwig Neresheimer* (GER) |
| Major Ritchie (BRI) Anthony Wilding (NZL) | — | Heinrich Kleinschroth (GER) *Hedwig Neresheimer* (GER) |
| Max Decugis (FRA) Maurice Germot (FRA) | — | Wallis Myers (BRI) Jessie Tripp (BRI) |
| Heinrich Kleinschroth (GER) Freidrich Rahe (GER) | — | Count Ludwig Salm (AUT) Elizabeth Ryan (USA) |
| Norman Brookes (AUS) Anthony Wilding (NZL) | — | Max Decugis (FRA) Elizabeth Ryan (USA) |
| Max Decugis (FRA) Nicholas Mishu (ROM) | — | Pierre Albarran (FRA) Suzanne Lenglen (FRA) |
| Francis Fisher (NZL) Major Ritchie (BRI) | — | Francis Fisher (NZL) *Winifred Beamish* (BRI) |
| Jack Hillyard (BRI) Resuge (FRA) | — | Jack Hillyard (BRI) *Phyllis Satterthwaite* (BRI) |
| Samuel Hardy (USA) Jack Hillyard (USA) | — | Samuel Hardy (USA) *Dorothea Chambers* (BRI) |
| Roger Danet (FRA) Malmstrom (SWE) | *Dorothea Chambers* (GBR) Kathleen McKane (GBR) | Charles Aeschliman (SUI) Suzanne Lenglen (FRA) |
| Henri Cochet (FRA) René Lacoste (FRA) | Suzanne Lenglen (FRA) Elizabeth Ryan (USA) | Henri Cochet (FRA) Suzanne Lenglen (FRA) |

**CANNES**  Beau Site Hotel  **Cannes Championships★**

| Year | Date | Men's Singles | Ladies' Singles |
|------|------|---------------|-----------------|
| 1925 | 23-29 March | ABANDONED AFTER FIRST ROUND OF THE TWO SINGLES EVENTS – RAIN | |
| 1926 | 22-28 March | Charles Aeschliman (SUI) | Lili de Alvarez (ESP) |
| 1927 | 21- 27 March | Henry Mayes (CAN) | Lili de Alvarez (ESP) |
| 1928 | 26 March-1 April | Henry Mayes (CAN) | Elizabeth Ryan (USA) |
| 1929 | 25-31 March | Emmanuel du Plaix (FRA) | *Sylvia Lafaurie (FRA)* |
| 1930 | 24 March | *Divided – by agreement* Wilbur Coen (USA) William Tilden (USA) | *Divided – by agreement* Paula von Reznicek (GER) Elizabeth Ryan (USA) |
| 1931 | 23-29 March | Hyotare Satoh (JPN) | Cilly Aussem (GER) |
| 1932 | 21-27 March | George Rogers (IRL) | Lolette Payot (SUI) |
| 1933 | 27 March-2 April | Franz Matejka (AUT) | Lolette Payot (SUI) |
| 1934 | 26 March-1 April | Giorgio de Stefani (ITA) | Jacqueline Goldschmidt (FRA) |
| 1935 | 25-31 March | Max Ellmer (SUI) | *Simone Mathieu (FRA)* |
| 1936 | 23-29 March | Fred Perry (GBR) | *Simone Mathieu (FRA)* |
| 1937 | 22-28 March | Adam Baworowski (POL) | Alice Weiwers (LUX) |
| 1938 | 28 March-3 April | George Rogers (IRL) | Jadwiga Jedrzejowska (POL) |
| 1939 | 27 March-2 April | Adam Baworowski (POL) | *Simone Mathieu (FRA)* |

Note: married ladies are shown in *italics*
★Cannes Championships from 1904
(H) = International Handicap events only

| Men's Doubles | Ladies' Doubles | Mixed Doubles |
|---|---|---|

DOUBLES ABANDONED – RAIN

| Men's Doubles | Ladies' Doubles | Mixed Doubles |
|---|---|---|
| René Gallepe<br>Erik Worm (DEN) | Elizabeth Bennett (GBR)<br>Elizabeth Ryan (USA) | Erik Worm (DEN)<br>Elizabeth Ryan (USA) |
| Henri Cochet (FRA)<br>Jack Hillyard (GBR) | Eizabeth Ryan (USA)<br>*Phyllis Satterthwaite* (GBR) | Erik Worm (DEN)<br>Elizabeth Ryan (USA) |
| Wilbur Coen (USA)<br>Emmanuel du Plaix (FRA) | *Sylvia Lafaurie* (FRA)<br>*Phyllis Sattherthwaite* (GBR) | René Gallepe (FRA)<br>*Sylvia Lafaurie* (FRA) |
| Wilbur Coen (USA)<br>William Tilden (USA) | Helen Jacobs (USA)<br>Elizabeth Ryan (USA) | William Tilden (USA)<br>Cilly Aussem (GER) |
| Myotare Satoh (JPN)<br>Jiro Satoh (JPN) | Cilly Aussem (GER)<br>Elizabeth Ryan (USA) | George Rogers (IRL)<br>Elizabeth Ryan (USA) |
| Charles Aeschliman (SUI)<br>Edouard Lotan (FRA) | *Doris Burke* (USA)<br>Muriel Thomas (GBR) | Charles Aeschliman (SUI)<br>Lolette Payot (SUI) |
| Franz Matejka (AUT)<br>George Rogers (IRL) | Cilly Aussem (GER)<br>Lolette Payot (SUI) | George Rogers (IRL)<br>Cilly Aussem (GER) |
| Herman Artens (AUT)<br>Franz Matejka (AUT) | Nancy Lyle (GBR)<br>Muriel Thomas (GBR) | Hector Fisher (SUI)<br>Muriel Thomas (GBR) |
| Max Ellmer (SUI)<br>Franz Matejka (AUT) | *Simone Mathieu* (FRA)<br>Muriel Thomas (GBR) | Edouard Lotan (FRA)<br>*Simone Mathieu* (FRA) |
| Franz Matejka (AUT)<br>Fred Perry (GBR) | *Simone Mathieu* (FRA)<br>Susan Noel (GBR) | Fred Perry (GBR)<br>*Simone Mathieu* (FRA) |
| Adam Baworowski (POL)<br>Georg von Metaxa (AUT) | *Greta Deutsch* (TCH)<br>Muriel Thomas (GBR) | Daniel Prenn (GER)<br>Joan Ingram (GBR) |
| Max Ellmer (SUI)<br>George Rogers (IRL) | Jadwiga Jedrzejowska (POL)<br>Muriel Thomas (GB) | Max Ellmer (SUI)<br>Alice Weiwers (LUX) |
| Jean Lesueur (FRA)<br>Karl Schroder (SWE) | *Simone Mathieu* (FRA)<br>Jacqueline Horner (FRA) | Karl Schroder (SWE)<br>*Simone Mathieu* (FRA) |

**CANNES** Beau Site Hotel New Year Tournaments

| Year | Date | Men's Singles | Ladies' Singles |
|------|------|---------------|-----------------|
| 1913 | 30 December–5 January (1912) | Hope Crisp (BRI) | Adele Topham |
| 1914 | 29 December–4 January (1913) | Gordon Lowe (BRI) | Suzanne Lenglen (FRA) |
| 1920 | 5-11 January | Major Ritchie (BRI) | Suzanne Lenglen (FRA) |
| 1921 | 3-9 January | Gordon Lowe (BRI) | Suzanne Lenglen (FRA) |
| 1922 | 2-8 January | Samuel Hardy (USA) | Elizabeth Ryan (USA) |
| 1923 | 1-7 January | Leighton Crawford (GBR) | Suzanne Lenglen (FRA) |
| 1924 | 31 December–6 January (1923) | Henry Mayes (CAN) | Elizabeth Ryan (USA) |
| 1925 | 29 December–4 January (1924) | Henry Mayes (CAN) | Elizabeth Ryan (USA) |
| 1926 | 28 December–3 January (1925) | Henry Mayes (CAN) | *Phyllis Sattherthwaite* (GBR) |
| 1927 | 27 December–2 January (1926) | Alan Behr (USA) | *Phyllis Satterthwaite* (GBR) |
| 1928 | 26 December–1 January (1927) | Henry Mayes (CAN) | Eileen Bennett (GBR) |
| 1929 | 17-23 December (1928) | Brame Hillyard (GBR) | Esna Boyd (AUS) |
| 1930 | 23-29 December (1929) | Paul Barrelet de Ricou (FRA) | Elizabeth Ryan (USA) |
| 1931 | 29 December–4 January (1930) | George Rogers (IRL) | Elizabeth Ryan (USA) |
| 1932 | 28 December–3 January (1931) | George Rogers (IRL) | Sheila Hewitt (GBR) |
| 1933 | 27 December–5 January (1932) | George Rogers (IRL) | *Phyllis Satterthwaite* (GBR) |
| 1934 | 25-31 December (1933) | Roger George (FRA) | Cosette Saint Omer Roy (FRA) |

Note: married ladies are shown in *italics*

| Men's Doubles | Ladies' Doubles | Mixed Doubles |
|---|---|---|
| — | — | — |
| — | — | — |
| ierre Albarran (FRA) / Iain Gerbault (FRA) | — | Pierre Albarran (FRA) / Suzanne Lenglen (FRA) |
| ancis Fisher (NZL) / ordon Lowe (BRI) | — | Wallis Myers (BRI) / Suzanne Lenglen (FRA) |
| muel Hardy (USA) / allis Myers (BRI) | — | Lord George Rocksavage (BRI) / Elizabeth Ryan (USA) |
| avid Morgan (GBR) / ouglas Watson (GBR) | — | Francis Fisher (NZL) / Suzanne Lenglen (FRA) |
| k Hillyard (GBR) / nry Mayes (CAN) | — | Charles Aeschliman (SUI) / Suzanne Lenglen (FRA) |
| rd George Cholmondeley (BR) / nry Mayes (CAN) | Suzanne Lenglen (FRA) / Elizabeth Ryan (USA) | Henry Mayes (CAN) / Elizabeth Ryan (USA) |
| arles Aeschliman (SUI) / rd George Cholmondeley (BR) | *Dorothy Coleman* / Eden Petchell (GBR) | Donald Greig (GBR) / *Phyllis Satterthwaite (GBR)* |
| né Gallepe (MON) / k Worm (DEN) | *Phyllis Satterthwaite (GBR)* / Madge Slaney (GBR) | Charles Aeschliman (SUI) / Eden Petchell (GBR) |
| arles Aeschliman (SUI) / rgio de Stefani (ITA) | Eileen Bennett (GBR) / Elizabeth Ryan (USA) | Jack Hillyard (GBR) / Elizabeth Ryan (USA) |
| arles Aeschliman (SUI) / rgio de Stefani (ITA) | Esna Boyd (AUS) / *Phyllis Satterthwaite (GBR)* | Rowley Scovell (GBR) / *Sylvia Lafaurie (FRA)* |
| arles Aeschliman (SUI) / los Magrane (ARG) | Elizabeth Ryan (USA) / *Phyllis Satterthwaite (GBR)* | Lord George Cholmondeley (GBR) / Elizabeth Ryan (USA) |
| arles Aeschliman (SUI) / k Worm (DEN) | *Mme Taunay (HOL)* / Muriel Thomas (GBR) | Charles Aeschliman (SUI) / Muriel Thomas (GBR) |
| dimir Landau (MON) / rge Rogers (IRL) | *Phyllis Satterthwaite (GBR)* / Muriel Thomas (GBR) | Charles Aeschliman (SUI) / Muriel Thomas (GBR) |
| uard Lotan (FRA) / rge Rogers (IRL) | *Phyllis Satterthwaite (GBR)* / Muriel Thomas (GBR) | George Rogers (IRL) / Muriel Thomas (GBR) |
| er George (FRA) / Hillyard (GBR) | *Phyllis Satterthwaite (GBR)* / Muriel Thomas (GBR) | Charles Aeschliman (SUI) / Muriel Thomas (GBR) |

## CANNES   Beau Site Hotel   New Year Tournaments

| Year | Date | Men's Singles | Ladies' Singles |
|------|------|---------------|-----------------|
| 1935 | 24-30 December (1934) | Max Ellmer (SUI) | *Simone Mathieu* (FRA) |
| 1936 | 30 December-5 January (1935) | Vladimir Landau (MON) | *Simone Mathieu* (FRA) |
| 1937 | 28 December-3 January (1936) | Kho Sin Kie (CHN) | *Simone Mathieu* (FRA) |
| 1938 | 27 December-2 January (1937) | George Rogers (IRL) | Alice Weiwers (LUX) |
| 1939 | 26 December-1 January (1938) | Constantin Tanacescu (ROM) | Alice Weiwers (LUX) |

## CANNES   Beau Site Hotel   Other tournaments

| Year | Date | Men's Singles | Ladies' Singles |
|------|------|---------------|-----------------|
| 1919 | 5-11 May | Pierre Albarran (FRA) | — |
| 1920 | 26 April-2 May | Alfred Hunter (BRI) | Suzanne Lenglen (FRA) |

## CANNES   Cannes LTC   Côte d'Azur Championships*

| Year | Date | Men's Singles | Ladies' Singles |
|------|------|---------------|-----------------|
| 1910 | 21-24 March | Artemas Holmes (USA) | *Countess Clara Schulenburg* (GE |
| 1911 | 27 March-2 April | Freidrich Rahe (GER) | *Hedwig Neresheimer* (GER) |
| 1912 | 18-24 March | Ferdinand Boelling (GER) | Blanche Colston (BRI) |
| 1913 | 14-15 February | Freidrich Rahe (GER) | Elizabeth Ryan (USA) |
| 1914 | 16-22 February | Anthony Wilding (NZL) | Elizabeth Ryan (USA) |
| 1920 | 22-28 March | Major Ritchie (BRI) | Elizabeth Ryan (USA) |
| 1921 | 21-27 March | Count Mimo Balbi (ITA) | Elizabeth Ryan (USA) |

*Côte d'Azur
Championships from
1911
Note: married ladies are
shown in *italics*

| Men's Doubles | Ladies' Doubles | Mixed Doubles |
|---|---|---|
| André Jacquemet (FRA)<br>Édouard Lotan (FRA) | Cosette Saint Omer Roy (FRA)<br>*Simone Mathieu* (FRA) | Vladimir Landau (MON)<br>Alice Weiwers (LUX) |
| Édouard Lotan (FRA)<br>Manca Amat (FRA) | Cosette Saint Omer Roy (FRA)<br>*Simone Mathieu* (FRA) | Manca Amat (FRA)<br>Alice Weiwers (LUX) |
| Kho Sin Kie (CHN)<br>Vladimir Landau (MON) | *Simone Mathieu* (FRA)<br>Susan Noel (GBR) | Vladimir Landau (MON)<br>*Mme S. Landau* (MON) |
| Max Ellmer (SUI)<br>George Rogers (IRL) | Cosette Saint Omer Roy (FRA)<br>Muriel Thomas (GBR) | George Rogers (IRL)<br>Alice Weiwers (LUX) |
| Gaston Medecin (MON)<br>René Gallepe (MON) | — | René Gallepe (MON)<br>Cosette Saint Omer Roy (FRA) |

| Men's Doubles | Ladies' Doubles | Mixed Doubles |
|---|---|---|
| - | — | — |
| Pierre Albarran (FRA)<br>Alain Gerbault (FRA) | — | Pierre Albarran (FRA)<br>Suzanne Lenglen (FRA) |

| Men's Doubles | Ladies' Doubles | Mixed Doubles |
|---|---|---|
| George Nettleton (USA)<br>Cedric Warburg (BRI) | — | *Divided – no time*<br>Ferdinand Boelling (GER)<br>*Countess Clara Schulenburg* (GER)/<br>Evan Gwynne Evans (BRI)<br>Rosamund Salusbury (BRI) |
| Theodore Mavrogordato (BRI)<br>Friedrich Rahe (GER) | — | Heinrich Kleinschroth (GER)<br>*Hedwig Neresheimer* (GER) |
| Wallis Myers (BRI)<br>George Simond (BRI) | — | Wallis Myers (BRI)<br>*Mrs Perrett* (BRI) |
|  | — | — |
| Craig Biddle (USA)<br>Anthony Wilding (NZL) | — | — |
| Francis Fisher (NZL)<br>Major Ritchie (BRI) | Suzanne Lenglen (FRA)<br>Elizabeth Ryan (USA) | Francis Fisher (NZL)<br>Winifred Beamish (BRI) |
| Charles Aeschliman (SUI)<br>Maurice Ferrier (SUI) | Suzanne Lenglen (FRA)<br>Elizabeth Ryan (USA) | Jack Hillyard (BRI)<br>*Phyllis Satterthwaite* (BRI) |

**CANNES**   Cannes LTC   **Côte d'Azur Championships★**

| Year | Date | Men's Singles | Ladies' Singles |
|------|------|---------------|-----------------|
| 1922 | 20-26 March | Henri Cochet (FRA) | Elizabeth Ryan (USA) |
| 1923 | 19-25 March | Henry Mayes (CAN) | *Phyllis Satterthwaite* (BRI) |
| 1924 | 17-23 March | Charles Aeschliman (SUI) | Elizabeth Ryan (USA) |
| 1925 | 16-22 March | René Lacoste (FRA) | Lili de Alvarez (ESP) |
| 1926 | 15-21 March | Henri Cochet (FRA) | Helen Wills (USA) |
| 1927 | 14-20 March | Henry Mayes (CAN) | Lili de Alvarez (ESP) |
| 1928 | 19-25 March | Henri Cochet (FRA) | Cilly Aussem (GER) |
| 1929 | 18-24 March | Emmanuel du Plaix (FRA) | Lili de Alvarez (ESP) |
| 1930 | 17-23 March | William Tilden (USA) | Cilly Aussem (GER) |
| 1931 | 16-22 March | George Rogers (IRL) | *Phyllis Satterthwaite* (GBR) |
| 1932 | 14-20 March | Ignacy Tloczynski (POL) | Jadwiga Jedrzejowska (POL) |
| 1933 | 20-26 March | Jozef Hebda (POL) | Lolette Payot (SUI) |
| 1934 | 19-25 March | Giorgio de Stefani (ITA) | Nancy Lyle (GBR) |
| 1935 | 11-17 March | Jacques Brugnon (FRA) | *Simone Mathieu* (FRA) |
| 1936 | 9-15 March | Josef Siba (TCH) | *Simone Mathieu* (FRA) |
| 1937 | 8-14 March | Kazimirez Tarlowski (POL) | Anita Lizana (CHI) |
| 1938 | 14-20 March | Adam Baworowski (AUT) | Jadwiga Jedrzejowska (POL) |
| 1939 | 13-19 March | Yvon Petra (FRA) | *Simone Mathieu* (FRA) |

★Côte d'Azur Championships from 1911
Note: married ladies are shown in *italics*

| Men's Doubles | Ladies' Doubles | Mixed Doubles |
|---|---|---|
| Henri Cochet (FRA) | — | Lord George Rocksavage (BRI) |
| Lord George Rocksavage (BRI) | | Elizabeth Ryan (USA) |
| Leighton Crawford (GBR) | Suzanne Lenglen (FRA) | Uberto de Morpurgo (ITA) |
| Wallis Myers (GBR) | Elizabeth Ryan (USA) | Suzanne Lenglen (FRA) |
| Charles Aeschliman (SUI) | Suzanne Lenglen (FRA) | Charles Aeschliman (SUI) |
| René Lacoste (FRA) | Elizabeth Ryan (USA) | Elizabeth Ryan (USA) |
| Charles Aeschliman (SUI) | Suzanne Lenglen (FRA) | Uberto de Morpurgo (ITA) |
| René Lacoste (FRA) | Elizabeth Ryan (USA) | Elizabeth Ryan (USA) |
| Charles Aeschliman (SUI) | Eileen Bennett (GBR) | Henri Cochet (FRA) |
| Henri Cochet (FRA) | Joan Ridley (GBR) | Helen Wills (USA) |
| Charles Aeschliman (SUI) | Eileen Bennett (GBR) | Uberto de Morpurgo (ITA) |
| René Gallepe (MON) | Elizabeth Ryan (USA) | Elizabeth Ryan (USA) |
| Charles Aeschliman (SUI) | Ermyntrude Harvey (GBR) | Charles Aeschliman (SUI) |
| Henri Cochet (FRA) | *Mme Taunay* (NED) | Cilly Aussem (GER) |
| Charles Aeschliman (SUI) | *Phyllis Covell* (GBR) | Charles Aeschliman (SUI) |
| René Gallepe (MON) | *Sylvia Lafaurie* (FRA) | *Sylvia Lafaurie* (FRA) |
| Wilbur Coen (USA) | Cilly Aussem (GER) | Takeichi Harada (JPN) |
| William Tilden (USA) | Elizabeth Ryan (USA) | Elizabeth Ryan (USA) |
| Jack Hillyard (GBR) | Cilly Aussem (GER) | Charles Aeschliman (SUI) |
| George Rogers (IRL) | Elizabeth Ryan (USA) | Lolette Payot (SUI) |
| Max Stolarow (POL) | *Mme Taunay* (NED) | Charles Aeschliman (SUI) |
| Ignacy Tloczynski (POL) | Muriel Thomas (GBR) | Lolette Payot (SUI) |
| Charles Aeschliman (SUI) | Eden Chew (GBR) | Charles Aeschliman (SUI) |
| Alan Gittings USA) | *Dorothy Winterbottom* (GBR) | Lolette Payot (SUI) |
| Charles Aeschliman (SUI) | *Simone Mathieu* (FRA) | Hector Fisher (SUI) |
| Edouard Lotan (FRA) | Muriel Thomas (GBR) | Muriel Thomas (GBR) |
| Jacques Brugnon (FRA) | *Simone Mathieu* (FRA) | Jacques Brugnon (FRA) |
| William Robertson (USA) | Kay Stammers (GBR) | *Simone Mathieu* (FRA) |
| Jacques Brugnon (FRA) | Edith Belliard (FRA) | Jean Lesueur (FRA) |
| Jean Lesueur (FRA) | Kay Stammers (GBR) | Kay Stammers (GBR) |
| Jacques Brugnon (FRA) | Jacqueline Goldschmidt (FRA) | Adam Baworowski (AUT) |
| Axel Schroder (SWE) | Simone Iribarne (FRA) | Simone Iribarne (FRA) |
| Jacques Brugnon (FRA) | Jadwiga Jedrzejowska (POL) | Jacques Brugnon (FRA) |
| Axel Schroder (SWE) | Muriel Thomas (GBR) | Jadwiga Jedrzejowska (POL) |
| Jean Lesueur (FRA) | Cosette Saint Omer Roy (FRA) | Pierre Pelizza (FRA) |
| Yvon Petra (FRA) | Alice Weiwers (LUX) | *Simone Mathieu* (FRA) |

## CANNES   Cannes LTC   Other tournaments

| Year | Date | Men's Singles | Ladies' Singles |
|---|---|---|---|
| 1921 | 17-23 January | Gordon Lowe (BRI) | Elizabeth Ryan (USA) |
| 1922 | 16-22 January | Charles Roupell (BRI) | Elizabeth Ryan (USA) |
| 1929 | 24-30 December (1928) | Giorgio de Stefani (ITA) | *Sylvia Lafaurie (FRA)* |
| 1935 | 15-21 April | George Godsell (GBR) | *Simone Mathieu (FRA)* |
| 1936 | 30 March -5 April | Fred Perry (GBR) | *Simone Mathieu (FRA)* |

## CANNES   Carlton LTC (Carlton Hotel)   International tournaments

| Year | Date | Men's Singles | Ladies' Singles |
|---|---|---|---|
| 1914 | 6-12 April | Anthony Wilding (NZL) | Suzanne Lenglen (FRA) |
| 1919 | 24 February- 2 March | Douglas Watters (USA) | Suzanne Lenglen (FRA) |
| 1920 | 16-22 February | Gordon Lowe (BRI) | Elizabeth Ryan (USA) |
| 1921 | 14-20 February | Gordon Lowe (BRI) | Suzanne Lenglen (FRA) |
| 1922 | 13-19 February | Charles Aeschliman (SUI) | Elizabeth Ryan (USA) |
| 1923 | 12-18 February | Henry Mayes (CAN) | Suzanne Lenglen (FRA) |
| 1924 | 11-17 February | Henry Mayes (CAN) | Elizabeth Ryan (USA) |
| 1925 | 9-15 February | Gordon Lowe (GBR) | Elizabeth Ryan (USA) |
| 1926 | 8-14 February | Uberto de Morpurgo (ITA) | Suzanne Lenglen (FRA) |
| 1927 | 17-23 January | Henri Cochet (FRA) | Diddie Vlasto (FRA) |

Note: married ladies are shown in *italics*

| Men's Doubles | Ladies' Doubles | Mixed Doubles |
| --- | --- | --- |
| Jack Hillyard (BRI) <br> Gordon Lowe (BRI) | — | Gordon Lowe (BRI) <br> Elizabeth Ryan (USA) |
| Samuel Hardy (USA) <br> Ernest Lamb (BRI) | — | Lord George Rocksavage (BRI) <br> Elizabeth Ryan (USA) |
| Giorgio de Stefani (ITA) <br> Rowley Scovell (GBR) | — | Charles Aeschliman (SUI) <br> *Sylvia Lafaurie* (FRA) |
| George Godsell (GBR) <br> Richard Turnbull (GBR) | *Divided* <br> *Paula von Stuck* (GER) <br> *Helen Turnbull* (GBR)/ <br> *Simone Mathieu* (FRA) <br> Alice Weiwers (LUX) | Edouard Lotan (FRA) <br> Simone Mathieu (FRA) |
| Fred Perry (GBR) <br> Max Ellmer (SUI) | *Simone Mathieu* (FRA) <br> Susan Noel (GBR) | Fred Perry (GBR) <br> *Simone Mathieu* (FRA) |

| Men's Doubles | Ladies' Doubles | Mixed Doubles |
| --- | --- | --- |
| Count Ludwig Salm (AUT) <br> Anthony Wilding (NZL) | — | Max Decugis (FRA) <br> Elizabeth Ryan (USA) |
| Watson Washburn (USA) <br> Richard Williams (USA) | — | Max Decugis (FRA) <br> Suzanne Lenglen (FRA) |
| Pierre Albarran (FRA) <br> Alain Gerbault (FRA) | — | Major Ritchie (BRI) <br> Elizabeth Ryan (USA) |
| Gordon Lowe (BRI) <br> John Rendall (BRI) | Suzanne Lenglen (FRA) <br> Elizabeth Ryan (USA) | Algernon Kingscote (BRI) <br> Suzanne Lenglen (FRA) |
| Charles Aeschliman (SUI) <br> Jack Hillyard (GBR) | Elizabeth Ryan (USA) <br> *Phyllis Satterthwaite* (GBR) | Alain Gerbault (FRA) <br> Elizabeth Ryan (USA) |
| Jack Hillyard (GBR) <br> Eliot Crawshay Williams (GBR) | Suzanne Lenglen (FRA) <br> Elizabeth Ryan (USA) | Uberto de Morpurgo (ITA) <br> Suzanne Lenglen (FRA) |
| Leonce Aslangul (FRA) <br> Leighton Crawford (GBR) | Suzanne Lenglen (FRA) <br> Elizabeth Ryan (USA) | Charles Aeschliman (SUI) <br> Suzanne Lenglen (FRA) |
| Henry Mayes (CAN) <br> Maj. Llewellyn Owen (GBR | Suzanne Lenglen (FRA) <br> Elizabeth Ryan (USA) | Charles Aeschliman (SUI) <br> Elizabeth Ryan (USA) |
| André Aron (FRA) <br> Félix Poulin (FRA) | Suzanne Lenglen (FRA) <br> Diddie Vlasto (FRA) | Uberto de Morpurgo (ITA) <br> Diddie Vlasto (FRA) |
| Jacques Brugnon (FRA) <br> Henri Cochet (FRA) | Elizabeth Ryan (USA) <br> *Phyllis Satterthwaite* (GBR) | Henri Cochet (FRA) <br> Elizabeth Ryan (USA) |

**CANNES  Carlton LTC (Carlton Hotel)  International tournaments**

| Year | Date | Men's Singles | Ladies' Singles |
|------|------|---------------|-----------------|
| 1928 | 6-12 February | Bela von Kehrling (HUN) | Elizabeth Ryan (USA) |
| 1929 | 4-10 February | Uberto de Morpurgo (ITA) | Eileen Bennett (GBR) |
| 1930 | 3-9 February | Giorgio de Stefani (ITA) | Elizabeth Ryan (USA) |
| 1931 | 2-8 February | George Rogers (IRL) | Elizabeth Ryan (USA) |
| 1932 | 1-7 February | George Rogers (IRL) | Elizabeth Ryan (USA) |
| 1933 | 6-12 February | Charles Aeschliman (SUI) | Sheila Hewitt (GBR) |
| 1934 | 5-11 February | Antoine Gentien (FRA) | Muriel Thomas (GBR) |
| 1935 | 4-10 February | Antoine Gentien (FRA) | *Simone Mathieu* (FRA) |
| 1936 | 3-9 February | André Martin-Legeay (FRA) | *Simone Mathieu* (FRA) |
| 1937 | 1-7 February | Vojtech Vodicka (TCH) | Simone Mathieu (FRA) |
| 1938 | 7-13 February | Kho Sin Kie (CHN) | Alice Weiwers (LUX) |
| 1939 | 6-12 February | Kho Sin Kie (CHN) | Alice Weiwers (LUX) |

Note: married ladies are shown in *italics*

| Men's Doubles | Ladies' Doubles | Mixed Doubles |
| --- | --- | --- |
| Placido Gaslini (ITA) | Eileen Bennett (GBR) | Erik Worm (DEN) |
| Bela von Kehrling (HUN) | Elsa Haylock (GBR) | Elizabeth Ryan (USA) |
| Charles Aeschliman (SUI) | Esna Boyd (AUS) | Uberto de Morpurgo (ITA) |
| Patrick Spence (RSA) | Betty Nuthall (GBR) | *Diddie Serpieri* (FRA) |
| Jacques Brugnon (FRA) | Sylvia Jung (FRA) | Henri Cochet (FRA) |
| Henri Cochet (FRA) | Elizabeth Ryan (USA) | Elizabeth Ryan (USA) |
| Jacques Brungon (FRA) | *Phyllis Satterthwaite* (GBR) | Alberto del Bono (ITA) |
| Henri Cochet (FRA) | Muriel Thomas (GBR) | Betty Soames (GBR) |
| George Rogers (IRL) | Elizabeth Ryan (USA) | George Rogers (IRL) |
| Erik Worm (DEN) | Muriel Thomas (GBR) | Elizabeth Ryan (USA) |
| Tino Jatta (ITA) | Dorothy Burke (USA) | Jacques Brugnon (FRA) |
| George Rogers (IRL) | Muriel Thomas (GBR) | Elizabeth Ryan (USA) |
| Jacques Brugnon (FRA) | Elizabeth Ryan (USA) | Jacques Brugnon (FRA) |
| Antoine Gentien (FRA) | Muriel Thomas (GBR) | Elizabeth Ryan (USA) |
| Henry Culley (USA) | *Simone Mathieu* (FRA) | Wilmer Hines (USA) |
| Wilmer Hines (USA) | Muriel Thomas (GBR) | *Phyllis Satterthwaite* (GBR) |
| Jacques Brugnon (FRA) | *Simone Mathieu* (FRA) | André Martin-Legeay (FRA) |
| William Robertson (USA) | *Phyllis Satterthwaite* (GBR) | *Simone Mathieu* (FRA) |
| Kho Sin Kie (CHN) | Lili de Alvarez (ESP) | Jacques Brugnon (FRA) |
| Vladimir Landau (MON) | Simone Mathieu (FRA) | Simone Mathieu (FRA) |
| Kho Sin Kie (CHN) | Cosette Saint Omer Roy (FRA) | Kho Sin Khie (CHN) |
| George Rogers (IRL) | Alice Weiwers (LUX) | Alice Weiwers (LUX) |
| Jacques Brugnon (FRA) | *Simone Mathieu* (FRA) | *Divided – no time* |
| Kho Sin Kie(CHN) | Gracyn Wheeler (USA) | Kho Sin Kie (CHN) |
| | | *Simone Mathieu* (FRA)/ |
| | | *two semi-finalists* |

## CANNES  Carlton LTC (Carlton Hotel)  New Year tournaments

| Year | Date | Men's Singles | Ladies' Singles |
| --- | --- | --- | --- |
| 1914 | 5-11 January | Anthony Wilding (NZL) | Suzanne Lenglen (FRA) |
| 1920 | 12-18 January | Major Ritchie (BRI) | Suzanne Lenglen (FRA) |
| 1921 | 10-16 January | Gordon Lowe (BRI) | Suzanne Lenglen (FRA) |
| 1922 | 9-16 January | Charles Aeschliman (SUI) | Elizabeth Ryan (USA) |
| 1923 | 8-14 January | Leighton Crawford (GBR) | Elizabeth Ryan (USA) |
| 1924 | 7-13 January | Henry Mayes (CAN) | Elizabeth Ryan (USA) |
| 1925 | 5-11 January | Henry Mayes (CAN) | Elizabeth Ryan (USA) |

## CANNES  Carlton LTC (Carlton Hotel)  Other tournaments

| Year | Date | Men's Singles | Ladies' Singles |
| --- | --- | --- | --- |
| 1920 | 12-18 April | Gordon Lowe (BRI) | *Sigrid Fick* (SWE) |
| 1921 | 11-17 April | Charles Aeschliman (SUI) | Suzanne Lenglen (FRA) |
| 1922 | 10-16 April | Alain Gerbault (FRA) | Sylvia Jung (FRA) |
| 1926 | 29 March-4 April | Charles Aeschliman (SUI) | Lili de Alvarez (ESP) |

Note: married ladies are shown in *italics*

| Men's Doubles | Ladies' Doubles | Mixed Doubles |
|---|---|---|
| Craig Biddle (USA) Anthony Wilding (NZL) | — | Anthony Wilding (NZL) Suzanne Lenglen (FRA) |
| Pierre Albarran (FRA) Alain Gerbault (FRA) | — | Major Ritchie (BRI) Elizabeth Ryan (USA) |
| Francis Fisher (NZL) Douglas Watson (BRI) | — | Francis Fisher (NZL) Suzanne Lenglen (FRA) |
| Francis Fisher (NZL) Harold Hunt (AUS) | — | Francis Fisher (NZL) Elizabeth Ryan (USA) |
| Charles Aeschliman (SUI) Francis Fisher (NZL) | Suzanne Lenglen (FRA) Elizabeth Ryan (USA) | Francis Fisher (NZL) Suzanne Lenglen (FRA) |
| Charles Aeschliman (SUI) Douglas Watson (GBR) | *Phyllis Covell* (GBR) Elizabeth Ryan (USA) | Jack Hillyard (GBR) *Phyllis Satterthwaite* (GBR) |
| Keats Lester (GBR) Jimmy van Alen (USA) | Suzanne Lenglen (FRA) Elizabeth Ryan (USA) | Henry Mayes (CAN) Suzanne Lenglen (FRA) |

| Men's Doubles | Ladies' Doubles | Mixed Doubles |
|---|---|---|
| Alfred Hunter (BRI) Gordon Lowe (BRI) | — | Gordon Lowe (BRI) *Sigrid Fick* (SWE) |
| Charles Aeschliman (SUI) Jack Hillyard (BRI) | — | Jack Hillyard (BRI) *Phyllis Satterthwaite* (BRI) |
| Charles Aeschliman (SUI) Ronaldo Boyd (ARG) | — | Jimmy van Alen (USA) Sylvia Jung (FRA) |
| Rene Grahn (FIN) Bertie Mayer (IND) | Suzanne Lenglen (FRA) *Phyllis Satterthwaite* (GBR) | Charles Aeschliman (SUI) *Phyllis Satterthwaite* (GBR) |

**CANNES** **Gallia LTC (Gallia Hotel)** **International tournaments**

| Year | Date | Men's Singles | Ladies' Singles |
|------|------|---------------|-----------------|
| 1924 | 21-27 January | Henry Mayes (CAN) | Elizabeth Ryan (USA) |
| 1925 | 19-25 January | Henry Mayes (CAN) | Elizabeth Ryan (USA) |
| 1926 | 25-31 January | Henri Cochet (FRA) | Helen Wills (USA) |
| 1927 | 31 January-6 February | Henri Cochet (FRA) | Elizabeth Ryan (USA) |
| 1928 | 30 January-5 February | Henri Cochet (FRA) | Eileen Bennett (GBR) |
| 1929 | 28 January-3 February | Henri Cochet (FRA) | Esna Boyd (AUS) |
| 1930 | 27 January-2 February | William Tilden (USA) | Elizabeth Ryan (USA) |
| 1931 | 26 January-1 February | Jacques Brugnon (FRA) | *Phyllis Satterthwaite* (GBR) |
| 1932 | 25-31 January | Jacques Brugnon (FRA) | Elizabeth Ryan (USA) |
| 1933 | 30 January-5 February | Jacques Brugnon (FRA) | Sheila Hewitt (GBR) |
| 1934 | 29 January-4 February | Giorgio de Stefani (ITA) | Muriel Thomas (GBR) |
| 1935 | 28 January-3 February | Antoine Gentien (FRA) | *Simone Mathieu* (FRA) |
| 1936 | 27 January-2 February | Jacques Brugnon (FRA) | *Simone Mathieu* (FRA) |
| 1937 | 25-31 January | Kho Sin Kie (CHN) | *Simone Mathieu* (FRA) |
| 1938 | 31 January-6 February | William Robertson (USA) | Alice Weiwers (LUX) |
| 1939 | 30 January-5 February | Kho Sin Kie (CHN) | Gracyn Wheeler (USA) |

Note: married ladies are shown in *italics*

| Men's Doubles | Ladies' Doubles | Mixed Doubles |
|---|---|---|
| eonce Aslangul (FRA) eighton Crawford (GBR) | Suzanne Lenglen (FRA) Elizabeth Ryan (USA) | Henry Mayes (CAN) Suzanne Lenglen (FRA) |
| ord George Cholmondeley GBR) Henry Mayes (CAN) | *Winifred Beamish (GBR)* *Phyllis Satterthwaite (GBR)* | Charles Aeschliman (SUI) Elizabeth Ryan (USA) |
| harles Aeschliman (SUI) enri Cochet (FRA) | Diddie Vlasto (FRA) *Phyllis Satterthwaite (GBR)* | Henri Cochet (FRA) Diddie Vlasto (FRA) |
| harles Aeschliman (SUI) enri Cochet (FRA) | Elizabeth Ryan (USA) *Phyllis Satterthwaite (GBR)* | Henri Cochet (FRA) Eileen Bennett (GBR) |
| harles Aeschliman (SUI) enri Cochet (FRA) | Ermyntrude Harvey (GBR) Elizabeth Ryan (USA) | Henri Cochet (FRA) Eileen Bennett (GBR) |

OUBLES ABANDONED – RAIN

| Men's Doubles | Ladies' Doubles | Mixed Doubles |
|---|---|---|
| ques Brugnon (FRA) enri Cochet (FRA) | *Sylvia Lafaurie (FRA)* Elizabeth Ryan (USA) | William Tilden (USA) Cilly Aussem (GER) |
| ques Brugnon (FRA) nmanuel du Plaix (FRA) | Elizabeth Ryan (USA) Lucia Valerio (ITA) | Jacques Brugnon (FRA) Elizabeth Ryan (USA) |
| ques Brugnon (FRA) nmanuel du Plaix (FRA) | Elizabeth Ryan (USA) Muriel Thomas (GBR) | George Rogers (IRL) Elizabeth Ryan (USA) |
| ques Brugnon (FRA) orge Rogers (IRL) | *Doris Burke (USA)* Muriel Thomas (GBR) | George Rogers (IRL) Elizabeth Ryan (USA) |
| ques Brugnon (FRA) toine Gentien (FRA) | Elizabeth Ryan (USA) Muriel Thomas (GBR) | Jacques Brugnon (FRA) Elizabeth Ryan (USA) |
| nry Culley (USA) lmer Hines (USA) | Simone Mathieu (FRA) Muriel Thomas (GBR) | Antoine Gentien (FRA) *Simone Mathieu (FRA)* |
| ques Brugnon (FRA) dré Martin-Legeay (FRA) | *Simone Mathieu (FRA)* *Phyllis Satterthwaite (GBR)* | André Martin-Legeay (FRA) *Simone Mathieu (FRA)* |
| ques Brugnon (FRA) lliam Robertson (USA) | — | Jacques Brugnon (FRA) *Simone Mathieu (FRA)* |
| o Sin Kie (CHN) orge Rogers (IRL) | Cosette Saint Omer Roy (FRA) Alice Weiwers (LUX) | *Divided – no time* André Jacquemet (FRA) Cosette Saint Omer Roy (FRA)/ Jacques Brugnon (FRA) *Simone Mathieu (FRA)* |
| ques Brugnon (FRA) o Sin Kie (CHN) | Cosette Saint Omer Roy (FRA) Alice Weiwers (LUX) | — |

| Year | Date | Men's Singles | Ladies' Singles |
|------|------|---------------|-----------------|
| 1904 | 22-28 March | Major Ritchie (BRI) | — |
| 1907 | 25-31 March | Major Ritchie (BRI) | *Countess Clara Schulenburg* (GER) |
| 1908 | 30 March-6 April | Anthony Wilding (NZL) | *Ruth Winch* (GBR) |
| 1909 | 27 March-3 April | Freidrich Rahe (GER) | Alice Greene (BRI) |
| 1910 | 24-30 March | Major Ritchie (BRI) | Rosamund Salusbury (BRI) |
| 1911 | TOURNAMENT NOT SCHEDULED | | |
| 1912 | TOURNAMENT NOT SCHEDULED | | |
| 1913 | 17-23 March | Gordon Lowe (BRI) | Elizabeth Ryan (USA) |
| 1914 | 31 March -5 April | Norman Brookes (AUS) | Elizabeth Ryan (USA) |
| 1920 | 5-11 April | Gordon Lowe (BRI) | *Madeline O'Neill* (BRI) |
| 1921 | 4-10 April | Henry Mayes (CAN) | *Divided* *Winifred Beamish* (BRI) *Phyllis Satterthwaite* (BRI) |
| 1922 | 3-9 April | Jean Borotra (FRA) | Sylvia Jung (FRA) |
| 1923 | 2-8 April | Brame Hillyard (GBR) | Elizabeth Ryan (USA) |
| 1924 | 31 March-6 April | Uberto de Morpurgo (ITA) | Lili de Alvarez (ESP) |
| 1925 | 26 January-1 February | Henry Mayes (CAN) | Elizabeth Ryan (USA) |
| 1926 | 18-24 January | Jacques Brugnon (FRA) | Helen Wills (USA) |
| 1927 | 10-16 January | Henri Cochet (FRA) | Diddie Vlasto (FRA) |
| 1928 | 23-29 January | Henri Cochet (FRA) | Elizabeth Ryan (USA) |

Note: married ladies are shown in *italics*

| Men's Doubles | Ladies' Doubles | Mixed Doubles |
|---|---|---|
| — | — | — |
| — | — | — |
| — | — | — |
| Artemas Holmes (USA)<br>Freidrich Rahe (GER) | — | — |
| Heinrich Kleinschroth (GER)<br>Robert Kleinschroth (GER) | — | Heinrich Kleinschroth (GER)<br>*Hedwig Neresheimer* (GER) |
| Heinrich Kleinschroth (GER)<br>Freidrich Rahe (GER) | — | Freidrich Rahe (GER)<br>*Countess Clara Schulenburg* (GER) |
| Max Decugis (FRA)<br>Alfred Dunlop (AUS) | — | Max Decugis (FRA)<br>Elizabeth Ryan (USA) |
| Francis Fisher (NZL)<br>Walter Ireland (GBR) | — | Francis Fisher (NZL)<br>*Winifred Beamish* (BRI) |
| Gharpur Singh (IND)<br>Das Narsingh (IND) | — | Jack Hillyard (BRI)<br>*Phyllis Satterthwaite* (BRI) |
| Jean Borotra (FRA)<br>Alain Gerbault (FRA) | — | Jean Borotra (FRA)<br>Suzanne Lenglen (FRA) |
| Jack Hillyard (GBR)<br>Lian Lezard (RSA) | Elizabeth Ryan (USA)<br>*Phyllis Satterthwaite* (GBR) | Frederick Scovel (USA)<br>Elizabeth Ryan (USA) |
| Uberto de Morpurgo (ITA)<br>Jimmy van Alen (USA) | Suzanne Lenglen (FRA)<br>Elizabeth Ryan (USA) | Antoine Gentien (FRA)<br>Nicole Descleres (FRA) |
| Charles Aeschliman (SUI)<br>Ernest Lamb (GBR) | Elizabeth Ryan (USA)<br>Diddie Vlasto (FRA) | Lord George Cholmondeley (GBR)<br>Elizabeth Ryan (USA) |
| Jacques Brugnon (FRA)<br>Francis Fisher (NZL) | Suzanne Lenglen (FRA)<br>Diddie Vlasto (FRA) | Jacques Brugnon (FRA)<br>Suzanne Lenglen (FRA) |
| Jacques Brugnon (FRA)<br>Henri Cochet (FRA) | Eileen Bennett (GBR)<br>*Phyllis Satterthwaite* (GBR) | Henri Cochet (FRA)<br>Diddie Vlasto (FRA) |
| Hermann Artens (AUT)<br>Count Ludwig Salm (AUT) | Elizabeth Ryan (USA)<br>*Phyllis Satterthwaite* (GBR) | Jack Hillyard (GBR)<br>Elizabeth Ryan (USA) |

**CANNES** Metropole LTC (Metropole Hotel) International tournaments

| Year | Date | Men's Singles | Ladies' Singles |
|------|------|---------------|-----------------|
| 1929 | 31 December–6 January (1928) | Uberto de Morpurgo (ITA) | Esna Boyd (AUS) |
| 1930 | 30 December–5 January (1929) | Paul Barrelet de Ricou (FRA) | Elizabeth Ryan (USA) |
| 1931 | 5-11 January | George Rogers (IRL) | *Hélène Nicolopoulo (GRE)* |

★ Transferred from Beaulieu LTC – Courts not ready
Note: married ladies are shown in *italics*

**CANNES** Metropole LTC (Metropole Hotel) Other tournaments

| Year | Date | Men's Singles | Ladies' Singles |
|------|------|---------------|-----------------|
| 1925★ | 22-28 December (1924) | Henry Mayes (CAN) | Elizabeth Ryan (USA) |

| Men's Doubles | Ladies' Doubles | Mixed Doubles |
|---|---|---|
| ...ck Hillyard (GBR) / ...berto de Morpurgo (ITA) | Esna Boyd (AUS) / *Phyllis Satterthwaite* (GBR) | Divided – no time<br>Franz Matejka (AUT)<br>Esna Boyd (AUS)/<br>Uberto de Morpurgo (ITA)<br>*Phyllis Satterthwaite* (GBR) |
| ...harles Aeschliman (SUI) / ...eorge Rogers (IRL) | Elizabeth Ryan (USA) / *Phyllis Satterthwaite* (GBR) | George Rogers (IRL)<br>Elizabeth Ryan (USA) |
| ...ck Hillyard (GBR) / ...adimir Landau (MON) | Elizabeth Ryan (USA) / *Phyllis Satterthwaite* (GBR) | George Rogers (IRL)<br>Elizabeth Ryan (USA) |

| Men's Doubles | Ladies' Doubles | Mixed Doubles |
|---|---|---|
| ...nry Mayes (CAN) / ...ncis Fisher (NZL) | Elizabeth Ryan (USA) / *Phyllis Satterthwaite* (GBR) | Arthur Yencken (GBR)<br>Elizabeth Ryan (USA) |

## CANNES  New Courts Club   International tournaments★

| Year | Date | Men's Singles | Ladies' Singles |
|------|------|---------------|-----------------|
| 1926 | 11-17 January | Henri Cochet (FRA) | *Phyllis Satterthwaite (GBR)* |
| 1927 | 24-30 January | Jacques Brugnon (FRA) | Elizabeth Ryan (USA) |
| 1928 | 16-22 January | Henry Mayes (CAN) | Eileen Bennett (GBR) |
| 1929 | 21-27 January | Uberto de Morpurgo (ITA) | *Sylvia Lafaurie (FRA)* |
| 1930 | 20-26 January | William Tilden (USA) | Elizabeth Ryan (USA) |
| 1931 | 19-25 January | George Rogers (IRL) | *Phyllis Satterthwaite (GBR)* |
| 1932 | 18-24 January | George Rogers (IRL) | Lucia Valerio (ITA) |
| 1933 | 23-29 January | George Rogers (IRL) | Sheila Hewitt (GBR) |
| 1934 | 22-28 January | Giorgio de Stefani (ITA) | Cosette Saint Omer Roy (FRA |

## CANNES  New Courts Club   Other tournaments

| Year | Date | Men's Singles | Ladies' Singles |
|------|------|---------------|-----------------|
| 1932 | 11-17 April | Jiro Satoh (JPN) | *Sylvia Henrotin (FRA)* |
| 1933 | 3-8 April | Franz Matejka (AUT) | Lolette Payot (SUI) |
| 1934 | 9-15 April | TOURNAMENT SCHEDULED BUT CANCELLED | |

★1932-1934
Mediterranean
Championships
Note: married ladies
are shown in *italics*

| Men's Doubles | Ladies' Doubles | Mixed Doubles |
|---|---|---|
| cques Brugnon (FRA) / enri Cochet (FRA) | Suzanne Lenglen (FRA) / *Phyllis Satterthwaite (GBR)* | Henri Cochet (FRA) / Suzanne Lenglen (FRA) |
| cques Brugnon (FRA) / enri Cochet (FRA) | Elizabeth Ryan (USA) / *Phyllis Satterthwaite (GBR)* | Erik Worm (DEN) / Elizabeth Ryan (USA) |
| ermann Artens (AUT) / ount Ludwig Salm (AUT) | Elizabeth Ryan (USA) / *Phyllis Satterthwaite (GBR)* | Henri Cochet (FRA) / Eileen Bennett (GBR) |

OUBLES ABANDONED – SNOW AND ICE

| Men's Doubles | Ladies' Doubles | Mixed Doubles |
|---|---|---|
| harles Kingsley (GBR) / illiam Tilden (USA) | *Sylvia Lafaurie (FRA)* / Joan Ridley (GBR) | William Tilden (USA) / Cilly Aussem (GER) |
| ck Hillyard (GBR) / eorge Rogers (IRL) | Elizabeth Ryan (USA) / *Phyllis Satterthwaite (GBR)* | *Divided – Rogers withdrew* Charles Aeschliman (SUI) Muriel Thomas (GBR)/ George Rogers (IRL) Elizabeth Ryan (USA) |
| berto del Bono (ITA) / eorge Rogers (IRL) | Elizabeth Ryan (USA) / Muriel Thomas (GBR) | George Rogers (IRL) / Elizabeth Ryan (USA) |
| adimir Landau (MON) / eorge Rogers (IRL) | Elizabeth Ryan (USA) / *Phyllis Satterthwaite (GBR)* | George Rogers (IRL) / Elizabeth Ryan (USA) |
| arles Aeschliman (SUI) / ouard Lotan (FRA) | Elizabeth Ryan (USA) / Muriel Thomas (GBR) | Wilmer Hines (USA) / Elizabeth Ryan (USA) |

| Men's Doubles | Ladies' Doubles | Mixed Doubles |
|---|---|---|
| orge Rogers (IRL) / Satoh (JPN) | *Sylvia Henrotin (FRA)* / Muriel Thomas (GBR) | Jiro Satoh (JPN) / *Sylvia Henrotin (FRA)* |
| arles Aeschliman (SUI) / ouard Lotan (FRA) | — | Charles Aeschliman (SUI) / Lolette Payot (SUI) |

**HYÈRES**  Hyères LTC (Golf Hotel)  International tournaments

| Year | Date | Men's Singles | Ladies' Singles |
|------|------|---------------|-----------------|
| 1910 | 31 March–5 April | John Flavelle (BRI) | *Regine Vlasto* (FRA) |
| 1911 | 3–9 April | Fredric Warburg (BRI) | *Emmeline Warburg* (BRI) |
| 1912 | 25 March–1 April | Count Ludwig Salm (AUT) | *Mrs Perrett* (BRI) |
| 1913 | 31 March–5 April | Hope Crisp (BRI) | E.M. White (BRI) |
| 1914 | 2–8 February | Gordon Lowe (BRI) | E.M. White (BRI) |
| 1920 | 9–15-February | Gordon Lowe (BRI) | *Winifred Beamish* (BRI) |
| 1921 | 31 January–6 February | Gordon Lowe (BRI) | *Blanche Colston* (BRI) |
| 1922 | 30 January–5 February | A. Resuge (FRA) | *Phyllis Satterthwaite* (GBR) |
| 1923 | 29 January–4 February | Jack Hillyard (GBR) | *Phyllis Satterthwaite* (GBR) |
| 1924 | 28 January–3 February | Jack Hillyard (GBR) | *Phyllis Satterthwaite* (GBR) |
| 1925 | 12–18 January | Lt René Jaurequiberry (FRA) | Cosette Saint Omer Roy (FRA |
| 1926 | 4–10 January | TOURNAMENT ABANDONED – BAD WEATHER, COURTS NOT AVAILABLE | |
| 1927 | 3–9 January | George Fletcher (GBR) | Mary Hartland (GBR) |
| 1928 | | TOURNAMENT NOT SCHEDULED | |

Note: married ladies are shown in *italics*

| *n's Doubles* | *Ladies' Doubles* | *Mixed Doubles* |
| --- | --- | --- |
| né Gheerbrandt (BEL)<br>Hitchcock (FRA) | — | — |
| dric Warburg (BRI)<br>Vlasto (FRA) | — | Fredric Warburg (BRI)<br>*Emmeline Warburg (BRI)* |
| unt Ludwig Salm (AUT)<br>arles Simond (BRI) | — | Count Ludwig Salm (AUT)<br>E.M. White (BRI) |
| pe Crisp (BRI)<br>offrey Youll (BRI) | — | Hope Crisp (BRI)<br>*Mrs Perrett (BRI)* |
| ig Biddle (USA)<br>hony Wilding (NZL) | — | *Divided*<br>Gordon Lowe (BRI)<br>Elizabeth Ryan (USA)/<br>Wallis Myers (BRI)<br>*A. Hall (BRI)* |
| brose Dudley (BRI)<br>rdon Lowe (BRI) | — | Ambrose Dudley (BRI)<br>*Winifred Beamish (BRI)* |
| L. Nouveau (FRA)<br>Resuge (FRA) | — | Jack Hillyard (BRI)<br>*Phyllis Satterthwaite (BRI)* |
| Hillyard (GBR)<br>Resuge (FRA) | — | Jack Hillyard (GBR)<br>*Phyllis Satterthwaite (GBR)* |
| me Hillyard (GBR)<br>Hillyard (GBR) | — | Jack Hillyard (GBR)<br>*Phyllis Satterthwaite (GBR)* |
| Hillyard (GBR)<br>est Lamb (GBR) | — | Jack Hillyard (GBR)<br>*Phyllis Satterthwaite (GBR)* |
|  | — | Lt René Jaurequiberry (FRA)<br>Miss Latty |
|  | — | Cyril Fletcher (GBR)<br>Mary Hartland (GBR) |

**HYÈRES** **New Courts Club** **International tournaments**

| Year | Date | Men's Singles | Ladies' Singles |
|------|------|---------------|-----------------|
| 1929 | 24-30 December (1928) | Jacques Brugnon (FRA) | Esna Boyd (AUS) |
| 1930 | 23-29 December (1929) | Johann Buss (GER) | Doris Metaxa (FRA) |

**JUAN-LES-PINS** **Juan-les-Pins LTC** **International Tournaments**

| Year | Date | Men's Singles | Ladies' Singles |
|------|------|---------------|-----------------|
| 1924 | 14-20 April | David Morgan (GBR) | *Sylvia Lafaurie* (FRA) |
| 1925 | 30 March-5 April | Jean Augustin (FRA) | Lili de Alvarez (ESP) |
| 1926 | 12-18 April | Pierre Landry (FRA) | *Dorothy Coleman* (GBR) |
| 1927 | 28 March-3 April | Erik Worm (DEN) | *Phyllis Satterthwaite* (GBR) |
| 1928 | 2-8 January | Henry Mayes (CAN) | Elizabeth Ryan (USA) |
| 1929 | 15-21 April | Emmanuel du Plaix (FRA) | *Sylvia Lafaurie* (FRA) |
| 1930 | 4-10 May | TOURNAMENT SCHEDULED BUT CANCELLED | |
| 1931 | 22-28 December (1930) | Charles Aeschliman (SUI) | Muriel Thomas (GBR) |
| 1932 | 21-27 December (1931) | Erik Worm (DEN) | — |
| 1932 | 4-10 April | Hyotare Satoh (JPN) | Ida Adamoff (FRA) |
| 1933 | 2-8 January | TOURNAMENT SCHEDULED BUT CANCELLED | |
| 1934 | 1-7 January | Charles Aeschliman (SUI) | Cosette Saint Omer Roy (FF |

Note: married ladies are shown in *italics*

| Men's Doubles | Ladies' Doubles | Mixed Doubles |
| --- | --- | --- |
| ...berto de Morpurgo (ITA) <br> ...ranz Matejka (AUT) | Esna Boyd (AUS) <br> *Phyllis Satterthwaite* (GBR) | Uberto de Morpurgo (ITA) <br> Esna Boyd (AUS) |
| . Duereux (FRA) <br> ...enri Reynaud (FRA) | — | Henri Reynaud (FRA) <br> *Regine Vlasto* (FRA) |

| Men's Doubles | Ladies' Doubles | Mixed Doubles |
| --- | --- | --- |
| ...ancis Fisher (NZL) <br> ...vid Morgan (GBR) | Suzanne Lenglen (FRA) <br> *Florence Gould* (GBR) | Alfred Hunter (GBR) <br> Lili de Alvarez (ESP) |
| ...rd George Cholmondeley (BR) <br> ...né Lacoste (FRA) | Lili de Alvarez (ESP) <br> *Phyllis Satterthwaite* (GBR) | Alfred Hunter (GBR) <br> Lili de Alvarez (ESP) |
| ...arles Aeschliman (SUI) <br> ...rre Landry (FRA) | — | Pierre Landry (FRA) <br> Lili de Alvarez (ESP) |
| ...k Worm (DEN) <br> ...né Gallepe (MON) | — | Erik Worm (DEN) <br> *Phyllis Satterthwaite* (GBR) |
| ...nry Mayes (CAN) <br> ...ell Andréws (NZL) | — | Eskell Andréws (NZL) <br> Elizabeth Ryan (USA) |
| | — | Rowley Scovell (GBR) <br> *Daisy Speranza-Wyns* (FRA) |
| ...arles Aeschliman (SUI) <br> ...k Worm (DEN) | — | Charles Aeschliman (SUI <br> Muriel Thomas (GBR) |
| ...arles Aeschliman (SUI) <br> ...k Worm (DEN) | — | — |
| ...tare Satoh (JPN) <br> ...rge Rogers (IRL) | *Sylvia Henrotin* (FRA) <br> Muriel Thomas (GBR) | Charles Aeschliman (SUI) <br> Muriel Thomas (GBR) |
| | — | — |

**JUAN-LES-PINS** Miramar LTC International tournaments

| Year | Date | Men's Singles | Ladies' Singles |
|------|------|---------------|-----------------|
| 1929 | 4–10 March | Henri Cochet (FRA) | Eileen Bennett (GBR) |
| 1930 | 7–13 April | William Tilden (USA) | Elizabeth Ryan (USA) |
| 1931 | 13–19 April | Hyotare Satoh (JPN) | Cilly Aussem (GER) |
| 1932 | 18–24 April | TOURNAMENT SCHEDULED BUT CANCELLED | |
| 1933 | 10–16 April | Jiri Satoh (JPN) | Muriel Thomas (GBR) |
| 1934 | 16–22 April | TOURNAMENT SCHEDULED BUT CANCELLED | |
| 1935 | 17–23 December (1934) | Edouard Lotan (FRA) | — |
| 1936 | TOURNAMENT NOT SCHEDULED | | |
| 1937 | 12–18 April | Edouard Lotan (FRA) | Susan Noel (GBR) |
| 1938 | 4–10 April | Jean Lesueur (FRA) | Alice Weiwers (LUX) |
| 1939 | 20–26 March | Adam Baworowski (POL) | Alice Weiwers (LUX) |

Note: married ladies are shown in *italics*

| Men's Doubles | Ladies' Doubles | Mixed Doubles |
|---|---|---|
| René Gallepe (MON)<br>Pierre Landry (FRA) | — | Henri Cochet (FRA)<br>Eileen Bennett (GBR) |
| Wilbur Coen (USA)<br>William Tilden (USA) | Cilly Aussem (GER)<br>Elizabeth Ryan (USA) | Wilbur Coen (USA)<br>Elizabeth Ryan (USA) |
| Ryotare Satoh (JPN)<br>Minoru Kawatji (JPN) | Cilly Aussem (GER)<br>*Sylvia Henrotin (FRA)* | Erik Worm (DEN)<br>*Sylvia Henrotin (FRA)* |
| Takishi Itoh (JPN)<br>Ryosuke Nunoi (JPN) | *Dorothy Burke (USA)*<br>Muriel Thomas (GBR) | Jiri Satoh (JPN)<br>*Dorothy Burke (USA)* |
| Edouard Lotan (FRA)<br>Gabriel Mercier (SUI) | — | — |
| Edmond Rivoire (FRA)<br>Phillipe Ville (FRA) | — | Edmond Rivoire (FRA)<br>Jeannette Poncelet (FRA) |
| *divided*<br>André Jacquemet (FRA)<br>Vladimir Landau (MON)/<br>Jean Lesueur (FRA)<br>Emmanuel du Plaix (FRA) | Simone Mathieu (FRA)<br>Muriel Thomas (GBR) | Jean Lesueur (FRA)<br>*Simone Mathieu (FRA)* |
| Vladimir Landau (MON)<br>Karl Schroder (SWE) | — | Christian Boussus (FRA)<br>Alice Weiwers (LUX) |

**MENTON**  Menton LTC  **Riviera Championships**

| Year | Date | Men's Singles | Ladies' Singles |
|------|------|---------------|-----------------|
| 1902 | 22-29 March | Willie Lemaire (BEL) | V. Henshaw (BRI) |
| 1903 | 17-24 March | Roy Allen (BRI) | Mildred Brooksmith (BRI) |
| 1904 | 18-25 February | Major Ritchie (BRI) | V. Henshaw (BRI) |
| 1905 | 23-28 February | Major Ritchie (BRI) | Amy Ransome (BRI) |
| 1906 | 5-9 March | Anthony Wilding (NZL) | Vera Warden (USA) |
| 1907 | 25 February-3 March | Major Ritchie (BRI) | Rosamund Salusbury (BRI) |
| 1908 | 2-9 March | Major Ritchie (BRI) | Maud Dillon (BRI) |
| 1909 | 1-7 March | Frederick Alexander (USA) | Rosamund Salusbury (BRI) |
| 1910 | 2-12 March | Max Decugis (FRA) | Rosamund Salusbury (BRI) |
| 1911 | 6-12 March | Anthony Wilding (NZL) | Jessie Tripp (BRI) |
| 1912 | 25 February-3 March | Roy Allen (BRI) | Madeline Rieck (GER) |
| 1913 | 3-9 March | Anthony Wilding (NZL) | Dagmar von Krohn (GER) |
| 1914 | 2-8 March | Anthony Wilding (NZL) | *Dorothea Chambers* (BRI) |
| 1919 | 10-16 March | Nicholai Mishu (ROM) | Suzanne Lenglen (FRA) |
| 1920 | 8-14 March | Nicholai Mishu (ROM) | *Winifred Beamish* (BRI) |
| 1921 | 7-13 March | Gordon Lowe (GBR) | Elizabeth Ryan (USA) |
| 1922 | 6-12 March | Rupert Wertheim (AUS) | Elizabeth Ryan (USA) |
| 1923 | 5-11 March | Gordon Lowe (GBR) | Suzanne Lenglen (FRA) |

Note: married ladies are shown in *italics*

| en's Doubles | Ladies' Doubles | Mixed Doubles |
|---|---|---|
| - | — | — |
| harles Allen (BRI)<br>oy Allen (BRI) | — | — |
| harles Allen (BRI)<br>oy Allen (BRI) | — | — |
| harles Allen (BRI)<br>oy Allen (BRI) | — | Roy Allen (BRI)<br>Mildred Brooksmith (BRI) |
| ajor Ritchie (BRI)<br>eorge Simond (BRI) | — | Anthony Wilding (NZL)<br>Vera Warden (USA) |
| ajor Ritchie (BRI)<br>eorge Simond (BRI) | — | Major Ritchie (BRI)<br>Rosamund Salusbury (BRI) |
| ajor Ritchie (BRI)<br>eorge Simond (BRI) | — | Major Ritchie (BRI)<br>Rosamund Salusbury (BRI) |
| ederick Alexander (USA)<br>allis Myers (BRI) | — | Wallis Myers (BRI)<br>Jessie Tripp (BRI) |
| ax Decugis (FRA)<br>ajor Ritchie (BRI) | — | Major Ritchie (BRI)<br>Rosamund Salusbury (BRI) |
| ajor Ritchie (GBR)<br>nthony Wilding (NZL) | — | Heinrich Kleinschroth (GER)<br>*Hedwig Neresheimer* (GER) |
| Moore (BRI)<br>eorge Simond (BRI) | — | Wallis Myers (BRI)<br>Jessie Tripp (BRI) |
| einrich Kleinschroth (GER)<br>eidrich Rahe (GER) | — | Heinrich Kleinschroth (GER)<br>Dagmar von Krohn (GER) |
| aig Biddle (USA)<br>nthony Wilding (NZL) | — | Anthony Wilding (NZL)<br>*Dagmar Murray* (GER) |
| erre Albarran (FRA)<br>, Fremaux (FRA) | — | Max Decugis (FRA)<br>Suzanne Lenglen (FRA) |
| ount Mimo Balbi (ITA)<br>W. Murray (BRI) | — | Ambrose Dudley (BRI)<br>*Winifred Beamish* (BRI) |
| mbrose Dudley (BRI)<br>ordon Lowe (BRI) | Suzanne Lenglen (FRA)<br>Elizabeth Ryan (USA) | Gordon Lowe (GBR)<br>Elizabeth Ryan (USA) |
| muel Hardy (USA)<br>k Hillyard (GBR) | Elizabeth Ryan (USA)<br>*Phyllis Satterthwaite* (GBR) | Jack Hillyard (GBR)<br>*Phyllis Satterthwaite* (GBR) |
| ighton Crawford (GBR)<br>k Hillyard (GBR) | Suzanne Lenglen (FRA)<br>Elizabeth Ryan (USA) | Randolph Lycett (AUS)<br>Elizabeth Ryan (USA) |

**MENTON**  Menton LTC  Riviera Championships

| Year | Date | Men's Singles | Ladies' Singles |
|------|------|---------------|-----------------|
| 1924 | 3-9 March | Gordon Lowe (GBR) | Suzanne Lenglen (FRA) |
| 1925 | 2-8 March | Gordon Lowe (GBR) | Elizabeth Ryan (USA) |
| 1926 | 1-7 March | Henri Cochet (FRA) | Helen Wills (USA) |
| 1927 | 28 February-6 March | Uberto de Morpurgo (ITA) | Elizabeth Ryan (USA) |
| 1928 | 5-11 March | Bela von Kehrling (HUN) | Lili de Alvarez (ESP) |
| 1929 | 4-10 March | Bela von Kehrling (HUN) | *Phyllis Covell* (GBR) |
| 1930 | 3-9 March | William Tilden (USA) | Cilly Aussem (GER) |
| 1931 | 2-8 March | Bela von Kehrling (HUN) | *Phyllis Satterthwaite* (GBR) |
| 1932 | 29 February-6 March | Roderich Menzel (TCH) | *Simone Mathieu* (FRA) |
| 1933 | 6-12 March | André Martin-Legeay (FRA) | *Simone Mathieu* (FRA) |
| 1934 | 7-12 March | Giorgio de Stefani (ITA) | *Sylvia Henrotin* (FRA) |
| 1935 | 5-10 March | Josef Caska (TCH) | *Simone Mathieu* (FRA) |
| 1936 | 2-8 March | Jean Lesueur (FRA) | Jadwiga Jedrzejowska (POL) |
| 1937 | 1-7 March | Karl Schroder (SWE) | Anita Lizana (CHI) |
| 1938 | 7-13 March | Karl Schroder (SWE) | Jadwiga Jedrzejowska (POL) |
| 1939 | 6-12 March | Franjo Puncec (YUG) | *Simone Laffargue* (FRA) |

Note: married ladies are shown in *italics*

| n's Doubles | Ladies' Doubles | Mixed Doubles |
|---|---|---|
| once Aslangul (FRA) ix Poulin (FRA) | Suzanne Lenglen (FRA) Elizabeth Ryan (USA) | Leonce Aslangul (FRA) Elizabeth Ryan (USA) |
| ndolph Lycett (AUS) erto de Morpurgo (ITA) | Suzanne Lenglen (FRA) Elizabeth Ryan (USA) | Randolph Lycett (AUS) *Joan Lycett* (GBR) |
| nri Cochet (FRA) erto de Morpurgo (ITA) | Lili de Alvarez (ESP) Diddie Vlasto (FRA) | Henri Cochet (FRA) Diddie Vlasto (FRA) |
| la von Kehrling (HUN) inrich Kleinschroth (GER) | Elsie Goldsack (GBR) Dorothy Shaw (GBR) | Bela von Kehrling (HUN) Lili de Alvarez (ESP) |
| la von Kehrling (HUN) k Worm (DEN) | Dorothea Chambers (GBR) Peggy Saunders (GBR) | Bela von Kehrling (HUN) Cilly Aussem (GER) |
| la von Kehrling (HUN) k Worm (DEN) | Marjorie Morrill (USA) Lucia Valerio (ITA) | Bela von Kehrling (HUN) Cilly Aussem (GER) |
| lbur Coen (USA) lliam Tilden (USA) | Cilly Aussem (GER) Elizabeth Ryan (USA) | Patrick Hughes (GBR) Elizabeth Ryan (USA) |
| la von Kehrling (HUN) orge Rogers (IRL) | Mary Heeley (GBR) Betty Nuthall (GBR) | Bela von Kehrling (HUN) Cilly Aussem (GER) |
| dré Martin-Legeay (FRA) dré Merlin (FRA) | *Simone Mathieu* (FRA) Colette Rosambert (FRA) | André Martin-Legeay (FRA) *Simone Mathieu* (FRA) |
| dré Martin-Legeay (FRA) n Lesueur (FRA) | *Simone Mathieu* (FRA) Elizabeth Ryan (USA) | Gottfried von Cramm (GER) Elizabeth Ryan (USA) |
| il Gabrowitz (HUN) a von Kehrling (HUN) | Elizabeth Ryan (USA) Muriel Thomas (GBR) | Jean Lesueur (FRA) *Sylvia Henrotin* (FRA) |
| nry Culley (USA) lmer Hines (USA) | Edith Belliard (FRA) *Simone Mathieu* (FRA) | Wilmer Hines (USA) *Simone Mathieu* (FRA) |
| ques Brugnon (FRA) n Lesueur (FRA) | Jadwiga Jedrzejowska (POL) Susan Noel (GBR) | Jean Lesueur (FRA) Kay Stammers (GBR) |

OUBLES ABANDONED AT SEMI-FINAL STAGE – RAIN

| | | |
|---|---|---|
| nri Bolelli (FRA) n Lesueur (FRA) | Rita Jarvis (GBR) Valerie Scott (GBR) | Henri Bolelli (FRA) Jadwiga Jedrzejowska (POL) |
| n Lesueur (FRA) on Petra (FRA) | Evelyn Dearman (GBR) Kay Stammers (GBR) | Yvon Petra (FRA) *Simone Mathieu* (FRA) |

## MENTON    International Mixed Doubles (Coupe des Nations)

| | | | | |
|---|---|---|---|---|
| 1924 | Henri Cochet (FRA)<br>Suzanne Lenglen (FRA) | | 1928 | Henri Cochet (FRA)<br>Paulette Marjollet (FRA) |
| 1925 | René Lacoste (FRA)<br>Suzanne Lenglen (FRA) | | 1929 | George Rogers (IRL)<br>*Phyllis Covell* (GBR) |
| 1926 | Henri Cochet (FRA)<br>Diddie Vlasto (FRA) | | 1930 | William Tilden (USA)<br>Elizabeth Ryan (USA) |
| 1927 | Frederick Scovel (USA)<br>Elizabeth Ryan (USA) | | 1931 | George Rogers (IRL)<br>Betty Nuthall (GBR) |

## MENTON    Menton LTC    Other tournaments

| Year | Date | Men's Singles | Ladies' Singles |
|---|---|---|---|
| 1922 | 23-29 January | Samuel Hardy (USA) | Margrethe Kahler (DEN) |

## MONTE CARLO    Various venues★    Monte Carlo Championships

| Year | Date | Men's Singles | Ladies' Singles |
|---|---|---|---|
| 1896 | 23-29 March | George Hillyard (BRI) | K. Booth (BRI)<br>or Mlle Guillon (FRA) |
| 1897 | 22-30 March | Reginald Doherty (BRI) | — |
| 1898 | 15-21 March | Laurence Doherty (BRI) | — |
| 1899 | 4-10 April | Reginald Doherty (BRI) | — |
| 1900 | TOURNAMENT NOT SCHEDULED | | |
| 1901 | 8-16 March | Laurence Doherty (BRI) | *Blanche Hillyard* (BRI) |
| 1902 | 1-8 March | Reginald Doherty (BRI) | *Countess Clara Schulenburg* (GER) |
| 1903 | 1-8 March | Reginald Doherty (BRI) | Toupie Lowther (BRI) |
| 1904 | 26 February-<br>6 March | Reginald Doherty (BRI) | Mlle de Robiglio (FRA) |

★ Venues:
1896-1905:
Hotel de Paris
1906-1914, 1920:
Condamine
1919, 1921-1927:
La Festa
1928:
La Festa Country Club
1929-1939: Monte Carlo
Country Club
1920-1939: Monte Carlo
Championships
Note: married ladies are
shown in *italics*

| 1932 | André Martin-Legeay (FRA)<br>*Simone Mathieu (FRA)* | 1936 | Jean Lesueur (FRA)<br>*Simone Mathieu (FRA)* |
| --- | --- | --- | --- |
| 1933 | André Martin-Legeay (FRA)<br>*Simone Mathieu (FRA)* | 1937 | Jacques Brugnon (FRA)<br>*Paulette de St Ferréol (FRA)* |
| 1934 | André Martin-Legeay (FRA)<br>*Sylvia Henrotin (FRA)* | 1938 | Ronald Shayes (GBR)<br>Peggy Scriven (GBR) |
| 1935 | Jacques Brugnon (FRA)<br>Edith Belliard (FRA) | 1939 | Yvon Petra (FRA)<br>*Sylvia Henrotin (FRA)* |

| *en's Doubles* | *Ladies' Doubles* | *Mixed Doubles* |
| --- | --- | --- |
| muel Hardy (UA)<br>ancis Waller (AUS) | — | Samuel Hardy (USA)<br>*Madeline O'Neill (GBR)* |

| *en's Doubles* | *Ladies' Doubles* | *Mixed Doubles* |
| --- | --- | --- |
| arry Bacon (BRI)<br>eorge Hillyard (BRI) | — | George Hillyard (BRI)<br>*Blanche Hillyard (BRI)* |
| eginald Doherty (BRI)<br>ount Victor Voss (GER) | — | — |
| urence Doherty (BRI)<br>eginald Doherty (BRI) | — | E. Robinson (BRI)<br>Vera Warden (USA) |
| eginald Doherty (BRI)<br>ount Victor Voss (GER) | — | — |
| urence Doherty (BRI)<br>eginald Doherty (BRI) | — | George Hillyard (BRI)<br>*Blanche Hillyard (BRI)* |
| eginald Doherty (BRI)<br>eorge Hillyard (BRI) | — | Reginald Doherty (BRI)<br>*Countess Clara Schulenburg (GER)* |
| dney Smith (BRI)<br>ank Riseley (BRI) | — | Sidney Smith (BRI)<br>*Ruth Winch (BRI)* |
| urence Doherty (BRI)<br>eginald Doherty (BRI) | — | Laurence Doherty (BRI)<br>K. Kentish (BRI) |

| Year | Date | Men's Singles | Ladies' Singles |
|------|------|---------------|-----------------|
| 1905 | 3-11 March | Laurence Doherty (BRI) | Dorothea Douglass (BRI) |
| 1906 | 22-28 February | Laurence Doherty (BRI) | Gladys Eastlake-Smith (BRI) |
| 1907 | 4-10 March | Major Ritchie (BRI) | Gladys Eastlake-Smith (BRI) |
| 1908 | 24 February-1 March | Anthony Wilding (NZL) | Gladys Eastlake-Smith (BRI) |
| 1909 | 22-27 February | Frederick Alexander (USA) | Alice Greene (BRI) |
| 1910 | 21-26 February | Max Decugis (FRA) | Rosamund Salusbury (BRI) |
| 1911 | 27 February-5 March | Anthony Wilding (NZL) | Rosamund Salusbury (BRI) |
| 1912 | 12-18 February | Anthony Wilding (NZL) | Jessie Tripp (BRI) |
| 1913 | 24 February-1 March | Anthony Wilding (NZL) | *Madeline O'Neill* (GBR) |
| 1914 | 23 February-3 March | Anthony Wilding (NZL) | *Dorothea Chambers* (BRI) |
| 1919 | 3-9 March | Nicholas Mishu (ROM) | Suzanne Lenglen (FRA) |
| 1920 | 1-7 March | Gordon Lowe (BRI) | Suzanne Lenglen (FRA) |
| 1921 | 28 February-6 March | Gordon Lowe (BRI) | Suzanne Lenglen (FRA) |
| 1922 | 27 February-5 March (some early matches played on Condamine courts) | Count Mimo Balbi (ITA) | Elizabeth Ryan (USA) |
| 1923 | 26 February-4 March | Gordon Lowe (GBR) | Kathleen McKane (GBR) |
| 1924 | 25 February-2 March (The men's singles and mixed doubles finals were decided at the Nice LTC because of rain) | Leighton Crawford (GBR) | Elizabeth Ryan (USA) |
| 1925 | 23 February-1 March | *Abandoned at semi-final stage – rain* | *Divided – rain* Winifred Beamish (GBR) Elizabeth Ryan (USA) |

★ Venues:

1896-1905: Hotel de Paris

1906-1914, 1920: Condamine

1919, 1921-1927: La Festa

1928: La Festa Country Club

1929-1939: Monte Carlo Country Club

1920-1939: Monte Carlo Championships

Note: married ladies are shown in *italics*

| Men's Doubles | Ladies' Doubles | Mixed Doubles |
|---|---|---|
| ...urence Doherty (BRI)<br>...eginald Doherty (BRI) | — | Roy Allen (BRI)<br>Dorothea Douglass (BRI) |
| ...urence Doherty (BRI)<br>...ilberforce Eaves (AUS) | — | Laurence Doherty (BRI)<br>Gladys Eastlake-Smith (BRI) |
| ...urence Doherty (BRI)<br>...ajor Ritchie (BRI) | — | Laurence Doherty (BRI)<br>Gladys Eastlake-Smith (BRI) |
| ...ajor Ritchie (BRI)<br>...nthony Wilding (NZL) | — | Laurence Doherty (BRI)<br>Gladys Eastlake-Smith (BRI) |
| ...urence Doherty (BRI)<br>...ajor Ritchie (BRI) | — | Wallis Myers (BRI)<br>Jessie Tripp (BRI) |
| ...anley Doust (AUS)<br>...allis Myers (BRI) | — | Max Decugis (FRA)<br>*Marie Decugis* (FRA) |
| ...ajor Ritchie (BRI)<br>...nthony Wilding (NZL) | — | Heinrich Kleinschroth (GER)<br>*Hedwig Neresheimer* (GER) |
| ...ax Decugis (FRA)<br>...aurice Germot (FRA) | — | Anthony Wilding (NZL)<br>Madaline Rieck (GER) |
| ...einrich Kleinschroth (GER)<br>...eidrich Rahe (GER) | — | Anthony Wilding (NZL)<br>Elizabeth Ryan (USA) |
| ...einrich Kleinschroth (GER)<br>...lix Poulin (FRA) | Elizabeth Ryan (USA)<br>Jessie Tripp (BRI) | Max Decugis (FRA)<br>Elizabeth Ryan (USA) |
| ...ax Decugis (FRA)<br>... Fremeaux (FRA) | Suzanne Lenglen (FRA)<br>Mlle G. Nativelle (FRA) | Max Decugis (FRA)<br>Suzanne Lenglen (FRA) |
| ...mbrose Dudley (BRI)<br>...ordon Lowe (BRI) | Suzanne Lenglen (FRA)<br>Elizabeth Ryan (USA) | Pierre Albarran (FRA)<br>Suzanne Lenglen (FRA) |
| ...gernon Kingscote (BRI)<br>...allis Myers (BRI) | Suzanne Lenglen (FRA)<br>Elizabeth Ryan (USA) | Algernon Kingscote (BRI)<br>Suzanne Lenglen (FRA) |
| ...ain Gerbault (FRA)<br>...n Samazeuilh (FRA) | Elizabeth Ryan (USA)<br>*Phyllis Satterthwaite* (GBR) | Rupert Wertheim (AUS)<br>Elizabeth Ryan (USA) |
| ...ain Gerbault (FRA)<br>...berto de Morpurgo (ITA) | Suzanne Lenglen (FRA)<br>Elizabeth Ryan (USA) | Erik Tegner (DEN)<br>Kathleen McKane (GBR) |
| ...once Aslangul (FRA)<br>...ighton Crawford (GBR) | Dorothy Shepherd-Barron (GBR)<br>Elizabeth Ryan (USA) | Ernest Lamb (GBR)<br>*Dorothea Chambers* (GBR) |

...OUBLES ABANDONED – RAIN

**MONTE CARLO**   **Various venues★**   **Monte Carlo Championships**

| Year | Date | Men's Singles | Ladies' Singles |
|------|------|---------------|-----------------|
| 1926 | 22-28 February | Bela von Kehrling (HUN) | Helen Wills (USA) |
| 1927 | 21-27 February | Bela von Kehrling (HUN) | Elizabeth Ryan (USA) |
| 1928 | 27 Feburary-4 March | Henri Cochet (FRA) | Eileen Bennett (GBR) |
| 1929 | 25 February-3 March | Henri Cochet (FRA) | Betty Nuthall (GBR) |
| 1930 | 24 February-2 March | William Tilden (USA) | Cilly Aussem (GER) |
| 1931 | 23 February-1 March | Henri Cochet (FRA) | *Simone Mathieu* (FRA) |
| 1932 | 22-28 February | Roderich Menzel (TCH) | *Simone Mathieu* (FRA) |
| 1933 | 27 February-5 March | Henry Austin (GBR) | Lolette Payot (SUI) |
| 1934 | 26 February-6 March | Henry Austin (GBR) | *Syliva Henrotin* (FRA) |
| 1935 | 25 February-4 March | Giovanni Palmieri (ITA) | *Simone Mathieu* (FRA) |
| 1936 | 24 February-1 March | Gottfried von Cramm (GER) | *Simone Mathieu* (FRA) |
| 1937 | 22-28 February | Gottfried von Cramm (GER) | *Hilde Sperling* (DEN) |
| 1938 | 28 February-6 March | Franjo Puncec (YUG) | Jadwiga Jedrzejowska (POL) |
| 1939 | 27 February-5 March | Pierre Pelizza (FRA) | *Hilde Sperling* (DEN) |

★ Venues:

1896-1905:
Hotel de Paris

1906-1914, 1920:
Condamine

1919, 1921-1927:
La Festa

1928:
La Festa Country Club

1929-1939: Monte Carlo
Country Club

1920-1939: Monte Carlo
Championships

Note: married ladies are
shown in *italics*

| Men's Doubles | Ladies' Doubles | Mixed Doubles |
|---|---|---|
| Bela von Kehrling (HUN)<br>Uberto de Morpurgo (ITA) | Hélène Contostavlos (GRE)<br>Helen Wills (USA) | Bela von Kehrling (HUN)<br>*Nelly Neppach* (GER) |
| Bela von Kehrling (HUN)<br>Uberto de Morpurgo (ITA) | *Dorothea Chambers* (GBR)<br>Elizabeth Ryan (USA) | — |
| Jack Hillyard (GBR)<br>Jan Kozeluh (TCH) | *Divided – no time*<br>Peggy Saunders (GBR)<br>Cristobel Hardie (GBR)/<br>*Phyllis Satterthwaite* (GBR)<br>Ermyntrude Harvey (GBR) | *Rain – final played at Menton LTC*<br>Henri Cochet (FRA)<br>Eileen Bennett (GBR) |
| Bela von Kehrling (GBR)<br>Uberto de Morpurgo (ITA) | Joan Fry (GBR)<br>Marjorie Morrill (USA) | Henri Cochet (FRA)<br>Eileen Bennett (GBR) |
| Wilbur Coen (USA)<br>Uberto de Morpurgo (ITA) | Simone Barbier (FRA)<br>Doris Metaxa (FRA) | René de Buzelet (FRA)<br>Doris Metaxa (FRA) |
| Hermann Artens (AUT)<br>Bela von Kehrling (HUN) | *Phyllis Satterthwaite* (GBR)<br>Muriel Thomas (GBR) | Henri Cochet (FRA)<br>*Eileen Fearnley Whittingstall* (GBR) |
| Jacques Brugnon (FRA)<br>Enrique Maier (ESP) | *Doris Burke* (USA)<br>Lucia Valerio (ITA) | Henri Cochet (FRA)<br>Colette Rosambert (FRA) |

DOUBLES ABANDONED – RAIN

| Men's Doubles | Ladies' Doubles | Mixed Doubles |
|---|---|---|
| Henry Austin (GBR)<br>George Rogers (IRL) | Elizabeth Ryan (USA)<br>Muriel Thomas (GBR) | Gottfried von Cramm (GER)<br>Elizabeth Ryan (USA) |
| Josef Caska (TCH)<br>Giovanni Palmieri (ITA) | *Simone Mathieu* (FRA)<br>Muriel Thomas (GBR) | Henry Austin (GBR)<br>Adeline Yorke (GBR) |
| Christian Boussus (FRA)<br>Jan Lesueur (FRA) | Simone Mathieu (FRA)<br>*Josanne de Meulemeester* (BEL) | André Martin-Legeay (FRA)<br>*Simone Mathieu* (FRA) |
| Ronald Butler (GBR)<br>Patrick Hughes (GBR) | *Simone Mathieu* (FRA)<br>*Hilde Sperling* (DEN) | *Divided – Four semi-finalists* |
| Kho Sin Kie (CHN)<br>George Rogers (IRL) | Jadwiga Jedrzejowska (POL)<br>Muriel Thomas (GBR) | Jozef Hebda (POL)<br>Jadwiga Jedrzejowska (POL) |
| Pierre Pelizza (FRA)<br>Yvon Petra (FRA) | *Simone Mathieu* (FRA)<br>*Hilde Sperling* (DEN) | Divided<br>André Martin-Legeay (FRA)<br>*Sylvia Henrotin* (FRA)/<br>Patrick Hughes (GBR)<br>*Simone Mathieu* (FRA) |

## MONTE CARLO

| | Butler International Trophy | Beaumont International Cup |
|---|---|---|
| 1925 | Uberto de Morpurgo (ITA)<br>Placido Gaslini (ITA) | — |
| 1926 | Uberto de Morpurgo (ITA)<br>Placido Gaslini (ITA) | Suzanne Lenglen (FRA)<br>Diddie Vlasto (FRA) |
| 1927 | Jacques Brugnon (FRA)<br>Henri Cochet (FRA) | *Elizabeth Corbiere* (USA)<br>Elizabeth Ryan (USA) |
| 1928 | René de Buzelet (FRA)<br>Henri Cochet (FRA) | *Dorothea Chambers* (GBR)<br>Ermyntrude Harvey (GBR) |
| 1929 | Jacques Brugnon (FRA)<br>Henri Cochet (FRA) | *Phyllis Covell* (GBR)<br>Betty Nuthall (GBR) |
| 1930 | Wilbur Coen (USA)<br>William Tilden (USA) | Simone Barbier (FRA)<br>*Simone Mathieu* (FRA) |
| 1931 | Enrique Maier (ESP)<br>Francisco Sindreau (ESP) | Betty Nuthall (GBR)<br>*Eileen Fearnley-Whittingstall* (GBR) |
| 1932 | Jacques Brugnon (FRA)<br>Henri Cochet (FRA) | *Simone Mathieu* (FRA)<br>Colette Rosambert (FRA) |

## MONTE CARLO  Various venues★  Easter tournaments

| Year | Date | Men's Singles | Ladies' Singles |
|---|---|---|---|
| 1919 | 21-26 April | — | — |
| 1920 | 3-9 May | TOURNAMENT SCHEDULED BUT CANCELLED | |
| 1921 | 18-24 April | Jack Hillyard (BRI) | Suzanne Lenglen (FRA) |
| 1922 | 17-23 April | Charles Aeschliman (SUI) | Suzanne Lenglen (FRA) |
| 1923 | 9-15 April | Jack Hillyard (GBR) | Lili de Alvarez (ESP) |
| 1924 | 7-13 April | Charles Aeschliman (SUI) | *Phyllis Covell* (GBR) |
| 1925 | 6-12 April | Henry Mayes (CAN) | *Phyllis Satterthwaite* (GBR) |
| 1926 | 5-11 April | Uberto de Morpurgo (ITA) | Lili de Alvarez (ESP) |

★ Venues:

1919-1927: La Festa

1928: La Festa Country Club

1929-1939: Monte Carlo Country Club

Note: married ladies are shown in *italics*

|      | **Butler International Trophy** | **Beaumont International Cup** |
|------|---------------------------------|-------------------------------|
| 1933 | Roland Journu (FRA) | *Dorothy Burke (USA)* |
|      | André Martin-Legeay (FRA) | *Elizabeth Ryan (USA)* |
| 1934 | Ladislav Hecht (TCH) | Muriel Thomas (GBR) |
|      | Roderich Menzel (TCH) | Adeline Yorke (GBR) |
| 1935 | André Martin-Legeay (FRA) | Muriel Thomas (GBR) |
|      | Jean Lesueur (FRA) | Adeline Yorke (GBR) |
| 1936 | André Martin-Legeay (FRA) | Edith Belliard (FRA) |
|      | Jean Lesueur (FRA) | *Simone Mathieu (FRA)* |
| 1937 | Gottfried von Cramm (GER) | *Colette Boegner (FRA)* |
|      | Henner Henkel (GER) | *Simone Mathieu (FRA)* |
| 1938 | Henri Bolelli (FRA) | *Colette Boegner (FRA)* |
|      | Pierre Pellizza (FRA) | *Simone Mathieu (FRA)* |
| 1939 | Jean Lesueur (FRA) | **Iliffe Cup** |
|      | Yvon Petra (FRA) | *Nellie Landry (FRA)* |
|      |  | *Simone Mathieu (FRA)* |

| n's Doubles | Ladies' Doubles | Mixed Doubles |
|-------------|-----------------|---------------|
| ·tram Marion Crawford | — | Bertram Marion Crawford (BRI) |
| ₹I) |  | Mlle Maubert (FRA) |
| H. Grace |  |  |
| ·arles Aeschliman (SUI) | — | Jack Hillyard (BRI) |
| ≮ Hillyard (BRI) |  | *Phyllis Satterthwaite (BRI)* |
| ·arles Aeschliman (SUI) | — | Alain Gerbault (FRA) |
| ·naldo Boyd (ARG) |  | Suzanne Lenglen (FRA) |
| ≮ Hillyard (GBR) | — | Charles Aeschliman (SUI) |
| ·arles Aeschliman (SUI) |  | Lili de Alvarez (ESP) |
| ·arles Aeschliman (SUI) | *Phyllis Covell (GBR)* | Charles Aeschliman (SUI) |
| ·on Roland de Graffenried | Edith Sigourney (USA) | Eleanor Goss (USA) |
| JI) |  |  |
| ·arles Aeschliman (SUI) | Suzanne Lenglen (FRA) | Lord George Cholmondeley (GBR) |
| n Tunis (USA) | *Phyllis Satterthwaite (GBR)* | Suzanne Lenglen (FRA) |
| ·erto de Morpurgo (ITA) | Suzanne Lenglen (FRA) | Uberto de Morpurgo (ITA) |
| ≮ Hillyard (GBR) | *Phyllis Satterthwaite (GBR)* | *Phyllis Satterthwaite (GBR)* |

**MONTE CARLO**  Various venues★  Easter tournaments

| Year | Date | Men's Singles | Ladies' Singles |
|------|------|---------------|-----------------|
| 1927 | 11-17 April | Erik Worm (DEN) | Lili de Alvarez (ESP) |
| 1928 | 9-15 April | René Lacoste (FRA) | Lili de Alvarez (ESP) |
| 1929 | 1-7 April | Erik Worm (DEN) | *Simone Mathieu* (FRA) |
| 1930 | 21-27 April | William Tilden (USA) | Lili de Alvarez (ESP) |
| 1931 | 6-12 April | Jiro Satoh (JPN) | Cilly Aussem (GER) |
| 1932★★ | 28 March-3 April | Beni Berthet (FRA) | Lolette Payot (SUI) |
| 1933 | 17-23 April | Jiro Satoh (JPN) | *Sylvia Henrotin* (FRA) |
| 1934 | 2-8 April | Wilmer Hines (USA) | *Sylvia Henrotin* (FRA) |
| 1935 | 22-28 April | *Divided – unfd. rain* <br> Jack Crawford (AUS) <br> Vivian McGrath (AUS) | *Simone Mathieu* (FRA) |
| 1936 | 13-19 April | Valentino Taroni (ITA) | *Simone Mathieu* (FRA) |
| 1937 | 30 March-4 April | Adam Baworowski (AUT) | Alice Weiwers (LUX) |
| 1938 | 18-24 April | Bernard Destremau (FRA) | *Simone Mathieu* (FRA) |
| 1939 | 10-16 April | Paul Feret (FRA) | *Simone Mathieu* (FRA) |

★ Venues:

1919-1927: La Festa

1928: La Festa Country Club

1929-1939: Monte Carlo Country Club

★★ 1932-1934: Beausoleil Championships

Note: married ladies are shown in *italics*

**PRIX DE FAMILLE**

| | |
|------|------|
| 1928 | F.F. Furnivall and Miss D. Furnivall (GBR) |
| 1929 | Eliot Crawshay-Williams and *Weeta Crawshay-Williams* (GBR) |
| 1930 | M. Sigart and Josanne Sigart (BEL) |
| 1931 | Beni Berthet and Rosie Berthet (FRA) |
| 1932 | Beni Berthet and Rosie Berthet (FRA) |
| 1933 | Fernand Henrotin and *Syliva Henrotin* (FRA) |
| 1934 | Max Ellmer and Miss Ellmer (SUI) |
| 1935 | René Mathieu and *Simone Mathieu* (FRA) |

| Men's Doubles | Ladies' Doubles | Mixed Doubles |
| --- | --- | --- |
| Charles Aeschliman (SUI)<br>...ck Hillyard (GBR) | Elizabeth Ryan (USA)<br>*Phyllis Satterthwaite (GBR)* | Erik Worm (DEN)<br>Elizabeth Ryan (USA) |
| ...ohn Hawkes (AUS)<br>...ck Crawford (AUS) | Lili de Alvarez (ESP)<br>*Phyllis Satterthwaite (GBR)* | John Hawkes (AUS)<br>Lili de Alvarez (ESP) |
| ...ené Gallepe (MON)<br>...rik Worm (DEN) | Elizabeth Ryan (USA)<br>*Phyllis Satterthwaite (GBR)* | George O'Connell (USA)<br>Elizabeth Ryan (USA) |
| ...illiam Tilden (USA)<br>...ilbur Coen (USA) | *Phyllis Satterthwaite (GBR)*<br>Josanne Sigart (BEL) | William Tilden (USA)<br>Lili de Alvarez (ESP) |
| ...an Lesueur (FRA)<br>...ntoine Gentien (FRA) | *Phyllis Satterthwaite (GBR)*<br>*Sylvia Henrotin (FRA)* | Jean Lesueur (FRA)<br>*Simone Mathieu (FRA)* |
| ...eorge Rogers (IRL)<br>...ul Feret (FRA) | Simone Mathieu (FRA)<br>Colette Rosambert (FRA) | André Martin-Legeay (FRA)<br>*Simone Mathieu (FRA)* |
| ...o Satoh (JPN)<br>...yosuke Nunoi (JPN) | *Sylvia Henrotin (FRA)*<br>Simone Barbier (FRA) | Charles Aeschliman (SUI)<br>Muriel Thomas (GBR) |
| ...harles Aeschliman (SUI)<br>...ector Fisher (SUI) | *Sylvia Henrotin (FRA)*<br>*Doris Andrus (USA)* | Hector Fisher (SUI)<br>*Doris Andrus (USA)* |
| ...ilmer Hines (USA)<br>...enry Culley (USA) | *Simone Mathieu (FRA)*<br>Edith Belliard (FRA) | Harry Hopman (AUS)<br>*Simone Mathieu (FRA)* |
| ...ul Feret (FRA)<br>...arcel Bernard (FRA) | *Simone Mathieu (FRA)*<br>Edith Belliard (FRA) | Marcel Bernard (FRA)<br>*Simone Mathieu (FRA)* |
| ...am Baworowski (AUT)<br>...org von Metaxa (AUT) | Joan Ingram (GBR)<br>*Phyllis Satterthwaite (GBR)* | Georg von Metaxa (AUT)<br>Joan Ingram (GBR) |
| ...rnard Destremau (FRA)<br>...toine Gentien (FRA) | Cosette Saint Omer Roy (FRA)<br>*Simone Mathieu (FRA)* | Antoine Gentien (FRA)<br>Alice Weiwers (LUX) |
| ...bert Abdesselam (FRA)<br>...ul Feret (FRA) | Cosette Saint Omer Roy (FRA)<br>Alice Weiwers (LUX) | Paul Feret (FRA)<br>Elfriede Kriegs-Au (AUT) |

**MONTE CARLO**   Various venues★   **Monaco Championships**

| Year | Date | Men's Singles | Ladies' Singles |
|------|------|---------------|-----------------|
| 1922 | 26 December–<br>2 Jan (1921) | Lord George Rocksavage (BRI) | *Phyllis Satterthwaite (BRI)* |
| 1923 | 25-31 December (1922) | Leighton Crawford (GBR) | *Phyllis Satterthwaite (GBR)* |
| 1924★★ | 24-30 December (1923) | Col. Charles Brierley (GBR) | Elizabeth Ryan (USA) |
| 1925 | 15 -21 December (1924) | Placido Gaslini (ITA) | Lili de Alvarez (ESP) |
| 1926 | 14-20 December (1925) | Jacques Brugnon (FRA) | *Divided – rain*<br>*Phyllis Satterthwaite (GBR)*<br>*Elizabeth Macready (FRA)* |
| 1927 | 20-26 December (1926) | Jacques Brugnon (FRA) | *Phyllis Satterthwaite (GBR)* |
| 1928 | 17-24 December (1927) | Henry Mayes (CAN) | Lili de Alvarez (ESP) |
| 1929 | 14-20 January | Uberto de Morpurgo (ITA) | Esna Boyd (AUS) |
| 1930 | 6-12 January | William Tilden (USA) | Elizabeth Ryan (USA) |

★ Venues:

1922-1927: La Festa

1928-1929: La Festa Country Club

1930: Monte Carlo Country Club

★★ Some matches played on Condamine Courts

Note: married ladies are shown in *italics*

**PRIX DE FAMILLE**

| | | |
|------|------|------|
| 1927 | Brame Hillyard and *Mrs Hillyard* (GBR) | |
| 1928 | Brame Hillyard and *Mrs Hillyard* (GBR) | |
| 1929 | Beverley Covell and *Phyllis Covell* (GBR) | |
| 1930 | John Pittman and *Elsie Pittman* (GBR) | |

| en's Doubles | Ladies' Doubles | Mixed Doubles |
|---|---|---|
| | — | — |
| k Hillyard (GBR) ighton Crawford (GBR) | — | Jack Hillyard (GBR) *Phyllis Satterthwaite* (GBR) |
| thur Lovibond (USA) k Hillyard (GBR) | — | Jack Hillyard (GBR) *Phyllis Satterthwaite* (GBR) |
| oberto Bocciardo (ITA) ount Leonardo Bonzi (ITA) | Lili de Alvarez (ESP) *Phyllis Satterthwaite* (GBR) | Bertram Marion Crawford (GBR) Lili de Alvarez (ESP) |
| ques Brugnon (FRA) ancis Fisher (NZL) | Suzanne Lenglen (FRA) *Phyllis Satterthwaite* (GBR) | Jacques Brugnon (FRA) Suzanne Lenglen (FRA) |
| ik Worm (DEN) ené Gallepe (MON) | *Phyllis Satterthwaite* (GBR) Eden Petchell (GBR) | Jacques Brugnon (FRA) *Phyllis Satterthwaite* (GBR) |
| *andoned – rain* | Lili de Alvarez (ESP) *Phyllis Satterthwaite* (GBR) | Jack Hillyard (GBR) *Phyllis Satterthwaite* (GBR) |
| ques Brugnon (FRA) atoine Gentien (FRA) | *Phyllis Satterthwaite* (GBR) Esna Boyd (AUS) | Charles Aeschliman (SUI) Esna Boyd (AUS) |
| illiam Tilden (USA) harles Kingsley (GBR) | *Phyllis Satterthwaite* (GBR) Elizabeth Ryan (USA) | — |

## MONTE CARLO    Condamine Courts    Monegasque Championships

| Year | Date | Men's Singles | Ladies' Singles |
|------|------|---------------|-----------------|
| 1931 | 16-23 February | Enrique Maier (ESP) | *Simone Mathieu (FRA)* |
| 1932 | 11-17 January | George Rogers (IRL) | Elizabeth Ryan (USA) |
| 1933 | 9-15 January | Vladimir Landau (MON) | *Phyllis Satterthwaite (GBR)* |
| 1934 | 8-14 January | Charles Aeschliman (SUI) | Cosette Saint Omer Roy (FRA) |
| 1935 | 7-13 January | Vladimir Landau (MON) | *Simone Mathieu (FRA)* |
| 1936 | 6-12 January | Gaston Medecin (MON) | *Simone Mathieu (FRA)* |
| 1937 | 4-10 January | Kho Sin Kie (CHN) | *Simone Mathieu (FRA)* |
| 1938 | 17-23 January | Kho Sin Kie (CHN) | Jeannette Poncelet (FRA) |
| 1939 | 2-7 January | Jean Borotra (FRA) | Alice Weiwers (LUX) |

## MONTE CARLO    Monte Carlo Country Club    Other tournaments

| Year | Date | Men's Singles | Ladies' Singles |
|------|------|---------------|-----------------|
| 1935 | 31 December–6 January (1934) | Jacques Bonte (FRA) | *Simone Mathieu (FRA)* |
| 1936 | 23-29 December (1935) | ABANDONED – VERY WET WEATHER | |
| 1936 | 12-18 January | Edouard Lotan (FRA) | *Simone Mathieu (FRA)* |
| 1937 | TOURNAMENT NOT SCHEDULED | | |
| 1938 | 24-30 January | Kho Sin Kie (CHN) | Alice Weiwers (LUX) |
| 1939 | 23-29 January | Constantin Tanacescu (ROM) | Alice Weiwers (LUX) |

Note: married ladies are shown in *italics*

| en's Doubles | Ladies' Doubles | Mixed Doubles |
|---|---|---|
| ristian Boussus (FRA) n Lesueur (FRA) | Cilly Aussem (GER) Lucia Valerio (ITA) | — |
| arles Aeschliman (SUI) ik Worm (DEN) | — | George Rogers (IRL) Elizabeth Ryan (USA) |
| arles Aeschliman (SUI) ouard Lotan (FRA) | — | Jack Hillyard (GBR) Elizabeth Ryan (USA) |
| arles Aeschliman (SUI) ilmer Hines (USA) | — | Vladimir Landau (MON) *Paulette de Saint Ferréol* (FRA) |
| adimir Landau (MON) ston Medecin (MON) | — | Vladimir Landau (MON) *Simone Mathieu* (FRA) |
| k Hillyard (GBR) dré Jacquemet (FRA) | — | Vladimir Landau (MON) *Simone Mathieu* (FRA) |
| ené Gallepe (MON) ston Medecin (MON) | — | René Gallepe (MON) *Simone Mathieu* (FRA) |
| o Sin Kie (CHN) orge Rogers (IRL) | — | Kho Sin Kie (CHN) Nancy Liebert (GBR) |
| Badin (ROM) nstantin Tanacescu (ROM) | — | Constantin Tanacescu (ROM) Alice Weiwers (LUX) |

| en's Doubles | Ladies' Doubles | Mixed Doubles |
|---|---|---|
| ouard Lotan (FRA) dré Jacquemet (FRA) | — | — |
| | — | Edouard Lotan (FRA) *Simone Mathieu* (FRA) |
| ston Medecin (MON) eco Noghes (MON) | Cosette Saint Omer Roy (FRA) Alice Weiwers (LUX) | Kho Sin Kie (CHN) Nancy Liebert (GBR) |
| orge Rogers (IRL) o Sin Kie (CHN) | Cosette Saint Omer Roy (FRA) Alice Weiwers (LUX) | George Rogers (IRL) *Simone Mathieu* (FRA) |

| Year | Date | Men's Singles | Ladies' Singles |
|------|------|---------------|-----------------|
| 1895 | 11-14 March | H. Thomas (FRA) | — |
| 1896 | — | — | — |
| 1897 | 15-21 March | Reginald Doherty (BRI) | — |
| 1898 | 7-16 March | Laurence Doherty (BRI) | — |
| 1899 | 13-19 March | Laurence Doherty (BRI) | Mildred Brooksmith (BRI) |
| 1900 | 19-31 March | Laurence Doherty (BRI) | *Countess Clara Schulenburg (GER* |
| 1901 | 18-24 March | Laurence Doherty (BRI) | *Blanche Hillyard* (BRI) |
| 1902 | 10-18 March | Laurence Doherty (BRI) | *Countess Clara Schulenburg (GER* |
| 1903 | 9-22 March | Laurence Doherty (BRI) | Toupie Lowther (BRI) |
| 1904 | 7-17 March | Laurence Doherty (BRI) | *Countess Clara Schulenburg (GER* |
| 1905 | 13-25 March | Laurence Doherty (BRI) | Constance Wilson (BRI) |
| 1906 | 12-19 March | Laurence Doherty (BRI) | Toupie Lowther (BRI) |
| 1907 | 11-17 March | Anthony Wilding (NZL) | Gladys Eastlake-Smith (BRI) |
| 1908 | 9-18 March | Anthony Wilding (NZL) | *Dorothea Chambers* (BRI) |
| 1909 | 8-15 March | Frederick Alexander (USA) | *Countess Clara Schulenburg (GER* |
| 1910 | 10-15 March | Max Decugis (FRA) | Rosamund Salusbury (BRI) |
| 1911 | 13-19 March | Anthony Wilding (NZL) | *Dagmar von Krohn* (GER) |
| 1912 | 4-10 March | Max Decugis (FRA) | Jessie Tripp (BRI) |
| 1913 | 10-17 March | Max Decugis (FRA) | *Dagmar von Krohn* (GER) |
| 1914 | 9-15 March | Anthony Wilding (NZL) | *Dorothea Chambers* (BRI) |

From 1899 – South of France Championships

★Venues:
1895-1921: Platz Mozart
1922-1939: Parc Imperial

Note: married ladies are shown in *italics*

| Men's Doubles | Ladies' Doubles | Mixed Doubles |
|---|---|---|
| — | — | — |
| — | — | |
| — | — | — |
| — | — | — |
| — | — | — |
| Laurence Doherty (BRI) Reginald Doherty (BRI) | — | — |
| Laurence Doherty (BRI) Reginald Doherty (BRI) | — | — |
| Laurence Doherty (BRI) Reginald Doherty (BRI) | — | — |
| Laurence Doherty (BRI) Reginald Doherty (BRI) | — | Reginald Doherty (BRI) *Countess Clara Schulenburg* (GER) |
| Laurence Doherty (BRI) Reginald Doherty (BRI) | — | Reginald Doherty (BRI) *Countess Clara Schulenburg* (GER) |
| Laurence Doherty (BRI) Reginald Doherty (BRI) | — | Reginald Doherty (BRI) *Countess Clara Schulenburg* (GER) |
| Laurence Doherty (BRI) Wilberforce Eaves (AUS) | — | Laurence Doherty (BRI) *Countess Clara Schulenburg* (GER) |
| Laurence Doherty (BRI) Major Ritchie (BRI) | — | Anthony Wilding (NZL) Gladys Eastlake-Smith (BRI) |
| Major Ritchie (BRI) Anthony Wilding (NZL) | — | Anthony Wilding (NZL) *Dorothea Chambers* (BRI) |
| Frederick Alexander (USA) Major Ritchie (BRI) | — | Laurence Doherty (BRI) *Countess Clara Schulenburg* (GER) |
| Max Decugis (FRA) Major Ritchie (BRI) | — | Artemas Holmes (USA) Mildred Brooksmith (BRI) |
| Major Ritchie (BRI) Anthony Wilding (NZL) | — | Max Decugis (FRA) *Marie Decugis* (FRA) |
| Max Decugis (FRA) Maurice Germot (FRA) | — | Wallis Myers (BRI) Jessie Tripp (BRI) |
| Friedrich Rahe (GER) Heinrich Kleinschroth (GER) | — | Count Ludwig Salm (AUT) Elizabeth Ryan (USA) |
| Craig Biddle (USA) Anthony Wilding (NZL) | — | Max Decugis (FRA) Elizabeth Ryan (USA) |

**NICE   Nice LTC   Various venues★   South of France Championships**

| Year | Date | Men's Singles | Ladies' Singles |
|------|------|---------------|-----------------|
| 1919 | 17-25 March | Max Decugis (FRA) | Suzanne Lenglen (FRA) |
| 1920 | 15-21 March | Count Mikhail Soumarokoff (RUS) | *Winifred Beamish* (BRI) |
| 1921 | 14-20 March | Count Mikhail Soumarokoff (RUS) | Suzanne Lenglen (FRA) |
| 1922 | 13-19 March | Count Mikhail Soumarokoff (RUS) | Elizabeth Ryan (USA) |
| 1923 | 12-18 March | Gordon Lowe (GBR) | Suzanne Lenglen (FRA) |
| 1924 | 10-16 March | René Lacoste (FRA) | Suzanne Lenglen (FRA) |
| 1925 | 9-15 March | René Lacoste (FRA) | Suzanne Lenglen (FRA) |
| 1926 | 8-14 March | Uberto de Morpurgo (ITA) | Helen Wills (USA) |
| 1927 | 7-13 March | Hermann Artens (AUT) | Lili de Alvarez (ESP) |
| 1928 | 12-18 March | Charles Aeschliman (SUI) | *Paula von Reznicek* (GER) |
| 1929 | 11-17 March | Emmanuel du Plaix (FRA) | *Paula von Reznicek* GER) |

(originally scheduled for February 11-17, but abandoned – snow)

| Year | Date | Men's Singles | Ladies' Singles |
|------|------|---------------|-----------------|
| 1930 | 10-16 February | William Tilden (USA) | Cilly Aussem (GER) |
| 1931 | 9-15 February | George Rogers (IRL) | *Phyllis Satterthwaite* (GBR) |
| 1932 | 8-14 February | Jacques Brugnon (FRA) | Elizabeth Ryan (USA) |
| 1933 | 13-19 February | George Rogers (IRL) | Sheila Hewitt (GBR) |
| 1934 | 12-18 February | George Rogers (IRL) | Muriel Thomas (GBR) |

From 1899 – South of France Championships

★Venues:
1895-1921: Platz Mozart
1922-1939: Parc Imperial

Note: married ladies are shown in *italics*

| Men's Doubles | Ladies' Doubles | Mixed Doubles |
|---|---|---|
| Max Decugis (FRA)<br>Georges Manset (FRA) | — | Max Decugis (FRA)<br>Suzanne Lenglen (FRA) |
| Pierre Albarran (FRA)<br>Alain Gerbault (FRA) | — | Pierre Albarran (FRA)<br>Suzanne Lenglen (FRA) |
| Alain Gerbault (FRA)<br>Count Mikhail Soumarokoff (RUS) | Suzanne Lenglen (FRA)<br>Elizabeth Ryan (USA) | Count Mikhail Soumarokoff (RUS)<br>Suzanne Lenglen (FRA) |
| Henri Cochet (FRA)<br>Lord George Rocksavage (GBR) | Suzanne Lenglen (FRA)<br>Elizabeth Ryan (USA) | Count Mikhail Soumarokoff (RUS)<br>Suzanne Lenglen (FRA) |
| Leighton Crawford (GBR)<br>Wallis Myers (GBR) | Suzanne Lenglen (FRA)<br>Elizabeth Ryan (USA) | Randolph Lycett (GBR)<br>Elizabeth Ryan (USA) |
| René Lacoste (FRA)<br>Jean Washer (BEL) | Suzanne Lenglen (FRA)<br>Elizabeth Ryan (USA) | Henri Cochet (FRA)<br>Suzanne Lenglen (FRA) |
| Charles Aeschliman (SUI)<br>René Lacoste (FRA) | Suzanne Lenglen (FRA)<br>Elizabeth Ryan (USA) | Charles Aeschliman (SUI)<br>Suzanne Lenglen (FRA) |
| Henri Cochet (FRA)<br>Uberto de Morpurgo (ITA) | *Dorothea Chambers* (GBR)<br>Ermyntrude Harvey (GBR) | Henri Cochet (FRA)<br>Diddie Vlasto (FRA) |
| Hermann Artens (AUT)<br>Count Ludwig Salm (AUT) | Elsie Goldsack (GBR)<br>Dorothy Shaw (GBR) | Charles Aeschliman (SUI)<br>Betty Nuthall (GBR) |
| Charles Aeschliman (SUI)<br>René Gallepe (MON) | Cilly Aussem (GER)<br>Betty Nuthall (GBR) | Charles Aeschliman (SUI)<br>*Elizabeth Corbiere* (USA) |
| Charles Aeschliman (SUI)<br>René Gallepe (MON) | *Phyllis Covell* (GBR)<br>Muriel Thomas (GBR) | Wilbur Coen (USA)<br>Cilly Aussem (GER) |
| Wilbur Coen (USA)<br>William Tilden (USA) | Phyllis Radcliffe (GBR)<br>Nancy Radcliffe Platt (GBR) | *Divided – no time*<br>Wilbur Coen (USA)<br>Cilly Aussem (GER)/<br>Eric Peters (GBR)<br>Joan Ridley (GBR) |
| Christian Boussus (FRA)<br>Emmanuel du Plaix (FRA) | Phyllis Satterthwaite (GBR)<br>Muriel Thomas (GBR) | Jack Hillyard (GBR)<br>Muriel Thomas (GBR) |
| Charles Aeschliman (SUI)<br>Edouard Lotan (FRA) | Elizabeth Ryan (USA)<br>Muriel Thomas (GBR) | Jacques Brugnon (FRA)<br>*Phyllis Satterthwaite* (GBR) |
| Charles Aeschliman (SUI)<br>Edouard Lotan (FRA) | Cilly Aussem (GER)<br>Elizabeth Ryan (USA) | Leonce Aslangul (FRA)<br>Margaret Scriven (GBR) |
| Henry Culley (USA)<br>Wilmer Hines (USA) | Elizabeth Ryan (USA)<br>Muriel Thomas (GBR) | Wilmer Hines (USA)<br>Muriel Thomas (GBR) |

**NICE   Nice LTC   Various venues★   South of France Championships**

| Year | Date | Men's Singles | Ladies' Singles |
|------|------|---------------|-----------------|
| 1935 | 11-17 February | Wilmer Hines (USA) | *Simone Mathieu* (FRA) |
| 1936 | 10-16 February | Jean Lesueur (FRA) | *Simone Mathieu* (FRA) |
| 1937 | 8-14 February | Kho Sin Kie (CHN) | *Simone Mathieu* (FRA) |
| 1938 | 14-20 February | Kho Sin Kie (CHN) | Gracyn Wheeler (USA) |
| 1939 | 13-19 February | Constantin Tanacescu (ROM) | *Simone Mathieu* (FRA) |

From 1899 – South of France Championships

★Venues:
1895-1921: Platz Mozart
1922-1939: Parc Imperial

**NICE   Nice LTC   Various venues★★   Other tournaments**

| Year | Date | Men's Singles | Ladies' Singles |
|------|------|---------------|-----------------|
| 1920 | 19-25 April | Gordon Lowe (BRI) | *Marcelle Gondoin* (FRA) |
| 1921 | 7-13 February | Gordon Lowe (BRI) | Suzanne Lenglen (FRA) |
| 1922 | 6-11 February | Count Mikhail Soumarokoff (RUS) | Elizabeth Ryan (USA) |
| 1923 | 5-11 February | Henry Mayes (CAN) | Suzanne Lenglen (FRA) |
| 1924 | 4-10 February | Leonce Aslangul (FRA) | Suzanne Lenglen (FRA) |
| 1925 | 8-14 December (1924) | Lyle Terrey (AUS) | *Phyllis Satterthwaite* (GBR) |
| 1925 | 2-8 February | Uberto de Morpurgo (ITA) | Suzanne Lenglen (FRA) |
| 1926 | 1-7 February | Uberto de Morpurgo (ITA) | Suzanne Lenglen (FRA) |
| 1927 | 7-13 February | Henri Cochet (FRA) | Eileen Bennett (GBR) |
| 1928 | 13-19 February | Henri Cochet (FRA) | Elizabeth Ryan (USA) |

★★ Venues:
1920-1922: Platz Mozart
1923-1939: Parc Imperial

★★★ 1933-1939:
Nice Championships

Note: married ladies are shown in *italics*

| en's Doubles | Ladies' Doubles | Mixed Doubles |
|---|---|---|
| cques Brugnon (FRA) | *Phyllis Satterthwaite (GBR)* | Jean Lesueur (FRA) |
| hristian Boussus (FRA) | Adeline Yorke (GBR) | Countess Gabriele Szapary (AUT) |
| ndré Martin-Legeay (FRA) | *Simone Mathieu (FRA)* | André Martin-Legeay (FRA) |
| an Lesueur (FRA) | Kay Stammers (GBR) | *Simone Mathieu (FRA)* |
| cques Brugnon (FRA) | Joan Ingram (GBR) | Jean Lesueur (FRA) |
| ho Sin Kie (CHN) | *Simone Mathieu (FRA)* | Joan Ingram (GBR) |
| cques Brugnon (FRA) | Jadwiga Jedrzejowska (POL) | Jacques Brugnon (FRA) |
| ho Sin Kie (CHN) | *Simone Mathieu (FRA)* | Jadwiga Jedrzejowska (POL) |
| ef Caska (TCH) | Cosette Saint Omer Roy (FRA) | Henner Henkel (GER) |
| dislav Hecht (TCH) | Alice Weiwers (LUX) | Gracyn Wheeler (USA) |

| n's Doubles | Ladies' Doubles | Mixed Doubles |
|---|---|---|
| | — | — |
| gernon Kingscote (BRI) | — | Algernon Kingscote (BRI) |
| rdon Lowe (BRI) | | Suzanne Lenglen (FRA) |
| in Gerbault (FRA) | — | Samuel Hardy (USA) |
| unt Mikhail Soumarokoff (US) | | Elizabeth Ryan (USA) |
| brose Dudley (GBR) | Suzanne Lenglen (FRA) | Henry Mayes (CAN) |
| in Gerbault (FRA) | Elizabeth Ryan (USA) | Suzanne Lenglen (FRA) |
| nce Aslangul (FRA) | *Dorothy Shepherd Barron (GBR)* | Charles Aeschliman (SUI) |
| est Lamb (GBR) | *Phyllis Satterthwaite (GBR)* | Suzanne Lenglen (FRA) |
| tram Marion Crawford (BR) | — | René Gallepe (MON) |
| né Gallepe (MON) | | M. Smailes (GBR) |
| ry Mayes (CAN) | Suzanne Lenglen (FRA) | Uberto de Morpurgo (ITA) |
| est Lamb (GBR) | Diddie Vlasto (FRA) | Suzanne Lenglen (FRA) |
| Hillyard (GBR) | Eileen Bennett (GBR) | Uberto de Morpurgo (ITA) |
| erto de Morpurgo (ITA) | Helen Wills (USA) | Suzanne Lenglen (FRA) |
| arles Aeschliman (SUI) | Eileen Bennett (GBR) | Henri Cochet (FRA) |
| ri Cochet (FRA) | *Phyllis Satterthwaite (GBR)* | Paulette Marjollet (FRA) |
| arles Aeschliman (SUI) | Eileen Bennett (GBR) | Henri Cochet (FRA) |
| a von Kehrling (HUN) | Elizabeth Ryan (USA) | Eileen Bennett (GBR) |

**NICE  Nice LTC  Various venues★★  Other tournaments**

| Year | Date | Men's Singles | Ladies' Singles |
|------|------|---------------|-----------------|
| 1929 | 11-17 March | (Date taken over by South of France Championships – abandoned due to snow, 11-17 February) | |
| 1930 | 10-16 March | William Tilden (USA) | *Simone Mathieu (FRA)* |
| 1931 | 9-15 March | Leonce Aslangul (FRA) | Betty Nuthall (GBR) |
| 1932 | 7-13 March | Giorgio de Stefani (ITA) | *Simone Mathieu (FRA)* |
| 1933★★★ | 13-19 March | Ignacy Tloczynski (POL) | Lolette Payot (SUI) |
| 1934 | 13-18 March | Giorgio de Stefani (ITA) | *Phyllis Satterthwaite (GBR)* |
| 1935 | 1-7 April | Karel Pachovsky (TCH) | *Simone Mathieu (FRA)* |
| 1936 | 6-12 April | Bernard Destremau (FRA) | *Simone Mathieu (FRA)* |
| 1937 | 15-21 March | Kho Sin Kie (CHN) | Jacqueline Goldschmidt (FRA) |
| 1938 | 11-17 April | Bernard Destremau (FRA) | *Simone Mathieu (FRA)* |
| 1939 | 3-9 April | Adam Baworowski (AUT) | *Simone Mathieu (FRA)* |

★★ Venues:
1920-1922: Platz Mozart
1923-1939: Parc Imperial

★★★ 1933-1939:
Nice Championships

Note: married ladies are shown in *italics*

**NICE  Nice Country Club  International tournaments**

| Year | Date | Men's Singles | Ladies' Singles |
|------|------|---------------|-----------------|
| 1914 | 16-26 March | Anthony Wilding (NZL) | *Dorothea Chambers (BRI)* |

| en's Doubles | Ladies' Doubles | Mixed Doubles |
|---|---|---|
| ...ilbur Coen (USA) | Cilly Aussem (GER) | William Tilden (USA) |
| ...illiam Tilden (USA) | Elizabeth Ryan | Cilly Aussem (GER) |
| ...harles Aeschliman (SUI) | Cilly Aussem (GER) | Jean Lesueur (FRA) |
| ...ck Hillyard (GBR) | Elizabeth Ryan (USA) | *Simone Mathieu* (FRA) |
| ...ector Fisher (SUI) | *Phyllis Satterthwaite* (GBR) | Hector Fisher (SUI) |
| ...harles Aeschliman (SUI) | Muriel Thomas (GBR) | Lolette Payot (SUI) |
| ...harles Aeschliman (SUI) | *Grete Deutsch* (TCH) | Charles Aeschliman (SUI) |
| ...oland Journu (FRA) | *Liesl Herbst* (AUT) | Lolette Payot (SUI) |
| ...ck Hillyard (GBR) | *Grete Deutsch* (TCH) | Edouard Lotan (FRA) |
| ...orgio de Stefani (ITA) | Toto Zehden (GER) | *Paulette de Saint Ferréol* (FRA) |
| ...dré Jacquemet (FRA) | *Simone Mathieu* (FRA) | Edouard Lotan (FRA) |
| ...ouard Lotan (FRA) | Muriel Thomas (GBR) | *Simone Mathieu* (FRA) |
| ...rnard Destremau (FRA) | Edith Belliard (FRA) | Paul Feret (FRA) |
| ...ul Feret (FRA) | *Simone Mathieu* (FRA) | *Simone Mathieu* (FRA) |
| ...am Baworowski (AUT) | Joan Ingram (GBR) | *Divided* |
| ...org von Metaxa (AUT) | Cosette Saint Omer Roy (FRA) | André Merlin (FRA) |
| | | Joan Ingram (GBR)/ |
| | | Max Ellmer (SUI) |
| | | Mlle A. Deivers (FRA) |
| ...n Lesueur (FRA) | Alice Weiwers (LUX) | Bernard Destremau (FRA) |
| ...o Sin Kie (CHN) | Cosette Saint Omer Roy (FRA) | *Arlette Halff* (FRA) |
| ...ul Feret (FRA) | Jacqueline Horner (FRA) | Antoine Gentian (FRA) |
| ...rl Schroeder (SWE) | *Simone Mathieu* (FRA) | *Simone Mathieu* (FRA) |

| ...n's Doubles | Ladies' Doubles | Mixed Doubles |
|---|---|---|
| ...x Decugis (FRA) | *Dorothea Chambers* (BRI) | Max Decugis (FRA) |
| ...rdon Lowe (BRI) | Elizabeth Ryan (USA) | Elizabeth Ryan (USA) |

**ST RAPHAEL**　**St Raphael LTC**　**International tournaments**

| Year | Date | Men's Singles | Ladies' Singles |
|------|------|---------------|-----------------|
| 1926 | 19-25 April | Arne Grahn (FIN) | Lili de Alvarez (ESP) |
| 1927 | 4-10 April | Erik Worm (DEN) | *Phyllis Satterthwaite (GBR)* |
| 1928 | 2-8 April | TOURNAMENT SCHEDULED BUT CANCELLED | |
| 1929 | 1-7 April | Charles Aeschliman (SUI) | — |
| 1930 | 31 March-6 April | William Tilden (USA) | Elizabeth Ryan (USA) |
| 1931 | 30 March-5 April | Hyotare Satoh (JPN) | Ida Adamoff (FRA) |

Note: married ladies are shown in *italics*

| Men's Doubles | Ladies' Doubles | Mixed Doubles |
|---|---|---|
| ne Grahn (FIN) | Mlle Durand-Viel (FRA) | Pescher (    ) |
| orn Thalbitzer (DEN) | *Mme Laty* | Lili de Alvarez (ESP) |
| ené Gallepe (MON) | Elizabeth Ryan (USA) | Erik Worm (DEN) |
| ik Worm (DEN) | *Phyllis Satterthwaite (GBR)* | Elizabeth Ryan (USA) |
| harles Aeschliman (SUI) | *Sylvia Lafaurie (FRA)* | Charles Aeschliman (SUI) |
| nmanuel du Plaix (FRA) | *Daisy Speranza-Wyns (FRA)* | *Sylvia Lafaurie (FRA)* |
| ilbur Coen (USA) | Cilly Aussem (GER) | William Tilden (USA) |
| illiam Tilden (USA) | Elizabeth Ryan (USA) | Cilly Aussem (GER) |
| o Satoh (JPN) | Elizabeth Ryan (USA) | Hyotare Satoh (JPN) |
| yotare Satoh (JPN) | Muriel Thomas (GBR) | Muriel Thomas (GBR) |

## Summer Tournament Venues 1928–1939

| Towns | Venues | Tournaments | Years |
|---|---|---|---|
| ANTIBES | Provençal LTC | International tournaments | 1931–1939 |
| CANNES | Cannes LTC | International tournaments | 1931–1939 |
| CANNES | Gallia LTC | International tournaments | 1928–1932 |
| CANNES | Metropole LTC (Metropole Hotel) | International tournaments | 1929 |
| CANNES | New Courts Club | International tournaments | 1931–1933 |
| JUAN-LES-PINS | Juan-les-Pins LTC | International tournaments | 1928–1933 |
| JUAN-LES-PINS | Miramar LTC | International tournaments | 1928–1939 |
| MENTON | Menton LTC | International tournaments | 1932–1939 |
| MONTE CARLO | Monte Carlo Country Club | International tournaments | 1930–1939 |
| VAL D'ESQUIÈRES | Hotel La Residence | International tournaments | 1935–1939 |

# Summer Tournament Schedule
# 1928–1939

## 1928
| | |
|---|---|
| August 6-12 | Juan-les-Pins, Juan-les-Pins |
| August 13-19 | Cannes, Gallia LTC |
| August 20-26 | Juan-les-Pins, Miramar LTC |

## 1929
| | |
|---|---|
| August 12-18 | Cannes, Gallia LTC |
| August 19-25 | Juan-les-Pins, Miramar LTC |
| August 26-September 2 | Cannes, Metropole Hotel |

## 1930
| | |
|---|---|
| August 4-10 | Juan-les-Pins, Juan-les-Pins |
| August 11-17 | Cannes, Gallia LTC |
| September 15-22 | Monte Carlo Country Club |

## 1931
| | |
|---|---|
| August 3-9 | Juan-les-Pins, Juan-les-Pins |
| August 10-16 | Cannes, New Courts Club |
| August 17-23 | Cannes, Gallia LTC |
| August 24-30 | Cannes, Cannes LTC |
| September 7-13 | Monte Carlo Country Club |
| September 14-20 | Cannes New Courts Club |
| September 28-October 4 | Antibes, Provençal LTC |

## 1932
| | |
|---|---|
| July 23-31 | Antibes, Provençal LTC |
| August 1-7 | Juan-les-Pins, Juan-les-Pins |
| August 8-14 | Cannes, New Courts Club |
| August 15-21 | Cannes, Gallia LTC |
| August 22-28 | Cannes, Cannes LTC |
| August 29-September 4 | Nice, Nice LTC, Parc Imperial |
| September 5-11 | Monte Carlo Country Club |
| September 12-18 | Menton, Menton LTC |
| September 19-25 | Cannes, New Courts Club |
| September 26-October 2 | Antibes, Provençal LTC |

## 1933

| | |
|---|---|
| May 29-June 4 | Cannes, Cannes LTC |
| July 24–30 | Antibes, Provençal LTC |
| July 31–August 6 | Juan-les-Pins, Juan-les-Pins |
| August 7-13 | Cannes, New Courts Club |
| August 14–20 | Cannes, Carlton |
| August 21-27 | Cannes, Cannes LTC |
| August 28-September 3 | Antibes, Provençal LTC |
| September 4-10 | Monte Carlo Country Club |
| September 11-17 | Menton, Menton LTC |
| September 18-24 | Cannes, New Courts Club |

## 1934

| | |
|---|---|
| July 9-15 | Antibes, Provençal LTC |
| August 13-19 | Antibes, Provençal LTC |
| August 20-26 | Cannes, Cannes LTC |
| September 3-9 | Monte Carlo Country Club |
| September 10-16 | Menton, Menton LTC |

## 1935

| | |
|---|---|
| July 29-August 4 | Juan-les-Pins, Juan-les-Pins |
| August 5-11 | Val d'Esquières, Hotel La Residence |
| August 12-18 | Antibes, Provençal LTC |
| August 19-25 | Cannes, Cannes LTC |
| August 26-September 1 | Monte Carlo Country Club |
| September 2-8 | Menton, Menton LTC |
| September 9-15 | Juan-les-Pins, Miramar LTC |

## 1936

| | |
|---|---|
| July 27-August 3 | Val d'Esquières, Hotel La Residence |
| August 3-9 | Juan-les-Pins, Miramar LTC |
| August 10-16 | Antibes, Provençal LTC |
| August 17-23 | Cannes, Cannes LTC |
| August 24-30 | Monte Carlo Country Club |
| August 31-September 6 | Menton, Menton LTC |

## 1937

| | |
|---|---|
| July-August 1 | Val d'Esquières, Hotel La Residence |
| August 2-8 | Juan-les-Pins, Miramar |
| August 9-15 | Antibes, Provençal |
| August 16-22 | Cannes, Cannes LTC |
| August 23-29 | Monte Carlo Country Club |
| August 30-September 5 | Menton, Menton LTC |

## 1938

| | |
|---|---|
| July 4-10 | Val d'Esquières, Hotel La Residence |
| July 25-31 | Cannes, Gallia LTC |
| August 1-7 | Juan-les-Pins, Miramar LTC |

| | |
|---|---|
| August 8-14 | Antibes, Provençal LTC |
| August 15-21 | Cannes, Cannes LTC |
| August 22-28 | Monte Carlo Country Club |
| August 29-September 4 | Menton, Menton LTC |

## 1939

| | |
|---|---|
| July 3-9 | Val d'Esquières, Hotel La Residence |
| July 31-August 6 | Juan-les-Pins, Miramar LTC |
| August 7-13 | Antibes, Provençal LTC |
| August 14-20 | Cannes, Cannes LTC |
| August 21-27 | Monte Carlo Country Club |
| August 28-September 4 | Menton, Menton LTC |

## Tournament Winners Summer 1928-1939

**ANTIBES** Provençal LTC  International tournaments

| Year | Date | Men's Singles | Ladies' Singles |
|---|---|---|---|
| 1931 | 28 September– 4 October | George Rogers (IRL) | Elizabeth Ryan (USA) |
| 1932 | 23-31 July | André d'Adhemar (FRA) | Leila Claude-Anet (FRA) |
| 1932 | 26 September– 2 October | John Gittings (USA) | Dvortsak (FRA) |
| 1933 | 24-30 July | TOURNAMENT SCHEDULED – NO INFORMATION AVAIL. | |
| 1933 | 28 August– 3 September | AlexAndré Goldryn (FRA) | *Divided* *Helen Dyson* (GBR) Joan Ingram (GBR) |
| 1934 | 10-15 July | Vladimir Landau (MON) | — |
| 1934 | 13-19 August | Vladimir Landau (MON) | Jacqueline Vives (FRA) |
| 1935 | 12-18 August | René Gallepe (MON) | *Simone Gorodnitchenko* (FRA) |
| 1936 | 10-16 August | Emmanuel du Plaix (FRA) | Alice Weiwers (LUX) |
| 1937 | 9-15 August | René Berthet (FRA) | Jacqueline Vives (FRA) |
| 1938 | 8-14 August | Roger George (FRA) | Jacqueline Horner (FRA) |
| 1939 | 7-13 August | George Godsell (GBR) | Jacqueline Vives (FRA) |

Note: married ladies are shown in *italics*

| Men's Doubles | Ladies' Doubles | Mixed Doubles |
|---|---|---|
| René Gallepe (MON) George Rogers (IRL) | Elizabeth Ryan (USA) Muriel Thomas (GBR) | George Rogers (IRL) Elizabeth Ryan (USA) |
| Léonce Aslangul (FRA) Edgar Ward (GBR) | — | Edgar Ward (GBR) Muriel Thomas (GBR) |
| ...llan ( ) ...hn Gittings (USA) | — | John Maurice, Duc d'Ayen (FRA) Blandin (FRA) |
| Vladimir Landau (MON) William Filmer-Sankey (GBR) | *Helen Dyson* (GBR) Joan Ingram (GBR) | Georges Glasser (FRA) *Helen Dyson* (GBR) |
| Vladimir Landau (MON) Gaston Medecin (MON) | — | — |
| Emmanuel du Plaix (FRA) Prince of Kutch (IND) | Cosette Saint Omer Roy (FRA) Alice Weiwers (LUX) | René Gallepe (MON) Cosette Saint Omer Roy (FRA) |
| ...B. Henderson (GBR) Teddy Tinling (GBR) | — | Vladimir Landau (MON) *Simone Gorodnitchenko* (FRA) |
| Paul Jourde (FRA) Emmanuel du Plaix (FRA) | — | Teddy Tinling (GBR) *Elizabeth Macready* (FRA) |
| Vladimir Landau (MON) Gaston Medecin (MON) | — | René Berthet (FRA) Jacqueline Vives (FRA) |
| ...B. Henderson (GBR) Teddy Tinling (GBR) | — | Teddy Tinling (GBR) Adeline Yorke (GBR) |
| George Godsell (GBR) Teddy Tinling (GBR) | — | Giuseppi Vastapane (ITA) Cosette Saint Omer Roy (FRA) |

**CANNES**   Cannes LTC   International tournaments

| Year | Date | Men's Singles | Ladies' Singles |
|------|------|---------------|-----------------|
| 1931 | 24–30 August | René Gallepe (MON) | *Mme Taunay* (HOL) |
| 1932 | 22–28 August | Alain Bernard (FRA) | Muriel Thomas (GBR) |
| 1933 | 29 May–4 June | Charles Aeschliman (SUI) | Cosette Saint Omer Roy (FRA |
| 1933 | 21–27 August | Paul Feret (FRA) | Cosette Saint Omer Roy (FRA |
| 1934 | 20–26 August | Emmanuel du Plaix (FRA) | Cosette Saint Omer Roy (FRA |
| 1935 | 19–25 August | Paul Feret (FRA) | Cosette Saint Omer Roy (FRA |
| 1936 | 17–23 August | Paul Feret (FRA) | Alice Weiwers (LUX) |
| 1937 | 16–22 August | Josef Siba (TCH) | Alice Weiwers (LUX) |
| 1938 | 15–21 August | Gaston Medecin (MON) | Alice Weiwers (LUX) |
| 1939 | 14–20 August | TOURNAMENT SCHEDULED BUT CANCELLED | |

Note: married ladies are shown in *italics*

| Men's Doubles | Ladies' Doubles | Mixed Doubles |
| --- | --- | --- |
| René Gallepe (MON) Count Mikhail Soumarokoff (RUS) | — | René Gallepe (MON) *Mme Taunay* (HOL) |
| *Divided* Morton Bernstein (USA) Emmanuel du Plaix (FRA)/ Max Guillemot (FRA) Jerome Mital (FRA) | — | Edgar Ward (GBR) Muriel Thomas (GBR) |
| John Gittings (USA) Edouard Lotan (FRA) | — | Charles Aeschliman (SUI) Cosette Saint Omer Roy (FRA) |
| Leonce Aslangul (FRA) Paul Feret (FRA) | — | Georges Glasser (FRA) *Helen Dyson* (GBR) |
| René Gallepe (MON) Max Guillemont (FRA) | Cosette Saint Omer Roy (FRA) Alice Weiwers (LUX) | Charles Aeschliman (SUI) Alice Weiwers (LUX) |
| Leonce Aslangul (FRA) Paul Feret (FRA) | — | Paul Feret (FRA) Cosette Saint Omer Roy (FRA) |
| Paul Feret (FRA) Vladimir Landau (MON) | *Paulette de Saint Ferréol* (FRA) Jacqueline Vives (FRA) | Paul Feret (FRA) Alice Weiwers (LUX) |
| Leonce Aslangul (FRA) Robert de Thomasson (FRA) | Cosette Saint Omer Roy (FRA) Alice Weiwers (LUX) | Teddy Tinling (GBR) Muriel Thomas (GBR) |
| Vladimir Landau (MON) William Filmer-Sankey (GBR) | — | *Divided – unfinished – no light* Roger George (FRA) Cosette Saint Omer Roy (FRA)/ Vladimir Landau (MON) Adeline Yorke (GBR) |

**CANNES**   Gallia  LTC   **International tournaments**

| Year | Date | Men's Singles | Ladies' Singles |
|------|------|---------------|-----------------|
| 1928 | 13-19 August | TOURNAMENT SCHEDULED – NO INFORMATION AVAILA | |
| 1929 | 12-18 August | Vladimir Landau (MON) | *Divided* Ninon Boilaive (FRA) Suzanne Versein (FRA) |
| 1930 | 11-17 August | Leonce Aslangul (FRA) | Ginette Sineux (FRA) |
| 1931 | 17-23 August | René Gallepe (MON) | Muriel Thomas (GBR) |
| 1932 | 15-21 August | Vladimir Landau (MON) | *Christiane Boyer* (FRA) |
| 1938 | 25-31 July | TOURNAMENT SCHEDULED – NO INFORMATION AVAILA | |

**CANNES**   Metropole LTC (Metropole Hotel)   **International tournaments**

| Year | Date | Men's Singles | Ladies' Singles |
|------|------|---------------|-----------------|
| 1929 | 26 August– 2 September | René Gallepe (MON) | *Phyllis Satterthwaite* (GBR) |

**CANNES**   New Courts Club   **International tournaments**

| Year | Date | Men's Singles | Ladies' Singles |
|------|------|---------------|-----------------|
| 1931 | 10-16 August | Emmanuel du Plaix (FRA) | Muriel Thomas (GBR) |
| 1931 | 14-20 September | Vladimir Landau (MON) | Elizabeth Ryan (USA) |
| 1932 | 8-14 August | Emmanuel du Plaix (FRA) | — |
| 1932 | 19-25 September | Vladimir Landau (MON) | *Paulette de Saint Ferréol* (FRA) |
| 1933 | 7-14 August | Vladimir Landau (MON) | Cosette Saint Omer Roy (FRA |

Note: married ladies are shown in *italics*

| Men's Doubles | Ladies' Doubles | Mixed Doubles |
| --- | --- | --- |
| René Gallepe (MON) | Ninon Boilaive (FRA) | Count A. Fabbricotti (ITA) |
| ack Hillyard (GBR) | Suzanne Versein (FRA) | *Jeanne Franke* (FRA) |
| — | — | — |
| René Gallepe (MON) | — | René Gallepe (MON) |
| Vladimir Landau (MON) | | *Mme Taunay* (HOL) |
| Vladimir Landau (MON) | — | — |
| William Filmer-Sankey (GBR) | | |

<br>

| Men's Doubles | Ladies' Doubles | Mixed Doubles |
| --- | --- | --- |
| René Gallepe (MON) | — | René Gallepe (MON) |
| ack Hillyard (GBR) | | *Phyllis Satterthwaite* (GBR) |

<br>

| Men's Doubles | Ladies' Doubles | Mixed Doubles |
| --- | --- | --- |
| René Gallepe (MON) | — | Emmanuel du Plaix (FRA) |
| Count Mikhail Soumarokoff (RUS) | | Muriel Thomas (GBR) |
| ntoine Gentien (FRA) | Elizabeth Ryan (USA) | George Rogers (IRL |
| an Lesueur (FRA) | Muriel Thomas (GBR) | Elizabeth Ryan (USA) |
| Morton Berstein (USA) | — | — |
| on. Esmond Harmsworth (GBR) | | |
| hn Gittings (USA) | — | Felix Poulin (FRA) |
| douard Lotan (FRA) | | *Paulette de Saint Ferréol* (FRA) |
| Morton Bernstein (USA) | — | — |
| mmanuel du Plaix (FRA) | | |

## JUAN-LES-PINS  Juan-les-Pins LTC  International tournaments

| Year | Date | Men's Singles | Ladies' Singles |
|---|---|---|---|
| 1928 | 6-12 August | TOURNAMENT SCHEDULED – NO INFORMATION AVAILA | |
| 1930 | 4-10 August | Leonce Aslangul (FRA) | Jacqueline Vives (FRA) |
| 1931 | 3-9 August | TOURNAMENT SCHEDULED – NO INFORMATION AVAILA | |
| 1932 | 1-7 August | André d'Adhemar (FRA) | Muriel Thomas (GBR) |
| 1933 | 31 July-6 August | Leonce Aslangul (FRA) | Muriel Thomas (GBR) |

## JUAN-LES-PINS  Miramar LTC  International tournaments

| Year | Date | Men's Singles | Ladies' Singles |
|---|---|---|---|
| 1928 | 20-26 August | René Gallepe (MON) | *Leslie Aeschliman* (USA) |
| 1929 | 19-25 August | René Gallepe (MON) | Jacqueline Vives (FRA) |
| 1935 | 29 July-4 August | TOURNAMENT SCHEDULED – NO INFORMATION AVAIL | |
| 1936 | 3-9 August | Edouard Robin (FRA) | Alice Weiwers (LUX) |
| 1937 | 2-8 August | Emmanuel du Plaix (FRA) | Alice Weiwers (LUX) |
| 1938 | 1-7 August | Roger George (FRA) | Jacqueline Horner (FRA) |
| 1939 | 31 July-6 August | Gaston Medecin (MON) | Alice Weiwers (LUX) |

Note: married ladies are shown in *italics*

| Men's Doubles | Ladies' Doubles | Mixed Doubles |
|---|---|---|
| ...eonce Aslangul (FRA) ...ean Parisot (FRA) | — | Vladimir Landau (MON) Jacqueline Vives (FRA) |
| ...ladimir Landau (MON) ...William Filmer-Sankey (GBR) | — | — |
| ...- | — | Paul Feret (FRA) Muriel Thomas (GBR) |

| Men's Doubles | Ladies' Doubles | Mixed Doubles |
|---|---|---|
| ...harles Aeschliman (SUI) ...ené Gallepe (MON) | — | Charles Aeschliman (MON) *Leslie Aeschliman (USA)* |
| ...ené Gallepe (MON) ...ck Hillyard (GBR) | — | René Gallepe (MON) *Mrs Jackson (GBR)* |
| ...ul Jourde (FRA) ...mmanuel du Plaix (FRA) | — | Maxime Belhommet (FRA) Jeannette Poncelet (FRA) |
| ...ollins (GBR) ...ladimir Landau (MON) | — | René Berthet (FRA) *Paulette de Saint Ferréol (FRA)* |
| ...- | — | — |
| ...harles Aeschliman (SUI) ...iuseppe Vastapane (ITA) | — | *Divided – abandoned – no light* Charles Aeschliman (USA) Cosette Saint Omer Roy (FRA)/ Giuseppe Vastapane (ITA) Alice Weiwers (LUX) |

**MENTON**   Menton LTC   International tournaments

| Year | Date | Men's Singles | Ladies' Singles |
|------|------|---------------|-----------------|
| 1932 | 12–18 September | "Page" | *Phyllis Satterthwaite* (GBR) |
| 1933 | 11–17 September | Vladimir Landau (MON) | *Phyllis Satterthwaite* (GBR) |
| 1934 | 10–16 September | TOURNAMENT SCHEDULED – NO INFORMATION AVAILA |  |
| 1935 | 2–8 September | Maj. Cartwright (GBR) | — |
| 1936 | 31 August–6 September | Vladimir Landau (MON) | — |
| 1937 | 30 August–5 September | René Gallepe (MON) | *Cosette Saint Omer Roy* (FRA) |
| 1938 | 29 August–4 September | Giuseppe Vastapane (ITA) | *Cosette Saint Omer Roy* (FRA) |
| 1939 | 28 August–4 September | TOURNAMENT SCHEDULED BUT CANCELLED |  |

Note: married ladies are shown in *italics*

| Men's Doubles | Ladies' Doubles | Mixed Doubles |
|---|---|---|
| Jack Hillyard (GBR)<br>Page" | — | Antoine Gentien (FRA)<br>*Phyllis Satterthwaite (GBR)* |
| AlexAndré Goldryn (FRA)<br>Vladimir Landau (MON) | *Phyllis Satterthwaite (GBR)*<br>Cosette Saint Omer Roy (FRA) | Vladimir Landau (MON)<br>*Phyllis Satterthwaite (GBR)* |
| — | — | — |
| Vladimir Landau (MON)<br>Gaston Medicin (MON) | — | — |
| René Gallepe (MON)<br>Vladimir Landau (MON) | Cosette Saint Omer Roy (FRA)<br>Alice Weiwers (LUX) | René Gallepe (MON)<br>Cosette Saint Omer Roy (FRA) |
| Victor Julien (FRA)<br>Giuseppe Vastapane (ITA) | — | Giuseppe Vastapane (ITA)<br>Cosette Saint Omer Roy (FRA) |

**MONTE CARLO**   Monte Carlo Country Club   International tournaments

| Year | Date | Men's Singles | Ladies' Singles |
|---|---|---|---|
| 1930 | 15-22 September | Robert de Thomasson (FRA) | Paulette Marjollet (FRA) |
| 1931 | 7-13 September | George Rogers (IRL) | Elizabeth Ryan (USA) |
| 1932 | 5-11 September | Antoine Genien (FRA) | Colette Rosambert (FRA) |
| 1933 | 4-10 September | Vladimir Landau (MON) | *Paulette de Saint Ferréol (FRA)* |
| 1934 | 3-9 September | Vladimir Landau (MON) | Edith Belliard (FRA) |
| 1935 | 26 August–1 September | Paul Feret (FRA) | Edith Belliard (FRA) |
| 1936 | 24-30 August | Gaston Medecin (MON) | Ann Marie Simon (FRA) |
| 1937 | 23-29 August | Gaston Medecin (MON) | Alice Weiwers (LUX) |
| 1938 | 22-28 August | Gaston Medecin (MON) | Alice Weiwers (LUX) |
| 1939 | 21-27 August | TOURNAMENT SCHEDULED BUT CANCELLED | |

**VAL D'ESQUIÈRES**   Hotel La Residence   International tournaments

| Year | Date | Men's Singles | Ladies' Singles |
|---|---|---|---|
| 1935 | 5-11 August | TOURNAMENT SCHEDULED – NO INFORMATION AVAILA | |
| 1936 | 27 July-3 August | Emmanuel du Plaix (FRA) | Jeannette Poncelet (FRA) |
| 1937 | 26 July-1 August | Emmanuel du Plaix (FRA) | Cosette Saint Omer Roy (FRA) |
| 1938 | 4-10 July | Gaston Medecin (MON) | Jeannette Poncelet (FRA) |
| 1939 | 3-9 July | Gaston Medecin (MON) | Alice Weiwers (LUX) |

Note: married ladies are shown in *italics*

| Men's Doubles | Ladies' Doubles | Mixed Doubles |
|---|---|---|
| Edouard Garcia (BRA) Edouard Lotan (FRA) | Jeanne Franke (FRA) Paulette Marjollet (FRA) | Maj. Cartwright (GBR) Jacqueline Vives (FRA) |
| Antoine Gentien (FRA) Jean Lesueur (FRA) | Edith Belliard (FRA) Elizabeth Ryan (USA) | George Rogers (IRL) Elizabeth Ryan (USA) |
| Roland Journu (FRA) ...osi ( ) | Rosie Berthet (FRA) Colette Rosambert (FRA) | Antoine Gentien (FRA) Colette Rosambert (FRA) |
| AlexAndré Goldryn (FRA) Vladimir Landau (MON) | *Helen Dyson (GBR)* Joan Ingram (GBR) | Vladimir Landau (MON) Joan Ingram (GBR) |
| ...ck Hillyard (GBR) Edouard Lotan (FRA) | — | — |
| René Gallepe (MON) Vladimir Landau (MON) | — | Paul Feret (FRA) Edith Belliard (FRA) |
| Vladimir Landau (MON) Gaston Medecin (MON) | — | Philippe Ville (FRA) Ann Marie Simon (FRA) |
| René Gallepe (MON) Aleco Noghes (MON) | Cosette Saint Omer Roy (FRA) Alice Weiwers (LUX) | René Gallepe (MON) Cosette Saint Omer Roy (FRA) |
| Vladimir Landau (MON) William Filmer-Sankey (GBR) | — | Jack Lysaght (GBR) Adeline Yorke (GBR) |

| Men's Doubles | Ladies' Doubles | Mixed Doubles |
|---|---|---|
| Emmanuel du Plaix (FRA) Paul Jourde (FRA) | — | Henri Raymond (FRA) Jeannette Poncelet (FRA) |
| Prince of Kutch (IND) Emmanuel de Plaix (FRA) | — | Emmanuel du Plaix (FRA) Alice Weiwers (LUX) |
| Pierre Pellizza (FRA) Prince Henry d'Orleans (FRA) | — | — |
| — | — | — |

**FRENCH PROFESSIONAL CHAMPIONSHIPS**   Bristol Cup   Various venues

| Year | Date | Venue | Singles Champion |
|------|------|-------|------------------|
| 1920 | 27-30 December | Beaulieu LTC | Romeo Aquarone (FRA) (Cannes, Carlton LTC) |
| 1921 | 22-25 December | Cannes, Cannes LTC | John Rendall (BRI) (Menton LTC) |
| 1922 | 21-24 December | Menton LTC | John Rendall (BRI) (Menton LTC) |
| 1923 | 20-23 December | Menton LTC | John Rendall (BRI) (Menton LTC) |
| 1924 | 25-28 December | Cannes, Metropole Hotel | Albert Burke (IRL) (Cannes, Carlton LTC) |
| 1925 | 24-27 December | Cannes, Carlton LTC | Albert Burke (IRL) (Cannes, Carlton LTC) |
| 1926 | 16-19 December | Cannes, Carlton LTC | Karel Kozeluh (TCH) (Beaulieu LTC) |
| 1928 | 12-15 January | Beaulieu LTC | Karel Kozeluh (TCH) (Beaulieu LTC) |
| 1929 | 10-13 January | Beaulieu LTC | Karel Kozeluh (TCH) (Beaulieu LTC) |
| 1930 | 16-19 January | Beaulieu LTC | Karel Kozeluh (TCH) (Beaulieu LTC) |
| 1931 | 15-18 January | Beaulieu LTC | Karel Kozeluh (TCH) (Beaulieu LTC) |
| 1932 | 7-10 January | Beaulieu LTC | Karel Kozeluh (TCH) (Beaulieu LTC) |

*...oubles Champions*

-

-

-

-

-

-

...rel Kozeluh (TCH)
...eph Kozeluh (TCH)

...pert Burke (IRL)
...artin Plaa (FRA)

...rel Kozeluh (TCH)
...artin Plaa (FRA)

# Country Abbreviations

| | | | | |
|---|---|---|---|---|
| ARG | Argentina | | IND | India |
| AUS | Australia | | ITA | Italy |
| AUT | Austria | | JPN | Japan |
| BEL | Belgium | | LUX | Luxembourg |
| BRA | Brazil | | MON | Monaco |
| BRI | British Isles | | NED | Netherlands |
| CAN | Canada | | NOR | Norway |
| CHI | Chile | | NZL | New Zealand |
| CHN | China | | POL | Poland |
| DEN | Denmark | | ROM | Romania |
| ESP | Spain | | RUS | Russia |
| FIN | Finland | | SRB | Serbia |
| FRA | France | | SUI | Switzerland |
| GBR | Great Britain | | SWE | Sweden |
| GER | Germany | | TCH | Czechoslovakia |
| GRE | Greece | | USA | United States |
| HOL | Holland | | YUG | Yugoslavia |
| HUN | Hungary | | | |

# Picture Credits

All images are from Wimbledon Lawn Tennis Museum and Kenneth Ritchie Wimbledon Library except:

Archive de Cannes – pages 14, 15
Harry Popp – pages 40, 199
Franco Alciati – pages 46, 85
Gem Hoahing – pages 55, 259, 288, 316,
Michael Sutter with Reserved rights – pages 70–71, 89, 143, 192, 193, 195, 203, 247, 283, 330,
Jean-Loup Coignard – page 109 (bottom)
Wikipedia Commons – page 139 (left)
Diane and Roger Aeschliman – pages 158, 173
Getty Images – pages 12, 167, back cover (bottom)
Carlton InterContinental Hotel – pages 311 (bottom), 317, 318, 319
Professor Kenneth McConkey/Felix Rosensteil's – page 211
Francis Carline, SNCF Society – pages 309, 310, 311 (top)
National Portrait Gallery – page 12
Gianni Clerici – page 108
Margaret Frith – page 109 (top)
James Johnson – page 161

# Index of Players
1883–1939

## MEN

Abdesselam, Robert (FRA) – 1939
Abe, Tamino (JPN) – 1930
Aeschliman, Charles (SUI) – 1921–34, 1939
Albarran, Pierre (FRA ) – 1920
Alexander, Frederick (USA) – 1898, 1905, 1909
Allen, Charles (BRI) – 1899, 1901–6, 1912
Allen, Roy (BRI) – 1899, 1901, 1903–6, 1912
Allison, Wilmer (USA) – 1936
Ambros, Eugene (TCH) – 1937
Andréws, Eskell (NZL) – 1928
Andréwes, C. (BRI) – 1909
Archibald, R.M. (GBR) – 1927
Aron, André (FRA) – 1926, 1927, 1936
Artens, Hermann ( AUT) – 1927–32, 1934–5
Asboth, Jozsef (HUN) – 1939
Aslangul, Leonce (FRA) – 1920, 1924, 1931, 1939
Attwood, T. (BRI) – 1887
Augustin, Jean (FRA) – 1925, 1931
Austin, Henry (Bunny) – (GBR) – 1930, 1933–5, 1938

Bacon, Harry (BRI) – 1889, 1891–4, 1896
Badin, M. (ROM)- 1938, 1939
Balbi di Robecco, Count Mimo (ITA ) – 1920–22
Ball-Green, George (BRI) – 1898
Barclay, Lewis (BRI ) – 1920
Barlow, Harry (BRI) – 1888, 1892, 1899
Barrelet de Ricou, Paul (FRA ) – 1928, 1930
Baworowski, Adam (AUT) – 1937, 1939
Beamish, Arthur (BRI ) – 1913
Beeckman, Livingston (USA) – 1887
Behr, Alan (USA) – 1927
Behr, Karl (USA) – 1912, 1927
Belhommet, Max (FRA) – 1937

Berger, Col. Arthur (GBR) – 1930
Bergman, Curt (SWE ) – 1911
Bernard, Marcel (FRA) – 1931, 1935, 1937
Berthet, Beni (FRA) – 1929, 1932
Biddle, Craig (USA) – 1911, 1914–15
Billington, Henry (GBR) – 1939
Blacker-Douglas, S. (BRI) – 1895
Blackwood-Price, C.W. (BRI) – 1897–8
Bocciardo, Roberto (ITA) – 1925
Boelling, Ferdinand (GER) – 1909–10, 1912
Bolelli, Henri (FRA) – 1938–9
Bonacossa, Alberto (ITA) – 1926
Bonte, Jacques (FRA) – 1935
Borotra, Jean (FRA) – 1922–3, 1926, 1937, 1939
Boussus, Christian (FRA) – 1927, 1929, 1931, 1933, 1935–9
Boyd, Ronaldo (ARG) – 1922
Breck, Henry (USA) – 1919
Brierley, Col. Charles (GBR) – 1924
Brook, E.W. (BRI) – 1889
Brookes, Norman (AUS) – 1913–14, 1924, 1928
Brugnon, Jacques (FRA) – 1926–39
Burke, Edmond (IRL) – 1935
Burke, Thomas (IRL) – 1900–03, 1905, 1915–17
Buss, Johann (GER) – 1928–30
Butler, Don (GBR) – 1937–8

Campbell – 1934
Campbell, Oliver (USA) – 1892, 1900
Canapele, Vanni (ITA) – 1936
Casdagli, Xenophon (BRI) – 1902
Caska, Josef (TCH) – 1935, 1939
Cazalet, Clement (BRI) – 1897, 1903–5, 1912–13
Cejnar, Frantisek (TCH) – 1937–8
Chalier, André (FRA) – 1898
Chalier, R, (FRA) – 1905
Chaytor, Thomas (IRL) – 1897

Chiesa, Hector (SUI) – 1929
Chippingdale, (BRI) – 1883
Cholmondeley (Rocksavage), Lord George
   (GBR) – 1923–8, 1930, 1937
Clark, Clarence (USA) – 1883
Clark, Joseph (USA) – 1883
Cochet, Henri (FRA) – 1922, 1924–33
Coen, Wilbur (USA) – 1929–30
Collinet, M. (BRI) – 1896
Coombe, Dennis (NZL) – 1939
Cordery, (BRI) – 1922
Corlett, G.R. (BRI) – 1889
Couiteas, Jean (FRA) – 1931
Cranston, William (USA) – 1897
Crawford, Jack (AUS) – 1928, 1935
Crawford, Leighton (GBR) – 1923–4,
   1926
Crisp, Hope (BRI) – 1913
Crispe, James (BRI) – 1891–2
Cumming, W. (USA) – 1925
Czetwertynski, Stanislav (POL) – 1926

Danet, Roger (FRA) – 1923
Davis, Dwight (USA) – 1901, 1919
d'Ainvelle, Fernand (FRA) – 1937
de Ahmerar, Andréa ( FRA ) – 1932
de Bertoult, Hubert (FRA) – 1908
de Bray, George (RUS) – 1907
de Galea, Christian (FRA) – 1937
de Garmendia, Basil (USA) – 1901–2
de Gladky, W. (RUS) – 1906
de Graffenried, Roland (SUI) – 1923
de Minerbi, Count Oscar (ITA) – 1931
de Morpurgo, Uberto (ITA) – 1923–7,
   1929–30, 1939
de Stefani, Georgio (ITA) – 1926–30,
   1932, 1934, 1936
de la Plane, Christian (FRA) – 1939
Decugis, Max (FRA) – 1905, 1907,
   1910–14, 1919–20
del Bono, Alberto (ITA) – 1929, 1931–2
del Frate, (FRA) – 1935
Dell, Burnham (USA) – 1919
Deloford, Murray (GBR) – 1939
Destremau, Bernard (FRA) – 1936,
   1938–9
Ditson, Edward (USA) – 1900
Dixon, Charles (BRI ) – 1913
Doherty, H.L. (Laurie) (BRI) – 1894,
   1897–8, 1900–5, 1907–9
Doherty, R.F. (Reggie) (BRI) – 1894,
   1897–1906, 1908
Doust, Stanley (AUS) – 1910

Druce, (BRI) – 1899
du Plaix, Emmanuel (FRA) – 1926–9,
   1931–2, 1934, 1938
Dubuc, Roger (FRA) – 1939
Dungyersky, Gyorgy (SRB ) – 1926
Dunkerley, R. (BRI) – 1915
Dunlop, Alfred (AUS) – 1911
Durrall, Jaime (ESP) – 1932–3
Dwight, James (USA) – 1883, 1886–7

Eaves, Wilberforce (BRI) – 1901, 1904,
   1906, 1908
Ellmer, Max (SUI) – 1932–8

Farrer, Claude (BRI) – 1883, 1885, 188,
   1890
Fassitt, F.L. (BRI) – 1896
Feret, Paul (FRA) – 1929, 1931–2, 1936,
   1939
Filmer-Sankey, William (GBR) – 1936
Fisher, Francis (NZL) – 1920–1
Fisher, Hector (SUI) – 1932–4
Flavelle, John (BRI) – 1910
Fomberlaux, André (FRA) – 1896
Forsmann, Penth (FIN) – 1938

Gabrowitz, Emil (HUN) – 1931–4
Gallepe, René (MON) – 1925, 1927–30,
   1937–9
Garcia, Edouard (BRA) – 1929, 1931–2
Gaslini, Placido (ITA) – 1925–6, 1928,
   1930–1
Geelhand, Pierre (BEL) – 1937
Gentien, Antoine (FRA) – 1924, 1928–9,
   1931, 1934–5, 1938–9
George, Roger (FRA) – 1931, 1934
Gerbault, Alain (FRA) – 1920–3
Germot, Maurice (FRA) – 1912, 1925
Gheerbrandt, René (BEL ) – 1910
Gittings, John (USA) – 1932–3
Goodbody, Manliffe (IRL) – 1891,
   1897–8, 1908, 1916
Gore, Arthur (BRI) – 1892, 1906
Grace, W.H. (BRI ) – 1919
Greig, Donald (GBR) – 1926
Grove, Harry (BRI) – 1885–9, 1891–2
Gwynne Evans, Evan (BRI) – 1904–5,
   1909

Haench, Louis (GER) – 1931
Harada, Takeichi (JPN) – 1930
Hardy, Sam (USA) – 1922
Hare, Charles (GBR) – 1937

Harrison, W.H. (BRI) – 1888
Harvey, M. (BRI ) – 1925
Hay-Gordon, J.R. (BRI) – 1898
Heath, Rodney (AUS) – 1911, 1913, 1925
Hebda, Josef (POL) – 1933, 1935, 1937–9
Hecht, Ladislav (TCH) – 1931–2, 1934, 1937–9
Henkel, Henner (GER) – 1936–7, 1939
Hillyard, Brame (GBR) – 1923–7, 1929–31, 1937
Hillyard, George (BRI) – 1892–4
Hillyard, Jack (GBR) – 1921, 1923–9, 1931, 1933–4, 1936
Hobart, Clarence (USA) – 1900
Holmes, Artemas (USA ) – 1909–10
Hopman, Harry (AUS) – 1928, 1935
Hughes, Pat (GBR) – 1929–30, 1937–9
Hunt, Harold ( AUS ) – 1922
Hunter, Alfred, ( BRI ) – 1913, 1920–4, 1930

Itoh, Erkishi (JPN) – 1933

Jacquemet, André (FRA) – 1934–6, 1938–9
Jauréguiberra Lt René (FRA) – 1925
Jamain, René (FRA) – 1938
Johnson, Col. Wait (USA) – 1919
Jourde, Paul (FRA) – 1932

Karsten, Willem (HOL) – 1933–4, 1936–7
Kawachi, Minoru (JPN) – 1931
Kennedy, A.E. (BRI) – 1889–90
Kho Sin Kie (CHN) – 1937–9
Kingscote, Lt Col Algernon (BRI) – 1921
Kingsley, Charles (GBR) – 1926, 1928–31
Kinzl, Rolf (AUT) – 1903
Kozeluh, Jan (TCH) – 1927–9, 1932
Kramet, A. ( USA ) – 1921
Kuhlmann, Fritz (GER) – 1929

Lacoste, René (FRA) – 1924–5, 1928
Lamb, Ernest (BRI ) – 1922, 1924–5
Lamperti, C. (ITA) – 1899
Landau, Vladimir (MON) – 1928, 1930–7, 1939
Landry, Pierre (FRA) – 1926–7, 1929, 1938
Larnard, William (USA) – 1919
Law, Bernard (USA) 1931
Leader, John (GBR) – 1932
Lee, Harry (GBR) – 1930
Lemaire de Warzee, Willie (BEL) – 1898–1900, 1902–3

Lester, Keats (GBR) – 1925, 1927, 1929
Lesueur, Jean (FRA) – 1930–1, 1933–9
Liddell, J. (BRI) – 1887
Lock, C.P. (GBR) – 1923
Lotan, Edouard (FRA) – 1931–7, 1939
Lovibond, Arthur (GBR) – 1924
Lowe, Gordon (BRI) – 1907, 1909, 1913–14, 1920–6
Lowry, J.N. (GBR) – 1924
Lund, Kai (GER) – 1936
Lycett, Randolph (GBR) – 1923, 1925–6
Lyle, Leonard (GBR) – 1921
Lysaght, Jack (GBR) – 1934

Macnamara, M.G. (BRI) – 1885, 1887, 1889–90, 1892–3
Madge, A.E. (BRI ) – 1906
Magrane, Carlos (ARG) – 1929, 1932
Maier, Enrique (ESP) – 1928, 1931–3
Malacek, Josef (TCH) – 1936
Malmstrom, Sune (SWE) – 1923–4
Malfroy, Camille (NZL) – 1936, 1939
Manset, Gerard (BRI ) – 1922
Mariani, Jean (FRA) – 1939
Mavrogordato, Theodore (BRI ) – 1911
Marsden, P. (BRI) – 1922
Marsalek, Forenc (TCH) – 1932
Martin-Legeay, André (FRA) – 1932–6, 1938–9
Matejka, Franz (AUS) – 1929–36
Matthey, Dean (USA) – 1919
Mayes, Henry (CAN) – 1921–8
McCormick, Allister (USA) – 1926
McGrath, Vivian (AUS) – 1935
Medecin, Gaston (MON) – 1934–9
Menzel, Roderick (TCH) – 1928, 1932, 1934
Mercier, Gabriel (FRA) – 1935
Merlin, André (FRA) – 1931–2, 1937
Miki, Ryuki (JPN) – 1933
Miller, B. (BRI) – 1891
Miller, Deane (USA) – 1891–3
Minerti, Count (ITA) – 1899
Mishu, Nicholas ( ROM ) – 1919–21, 1924
Mitic, Dragutin (YUG) – 1938–9
Moore, C. (BRI ) – 1912
Morgan, David (BRI) – 1922–4
Morier, G.M. (SUI) – 1922
Morrice, David (CAN)- 1926
Mulholland, A.J. (BRI) – 1883, 1886
Muller, Otto von (GER ) – 1905
Murray, C.W. (BRI ) – 1920, 1922

Myers, Wallis (BRI) – 1909–12, 1921–2, 1925, 1927–8, 1937

Nadin, Henry Guy (BRI) – 1891
Nettleton, G.H. (USA ) – 1910
Nicolaides, M. (GRE) – 1930
Nielsen, J. ( BRI ) – 1922
Nisbet, Harold (BRI) – 1897
Noghes, Aleco (FRA) – 1935–8
Nunoi, Ryosuke (JPN) – 1933
Nystrom, Sven (SWE) – 1937

Ohta, Yoshiro (JPN) – 1929
Olliff, John (GBR) – 1931, 1933
Owen, Llewellyn (GBR) – 1930

Pachovsky, Karel (TCH) – 1935
Palmieri, Giovanni (ITA) – 1935–7
Parke, James (BRI) – 1913
Patterson, Gerald (AUS) – 1928
Payn, Frederic (BRI) – 1904
Payne, Capt. Frank (USA)- 1919
Pellizza, Pierre (FRA)- 1938–9
Pennington, (BRI) – 1887
Pentecorvo, Gilberto (ITA) – 1939
Perry, Fred (GBR) 1936
Peters, Eric (GBR) – 1928–30, 1932, 1938–9
Petra, Yvon (FRA) – 1939
Poulin, Felix (FRA) – 1913–14, 1921
Powell, Robert (CAN ) – 1907, 1909, 1917
Prenn, Daniel (GER) – 1930, 1937
Puncec, Ferenc (YUG) – 1936, 1938

Quist, Adrian (AUS) – 1935

Rahe, Friedrich (GER) – 1909, 1911, 1913, 1933
Ramaswami, Cotah ( IND) – 1921
Redl, Hans (GER) – 1939
Renard, A. (FRA) – 1929
Renault, Marcel (FRA) – 1931
Rendall, Major John (BRI) – 1921
Renshaw, Ernest (BRI) – 1883, 1885, 1888, 1890, 1892–4, 1897–9
Renshaw, William (BRI) – 1883, 1885, 1887–9, 1891–4
Resuge, A. (FRA) – 1913, 1921–2
Rhodes, Daniel (USA) – 1907
Riseley, Frank (BRI) – 1903, 1905, 1914
Ritchie, Major (BRI) – 1903–11, 1920, 1923
Ritchie, Richard (GBR) – 1938

Rivoire,Edmond (FRA) – 1937
Robertson, William (USA) – 1935–8
Robinson, E.D. (BRI) – 1905
Robinson, Julien (BRI) – 1886–7, 1892
Rocksavage (Cholmondeley), Lord George (BRI) – 1912, 1921–2
Rogers, George Lyttleton (IRL) – 1927–34, 1938–9
Rohrer, Friedrich (GER) – 1924
Rouillot, Jean (FRA) – 1933
Roupell, Charles ( BRI) – 1922

Samazeuilh, Jean (FRA) – 1922
Sanderson, K. (BRI ) – 1905
Sanglier, Jacques (FRA) – 1939
Satoh, Hyotare (JPN) – 1930–2
Satoh, Jiro (JPN) – 1933
Saulter, G.A. (GBR ) – 1924
Schroder, Karl (SWE) – 1937–9
Scovel, Frederick (USA) – 1923, 1927
Scovell, Rowley (GBR) – 1929
Sears, Richard (USA) – 1883–4, 1886
Shaffi, Laurie (GBR) – 1939
Shayes, Ronald (GBR) – 1938
Siba, Josef (TCH) – 1936
Simond, George (BRI) – 1904–9, 1912, 1915–16
Sindreu, Francisco (ESP) – 1931
Slack, Dennis (GBR) – 1939
Slocum, Henry (USA) – 1904
Smedsrud, A. (NOR) – 1939
Smith, Sidney (BRI) – 1903, 1905
Soumarokoff, Count Mikhail (RUS ) – 1920–3
Spychala, Czeslaw (POL) – 1938
Stanley, Arthur (BRI) – 1883, 1886–7, 1889–90, 1904
Stewart, Rhinelander (USA) – 1890
Stolarow, Maks (POL) – 1932
Straten D. (USA) – 1925
Stubbs, (BRI) – 1885
Sweet, Charles Lacy (BRI) – 1886
Sydow, H. (AUT) – 1927

Tanacescu, Constantin (ROM) – 1938–9
Tarlowski, Kazimierz (POL) – 1936–7
Taroni, Valentino (ITA) – 1936, 1938
Taylor, A. (BRI) – 1900
Taylor, G.H. (BRI) – 1885
Taylor, W.C. (BRI) – 1886
Tegner, Erik (DEN) – 1923
Terrey, Lyle (AUS) – 1925
Teschmacher, Diederik (NED) – 1937

Tilden, Bill (USA) – 1930
Tilney, Norcross (USA) – 1936
Timmer, Henk (HOL) – 1933
Tloczynski, Ignacy (POL) – 1931–3, 1938
Tuebben, Dr Herbert (GER) – 1935
Turnbull, Donald (AUS) – 1935

Ulrich, Einer (DEN) – 1927
Uthmoller, H. (GER) – 1932

van Alen, Jimmy (USA) – 1921–2, 1924–5
van Swol, Hans (NED) – 1939
Ville, Phillipe (FRA) – 1937
Vodicka, Vojtech (TCH) – 1937
Voight, Charles (USA ) – 1905
von Cramm, Gottfried (GER) – 1933–5, 1937
von Kehrling, Bela (HUN) – 1926–34
von Metaxa, Georg (AUT) – 1937, 1939
von Planner, Richard (AUS) – 1935
Voss, Count Victor (GER) – 1895–1900

Walker, Glen (BRI ) – 1921
Wallen, Ake (SWE) – 1938
Warburg, Fredric (BRI) – 1911

Warwick, (USA) – 1932
Washburn, Watson (USA) – 1919
Washer, Jean ( BEL) – 1924
Watson, Douglas (GBR) – 1921, 1923–5
Watters, Douglas (USA) – 1919
Weir, C.B. (BRI) – 1900
Wertheim, Rupert (AUS ) – 1922
Whiteway, L.L. (BRI) – 1895–6
Whiteway, P. (BRI) – 1896
Wilding, Tony (NZL) – 1906–9, 1911–15
Williams, B.I. (BRI ) – 1919
Williams, Richard (USA ) – 1911–12, 1919
Wills, Ernest (BRI) – 1899, 1900, 1905–6
Winkworth, Stephen (BRI) – 1885, 1890–2
Winthrop, B. (BRI) – 1887
Worm, Erik (DEN) – 1927–9, 1931–2
Wrenn, George (USA) – 1919
Wright, Adam (USA) – 1892–3, 1897
Wright, Beals (USA) – 1907
Wright, H. (BRI) – 1891
Wright, Hornsby (GBR) – 1935
Wright, Irving (USA) – 1907
Wright, Marion (USA) – 1891, 1897
Wuarin, Jean (SUI) – 1930

## LADIES

Adamoff, Mlle Ida (FRA) – 1930–3
Aeschliman, Mrs Leslie (Bancroft) (USA) – 1925–6
Andrus, Miss Dorothy (Burke) (USA) – 1931, 1934
Aussem, Frl Cilly (GER) – 1928–30
Aylmer, Miss (BRI) – 1922

Bancroft, Miss Leslie (USA) – 1923
Barbier, Mlle Simone (FRA) – 1929–30, 1933, 1935
Barger-Wallach, Mrs Maud (USA) – 1912
Beamish, Mrs Winifred, (BRI) – 1920–3, 1925
Beckingham, Miss Claire (GBR) – 1927
Belliard, Mlle Edith (FRA) – 1932–3, 1935–6
Berthet, Mlle Rosie (FRA)- 1930–2
Bennett, Miss Eileen (GBR) – 1925–9
Boegner, Mme Colette (Rosambert) (FRA) – 1937–8
Booth, Miss K. (BRI) – 1895–6
Bosworth, Miss E (BRI) – 1899

Bougeois, Mlle Yvonne (FRA) – 1924–6
Bouman, Miss Kea (HOL) – 1928
Boyd, Miss Esna (AUS) – 1929
Bramley Moore, Mrs (GBR) – 1927
Bristed, Miss Grace (USA) – 1922
Brooksmith, Miss Mildred (BRI) – 1897, 1899, 1901–3, 1905, 1910–11
Brown, Miss Nina (GBR) – 1939
Bryan, Miss Constance (BRI)- 1883, 1887, 1889
Burke, Mrs Dorothy (Andrus) (USA) – 1932

Cadle, Miss Lesley (GBR) – 1923–6
Cazalet, Mrs T. (GBR) – 1928
Chalier, Miss M (FRA) – 1898–9
Chambers, Mrs Dorothea (Douglass) (BRI) – 1908, 1914, 1920–5, 1927–8
Charpenal, Mlle Aimée (FRA) – 1931
Clarke-Jerroise, Mrs Gladys (GBR) – 1934
Claude Anet, Mlle Leila (FRA) – 1931–2
Cochet Mme Aimée (Charpenal) (FRA) – 1934

Coleman, Mrs Dorothy (GBR) – 1926–7

Colston, Mrs Gladys (Duddell) (BRI) –
1911–12, 1921

Contostavlos, Mlle Hélène (FRA) – 1924,
1926–8

Corbiere, Miss Elizabeth (USA) – 1927–8,
1932

Covell, Mrs Phyllis (Howkins) (GBR) –
1924, 1929

Craddock, Mrs Doris (GBR) – 1923

Churchill, Mrs Clementine (GBR) –
1923

Crawshay-Williams, Mrs Weeta (GBR) –
1935, 1939

Crosfield, Lady Domini (BRI) – 1912,
1923, 1925–7, 1937

Crundall-Punnett, Mrs Eveline
(Nutcombe Quicke) (GBR) – 1925

Czery, Miss Katalin (HUN) – 1907


d'Hannoncelles, Mlle Emilie (FRA) –
1936

d'Orléans, Princess Anne (Orbrag) (FRA)
– 1939

de Alvarez, Srta Lili (ESP) – 1923–30,
1935

de Meulemeester, Mme Josane (Sigart)
(BEL) – 1936

de Robiglio, Mlle (FRA) – 1903–4

de Saint Ferréol, Paulette (FRA) – 1933–9

Dearman, Miss Evelyn (GBR) – 1939

Debenham, Miss (BRI)- 1899

Descleres, Mlle N. (FRA) – 1924

Deutsch, Frau Grete (TCH) – 1933–8

Dillon, Miss Evelyn (BRI) – 1908

Dillon, Miss Maude (BRI) – 1908

Dod, Miss Lottie (BRI) – 1902

Douglass, Miss Dorothea (BRI) – 1905

du Cross, Mlle Pat (FRA) – 1926

Duddell, Miss Gladys (BRI) – 1901

Dyas, Miss Ruth (BRI) – 1897


Eastlake Smith, Miss Gladys (BRI) –
1905–8

Ellis, Mrs M.F. (GBR) – 1924

Emmanuelli, Mme (FRA) – 1939

Endicott, Mrs (GBR) – 1928

Faber, Miss (BRI) – 1899


Fearnley Whittingstall, Mrs Eileen
(Bennett) (GBR) – 1931

Fick, Mrs Sigrid (SWE) – 1920–1

Fry, Miss Joan (GBR) – 1929

Glover, Mrs Nancy (Lyle) (GBR) – 1939

Goldsack, Miss Elsie (GBR) – 1927

Goldschmidt, Mlle Jacqueline (FRA) –
1932–5, 1937–9

Gondoin, Mme Marcel le (FRA) – 1920

Goss, Miss Eleanor (USA) – 1921–4

Gould, Mrs Florence ( USA) – 1924

Greene, Miss Alice (BRI) – 1909

Grioni, Sta Guiliana (ITA) – 1935

Guillen, Miss  (BRI)  – 1896

Gurney , Miss E. (BRI) – 1887


Halff, Mme Arlette (FRA) – 1938

Hampshire, Miss (BRI) – 1907

Hardie, Cristobel Miss (GBR) – 1925,
1927–8

Hardwick, Miss Mary (GBR) – 1933–4,
1937

Hartland, Miss Mary (GBR) – 1927

Harvey, Miss Ermyntrude (GBR) –
1924–6, 1928, 1930

Haycraft, Mrs Olga (GBR) – 1935–6,
1938

Haylock,Mrs Elsa (GBR) – 1926

Heeley, Miss Mary (GBR) – 1931

Henrotin, Mme Sylvia (Jung, Lafaurie)
(FRA) – 1931–4, 1939

Henshaw, Miss V. (BRI) – 1902, 1904

Herbst, Frau Lisel (AUT) – 1933

Hewitt, Miss Sheila (GBR) – 1932–3

Hillyard, Mrs Blanche (BRI) – 1896,
1901–2

Hirsch, Miss Carolyn (USA) – 1930

Hoahing, Miss Gem (GBR) – 1933–6,
1938

Hobson, Miss Betty (GBR) – 1934

Holman, Miss Dorothy (GBR) – 1939

Horner, Mlle Jacqueline (FRA) –
1934–9

Howkins, Miss Phyllis (BRI) – 1921

Hudd, Miss (BRI)- 1899

Huntbach, Miss Denise (GBR) – 1937

Hunt, Miss N. (GBR) – 1927

Hutchings, Miss Iris (GBR) – 1935–9


Ingram, Miss Joan (GBR) – 1934, 1937

Iribarne, Mlle Simone (FRA) – 1937


Jacobs, Miss Helen (USA) – 1930

Jarvis, Miss Rita (GBR)  – 1938

Jedrzejowska, Miss Jadwiga (POL) – 1932,
1936–9

Jung, Mlle Sylvia (FRA) – 1922

Kahler, Miss Margrethe (DEN )- 1922
Keays, Mrs W.P. (GBR) – 1924, 1926
Kentish, Miss K. (BRI) – 1904
Kops, Mme Bruyn (DEN) – 1931
Kormoczy, Miss Susie (HUN) – 1939
Korotvicova, Mme Albina (TCH) –
 1930–1
Kovac, Mlle Hella (YUG) – 1938–9
Kriegs Au, Frl Elfriede (GER) – 1939

Lafaurie, Mme Sylvia (Jung) (FRA) –
 1924, 1926–7, 1929–30
Laffargue, Mme Simone (Iribarne) (FRA)
 – 1939
Lamplough, Mrs Gladys (Eastlake Smith)
 (BRI) – 1908
Landry, Mme Nelly (FRA) – 1939
Laverton, Mrs Margaret (BRI) – 1913–14
Lebailly, Mme Marguerite (FRA) – 1939
Lermitte Miss Violet (GBR) – 1939
Liebert, Miss Nancy (GBR) – 1937–8
Lizana, Sta Anita (CHI) – 1937
Louvean, Mme (FRA) – 1935
Lowenthal, Frl Annemarie (GER ) – 1929,
 1933
Lowther, Toupie (BRI) – 1903, 1906–7
Lumley-Ellis, Miss Sylvia (GBR) – 1927
Lycett, Mrs Joan (GBR) – 1925–6
Lyle, Miss Nancy (GBR) – 1934

Macready, Mrs Elizabeth (FRA) – 1926
Madarasz, Miss Margit (HUN) – 1907
Mallory, Mrs Molla (USA) – 1923
Mariollet, Mlle Paulette (FRA) – 1928
Martin, Miss Louise (BRI) – 1902
Mathieu, Mme Simone (FRA) – 1929–39
Maynard, Miss Sally (GBR) – 1926
McAlpine, Miss J. (GBR) – 1934
McKane, Miss Kathleen (GBR) – 1923
Metaxa, Mlle Doris (FRA) – 1930–1
Meunier, Mme René (FRA) – 1931
Miles, Miss (BRI) – 1897, 1904
Morrill, Miss Marjorie (USA) – 1928
Morris, Mrs (GBR) – 1927
Mumford, Miss Isabella (USA) – 1926

Nepach, Frau Nelly (GER) – 1926
Nerescheimer, Frau Hedwig (GER) –
 1906, 1910
Neufeld, Mlle Arlette (FRA) – 1930

Neville-Smith, Mrs Annie (GBR) –
 1925

Nicolopoulo, Mme Hélène (Contostavlos)
 (FRA) – 1931
Noel, Miss Susan (GBR) – 1931, 1935–8
Norman, Miss Mary (GBR) – 1937
Nutcombe Quicke, Mrs Eveline (BRI) –
 1908–11
Nuthall, Miss Betty (GBR) – 1927–9,
 1931, 1938

O'Connell, Miss Patricia (GBR) – 1938
O'Neill, Mrs Madeline (BRI) – 1913,
 1920–3
Owen, Miss Dawn (GBR) – 1936
Owen, Miss Pat (GBR) – 1936
Owen, Mrs Violet (GBR) – 1930

Payot, Mlle Lolette (FRA) – 1929,
 1931–3
Perrett, Mrs (BRI) – 1912
Petchell, Miss Eden (GBR) – 1926–8
Peteri, Mrs Ilona (HUN) – 1926
Pillans, Miss Helen (BRI) – 1899
Pillans, Miss Katie (BRI) – 1899
Pitman, Mrs L. (GBR) – 1926
Pittman, Mrs Elsie (Goldsack) (GBR) –
 1930
Poncelet, Mlle Jeannette (FRA) – 1935,
 1938–9
Pons, Sra Bella (ESP) – 1928
Porakova, Mlle Eva (TCH) – 1939

Ransome, Miss Amy (BRI) – 1904–6,
 1910
Radcliffe, Miss Nancy (GBR) – 1930
Radcliffe, Miss Phyllis (GBR) – 1930
Riboli, Sig.na Elsa (ITA) – 1931–2
Riddell, Miss Mona (GBR) – 1934
Ridley, Miss Joan (GBR) – 1926, 1930,
 1934
Rieck, Frl Magdaline (GER) – 1912
Riseley, Miss Edith (BRI) – 1899
Roberg, Miss Gull (SWE) – 1937
Rooke Miss (BRI) – 1897, 1904
Rose, Mrs E.S. (BRI) – 1910
Rosambert, Mlle Colette (FRA) – 1930–2,
 1934
Rost, Frl. Irmgard (GER) – 1935
Roundway, Lady Gladys (Duddell,
 Colston) (GBR) – 1928, 1937
Ryan, Miss Alice (USA) – 1913
Ryan, Miss Elizabeth (USA) – 1913–14,
 1920–34

Saint Omer Roy, Mlle Cosette (FRA) – 1925, 1931–9

Salusbury, Miss Rosamund (BRI) – 1906–11

Sander, Frl E. (GER) – 1931

Satterthwaite, Mrs Phyllis (BRI) – 1920–37, 1939

Satzger, Frau Hedwig (Neresheimer) (GER) – 1912

Saunders, Miss Margaret (Peggy) (GBR) – 1928

Schulenburg, Countess Clara (GER) – 1897–1909, 1919

Scott, Miss Valerie (GBR) – 1938

Scriven, Miss Margaret (Peggy) (GBR) – 1933, 1938

Septier, Mlle M. (FRA) – 1921

Serpieri, Mme Diddie (Vlasto) (FRA) – 1929

Shaw, Miss Dorothy (GBR)  – 1927

Shepherd, Miss Dorothy (BRI) – 1920

Shepherd-Barron, Mrs Dorothy (Shepherd)(GBR) – 1924, 1926

Sigart, Mlle Josane (BEL) – 1930

Shirley, Miss (GBR) – 1926

Slaney, Miss Madge (GBR) – 1927–8, 1930

Smailes, Miss M. (BRI) – 1922–3

Smallwood, Mrs (GBR) – 1934

Soames, Miss Betty (GBR) – 1931

Somogyi, Miss Klara (HUN) – 1939

Speranza-Wyns, Mme Daisy (FRA) – 1929

Sperling, Frau Hilde (DEN) – 1937, 1939

Stammers, Miss Kay (GBR) – 1935–6, 1939

Stein, Frl (GER) – 1937

Sterry, Mrs Gwen (GBR) – 1928

Stuart, Miss M. (BRI) – 1914

Szapary, Countess Gabriele (AUT) – 1934–5

Taunay, Mme (HOL) – 1926–7, 1929, 1931

Thomas, Miss Muriel (GBR) – 1929, 1931–5, 1937–9

Topham, Miss Adele (BRI) – 1913–14

Topham, Miss Doris (BRI) – 1913

Towler, Miss M. (BRI) – 1913

Tripp, Miss Jessie (BRI) – 1908–9, 1911–14

Tripp, Miss Margaret (BRI) – 1911–12, 1922–6

Valerio, Sig.na Lucia (ITA) – 1928, 1930–2, 1934–5

Vlasto, Mlle Diddie (FRA) – 1923–7

Vlasto, Mlle Régine, (FRA) – 1930

Vlasto, Mme Régine  (FRA) – 1910

von Krohn, Frl Dagmar (GER) – 1911, 1913

von Reznieck, Baroness Paula (GER) – 1928–30

von Stuck, Frau Paula (GER) – 1935

Warburg, Mrs Emmeline (BRI) – 1911

Ward, Miss M. (BRI) – 1914

Warden, Miss Vera (USA)– 1906

Watson, Miss Maud (BRI) – 1887

Weekes, Miss Penny (GBR) – 1937

Weivers, Mlle Alice (LUX) – 1934, 1939

Wheeler, Miss Gracyn (USA) – 1938–9

White, Miss E.M. (BRI) – 1912–13

Whitmarsh, Miss Mary (GBR) – 1938

Wills, Miss Helen (USA) – 1926

Wilson, Miss Constance (BRI) – 1905

Winch, Mrs Ruth (BRI) – 1903–4, 1906–10, 1914

Woolrych, Miss Honor (BRI) – 1922, 1925–6

Wright, Miss Audrey (GBR) – 1924, 1926

Yorke, Miss Adeline (Billie) (GBR) – 1934

Young, Mrs (GBR) – 1926

Zenden, Frl Totta (GER) – 1934

Alan Little began collecting books on tennis in his teens. He was a contributor to 'Lawn Tennis & Badminton' (1960-1969) and Editor of 'Tennis World' (1969-1977). A member of the Lawn Tennis Writers' Association of Great Britain since 1974, he was recipient of the Association's Annual Award in 2008. He founded the Kenneth Ritchie Wimbledon Library at Wimbledon Lawn Tennis Museum and has been its Honorary Librarian ever since. He is the author of many tennis books including 'Wimbledon Gentlemen's and Ladies' Singles' (2006, 2012), 'Suzanne Lenglen – Tennis Idol of the Twenties' (1988, 2007), 'Tennis and the Olympic Games' (2009), 'The Olympic Tennis Event at Wimbledon' (2012), 'Wimbledon Compendium' (annually from 1991). He has witnessed every Gentleman's Singles final at Wimbledon since 1950 and was made an Honorary Member of the All England Lawn Tennis Club in 1985. In the 2014 New Year's Honours List, he was awarded the MBE for services to tennis.